THE FLIGHT
FROM TRUTH

Random House
New York

Jean-François Revel

THE FLIGHT FROM TRUTH

The Reign of Deceit in the Age of Information

Translated from the French by Curtis Cate

Library of Congress Cataloging-in-Publication Data
Revel, Jean François.
[Connaissance inutile. English]
The flight from truth/Jean-François Revel; translated from the
French by Curtis Cate.—1st ed.
p.   cm.
Translation of: La connaissance inutile.
Includes bibliographical references and index.
ISBN 0-394-57643-8
1. Truthfulness and falsehood. 2. World politics—1985–
1. Title.
BJ1422.R3913 1991   177'.3—dc20   89-43438

TO OLIVIER TODD

Contents

Introduction to the English Language Edition

This is not a book about politics, nor is it a book about journalism or about relations between East and West, nor is it a book about the Left, even though many of the examples I have furnished are drawn from one or another of these fields, as well as from others. My principal aim has been to examine the various reasons why human beings so frequently neglect the genuine knowledge that is available to them and prefer to base their conceptions and their actions on false information, even though it is often against their interest to do so. This paradoxical behavior is neither new nor peculiar to our age; but in the twentieth century it has assumed a new intensity, and its absurdity seems all the more mysterious since no civilization has been as organized around knowledge as ours is, or been called upon to function more intensively with and through the use of knowledge in all of its diverse forms, in all of its diverse branches, side paths, or applications. By these I mean, specifically, the realms of science, technology, education, information, and democracy (which presupposes education and information)—for all of which the press, radio, and TV act as planetary amplifiers. Why then is there such an inherent contradiction in human behavior with regard to knowledge and its uses? And is the falsification of knowledge compatible with the survival of a culture founded on knowledge?

Often an author encounters reactions or objections relating to the particular examples he furnishes, but not to the general idea these examples illustrate. Thus in this book I write about Marxism because this ideology has played a dominant role throughout the second half of the twentieth century. However, if I dwell on Marxism, it is primarily to be able to study the structure and function of ideology *in general.* I could just as easily have taken as an example the scholastic-Aristotelian ideology that dominated Europe from about 1550 to 1650 and described the fight it put up in order to resist the rise of modern science. It was, however, simpler to take Marxism as an example because this system is familiar to the contemporary reader, it affects historical and cultural events known to us all, and because—though by and large it has been discredited—it still goes on influencing many of our modes of thought (a phenomenon I have called "ideological afterglow"). But the essential question is one of determining *why such ideologies exist,* what they consist of, why and for what purpose they impose themselves notwithstanding their falseness and harmfulness and finally in what reincarnations and metastatic disguises they reappear when they have supposedly or seemingly disappeared.

In addition to the confusion between idea and example, public debate is often vitiated by the fact that the idea being discussed is rarely the one that has been expressed. For example, in April 1989 Stephen Rosenfeld wrote in *The Washington Post* that "Conservatives of Jean-François Revel's and Jeane Kirkpatrick's stripe lean to a view that Gorbachev is employing his 'prodigious Machiavellian charm' in a peace offensive meant to disarm, first politically but also militarily, the countries that surround his. In this view, the Soviets, in pulling out of Afghanistan, are merely sacrificing a pawn for the sake of strategic gains in, primarily, Europe."* Rosenfeld was referring to an article entitled "Is Communism Reversible?," first published in the autumn 1988 issue of *Politique Internationale* and later reprinted in an English translation in the January 1989 issue of *Commentary.* Nowhere in this article did I present the Soviet withdrawal from Afghanistan as being a "ruse" or a "trap." Nowhere did I employ the image of a "pawn" cleverly sacrificed by a consummate chess player. I forthrightly declared that the Soviets had left because they were beaten militarily.† The question I did raise was this: How and why is it that they have managed to transform this strategic defeat into a political victory? Through what mysterious magic were they able in so doing to robe themselves in an aura of moral merit after having massacred one and a half million civilians and having forced another five million to flee the country and seek refuge abroad? I have never for one moment doubted that the Soviets were forced to leave. As for Gorbachev's "Machiavellian charm," it was mentioned in

---

*Stephen Rosenfeld, "Does Gorbachev No Longer Want Us In?" *The Washington Post,* April 28, 1989.

†Beaten militarily in the precise sense established by Clausewitz: "War is an employment of force whereby we seek to force the adversary to submit to our will." It is obvious that the Soviets did not succeed in forcing the Afghan people to submit to their will; therefore they lost the war.

another context having to do with his relations with the Western press and media. I used this expression in my *Commentary* article with regard to the continuing disarmament negotiations and to the talent Gorbachev was displaying in striving to separate West Germany from the rest of Western Europe, and Europe from the United States.

The fact is that we do not use our minds to seek out the truth or to establish particular facts with absolute certainty. Above all and in the great majority—if not the totality—of cases, we use our intellectual faculties to protect convictions, interests, and interpretations that are especially dear to us. This approach is particularly prevalent in matters of politics or ideology, sectors in which it is difficult or impossible to attain a high degree of demonstrable truth. But if it is less frequently found in strictly scientific fields, it is not because scientists are virtuous; it is because the very nature of scientific knowledge imposes limits on falsification and deception. In their subjective behavior and personal relationships scientists, it must be said, hardly differ from politicians.

In 1983 and 1984, to cite a particular case, a violent argument arose between an American and a French laboratory: Which of the two had been the first to discover the AIDS virus? The debate was marked by "low blows" and even allegations of thefts worthy of the stock market wars that financiers wage against each other with the help of "insider trading" tips and so on.* Finally the two rivals, Robert C. Gallo and Luc Montagnier, whose quarrel might have ruined their chances of obtaining a joint Nobel Prize in Physiology and Medicine, wrote an article for *Scientific American*—a charming account of the discovery of the virus from which all traces of their bitter quarrel were calmly erased. Again, there is nothing particularly new in this "prophylactic" approach to scientific history. In the nineteenth century Claude Bernard, a fount of inspiration for experimental biologists, claimed that scientists had a right to indulge in such historical reconstructions for pedagogic reasons, the aim being to efface for posterity the often chaotic and groping progress of experimentation and the painful conflicts it can engender.

The year 1988 was marked by a similar hubbub provoked by the "discovery," made by a French scientist, Dr. Benveniste, that water molecules possess "memory." After the prestigious magazine *Nature* had publicized what it regarded as a major discovery, thus virtually guaranteeing its authenticity, it had the discovery subjected to other

*See Mirko D. Grmek, *Histoire du SIDA* ("The History of AIDS") (Paris: Plon, 1989), in particular pp. 116–17 of Chapter 6, which is devoted to this "Franco-American dispute."

tests, which proved that Dr. Benveniste's claims were bogus. The editor of *Nature,* John Maddox, then declared that he had published the article for didactic reasons, in order to teach the reading public how adventurous and full of perils scientific research can be. Benveniste, for his part, riposted in *Le Monde* with a denunciation of these inquisitorial methods, which he described as being "identical to those of the Gestapo." Here, as one can see, we are far removed from the serenity that is supposed to reign in scientific circles!

Scientists themselves often attribute the theories or objections of their colleagues to motivations having nothing to do with a love of knowledge. Thus there was talk of a witch-hunt in May 1989 when the National Institutes of Health launched an investigation into a 1986 article in *Cell* coauthored by Dr. David Baltimore, a Nobel Prize winner for medicine. There were allegations, later found to be true, that Dr. Baltimore's coauthor Dr. Imanishi-Kari had faked some of the dates on which the article was based.* Baltimore, however, strongly defended the article and his colleague throughout the investigation, because, he later explained, he felt that it was he more than Imanishi-Kari who was the real target of the investigation. All talk of a "witch-hunt" in this case was unjustified. Why should such an article by any scientist be immune from investigations concerning the honesty of the experiments on which it is based? As Robert E. Pollack, a biologist and dean of Columbia University, pointed out in *The New York Times:* "Science differs from politics, or religion, in precisely this one discipline: we agree in advance to simply reject our own findings when they have been shown to be in error. There is no shame to this. The freedom to make mistakes and admit them is at the core of the scientific process." All of this is true enough. However, Dr. Pollack was a bit hasty in confusing the right to make mistakes with the right to indulge in fraud. That was the charge made in the course of the NIH's investigation, which spoke of fraud, not of errors. In pretending not to understand the distinction, Pollack himself furnished an example of a certain insincerity—which was the last thing needed in this particular instance.

Accusations of fraud are constantly being made in the internal debates of the scientific community. It is a rare issue of *Nature* in which a possible case of fraud is not brought to light. For example, in its April 20, 1989, issue, John Talent, an Australian paleontologist from the University of New South Wales, published an article picturesquely entitled "The Case of the Peripatetic Fossils," which had the following headline:

The New York Times, April 30, 1989; *Nature,* May 4 and 11, 1989.

"Through the activities of one Indian scientist, paleontological literature on the Himalayas has become shot through with disinformation."
The article, which was, one must admit, very detailed and convincing,
was backed up—this in itself was exceptional—by an editorial vigorously supporting the accusations. "Paleontology," wrote *Nature*, "is
renowned for spectacular deceptions, among which 'Piltdown Man' is
generally the best known, but the trouble caused in the Himalayas by
the activities of Professor Viswa Jit Gupta of the Punjab University of
Chandigarh will cast a longer shadow, as Dr. John Talent shows. For
there was only one Piltdown skull which many, from the outset, believed
to be a hoax. Gupta's cumulative joke, going back over a quarter of a
century, will be excised from the record only with much greater difficulty."

The following issue (April 27, 1989) reported Professor V. J. Gupta's
denial of the charges and quoted his reply: "Talent's outburst was
motivated by a malicious intent to take revenge for personal rivalry and
professional jealousy over the past 20 years." Particularly striking is the
"scientific" density of this reply. It all sounds like a no-holds-barred
scrap between two ballerinas from the Paris Opera, or, rather, from the
Crazy Horse Saloon.

But the scandal that overshadowed all others during the spring of 1989
was the one provoked by an experiment in "cold fusion," which ceased
overnight to be the select property of scientific journals and made media
headlines all over the globe. As soon as Dan Rather had announced on
the March 23 "CBS Evening News" that two obscure scientists from the
University of Utah had perhaps succeeded in carrying out *in vitro* a
nuclear fusion process capable of supplying an unlimited supply of
energy, scientists from all over the world chimed in to say that they too
had tried the same experiments and obtained identical results! Soon,
however, it was revealed that these experiments could not be reproduced
under rigorously controlled conditions. A few weeks were enough to
unmask the hoax, or the incompetence—or simply the mistake—of the
two scientists.*

It is here that we can measure a characteristic superiority of the exact
sciences over the social sciences or politics. In politics an error or hoax
of this importance could have lasted for centuries without the lessons
of reality being able to furnish a sufficiently clear refutation to silence

---

*Nature, April 20 and 27, 1988, May 4 and 9, 1989; *Time* and *Newsweek*, May 8, 1989.
Which did not keep the Madrid weekly *Cambio 16* from announcing pompously in its May
15 issue: "Spain has accorded itself a one-month delay to verify the discovery."

its partisans. In the social sciences it is what people _want_ to see proved
that becomes the main criterion of the "truth." It is interesting to note
that, with regard to Margaret Mead, whom I mention in Chapter 9, an
anthropologist, Adam Kuper, could write of her work in _Nature_ (April
6, 1989): "The public has been led to believe that if Mead is shown to
be wrong about adolescent girls in Samoa, this will have decisive implications for debates about how far our capacities and characters are
shaped by experience, especially childhood experience, and how far they
are fixed by heredity." Kuper here was aiming his remarks at a book
published by Derek Freeman.* The question as to whether or not Margaret Mead deliberately embellished her description of the adolescent
period of Samoan girls is now of secondary importance. The vital issue
is an _ethical_ choice between biological fatality (hereditary factors) and
cultural relativism (social influences). The distinction between the exact
and the approximative sciences has nothing to do with the varying
degrees of intellectual probity of those who practice them, but is linked
to their fundamental structure. In the approximative sciences verification and refutation can be indefinitely delayed and contested. Not so in
the exact sciences. Yet even in the exact sciences falsifications do
exist—a phenomenon that indicates among those who commit such
"errors" an almost pathological indifference to truth, even among the
most brilliant scientists, who must realize that inevitably they will be
unmasked. This is what Efraim Racker, a research scientist in biochem-
istry at Cornell University, had to say on the subject in pointing out that
in cases of fraud the faker is not the only one responsible. Equally
responsible are supervisors and team assistants, university staffs and
financial backers, the U.S. administration and Congress, and finally the
press. The author even ventured to write: "I wish we could persuade
Congress to think of curbing inaccurate and sensational journalistic
versions of the truth; there must be freedom of the press but without the
freedom to distort and invent."† What a program! The author seems to
have forgotten that he is attacking the First Amendment; for a call for
"freedom of the press but without the freedom to distort and invent"
is a demand that could be applied to all spheres of public expression and
not simply to scientific information. Unfortunately, it is impossible to
implement such a demand without infringing on the freedom of the
press. For what authority could be regarded as sufficiently competent

*Derek Freeman, _Margaret Mead and Samoa: The Making and Unmaking of an Anthropo-
logical Myth_ (Cambridge, Mass.: Harvard University Press, 1983).

†Efraim Racke, "A View of Misconduct in Science," _Nature,_ May 11, 1989.

and honest to decide beyond the shadow of a doubt that "distortion or invention" has occurred? This is a Utopian demand.

Nature itself occasionally indulges in abuses of trust by using its international prestige in scientific matters to publish articles of purely political opinion that have nothing to do with science and which are more appropriate to the opinion pages of a daily newspaper. For example, the editorial in the April 13, 1989, issue—"Gorbachev Needs an Answer"—presents a thoroughly respectable point of view on disarmament, but one that is totally lacking in scientific rigor. Equally subjective is another article (in the April 27, 1989, issue) entitled "NATO Should Modernize Its Weapons—How to Lose with Nothing to Lose." Such editorial columns may be correct or not—that is not the issue. What is debatable is the context, which makes them look like scientific communications.

I hope that these examples help to explain the central thesis of this book—that a concern for the truth is not the principal guide of Man's intellectual activity, even in the sciences, where methodological precision makes it extremely hard to get away with fraud.

In its May 18, 1989, editorial, *Nature* returned to the case of the Nobel Prize winner David Baltimore, who had been summoned to appear before a House of Representatives committee of inquiry chaired by Representative John Dingell, in order to answer charges that he had made use of his prestige to promote the authors of an article published in *Cell* that was thought to contain fraudulent claims. After declaring, predictably enough, that "formal Congressional inquiries are not the best way of refereeing research reports," the editorial went on: "That is not to say that formal mechanisms for regulating quality and accuracy have no place in science. . . . The moral for science is that when, for whatever reason, the informal mechanisms for telling what is good and what less good have to be replaced by more formal mechanisms for inquiring into allegations or more serious wrongdoing, the formal mechanisms should be rigorous and should be prosecuted with zeal. . . . The scientific community has rallied to Baltimore's defense; the Dingell committee will have been inundated with mail (not always flattering) this past week. . . . But the community, in defending one whom it rightly considers a true hero, should not make his mistake of defending what need not have been defended."

These well-balanced considerations make it quite clear that the intellectual faker exists even in science, notwithstanding the almost absolute certainty that sooner or later he will be unmasked. To discourage him, the normal, "informal" way of eliminating bad research to the advantage of good research by a process of natural decantation does not suffice. Hence the need to add "formal," one might say "disciplinary," bodies entrusted with the mission of ferreting out and repressing fraud. Finally, it is significant that the scientific community sided with Baltimore without considering the fundamental issue. In this respect scientific researchers do not behave any differently from intellectuals as a whole; they tear one another apart, but collectively they feel they have a statutory right to be exempt from criticism by the rest of the human species. This said, their field of action lends itself far less than others to imposture, and above all to its indefinite prolongation.

In all other domains, which are rarely or never sanctioned by decisive proofs, people battle all the more freely for their particular cause, their interests, their prejudices, and not for the truth, since they enjoy a great latitude in selecting arguments, neglecting or inventing facts, or at least interpreting information in such a way that it reinforces their convictions and their case. Hence the chaotic, interminable, and forever uncertain character of political, philosophical, moral, historical, and economic controversies. This is not to say that these sectors of knowledge are fated by nature to be arenas of arbitrary judgment. On the contrary, I am persuaded that the degree of precision possible in everyday affairs far exceeds what we actually attain. But to be able to attain this precision and to be able fully to use the knowledge available to us, in order to reach a consensus based on the closest possible approximation to the truth, our civilization still lacks one essential ingredient: sincerity. A sizable segment of the knowledge we could employ remains unused because of this lack. And this lack of sincerity has grave consequences in practice—for example, in the agricultural sector of underdeveloped countries, where, despite all the negative evidence accumulated over the past twenty or thirty years, calls for "agrarian reform" continue to be made, even though such experiments have almost invariably resulted in the creation of cooperatives run by totally inept urban bureaucrats.

The fundamental question posed by *La Connaissance inutile* (the virtually untranslatable French title of my book, most closely rendered in English as "useless knowledge") thus boils down to this: Has Man, thanks to his ability to undertake an anticipatory analysis on the basis of information permitting him to effect a correct diagnosis, ever averted or shortened a disastrous experiment? Has he not, more often, pursued the disastrous experiment right up until the culminating, disintegrating catastrophe—which is to say, *behaving as though he were not an intelligent being* and as though he lacked the necessary knowledge and capacity to envisage potentially disastrous outcomes? From Alcibiades' reck-less expedition against Syracuse in the year 415 B.C. down to Napoleon's catastrophic Russian campaign of 1812 and Hitler's repeat performance in 1941, history is full of examples of political leaders who ruined themselves and their countries by their pigheaded insistence on pursuing insane projects despite expert warnings and a wealth of admonitory information. But we would do well to remind ourselves that the old Latin saying "Whom the gods would destroy, they first make mad" applies not only to dictators and autocrats, but also to democratic leaders, such as Neville Chamberlain and his pacifistic colleagues, who thought Adolf Hitler could be appeased, or, to move closer to the present, President François Mitterrand, who after his electoral triumph in 1981 refused to listen to economic reason and launched France on a suicidal policy of bank nationalizations, which resulted in three successive devaluations of the franc.

Reflection, when preceding action, offers one principal advantage: it allows us to gain time, to spare ourselves predictable vicissitudes, to avoid having to *live* bad solutions, which need only to be *thought* about seriously for it to become obvious how bad they are. If through hypocrisy or ideological fanaticism we do not employ thought toward this end, above all in the field of politics; if we are content to be swept along to the very end of risky experiments before being able to judge them at last (and when it is too late), as we have so often done in the course of the twentieth century; then one may well ask what point there is in possessing the faculty of knowledge or an abundance of information.

Let us take, for example, the negative view of communism that began to prevail in the West during the 1980s. It was not due to our better understanding of the phenomenon. It was not until the communist world had begun to proclaim its bankruptcy that much of the West perceived what was going on. Many of the Western sovietologists and columnists who since 1985 have been pontificating about the "economic failure of communism" did not reach this new conclusion by examining the facts, which had long been available to the world but which they preferred not to look at; they based their assertions on statements made by Mikhail Gorbachev himself. Similarly, after Mao's death, the sinologists changed their minds only after the Chinese leaders themselves had changed their tune.

The same specialists and columnists were those who claimed that the countries of the West should not adopt a "confrontational" attitude toward the USSR at the very moment when Soviet forces were invading Afghanistan and landing troops in various parts of Africa, when the

Soviets were promoting subversion in Central America and threatening Western Europe with a wave of terrorism and the deployment of SS-20 intermediate-range missiles. What relation did this fanciful advice have to what was actually going on?

Prior to this, a hate campaign, full of calumnies and shocking distortions of his thinking, had been launched against Aleksandr Solzhenitsyn in the West, particularly at U.S. universities. There was a specific cause for this phenomenon: most American sovietologists upheld the view that basically the USSR had succeeded. Solzhenitsyn, on the other hand, had repeatedly denounced the Soviet Union as a radical failure. Today Gorbachev himself has more or less endorsed Solzhenitsyn's indictment. So how do U.S. sovietologists react to this new turn of events? They say that Gorbachev is right, and that he must be supported. But do they apologize to Solzhenitsyn and admit their past errors? Not in the least. They have always adhered to the official Soviet "truth" of the moment, no matter what that might be. And so they carry on as before. But such "truth" has nothing to do with historical truth, as we understand it in the West—the kind which, though quite modest and relative, can at least be apprehended with truly scientific scruples, if not with utter certainty.

The censorious "moralists" who ask us to place an *a priori* trust in *perestroika* and *glasnost* have not changed their attitudes. They were the same ones who, fifteen years ago, asked us in advance to trust the USSR of Brezhnevite stagnation and so-called détente. Those who fifteen years ago were taking us to task for saying that communism was a failure are those who are now reproaching us for the lukewarmness of our faith in Gorbachev, the man who has admitted that communism is a failure. They don't seem to realize that what Gorbachev is saying today makes their arrogance of fifteen years ago look ridiculous. And they don't seem to understand that the behavior we should rid ourselves of in such cases is precisely this blind faith, this ecstatic veneration—whether the object of this adoration be Gorbachev, Brezhnev, Mao, Khrushchev, Castro, Stalin, or Lenin. It is not a question of determining whether one should "believe" or not "believe" in this or that. Belief is of little value in political analysis, and when the object of the hero-worship changes or, let's say, perhaps even turns out to be an improvement on the past, the ecstatic believer is no more lucid or competent. The only value that can be attached to this kind of thinking is what it tells us about the believer, not about things as they really are.

Furthermore, the forming of opinions and the evaluation of ideas are today hampered by the oversimplifications brought about by mass communications. Every advantage offers a danger as well. The advantage is that cultural and ideological issues—debated at public meetings, reported by the press, and transmitted on TV screens—reach the ears of millions of people. The disadvantage is that inevitably these millions retain only summary notions of these debates, in particular striking phrases that are supposed to sum up the gist of what has been said, but only too often caricature and deform it. Admittedly, more people than ever read books, but there are many more who entertain opinions about books they have never read and think themselves fully justified in their opinions.

I myself am a partisan of mass culture. It is incontestably a progress made possible by the democratic process. However, we should also understand its negative implications. Before the development of today's media complex, people read or did not read books. In the latter case they did not think that they could know and judge what was in them, and accordingly militate for or against the ideas they contained. Most frequently, in fact, they were not even aware of their existence. To be sure, certain persons who had not read a particular book could nevertheless hear it discussed in some circle or salon and then peddle a good or poor opinion about it, but this worldly affectation of culture represented a rather limited social bane, offensive though it was. This particular ill is far more widespread now, for judgments based on hearsay are shared by tens, indeed hundreds, of millions of TV "idea consumers" who have never had direct, autonomous contact with these ideas as they were originally expressed. I am not proposing that we should reverse gears—something that is impossible, in any case. I am not an elitist. What needs to be done in order to curb this curse is to progress further still and to increase the taste for genuine culture, notably through education, founding it on the personal reading of basic texts rather than on hearsay culture.

It is certainly no exaggeration to claim that today, even among the book-reading public, the vast majority of persons who express an opinion about a certain book have not read it, even when it becomes a best-seller. Their opinions are based on casual talk or on articles that rarely provide detailed analyses or sincere, competent, critical evaluations. At times the authors of such articles want above all to air their own opinions on the subject, or else they provide a superficial résumé of the book they have read, or they adopt a militant attitude toward the book, wishing either to promote or to destroy it. A book's commercial success does not correct this false perception. Whether a book sells ten copies or a million, we shall have the same proportion of adepts of hearsay culture—a hundred "well-informed nonreaders" in the first instance, ten million in the second.* Even interviews, symposia, and conferences modify this phenomenon of oversimplification only slightly. In an interview the questioner almost always plies a writer with questions he has already answered in the book, rather than new questions that would force him to develop his line of thought and make it more precise. What the interviewer seeks is a rapid résumé of the work by the author himself. The purpose of the interview is not to extend but to replace the reading of the book, with phrases as simple and as short as possible, and without overextensive argumentation, particularly on radio and television. The danger in all this is that the reader or TV viewer will acquire the impression of having understood the work as though he had read and thought about it. When listening to an author who is delivering a lecture, or when reading his remarks, the readers, listeners, or viewers have the illusion that they have picked up as much as they would have if they had actually read the book. This of course is an impossibility with any serious or complex work. Yet the illusion is so deeply rooted that authors are constantly being asked to sum up in a few words not only a work already published but also future books.

Any author attending a reception knows ahead of time that several times he will be asked, "Tell me, what are you working on now?" To try to wriggle out by arguing that it is difficult to talk intelligently about such matters at a cocktail party is likely to leave the questioner both annoyed and unbelieving. Even in a serious conversation or when trying to explain the contents, a writer has time only to provide a few vague, terribly simplified indications as to the *conclusions* of the book, *without entering into details of the arguments leading up to them.* But the arguments are in fact what matter most in any intellectual work. Without them, the conclusions drawn are arbitrary opinions, which float in the air, cut off from their roots, and are devoid of all educational value. The danger posed by a civilization based on rapid communication is that it may replace a culture of information with a "culture of affirmation." The public gradually comes to feel that rational thought is no more than a mosaic of interchangeable affirmations from among which each person is free to choose according to his or her subjective preferences. The whys and wherefores, the subtle restrictions and nuances disappear.

*After *Foreign Affairs,* in the spring and summer of 1980, provoked an uproar by publishing a long article by Solzhenitsyn, John R. Dunlap contributed a letter (published in the autumn 1980 issue) in which he said that he had often had discussions with cultivated persons who told him that "as a matter of principle" they did not read Solzhenitsyn. On the other hand, they welcomed articles and reviews hostile to Solzhenitsyn.

As a result, in this "culture of affirmation," an intellectual debate often consists of "refuting" theories an author has never upheld, or at any rate not in the simplified form this kind of hearsay culture engenders. At this point I hope I may be forgiven for speaking briefly about myself; but since I don't live in the United States, I rarely have a chance to thank people there for their praise or reply to criticisms published about my books. One of these criticisms, inspired by recent changes that have taken place or been announced in the communist world, consists of objecting: "You have said that communism is indestructible and that the democracies would perish, but it's the very opposite that is now occurring."

In fact, ever since *Without Marx or Jesus,* * I have always maintained that communism was not viable and *could not* work. It was not I, but a large number of U.S. sovietologists and sinologists, who for years kept claiming that communist countries were succeeding and that conditions in communist societies were improving. Those who used to attack me because I condemned communism as being a hopeless dead end now accuse me of having been mistaken, at the very moment when communism is collapsing! In *Without Marx or Jesus* I asserted (1) the absolute nonviability and irremediable failure of communist economies, including the "alternative" models to be found in Cuba, China, Yugoslavia, Hungary, and the Czechoslovakia of the "Prague Spring" of 1968; (2) the nonviability of collectivist socialism in the Third World—at that time a new theory, but one that, twenty years later, has largely been accepted; and (3) the superiority of "democratic capitalism" and of the Western democratic systems as being the sole sources of modern revolutions (of a new variety), as opposed to Marxist or religious pseudorevolutions (the Islamic revolution in Iran has since provided a dramatic illustration of the regressive character of fundamentalist religious "revolutions" when applied to politics).

On the other hand, the question I raised in *How Democracies Perish* (first published in French in 1983) was *why a system that had proved itself a chronic failure from the outset has almost always triumphed in the sphere of foreign policy,* to the detriment of the democratic system, which was a going concern. Unfortunately, I have not changed my viewpoint on this matter as much as I would have liked. In 1985, when he came to power, Mikhail Gorbachev declared officially that communism as an economic system was a failure. He launched *perestroika,* or the "restructuring" of this system, but in 1989 he acknowledged that this

*Jean-François Revel, *Without Marx or Jesus* (New York: Doubleday, 1971).

restructuring has also failed. Nevertheless, Gorbachev almost succeeded in convincing the democracies that the Soviet menace was waning and that a strong defense was consequently unnecessary. All that time he has been working for the separation of West Germany from its other European allies, accompanied by the beginning of an uncoupling of Western Europe and the United States. The dream nurtured by Stalin, Khrushchev, Brezhnev, and Gromyko—of isolating Western Europe strategically—no longer seems unrealizable.

The mental mechanisms that have pushed the democracies into this position of inferiority are the same as those I described in *How Democracies Perish*. The Gorbachev cult has only too often plunged us into a kind of mental paralysis and idolatry. The democracies do not recognize that the fundamental principles of Soviet foreign policy, under its new guise, remain the same. An idea is not truly understood as long as it has been grasped in only one of its manifestations. In such cases, a new incarnation of the principle can even look like its negation.

Even in Afghanistan, as I have said, Gorbachev managed to transform a military defeat into a political, and even a moral, victory. He has done better than that; for he has so well equipped and trained the Afghan communist army that the pro-Soviet regime did not collapse immediately after the departure of the Red Army.

I should add that the title *How Democracies Perish* is not *How Democracies Will Perish*. In that book I indicated the way in which the democracies may come to grief; I did not recommend it. If I explained the *modus operandi,* it was precisely in the hope that the democracies would stop behaving in this way. I would like to stress the point, too, that my books are not purely descriptive. They are designed to make people think and change their minds, and thus to influence the course of events by forestalling the evil they denounce. It is said of certain books and utterances that they are "self-fulfilling prophecies." The ambition of my own is that they should prove to be self-destroying prophecies. I am not immodest enough to believe that they have been able to change anything by themselves. But they are part of a vast current—which was born in the mid-1970s and which since then has assumed a great scope and force—in favor of democracy and against totalitarianism. The representatives of this current have sometimes suffered the affront of being classified as belonging to the "extreme Right." Inasmuch as the spirit of the Left, if the term still means anything at all, has always been and should have been to militate in favor of freedom and prosperity, our descendants may one day be surprised to discover that our age classified as belonging to the "Right" human beings who were battling for democratic and prosperous societies, and as belonging to the "Left" the advocates of societies where dictatorship, along with penury, reigned supreme.

Here too we are confronted by another mystery. Why, for so long, has the ideological ascendancy of Marxism made itself felt in democratic societies? Why have human beings, and above all intellectuals, who are fortunate enough to live in the freest and richest countries history has ever known, carried on as if they wanted to live and above all to make their fellow citizens live in impoverished totalitarian societies? Why, even if they didn't literally want to force them to live under such conditions, did they systematically hold up those societies as superior to our own? This was the mystery I sought to examine, if not to explain, in *The Totalitarian Temptation,* which dates from 1975. Since then, the ideological domination of Marxism has greatly declined in the West, even though it frequently reappears under other disguises. For let us not imagine that the totalitarian mentality is restricted to Nazism and communism. It is an eternal phenomenon, and it will perennially have to be combated, thwarted, analyzed, and paralyzed. But what is amusing, in the context of a civilization of communication, is that when *The Totalitarian Temptation* was published in the United States, an important literary critic wrote in *The New York Times Book Review* that essentially the book amounted to an attack on—Eurocommunism!

Eurocommunism was then the latest intellectual gimmick, a fashionable notion that enjoyed far more success in American universities than it did in European communist parties. But no matter what people may have thought, one thing—to me at least—was certain: Eurocommunism was not the subject of my book. At the request of my U.S. publisher, who wanted to make my work more "up to date," I had added an epilogue on this ephemeral subject, but this *hors d'oeuvre* (or perhaps I should say, dessert), written in September 1976, was marginal compared to the central theme of the book, which was intended to illuminate a general problem and not a particular, topical, and highly temporary phenomenon. This was also a distortion due to a media-minded civilization—the tendency to mistake a fragment for the whole and to focus on the final hundredth of a second of the present moment as though it were as important as the whole of human history. How many times have I not heard people say, "After Mr. X's latest speech . . ." or "After last Wednesday's article in *Pravda,* don't you feel obliged to alter your book?" Thanks to this lack of perspective, a "mediatic" culture can perceive only *one event at a time—the latest—*unlinked to others, to the past, to the context. To it every moment seems to be a "great turning point" of history.

Here is another example of characteristic and chronic oversimplification—an objection that has frequently been thrown at me since Gorbachev came to power: "You have upheld the irreversibility and indestructibility of communist systems, to the detriment of democracy. But communism is everywhere in a state of crisis or undergoing reforms, and democracy is triumphing." This was not exactly what I wrote in *How Democracies Perish.* I have never thought communist systems were eternal. What human reality is? What I tried to show was that communist systems, considered in terms of sheer power and as political machines rather than as social realities, had displayed an *exceptional* longevity and a resistance to failure, to setbacks, to massive unpopularity that has been far superior to those of any other political system, including democratic systems and even conventional or traditional authoritarian systems. What noncommunist regime could have lasted for so many years while inflicting on its people the sufferings, the famines, the persecutions that Ceauşescu inflicted on the Romanians, Mengistu on the Ethiopians, Castro on the Cubans, and above all, of course, which the Russian and Chinese Communist parties have inflicted on their respective peoples? Under all other kinds of regimes we would have witnessed revolutions or coups d'état for far less. What political leader other than Stalin could have remained at the head of his country after the gigantic military defeats of 1941, due to his lack of foresight and incompetence, and to the shortage of able generals, most of whom he had had shot? How was such survival possible against such a record of failures? I tried to explain it by showing how, from the moment a communist regime seizes power (we saw this happen again from 1978 on in Afghanistan, and from 1980 on with the Sandinistas in Nicaragua), it seeks to set up an irreversible situation, to eliminate all forms of replacement and all alternative solutions from the society it dominates. Communism is a machine for vitiating human society. When classic dictatorships disappear—Franco in Spain, Marcos in the Philippines, Zia in Pakistan, Pinochet in Chile—there are still organized social and political groups capable of taking over. With but very rare exceptions—such as the Catholic Church and Solidarity in Poland—almost all communist regimes eliminate the forces of alternance, thus creating a lack of replacement solutions for times of crisis. The only emergency exits that remain open then seem to be brutal repression or anarchy, since no one outside the Communist Party has the means of assuring the continuity of the state and the conduct of affairs, which the Party itself has become powerless to control.

Ever since the first communist regimes were set up, Western analysts have tended to confuse popular revolts or the beginnings of economic liberalization with a *finished* process of democratization. As soon as things begin to move, there are cries of "This is it! It's happened!" The miracle has taken place, all we need do is sit back and applaud. For example, during the first three weeks of May 1989 most of the daily papers and newsmagazines of the West proclaimed the "return of liberty" to China in bold headlines, as though this had definitely been established. President Mitterrand even compared the Chinese students' and workers' uprising of 1989 to that of the French people in 1789, as though a radical change of regime had taken place in China too. When, after having vainly tried for several weeks to neutralize the demonstrators without shedding blood, the Chinese leaders finally decided on June 3–4 to have soldiers open fire on them, people in the West did not stop to ask themselves if their theory of a Chinese "democratic revolution" had by any chance been false. Could interpretative schemas borrowed from the history of societies other than communist societies be applied to the latter? Aren't we dealing, in the case of communism, with societies of a radically new type, in which so far we have never in fact observed a complete change of regime? These questions were hardly raised, and those who raised them were looked upon as reactionary diehards.

Rarely has the international press indulged in so many gratuitous suppositions and forged more fanciful theories than in that May of 1989. The crowning touch was provided by the "great liberal," Deng Xiaoping, the master of the "economic revolution," who, along with Premier Li Peng, finally ordered the massacre. Had anyone ever asked what might happen the day this economic revolution collided headlong with the political system and a choice would have to be made between the two? Simply raising the objection was enough to be lumped together with those obtuse souls who refuse to accept that communism can change. Did we have a single precedent to guide us? In the above-mentioned article published by *Commentary,* I undertook to reply to an author who had written in 1988 that China was "halfway across the ford" that in the case of communist reforms it is always the second half of the passage that is the most difficult to negotiate. All previous precedents had been negative, the latest having been the dismissal of Hu Yaobang in January 1987. I do not claim and I do not believe things will always turn out in such a negative fashion. But in the meantime, that was the way things always had gone. We should have been more cautious before proclaiming the "victory of democracy," realizing that a "transition to democracy" in a communist country could not be easy to accomplish, that we were on largely unexplored territory with no map to guide us. Nevertheless, the bloody repression in early June took most Westerners by surprise.

This bloodbath, furthermore, was not a passing spasm due to a momentary panic on the part of the authorities. It was followed by a reversion to mass terror in the purest Stalinist and Maoist tradition: a systematic manhunt, mass arrests, a roundup of all suspects, calls for denunciations of wanted individuals, the public humiliation of "guilty" trouble-makers, the diffusion of televised close-ups of the suspects to enable the public to recognize them and hand them over to the police, the blackmail of families to force them to denounce their "counterrevolutionary" kinsfolk—so many "lessons" administered to the people over the length and breadth of China, according to the model of the Great Terror perfected at the time of the Moscow show trials of 1937.

I might add that one of the dogmas of Western sovietology for the past fifteen years at least (and this despite the Cambodian, Vietnamese, and Ethiopian "exceptions") is that communism has definitely broken with Stalinism and that a relapse into mass terror is unthinkable, above all in Deng Xiaoping's China, the very model of a "liberalization" process.

In dealing with communism, we would do well to beware of snap judgments. Why? For this simple reason: since 1917, the year that saw the birth of the first communist state, we of the democracies have never stopped fooling ourselves regarding the exact nature of communism. It is thus unclear why, thanks to some miracle, we should have become infallible since 1985. Some may reply: it is because of *glasnost,* because today we have more information—which is true. But there was no dearth of information before that date. Neither the Soviet nor the Chinese regime distributed this information willingly, but still, we had plenty available. The trouble was that we either did not use it or thought it too implausible to be believed. A strange phenomenon, indeed—for the errors did not simply emanate from communists and fellow travelers, they also came from politicians and intellectuals who were hostile to communism but who were mistaken, through sheer gullibility or analytical mistakes. Why should we be exempt from such errors today?

Another major cause of the exceptional longevity of communist systems is found in the naïveté of democratic countries, which not only keep believing from week to week that these systems are now cured of the totalitarian virus, but which, instead of exploiting their weaknesses and failures in order to encourage change, seek to help them surmount their difficulties and to aid them when they are threatened from within. I furnished many examples of this naïveté in *How Democracies Perish.* What I emphasized in that book was the illogical contrast between the vulnerability of the system that functions best—democratic capitalism—and the durability in time of the system that does not function at all—socialism. I am referring once again to the *political* system of communism, which is extraordinarily resistant, and not to the socioeconomic system, which is a chronic shipwreck. According to normal criteria of success, the Soviet regime should have collapsed in 1921, given the mass of catastrophes it had engendered and its manifest inability to govern any country for its welfare and improvement. That this "nightmare," as the Russians now openly call it, should have been prolonged to the end of our century is incomprehensible without some explanation. I sought to provide it. Fortunately, analyzing the reasons for an abnormal duration is not the same as proclaiming its absolute perpetuity.

However, I must admit that I did not suspect that the generalized failure of communism, notably its economic failure, would reach such abysmal depths as those of the 1985–90 period. Doubtless influenced by the optimism of specialists and Western newspapers, I did not dare believe that Marxist societies had reached a virtually terminal state, one that was revealed to us in 1985 by Gorbachev, who later contributed to making things worse. Paradoxically but also typically, it was precisely those who previously attacked me, objecting that communism was perfectly viable economically, who now criticize me, just when it is collapsing, for having judged it too favorably. Personally, I have never doubted that communism was *The Great Failure*—to borrow the title of a masterly book written by Zbigniew Brzezinski, who nonetheless underestimated the possibility of a totalitarian revival in China.* What I found mystifying about communism, in addition to its ability to resist internal crises, was how this system, which had failed from the outset, had managed to win so many diplomatic and ideological victories against the democracies and its own society, which it had destroyed. We should not forget the very grave dangers to which the democracies were exposed during the period of so-called détente—an obscene word which nobody in the United States now dares to utter, after the bitter experience of the gigantic strategic, economic, and political swindle to which it gave rise. But let us recall that in the 1970s and even at the time of Andropov, at

*Zbigniew Brzezinski, *The Great Failure* (New York: Charles Scribner's Sons, 1989).

the moment of the Euromissile crisis of 1983, one could not submit the notion of "détente" to rational examination without being branded a "cold warrior" and subjected to a broadside cannonade as a "neoconservative of the far Right."

It is the same today with regard to Gorbachev's weekly initiatives, as soon as we seek to weigh what is serious and what is not serious in his ceaseless "overtures," what might be in the interest of the West and what we would do well to treat warily. The psychological vulnerability of the democracies is part of their makeup, and Gorbachev has been able to exploit it as surely, though in other ways, as his predecessors. At the conclusion of his triumphal trip to Bonn on June 12–15, 1989, Gorbachev put in a plea for a "great Europe without frontiers." This grandiose vision was above all directed against the European Economic Community. During this visit Gorbachev alluded only vaguely to the possibility of tearing down the Berlin Wall, while at the same time evoking the "threat" of a "new wall" destined to render impenetrable a fortress now under construction. This was an allusion to the single European market that is being prepared for the year 1993. Here too the old communist objective of impeding the unification of Western Europe, in particular by luring the Federal Republic toward the East, continued to be Gorbachev's aim, just as it had been that of his predecessors.

All this, and in particular the mystic transports of delight and the irrational rapture with which the people of West Germany greeted Gorbachev during that visit, bodes ill for the future of democracy. Moribund but incapable of dying, communism seems able neither to cure itself nor to pass away. Around it, under it, in its very bosom, efforts have been made to disconnect all of the feeding tubes that have been maintaining it artificially, but these efforts have met with virtually no success. This operation admittedly presents problems, depending on what latitudes and regions of the globe are concerned. For the 2 billion human beings who are still under the grip of communism, extricating oneself from the system cannot be undertaken in the same way everywhere. It is thus not communist *society* that conceived of itself as being irreversible; on the contrary, that society never stops decomposing and erupting. It is the political system of totalitarianism, constructed to eliminate alternative solutions.

Today the new, all-important fact is the depth of the crisis that renders unendurable the contrast between political irreversibility and social mutation. The anticommunist uprisings, their aspirations toward liberty and democracy, reveal a need to do away with this contradiction, which will remain largely insoluble unless and until the keys of political alternation are once again found or invented. This will not be easy. Since the very notion of a government as being the reflection and the instrument of the demands of society is, by definition, incompatible with the nature of totalitarian power, what easy exit, what breach can be found to make an escape from such a carefully sealed enclosure?

It is interesting to note that Chinese communism ran into a political impasse after having succeeded relatively well in its economic reforms, whereas Soviet communism has run into an economic impasse after having with a certain boldness launched a spectacular political reform and a vast liberalization of expression and information. Doubtless this is the case because, no matter how one tries to cure it, a totalitarian system cannot be cured unless it is changed completely—or, in a word, done away with. Failing which—and this could be the fate of China and even of the Soviet Union—a long period of dislocation, chaos, and anarchy is bound to ensue.

The revolutions at this end of the twentieth century are anticommunist. Poor Marx! Today it is against socialism that the masses, in particular the youth, are revolting. But the left-wing and the "radical chic" intelligentsia of the West, after having long upheld and justified Stalinist regimes, continues to regard itself as the only group entrusted with a universal liberating mission, and it goes on damning as "reactionaries" and as members of the "new Right" those intellectuals who have always fought on behalf of democracy and freedom. If the students who were massacred in Peking in early June 1989 were of the "new Right," that would be one thing. But if they are regarded as genuine freedom fighters and victims of totalitarianism, and if there is a consensus of opinion for considering them as such—which seems to be the case—then Simon Leys, Solzhenitsyn, and a few others have a right to expect apologies. More generously inclined than the West's pigheaded Left, the Soviet authorities, in the spring of 1989, were considering the possibility of offering apologies to the author of *The Gulag Archipelago.* *

Totally different is the state of mind of leftists in the West, or at least of those who are the most radically inclined. Thus *The Nation,* which has remained an intellectual bastion for rad chic fanatics and a stronghold of procommunist sovietology, thought it quite normal in the spring of 1988 to publish an article that must have delighted the conservative diehards in Moscow and particularly the top hierarchy of the KGB

*This may sound incredible, but it is the strict truth, confirmed for me by a Frenchman of Russian origin who was told this by responsible persons during a trip to Moscow in April 1989.

since it denounced the Center for Democracy, which had been set up in the United States by Russian dissident exiles closely linked to Sergei Grigoriantz's *Glasnost* periodical in the USSR. *Glasnost,* which has had some trouble surviving (having more than once suffered police raids, with seizures of entire issues as well as printing material), is the only publication in the Soviet Union that is truly independent of the regime. Many newspapers, weeklies, and monthlies now support Gorbachev's reforms, convinced that to return to the intellectual aridity of the Brezhnev era would be a national catastrophe, but they are also careful not to be too sharply critical of the Soviet Union's new president. *Glasnost* alone has remained ruggedly independent by refusing to compromise on fundamental principles. However, the article published by *The Nation*—which was offered to *Literaturnaya Gazeta* even before it appeared in the USA (!) and which was immediately picked up and translated by several Soviet newspapers—accused the Center for Democracy, and thus *Glasnost,* of being indirectly subsidized by the CIA via the National Endowment for Democracy, which, according to *The Nation,* promotes "a program that more closely resembles intelligence-gathering than human-rights work." The consequences of this cascade of calumnies were not long in coming: Sergei Grigoriantz and his friends were the targets of systematic persecutions and were subjected to all kinds of harassment by the Soviet authorities. Indeed, in an interview granted to *The Washington Post,* published on May 22, 1988, Mikhail Gorbachev personally denounced *Glasnost* in mendacious terms as a "parasite funded by the West." Thus leftists in the West were able to culminate their illustrious careers as "progressives" by acting as police informers for the Soviet KGB and the Kremlin.*

Just as I have long believed in the chronic economic failure of communism, so I have never doubted that the populations forced to submit to the communist yoke find it unbearable. Brute force, police repression, concentration camps, and omnipresent fear alone, I was convinced, have kept such captive peoples from revolting against their masters more often. It was not I who asserted that they were satisfied with their lot. Quite a number of sovietologists had invented a theory according to which communism provided these populations with a realistic measure of personal security, along with a modest but regular improvement in the standard of living—satisfactions which, though mediocre in appearance, were more equitably distributed and basically more solid and

---

*Kevin Coogan and Katrina van den Heuvel, "U.S.A. Funds for Soviet Dissidents," *The Nation,* March 19, 1988.

durable than the chaotic ups and downs and deceptive illusions of democratic capitalism. Recent events in Poland, East Germany, Czechoslovakia, Romania, Bulgaria, the USSR, and China have shown the emptiness of this theory. As soon as the populations of communist countries glimpse the possibility of rebelling without risking too ferocious a repression—and sometimes they have even been willing to take this risk—they unequivocally manifest their detestation for the system. Yet notwithstanding the intensity of this popular rejection and the depth of the crisis in which it now finds itself, communism everywhere displays an astounding capacity for resistance. As I write these lines in the summer of 1989, not a single communized country has yet succeeded in freeing itself completely. The Vietnamese, notwithstanding the collapse of their economy, have succeeded in consolidating their military grip on Cambodia while officially "evacuating" this neighboring country. The "simultaneous" evacuation of Angola by Cubans and South Africans in 1988 resulted in the sole departure of the latter. The regime in Luanda remained a communist regime, with no immediate prospect of free elections in the country.* Once again communism's capacity for survival on the geostrategic level remained impressively strong. Only the incomprehension, complacence, and complicity of the democracies have made it possible for communism, despite its extravagant absurdities, to last as long and to extend itself as far afield as it has. The problem, in a sense, is not that of communism—it is that of the democracies.

For it is more than likely that once the communist adversary has been weakened or has disappeared from the scene, the democracies would behave toward another adversary in much the same way, displaying the same ignorance, the same inconsistencies, the same cowardice that in the past they displayed toward Nazism. As Francis Loewenheim reminds us: "From the early 1930s, the democracies—politicians, media, schools—played straight into Hitler's hands. In the midst of the worst

---

*The agreement reached in Zaire on June 22, 1989, between Jonas Savimbi's UNITA and the communist government of Luanda contains certain positive features, such as the promise to integrate UNITA partisans into various levels of the Angolan administration. But the agreement also contains a glaringly negative feature: the implicit recognition of the communist regime despite its *illegitimate* origins (see Chapter 8) and its economic and military setbacks. The promise of elections to be held within two years echoes a similar promise made back in 1975—and never kept. If such elections now take place, they will be held under the control of the Luanda government. No precise date has been fixed for the departure of *all* Cuban troops, whereas the South Africans evacuated Angola in 1988. In view of the communist regime's lackluster record, this accord may be regarded as a major diplomatic success, particularly since it has been accompanied by new promises of Western credits. It is probably fair to say that only a communist regime, in such conditions, could have succeeded in obtaining such manifest advantages.

modern depression, they were consumed by pacifist guilt and self-doubt over the Great War and the peace treaties that followed. They were prepared to make significant concessions to Germany. They failed to recognize that Hitler's goals were light-years beyond those of the Weimar Republic he had destroyed. Did the democracies know what was afoot in Germany? They did not lack published evidence. What they lacked was a willingness to understand the policies that Hitler made no attempt to disguise."*

In this passage we find described the same kind of casual neglect and willful ignorance of *information* that has characterized the behavior of the democracies over and against communism since the end of World War II, along with a blind trust in the magic power of unilateral concessions as a means of appeasement. If this behavior has not resulted in the victory of communism, it is certainly not because of the tactical cleverness or the political intelligence of the democracies; it is because communism began, on its own, to collapse from within. This happy accident, if it attains its final stage, will not occur because the democracies as a whole have analyzed and managed the communist phenomenon correctly. It will occur in spite of them. Communism is such a wretched system that it will crumble notwithstanding the deliberate or unwitting, active or passive aid that the democracies have continued to contribute, and which, led in particular by the Federal Republic of Germany, they continued to provide throughout 1989. Thus, were another totalitarian menace of a different sort to present itself later on, the democracies might very well commit the same errors and display the same weaknesses, always for the same, unchanging reason: their unwillingness to face harsh facts and their inability to use the knowledge, the notions, and the information they have readily available and to draw the appropriate conclusions.†

Through an unexpected paradox of history, one of the men who has the most clearly understood that the present-day world cannot be managed by persisting forever in generalized falsehood is Mikhail Gorbachev. What is the underlying meaning of *glasnost,* if not the public recognition of the principle that a society that does not accept the truth about itself is a society that will destroy itself? It is revealing that this awareness should have surfaced in the very society that promoted the systematic use of falsehood more than any other, and which paid the

*Francis Loewenheim, "Democracies Never Again So Weak?" *International Herald Tribune,* April 20, 1989.

†This Introduction was written prior to Saddam Hussein's invasion of Kuwait.

price for it by developing a numbing necrosis in all of its vital functions. In effect, Mikhail Gorbachev has implicitly acknowledged that Solzhenitsyn and Boris Souvarine were right, as were all those sovietologists who have been so stupidly labeled "conservative"—Robert Conquest, Michel Heller, Martin Malia, Adam Ulam, Richard Pipes, Alain Besançon, and Branko Lazitch.

This said, the main evil in democratic countries and in countries that are neither democratic nor totalitarian (this being the most populous category) is not the absolute lie, fashioned and decreed by communist regimes. Rather, it is a kind of confused half lie (or half truth), inside of which the information, disinformation, and misinformation that nourish public debates splash and thrash around. As noted, public debates are often vitiated by excessive haste and trivialization, with ideas discussed that are either distortions of those that people are supposed to be discussing or amputated fragments of the ideas and examples that illustrate them. For example, this book has been interpreted by many European reviewers as being a work aimed "against" journalism, whereas journalism is in fact only one aspect of a far vaster inquiry. Furthermore, to claim that we journalists sometimes fool our readers by professional incompetence or ideological dishonesty is no more an attack against "journalism" as such than a campaign against bad doctors and bad hospitals is an attack against "medicine" or "health."

Another, more "philosophical" way of criticizing this book has been to accuse it of expressing an overly simpleminded confidence in rationalism, too literally derived from the eighteenth-century Age of Enlightenment. This is truly a disconcerting objection, for what marked the spirit of the Enlightenment was precisely a burning faith in the omnipotence of knowledge. The truth, it was thought in the eighteenth century, is difficult of access because "prejudices," "superstitions," and forms of censorship hinder one's approach to it. But for the philosophers of the Enlightenment it naturally followed that once the obstacles have been overcome and we are in possession of the truth, we will mold our conduct and the governance of society accordingly. However, the main thesis of this book is exactly the contrary. It is based on the cultural contradiction that separates accessibility to knowledge from the irrationality of human behavior. If I effectively adhere to the tradition of the Age of Enlightenment, it is because I believe that only truth and knowledge can serve as a sound guide for action, for the common welfare of mankind. But over and against the cultural optimism of the Enlightenment philosophers, I do not believe that there is an automatic link leading from true knowledge to sound action. I believe this link can be established only through persistent, willful effort, intellectual rigor, mental discipline—in short, that the link is anything but natural. I also think that the hour has struck and that this effort must now be made for the survival of mankind. Illness, as Proust liked to say, is the best doctor, for it is the only reminder that can really force us to take care of our health. Are we sick enough to be forced to follow this rule?

I should reply to the question raised at the start of this book. Does our good fortune in having at our disposal an incomparably greater wealth of knowledge and information than was available three centuries, or a mere two years, or even six weeks ago cause us to be wiser in our decision making? For the time being, the answer is no. But this answer could change.

It is not, I must insist, a question of determining whether our knowledge has increased or not. It is clear enough that knowledge, and particularly scientific knowledge, continues to increase uninterruptedly. The decisive question concerns the place that knowledge and what might be called "solid information" occupy in the guiding of day-to-day action. The conclusion I draw from a cursory examination of this problem is that knowledge plays a part only when it is not blocked by some sterile prejudice. In other words, error, based on dogmatic "principles" and unworkable "solutions," is generally preferred to effective action based on knowledge and solid information. Needless to say, no one opposes improvements in the technology available to dental surgeons or to construction engineers, even though (I will furnish several examples) science or "trivial" truth do not always emerge victorious in their battles with prejudices. Sometimes in practice—one has only to think of the "Copernican revolution" or Einsteinian relativity—a scientific truth finally manages to impose itself. But like the more trivial versions of the truth that guide our daily lives, it participates only partially and above all *in good time* for the elaboration of a vision of the world which molds public opinion and weighs on the course of events. For that is the decisive factor which modifies the influence knowledge can exercise in human affairs: the element of time. To understand what needs to be done too late—at least for taking effective action—is almost the same as not to understand.

Will we succeed in taking this giant step in human history, this new, "neolithic" revolution—that is, by harmonizing our knowledge with our ways of behaving? If I have momentarily answered this question with "no," I must add that there are signs that permit me to say that in certain cases we *have* taken this step and have shown that we know how to modify our behavior. For example, the manner in which the world economic crisis of 1973 onward was handled shows that the governments in the most developed countries had learned the lessons of errors committed in the 1930s. They did not, like their predecessors, close their borders, raise tariff barriers, asphyxiate the world economy through protectionist measures, forcibly reduce the workweek (as the French socialists did in 1936) in the illusory belief that this was the best way to create more jobs—all of which were mistakes that in the 1930s helped to transform a momentary breakdown into an international cataclysm. This, then, is an example of acquired experience being harnessed to action for the benefit of all.

We should, however, note that some leaders aggravated the crisis by resorting to Keynesianism, which in the 1960s had revealed itself to be an insufficient guide for the solution of all economic problems, and by propagating hostility to economic liberalism, considered to be harmful to the weak and the poor, when in fact it was saving people from poverty. Nor should we forget that in 1988, at the end of his second four-year term, Ronald Reagan was regarded by most of the "eggheads" of the planet as a perfect imbecile and a heartless foe of the poor, when in fact he was struggling to keep the U.S. Congress from adopting protectionist legislation, a sinister holdover from the 1930s. On the other hand, the "liberals" of the Democratic Party and the trade unions, eager to see the tariff barriers raised—an expert recipe for increasing unemployment, retarding the country's technological advances, and adding to the economic suffocation of the Third World—enjoyed the reputation of being generous philanthropists and supporters of the weak and the impoverished! Still, the important thing is that between 1974 and 1984, when the industrial world finally emerged from the economic crisis, the principal actors on the whole saw and acted correctly, even if certain pontificators continued to think and talk rubbish.

The new, serious phenomenon we have witnessed since the early 1980s is that whereas democratic capitalism was overcoming its crisis and exhibiting a new vitality, the communist world was entering the gravest crisis in its history, marked by the evident shipwreck of the Soviet economy. Gorbachev was essentially the product of this contrast. As Françoise Thom has written, Gorbachev's emergence was in a way a consequence of Reagan's success.*

Contemporary man's conversion to truly intelligent action has not yet been accomplished, but it is possible. It has not yet been massively realized, but it can be. Should the contrary occur, our civilization cannot

*Françoise Thom, *Le Moment Gorbachev* (Paris: Hachette-Pluriel, 1989).

avoid regressing toward methods of management in which knowledge is not necessary. Such methods exist. In such a civilization we would doubtless be less effective in practical matters but perhaps happier, if it be true that man's happiness depends less on what he is than on what he fancies himself to be. However, soon enough it will be necessary to advance or to regress, for we cannot forever go on resisting the pathogenic tension inflicted on us by our hybrid culture, in which each of our states of consciousness is divided between what we know and at the same time deny to be true, and in which every honest soul is condemned, as Emile Cioran has put it, to oscillate "between opportunism and despair"—and, I would add, between cynicism and contrition.

THE FLIGHT
FROM TRUTH

CHAPTER 1

On Our Resistance to Information

The foremost of all the forces that drive the world is falsehood. More than any before it, twentieth-century civilization has depended on information, teaching, science, culture—in short, on knowledge, as well as on a system of government which, by its very definition, seeks to make knowledge available to all: democracy. Clearly, freedom of information, like democracy itself, has known enormous variations in its practical application from one country to the next. Few are the countries in which both have managed to get through the century without an interruption, or indeed without an outright suppression, lasting several generations. But no matter how intermittent the part information plays in influencing the persons who determine the course of events (i.e., political leaders) and those who react to those events, it is today unquestionably more important, more constant, and more widely diffused than in earlier times. Those who act have better data on which to base their actions, and those on the receiving end are much better informed about what those who act are doing.

It is therefore interesting to inquire whether this preponderance of available knowledge—with its detail, its abundance, its ever broader and swifter dissemination—has enabled humanity to guide itself more judiciously than in the past. The question is all the more important since the perfecting and accelerating of the techniques of transmission and the steady increase in the number of individuals who benefit from them will make the twenty-first century an age in which, even more than in the twentieth, information will be a central element of civilization.

Our century has witnessed a notable increase of knowledge along with a similar increase in the number of human beings who have access to that knowledge. In other words, knowledge—and in particular scientific knowledge—has increased, and it has been accompanied by an enormous expansion in the volume of information making it available to the general public. To begin with, the educational process is being prolonged ever further, into late adolescence, and various forms of education are being made available to adults. At the same time, the tools of mass communication have been multiplying and now shower us with words and images to a degree inconceivable in the past. Whether it is to popularize the news of a scientific discovery and the technical prospects it opens up, to announce a political event, or to publish figures enabling one to analyze an economic situation, the universal information machine is becoming more and more egalitarian and generous, ceaselessly reducing the old discrimination between the elite in power, who knew little, and the common run of the ruled, who knew nothing. Now both know—or can know—a great deal. The superiority of our century over preceding centuries seems to be due to the fact that those in positions of authority in all walks of life have increasingly had at their disposal a far greater and more abundant fund of information and knowledge with which to prepare their decisions, while the public is receiving an abundance of information which should enable it to judge the correctness or wisdom of those decisions. Such an auspicious convergence of favorable factors should logically have engendered a prodigious improvement in the human condition. But has this happened?

To answer "yes" would be frivolous. Ours has been one of the bloodiest centuries in human history, marked by the vast scope of its oppressions, persecutions, exterminations. It is the twentieth century that invented, or at least systematized, genocide, the concentration camp, the extermination of entire peoples by organized famine, which conceived in theory and instituted in practice the most advanced systems of bondage that have ever been devised to crush such huge numbers of human beings. These astonishing achievements would appear to undermine the notion that our age has seen the triumph of democracy. And yet, in spite of everything, our age has seen just that, and for two good reasons. Notwithstanding many setbacks, the century is moving toward its close with a greater number of democracies, and these in far better working order, than at any other moment of history. Furthermore, even though flouted and abused, democracy has imposed itself on nearly everyone as the theoretical norm. The divergences concern methods—the "false" or "true" application of the democratic principle. Even if we deplore the mendacious character of tyrannies that claim to operate in the name of a supposedly genuine democracy or with the promise of a "perfect" democracy forever just over the horizon, we must readily admit that the species of dictatorial regimes that were founded on the explicit, doctrinal rejection of democracy disappeared with the collapse of Fascism in 1945 and of Francoism in 1975. Those that remain are marginal.

Recently tyrannies have at least been reduced to justifying themselves in the name of a morality they violate and have been driven to verbal acrobatics which, given their monotonous implausibility, take in fewer dupes each day. The employment of this double-talk does not affect the problem of the effectiveness of information. Totalitarian leaders, who try to control everything, have as much information at their disposal as do democratic leaders, even if they desperately try to keep it from their subjects, albeit with incomplete success. The economic failures of communist countries, for example, have not stemmed from the fact that their leaders were ignorant of the causes. In general, they have known the reasons well and occasionally, obliquely, they have admitted as much. But they have not wanted to, and could not, suppress those causes, at least not completely, and often they have done no more than attack the symptoms, fearing to jeopardize a political and social system more precious in their eyes than economic success. In such cases, the reason for the ineffectiveness of information itself is understandable. One can always refrain from using what one knows. Frequently in the life of societies, as of individuals, the truth is ignored because drawing the pertinent conclusions would be contrary to one's interests.

Nevertheless, the inability of information to influence actions, or simply convictions, would be a commonplace misfortune were it due merely to censorship, hypocrisy, and falsehood. It would still be comprehensible if to those causes were added the mechanisms of intellectual dishonesty so pointedly exposed over the ages by moralists and playwrights, novelists and psychologists. Still, it is surprising to see how all-pervasive these mechanisms of bad faith have become, in what is now a veritable global industry of communication. The public's perfunctory opinion of journalists as well as politicians is usually severe; it tends to regard dishonesty as a kind of second nature existing in most of those whose mission it is to inform, to think, to speak, to manage. Could it be that the very abundance of accessible knowledge and available information arouses in some minds a desire to bury them rather than use them? Could it be that the insidious invasion of the truth here and there unleashes resentment rather than satisfaction, a sense of peril rather than of power? How can we explain the rarity of accurate and precise information in free societies, where those who are curious have ready access to information and where most of the material obstacles to the diffusion of knowledge have disappeared? Yes, by raising such questions one approaches the misty banks of the real mystery.

"Open" societies, to adopt the adjective used by Henri Bergson and Karl Popper, are both the cause and the effect of freedom to inform and to inform oneself. Yet those who gather information frequently seem moved by a desire to falsify the evidence, and those who receive to elude it. In such societies the duty to inform and the public's right to information are endlessly invoked. But journalists (and of course politicians) are as ready to betray this duty as their clients are reluctant to take advantage of their right. In the hypocritical game played out by the partners in this informational comedy, producers and consumers pretend to respect each other, whereas in fact they fear and in some cases despise each other.

Only in open societies can one observe and measure the genuine zeal human beings show for saying and welcoming (or ignoring) the truth, since its circulation is unhampered by anything but themselves. But— and this is not the least intriguing aspect of this situation—how can they so often act against their own interests? For democracy cannot thrive without a certain diet of truth. It cannot survive if the degree of truth in current circulation falls below a minimal level. A democratic regime, founded on the free determination of important choices made by a majority, condemns itself to death if most of the citizens who have to choose between various options make their decisions in ignorance of reality, blinded by passions or misled by fleeting impressions. If in a democracy information is so free, so sacred, it is because it can thwart everything that obscures the judgment of the citizens, the ultimate deciders and judges of the public weal. But what happens if the judgment of the judges is obscured by the nature of the information dispensed? For let us be honest in facing this fundamental fact: those who cultivate competence, accuracy, and intellectual honesty tend to be the smallest segment of the journalistic community, their audience the smallest sector of the public. Only too often the big newspaper stories, the televised documentaries or debates, the press campaigns that generate the greatest heat and dust turn out to be of an informational poverty matched only by the inherent fraudulence of sensation seeking. Even what is popularly called "investigative journalism," which is praised as the very model of courage or intransigence, is significantly swayed by motivations that are not always determined by the disinterested cult of full and fairly interpreted information. Often a particular dossier is brought to light less for its intrinsic merit than because it is capable of destroying a particular statesman or politician. This or that other dossier, of infinitely greater import for the general welfare, is neglected or sidetracked because it lacks any immediate personal, partisan, or popular utility.

Whatever may be said about journalism (and I shall say a great deal), we should beware of incriminating journalists. If, indeed, far too few of them live up to the theoretical ideal, it is, I must insist, because they get precious little encouragement from the public; and so it is to the general public, and thus to each one of us, that one must look for the causes of the supremacy of incompetent or unscrupulous journalists. The supply is determined by the demand. But the demand, in matters of information and analysis, emanates from our own convictions. And how are these formed? We adopt our most cherished preferences in such a welter of approximation, prejudice, and passion that later, when confronted by a novel fact, we sniff at it and weigh it less for its exactness than for its capacity to serve or to counter our system of interpretation, our sense of moral comfort, our attachment to a network of personal relationships and loyalties. According to the laws that govern the mixture of words, attachments, wishes, hatreds, notions, and fears that we call "opinion," a fact is neither real nor unreal; rather, it is desirable or undesirable. It serves as an accomplice or plotter, as an ally or adversary, not as an object that needs to be known. At times we even elevate this priority of possible utilization over readily available knowledge to the status of a doctrine, thus justifying it in principle.

That our opinions, no matter how disinterested, stem from diverse influences among which a genuine knowledge of the subject or of the objective situation is often in last place—behind beliefs, cultural factors, chance, appearances, different forms of bias, the desire to see reality conform to our prejudices, mental laziness—none of this is really new. Such has been the case since the day Plato taught us the difference between opinion and science. And indeed, the novelty is even less today, inasmuch as the development of science since Plato's time has steadily accentuated the distinction between the verifiable and the unverifiable, between a process of reasoning that is demonstrable and one that is not. But simply to realize that we are now living in a world fashioned more than ever by the applications of scientific research is not to guarantee that more human beings than ever think in scientific terms. Most of us use tools fashioned by science, take care of our health thanks to science, have or do not have children thanks to science, without, intellectually speaking, having anything to do with the scientific disciplines responsible for the discoveries from which we benefit. In addition, even the tiny minority of persons who are engaged in those disciplines acquire their nonscientific convictions in irrational ways. By virtue of its specific nature, scientific work imposes criteria that cannot in the long run be eluded. In the same way a sprinter, no matter how crazy or stupid he may be outside, accepts the rational law of the stopwatch once he has entered the stadium. There would be no point in his copying the politician or the artist by putting up posters or advertisements, or by holding public meetings in order to proclaim himself a world champion and to announce that he can run the hundred-meter dash in eight seconds, when everyone can verify the fact that he has never been clocked under eleven seconds. Though obliged by the rules of the track to behave rationally, he is, however, quite capable of running down an ascending escalator. A great scientist can forge his political and moral opinions in just as arbitrary a fashion and under the sway of considerations that are as insane as those that move human beings who have no experience of scientific reasonining. There is in his internal makeup no necessary osmosis between the mental activity to which he is constrained by his discipline—to make no assertion without proof—and his opinions on current affairs and everyday matters, where he is subject to the same enthusiasms and prejudices as any other man. Like him and in just as unforeseeable a way, he can incline toward common sense or extravagance and turn his back on the evidence when it counters his beliefs or preferences or sympathies.

To live in an age modeled by science does not, consequently, render any of us much more likely to behave in a scientific manner—outside of those fields and conditions in which the constraint of scientific procedures reigns supreme. When he has a choice, Man is today neither more nor less rational and honest than he was in epochs designated as prescientific. To return to the previously mentioned paradox, one can even argue that intellectual incoherence and dishonesty are more alarming and serious nowadays since, in the case of science, we have before us a model of what rigorous thinking can be. But the scientific researcher is not by nature a more honest man than the ignoramus. He is somebody who has voluntarily locked himself inside rules that condemn him, so to speak, to honesty. A particular ignoramus may temperamentally be more honest than such-and-such a scientist. In disciplines that cannot by their very nature provide total demonstrable constraint, imposing itself from outside on the researcher's subjectivity—for example, the social sciences and history—we often see, alas, the flourishing of light-headedness, insincerity, the ideological manipulation of facts, and the tendentiousness of clan rivalries, which occasionally take precedence over the pure love of truth by which such researchers are supposedly consumed.

It is well to recall these elementary caveats, for we shall understand nothing of the torments of our supposedly scientific age unless we realize that when we speak of "scientific behavior" we should not refer exclusively to those mental procedures that are, strictly speaking, the properties of scientific research. To behave scientifically—that is, by combining rationality and honesty—means not to express an opinion about a question without considering all of the information at one's disposal, without deliberately eliminating anything, without deforming or expurgating a a single element, and after reaching as best and as honestly as one can the conclusions that seem called for. Nine times out of ten the available information will not be complete enough or its interpretation sufficiently rigorous to lead to a certainty. But if the final judgment rarely has a completely scientific character, the attitude leading toward it can always have this character. The Platonic distinction between opinion and science—or, to put it better (in my opinion), between conjectural judgment *(doxa)* and certain knowledge *(episteme)*—is based on the raw material about which one opines and not on the attitude of the person formulating the opinion. Whether it is a matter of simple opinion or certain knowledge, in both cases Plato assumed that logic and intellectual honesty prevail. The difference springs from the fact that certain knowledge is derived from things that lend themselves to irrefutable demonstration, whereas opinion roams through regions where all we can do is collect a bundle of likelihoods. It is nonetheless true that an opinion, even when merely plausible and bereft of absolute certainty, can (or cannot) be forged in as rigorous a manner as possible on the basis of an honest examination of all accessible data. Conjecture is not the same as arbitrary judgment. It requires no less probity, no less exactitude, no less erudition than science. On the contrary, it may require even more, given that the virtue of prudence constitutes its principal safeguard.

Respect for the truth—or its least imperfect approximation—and the wish to use the information at our disposal in an honest manner spring from personal inclinations that are quite independent of the state of contemporary science. In all probability the percentage of human beings possessing such inclinations was not appreciably smaller in prescientific periods than it is today. Or rather, one would like to know if the existence in our present-day world of a definite standard of certain (i.e., scientific) knowledge has necessarily resulted in the appearance among us of a higher percentage of persons inclined to think rationally. Before hazarding an answer to this question, let us simply remind ourselves that in any case far and away the largest number of issues about which contemporary mankind forms its convictions and takes its decisions belongs to the conjectural sector of human thought and not to the scientific one. We nevertheless enjoy a considerable superiority over those who lived before us, for in this same conjectural sector we can exploit a wealth of information that was unknown to them. Thus, quite apart from the advantages of science, our chances are greater than ever, in other fields as well, of arriving at what Plato called "true opinion"— that is, of conjecture which, although not based on a binding demonstrability, is nonetheless correct. But do we profit as much as we should from such opportunities? On the answer to this question depends the survival of our civilization.

CHAPTER 2

What Is Our Civilization?

I t might seem pointless to speak of "our" civilization. Humanity
cannot be thought of as comprising one civilization by any reasonable standard—be it political institutions, wealth and technology,
civil and penal laws, customs—let alone in terms of beliefs, religion,
morals, art. In addition, the tendency since the middle of the century
to insist on a nation's or a people's cultural diversity, particularity, and
(that revealing catchphrase) "identity" has prevailed over an acceptance
of certain virtually universal criteria of civilization, however vaguely
expressed. Decolonization has further spurred the rejection of what is
all too simply called the "Western model," this model being thought of
as a recipe for economic development and as exhibiting an attachment
to "rational" modes of thought which even the West contests. In fact,
many voices in the West have humbly endorsed the condemnation of
ethnocentrism, the relativization of cultures, and the proclaimed equivalence of all forms of morality. Paradoxically, Westerners have been
almost alone in doing so; the spokesmen of non-Western cultures, at

least in their most strident proclamations, seem to have appropriated and extolled the ethnocentric intolerance that was the rule in human communities of the past, condemning the way of life of others, and especially the "Western model," as foolish, impure, indeed impious. This has been particularly true of Islam, in the more virulent manifestations of its modern renascence, but not only of Islam.

It thus seems an ill-chosen moment to speak of a common civilization, since human beings once again are willfully rushing toward fragmentation, glorifying a reciprocal, obtuse incomprehension of cultures different from their own. Have we ever been further removed from a universally shared system of values? Yet this flagrant contradiction is merely superficial. No matter how diverse, all civilizations today coexist in some form of perpetual interaction, the combined effects of which affect them more in the long run than their individual particularities. The existence of this interaction in the economic, geopolitical, and geostrategic fields is now taken for granted. On the other hand, despite all the loose talk on the subject, few persons seem to realize to what extent information has become the principal instrument, the permanent agent and mirror of the planet's omnipresence for all those who inhabit it, not through the provision of accurate information—there precisely is the problem—but thanks to a continuous torrent of messages, which begins by submerging individual minds from early schooling on; for teaching is neither more nor less than one of the ways in which information is dispensed. At any given moment, contemporary Man has an image of the world and of his own society in that world. He acts and reacts with reference to that image. He accepts its implications willingly, passively, or grudgingly, or revolts against them. The more twisted and distorted the picture, the more dangerous his actions and reactions can become, both for himself and for others. But except for extreme, increasingly rare cases of primitive tribes or groups living in almost total isolation from the rest of the world, it is simply impossible for the average person today not to have some global conception of the planet on which he lives.

The claim of Third World countries to their own "cultural identity" enables the ruling minorities in many of them to justify, among other things, the censorship of information and the exercise of dictatorship. Under the pretext of protecting their peoples' "cultural purity," these leaders do their utmost to keep them ignorant of what is going on in the world and what the rest of the world thinks of them. They let a trickle of news seep through, inventing, when necessary, scraps of information that permit them to mask their own failures and to perpetuate their impostures. But the very zeal they display in seeking to intercept, falsify, or fabricate information reveals how dependent they know themselves to be on information control—even more, if it were possible, than on their hold over the economy or the army. How many heads of state in our time have owed their renown not to what they were actually doing but to what they got people to say they were doing!

The suppression or destruction of accurate information and the fabrication and dissemination of false "information" thus result from a carefully calculated, rational analysis in perfect conformity with the rationalized "Western model" such leaders supposedly reject. In the West it has long been understood that in a society which lives and breathes and is animated by the flow of information, the power to regulate this flow is decisive. On this point at least, the self-proclaimed protectors of cultural identity have had no trouble heeding the lessons provided by Western "rationality."

As for the irrationality of the West, we have only to think of our continuing philosophical controversies over the nature of "rationalism." That after three millennia of philosophical discussion, persons trained in the traditions of the West should not have rid themselves of the vice of bandying about abstract notions without having properly defined them proves that a civilization can be constructed on modes of thought that are practiced by only a tiny minority of its members. In particular, present-day philosophers, so eager to show off but forgetful of the rudimentary techniques of discussion and intellectual investigation taught us by Plato and Aristotle, have not helped their contemporaries to indulge in serious reflection. We should not, therefore, be surprised to see how often an exchange of viewpoints concerning elementary concepts bogs down in the most dismaying confusion.

But, it may be objected, why is serious reflection so necessary? I accept the objection; there is no obligation to reflect seriously except with respect to certain clearly determined objectives. The construction of an airplane is not something that necessarily follows from any imperative inherent in the human condition. An airplane is something one can do without. But if you do decide to construct an airplane capable of flying, you will not be able to do so if you do not observe rational norms based on previous experience. Which, however, fortunately does not mean that rationality must govern all the activities of an aeronautical engineer; he or she can paint, compose or listen to music, or practice a religion without ceasing to design airplanes. Let's hope Mexicans will not become "rational" in questions of art; but I doubt that Mexico's financial system can be improved except through rational calculations.

It may surprise me to discover that a Singhalese finance minister, who happens to be a friend of mine, consults a sorcerer in order to remove the spell cast on his mother-in-law; but his "cultural identity" in such a matter neither concerns nor worries me, though it strikes me as being irrational and ineffective, even with regard to the problem of the mother-in-law. On the other hand, when this same minister takes part in a conference held by the International Monetary Fund, he involves himself in and can in no way wriggle his way out of a universal context of economic rationality. In his professional capacity he approves of its axioms. Were he to reject to them, he would exclude himself from the system or paralyze its local application and benefits. In the rational sphere he can only act rationally; but life, of course, has many other spheres.

This distinction does not mean that every person unfailingly behaves in a rational manner, even in those fields that can and should be governed solely by reason. If so, mankind would long since have spared itself certain harsh consequences. But often humanity does not act as much as is commonly supposed in accordance with rational interests. Human beings frequently display a disconcerting "disinterestedness," as witness the fact that they keep stubbornly engaging themselves in all sorts of imbecilic enterprises for which they pay dearly. Rationality? Many of Man's activities are not dependent on it, and even in those that are dependent on it, we persistently wander off the path of reason every time we think we can get away with it.

It is shameful to have to insist on such truisms. This is because the meaning of the word "rationalism" keeps being altered. It might, for example, refer to the great metaphysical systems of the seventeenth century, and, as in the case of Descartes and Leibniz, signify that the universe is rational because God himself is Reason. A century later, it embraced the contrary notion, with the result that the "cult of Reason" assumed an antireligious and atheistic connotation. Reason then became the human faculty *par excellence:* "Enlightenment" was opposed to "superstition," to barbarism, to "liberty-killing" restrictions not authorized by any law. Universal and identical for all human beings, as long as its transparency remained untroubled, Reason alone, according to this philosophy, was capable of explaining nature, formulating moral laws, defining a political system, guaranteeing both human rights and the legitimate authority of governments. Then, from the start of the nineteenth century—which is when the word acquired widespread currency—the champions of rationalism were above all the enemies of dogma and the faithful followers of Science.

Even if it has quite recently lost its antireligious character, the intellectual and moral conception of rationalism, inherited from the age of the Enlightenment, remains one of the intellectual buttresses of our contemporary world. When a stricken country needs medicines and foodstuffs, it appeals to the rationality of the West, not to its own cultural identity. The rational serves as an explicit or implicit yardstick each time a petition is signed against some oppression, a violation of human rights, a persecution, a coup d'état, a dictatorship, racial discrimination, war, social or economic injustice. Needless to say, most societies, governments, parties, and coteries employ this yardstick to judge and condemn others rather than themselves. Nevertheless, rationality is the yardstick they accept, even if they cheat outrageously in the way they use it.

During the nineteenth and twentieth centuries the word "rationalism" was used pejoratively and in yet another sense—to designate the type of narrow-mindedness that in French is derisively called "scientism." This consists of reducing all activities of the mind to their purely logical components, and of ignoring the originality and function of myth, poetry, faith, ideology, intuition, passion, the cult of beauty or even the thirst for the evil and the hideous, the craving for servitude, the fondness for error. However, from a critique of such narrow-mindedness it is all too easy to drift toward the more or less corollary thesis, that in the final analysis there is no fundamental difference between rational and other modes of behavior. Or, to put it more clearly, there are no forms of behavior that are truly rational, no forms of knowledge that are truly scientific. All behavior is then regarded as irrational, and all elements of knowledge regarded as of equal value. So-called rational behavior is such only in appearance, while points of view are assumed to be the result of choices that are always emotively and ideologically inspired.

Even if this last hypothesis were well founded, it would in no way diminish the rational character of certain modes of behavior or the superior efficacy of certain forms of knowledge. Even if a "scientist" sectarianism prompts me to explain my attack of flu as resulting from a virus rather than from a curse cast on me by an evil-intentioned neighbor, I shall surely increase my chances of getting well by attacking the virus rather than my neighbor. Although there are millions of human beings, some of them to be found in the very citadels of Western rationalism, who believe or fancy that they believe in astrology, the same persons, when confronted with the prospect of fire or earthquake, go to consult their insurance broker rather than their astrologer. The fiercest defender of the "occult sciences" will, before taking to the road for a long trip, entrust the inspection of his car to a mechanic rather than to a magician. In the same way the intellectual and political leaders of societies that exalt their anti-Western "cultural identity" live and function simultaneously in two spheres: in a verbal sphere, where they spend their time proclaiming their "cultural identity," and in an operational sphere, where they know perfectly well that imported tractors and fertilizers are of greater benefit to their agriculture than ethnocentric speeches.

Only too often, in practice, the incantatory, and more particularly the ideological, dimension prevails over rationality. But sooner or later the dire consequences of this preference ineluctably exact their cruel toll. Sometimes those responsible for this kind of error, or their successors, end up denouncing ideology, if not always correcting it. Such recantations are periodically heard in communist lands and Third World countries—for example, in the wake of blunders committed in the name of "autocentric development." The loudspeaker used by ideologists playing up their "cultural identity" or the "marvels" of socialism is replaced, when needed, by another that is attuned to economic rationality. I know one head of state who is able, in the morning, to deliver a flaming diatribe against multinational corporations and, on the evening of the same day, to deploy all his charm and efforts to persuade the chairman of one of those multinational corporations to come, invest, and set up a subsidiary in his country. What is involved here is less a contradiction than a doubling of one's personality. This leader must first make a symbolic sacrifice to the lyricism of Third World mythology, then, in order actually to improve his country's lot, he has to go to work and reintegrate the logical universe in order to attract foreign capital. No matter how great the ideological blindness and the excesses of local propaganda, there now exists for the first time a common fund of worldwide information—about fertilizers, investment capital, health-protecting measures—on which all governments can draw, at least intermittently, and on which even the most lunatic leaders are occasionally forced to rely. Every country in the world today lives under the influence of this worldwide stock of information—benefiting from it, rejecting it, or trying to adulterate it for its own purposes, but without ever managing to escape this influence or the backlash that occurs when it does so.

Without oversimplification one can thus speak of "our civilization" with reference to a relative unity of behavior, even though it is rent by myriad antagonisms and differences. Not so long ago the inhabitants of certain regions of the globe did not even suspect the existence of other parts, and when they came to do so, they had but a hazy notion of what went on in such distant, accidentally heard-of regions. Compared to yesterday's fragmentation of the globe into isolated areas, separated by a complete absence or extreme rarity of communication, our world tends to be a whole—not, to be sure, a unified whole, but one whose various components interact at every minute of the day or night thanks to and through the force of information. For this reason its future depends, to a far greater degree than is generally realized, on the correct or incorrect, honest or dishonest use of information.

What, then, is the destiny of information in this civilization that lives off it and by it? What purpose does it serve, and how do people use it—for good or ill, for success or failure, for or against oneself, to teach or deceive others, for further understanding or to foment friction, to nourish or starve, subjugate or free, humiliate or respect human beings?

This question cannot, to be sure, be posed or answered in the same way everywhere. The answer will depend on whether one is dealing with leaders or subjects, with democratic or totalitarian regimes, with traditional authoritarian societies or modern dictatorships, with secular or theocratic lands, and among the latter with those that are intolerant or those that are opening up to religious pluralism, with countries that long since achieved a high degree of education or those that still suffer from inadequate schooling, with those that enjoy a high density of newspapers and other media or those where they are rare and where what they serve up is threadbare and shoddy.

Nor can the question be posed in the same way unless we decide whether it applies to intellectuals or to persons who have neither the free time, nor the pretensions, nor the responsibility for gathering, verifying, and interpreting information, deriving therefrom the notions that influence public opinion. Notwithstanding these differences, something radically new obtrudes. The difficulty of clearly discerning choices and acting judiciously is no longer due to a lack of information. Information exists in abundance. Information is the tyrant of the modern world, but it is also its servant. Admittedly, we are far from knowing everything we need to know in order to understand and to act in every case. But there are even more striking and sobering cases in which we judge, decide, take personal risks and expose others to them, convince other persons and urge them to make up their minds, basing our decisions and actions on information we know to be false—

or at least without paying sufficient heed to information that is absolutely reliable, which we could use if we really desired it, demanded it, worked to get it. Today, as yesterday, Man's major foe is deep within him. But the enemy is no longer the same. Formerly it was ignorance; today it is falsehood.

CHAPTER 3

On Simple Lies

The notion of falsehood may seem too crude, too rudimentary to fit the vast variety of ways in which information is resisted. It cannot cover all of them, I admit. Between unwitting error and deliberate deceit there are all sorts of hybrid forms in which the two are mixed in any number of blends.

It requires little introspection to realize how important is the part played in our psychic makeup by the delicate partnership of mendacity and sincerity when the need to believe is stronger than the desire to know, by bad faith and lack of honesty when instinctively we hide the truth from ourselves in order to reinforce our apparent firmness in denying it before others. Then there is our reluctance to admit an error, except when we can impute it to some good quality or intention. Above all, there is our capacity for mentally absorbing those systematized explanations of reality we call ideologies, those machines of selection that are designed to sift out facts favorable to our convictions and to reject the rest.

These aspects of our spiritual life have inspired so many sardonic or bitter reflections, so many penetrating analyses and piquant quips on the part of philosophers, historians, moralists, and sociologists, that we have grown somewhat thick-skinned about the barefaced, deliberately indulged-in lie. We tend to underestimate the importance of its role in everyday life. For we would do well to remember that all such mental and moral maneuvers and contortions have a common motivation: to save us the trouble of using information, and in particular to keep it from being used and thus allowed to circulate. For this purpose the simple lie offers the most economical means. No matter how beguiling the ingenious figures of the perennial ballet which, since time immemorial, human beings have been dancing in order to avoid the truth even when it looms directly in our path, we are honor-bound to admit that it is more convenient to get rid of it before it becomes visible. Ideological fixations and insincerity are complex solutions to truth avoidance; they are costly in energy, in time, and even in intelligence. Their employment is thus justified only in cases where the straightforward lie fails. Such failures, however, are far fewer than many naïve souls would have us believe.

In the exact sciences, no simple lie can in the long run last. Hoaxes occasionally occur; they can fool the scientific community for a while, but in the end they are relegated to the realm of psychopathology. Deep down the authors know that they will soon be exposed as frauds and that they will have to pay for ephemeral glory with definitive dishonor. Rare is the case when a scientific hoax enjoys a long run of official favor—as happened with T. D. Lysenko's biological theories from 1935 to 1964, when they imposed themselves, or rather were imposed, on the entire Soviet Union by its totalitarian regime. But Lysenko never enjoyed the slightest credit in international scientific circles. Lysenko, who rejected the chromosome theory, who denied the existence of genes, and who stigmatized in grotesque terms the "Fascist and Trotskyist-Bukharinist deviation of genetics," owed the local hegemony of his crazy biology less to his cleverness as an imposter than to the political volition of Stalin and Khrushchev. It was a success of the regime rather than of mere charlatanism, a triumph of brute force over scientific talent. Even so, it represented an exceptional success for falsehood. For thirty years a vast population, cut off from all external scientific information, was obliged to accept the dream of a madman because it was supported by the dictates of a totalitarian state. Meanwhile, "dissident" biologists were persecuted, jailed, deported, shot. School textbooks, encyclopedias, and university courses were purged of references to other biological theories, condemned out of hand as "bourgeois science"—as opposed to "proletarian science." The ultimate miscarriage of this intellectual lie was revealed by the disastrous effects of Lysenkoism on Soviet agriculture. Stalin and Khrushchev ruined their agriculture by every means they could, including pseudoscientific ones. For Lysenko's "agrobiology," decreed to be the agronomic gospel of the State, preached the uselessness of fertilizers and forbade hybrid cross-fertilization, it being common knowledge, according to this doctrine, that one species can transform itself into another without cross-fertilization—rye into wheat, cabbage into turnip, the pine tree into the fir, and vice versa. The "great leader" forced Soviet peasants to produce the "forked wheat of the Pharaohs," with the result that output dropped by half, having already been seriously diminished by the collectivization of arable land.* The Lysenkoan tragicomedy is the strange story, barely believable in our century, of a policy being imposed on a country by much the same compulsory means as those used, say, for the prohibition of alcohol in the United States—but with a far higher coefficient of enforcement, the police agencies of a totalitarian state being incomparably more efficient than those of a democracy.

If, in a democracy, no hoax in the exact sciences can, through authoritarian means, long remain official, universal, compulsory doctrine, in the social sciences (history, economics, sociology, etc.), which are governed by less rigorous tests, public opinion can be deceived without the exercise of State pressure. This does not not mean that other restraints or pressures do not operate. Professors in senior university posts can practice forms of hierarchical constraint by promoting their particular concepts and disciples. But these are incidental factors, which cannot be compared to the persuasive force that emanates from a pseudo-demonstration.

Let us take a classic example—the birth during the nineteenth century of one of the most deadly scientific falsehoods of modern times: the Aryan myth. The study of Sanskrit and the structural kinships revealed by philological comparisons had permitted the identification of a group of related languages that came to be called Indo-European. This discovery prompted several generations of scientists to postulate, behind this vast linguistic unity, the corresponding unity of a racial substratum. Thus was fabricated the concept of "Aryans"—an Asiatic, vaguely Indo-Persian race, who conveniently supplied a surprising foundation

*Zhores Medvedev, *The Rise and Fall of T. D. Lysenko,* trans. I. M. Lerner (New York: Columbia University Press, 1969).

for proclaiming the superiority . . . of the Germanic peoples! Europe thus gave itself ancestors to whom were opposed another gratuitous scientific fantasy—the creation of a "Semitic" race, inferred from certain similarities noted in a group of languages but otherwise bereft of any serious anthropological support. Yet this theory, albeit challenged and discredited in the early twentieth century, went on to have a tragic influence on the fate of tens of millions of human beings because, like Lysenkoism, it became the official doctrine of a totalitarian power, the Nazi Reich, and was imposed by force.

Fortunately, in the democracies, scientists cannot harness an omnipotent state to the service of their ideas. However, they do not hesitate to use the prestigious power of the university and that of the intellectual establishment, which, though more limited, is nonetheless real. For example, during the twentieth century certain sociologists in France (and elsewhere) have interpreted the findings of scholastic investigations to prove, with the help of figures, that the students in the upper grades of secondary schools who then went on to universities all came from the "bourgeoisie" or middle class. This gave substance to the idea that education in liberal societies, far from fulfilling the equalizing function it was supposed to serve in an increasingly democratic context, had instead become an instrument for assuring the transmission of power from one generation to the next within the ranks of the dominant class. No attempt was made to extend the analysis farther back to the grandparents' generation, for this would have destroyed an already fragile thesis based on a discrete filtering of the data collected about the parents' generation.

The authors of this inquiry also casually disregarded those "bourgeois" elements who were unable to complete their secondary studies and who for that reason could not go on to a university education. A complete and honest picture, extended over two to three generations, would have revealed a twofold movement: an ascensional movement on the part of students from the poorest social strata toward diplomas offering them access to middle- or high-ranking careers, and a "fall" of children born into well-to-do families toward middling or mediocre occupations, less good in any case than those of their parents, due to their failure to obtain the needed diplomas. An exact analysis would have brought out the concurrent action of two factors in professional advancement based on classroom studies: an undeniable social factor that provides the children of well-to-do and more cultivated families with more favorable conditions for getting ahead than the others, and a personal factor attesting to natural gifts, intelligence, and a determined desire to learn. Does the second factor, in the course of historical evolution and as education is gradually democratized, become a greater determinant than the first? This is, I think, the crucial question. The theory based on the purely socioeconomic origins of scholastic and university success was buttressed by a tacit assumption denying inequality, and even any marked diversity, in natural gifts among children. According to this theory, there are not, nor should there be, good and bad students; there are only victims or beneficiaries of social injustice. As one can see, the first falsehood, which denies any equalizing effect in an increasingly democratic educational system, leads straight to the second falsehood, which denies that certain students have a greater disposition than others for intellectual work. Every effort had to be made to mask the fact that many children from low-income families are more successful in their studies and careers than many children from upper-class families. To obscure this truth, certain "progressive" pedagogues, moving from theory to practice, have even gone as far as to propose educational changes expressly conceived to keep the most gifted and hard-working children from advancing more rapidly than others. Inasmuch as every superior student is suspected of being so because he or she belongs to the privileged class, and since the good student who happens not to belong to this class undermines the theory, it is necessary—we shall see later exactly how—for all students to become "bad," so that all may start out on an equal footing toward a radiant, egalitarian future.

Although the dividing line in the social sciences between the flagrant lie and the more or less conscious ideological distortion (which is a different phenomenon) remains vague, we can speak of falsehood when we encounter a palpable falsification of figures, facts, or data. There is one sector in which the science of economics has brought forth a tropical profusion of such falsehoods—the one that deals with underdeveloped countries. It was political motives, more than humane ones, that inspired the fashionable imposture known as "Third Worldism." But it was "scientific" falsehoods invented or adopted by certain economists, demographers, and agronomists that provided this imposture with the many slogans that have supported and promoted it. Phrases such as "tens of millions of the world's children die each year of undernourishment"; "the world's food situation is steadily deteriorating"; "rich countries are getting richer and richer, poor countries poorer and poorer"; "each day there is greater poverty in the Third World"; "the rich man's cow eats the poor man's grain"; "an unfair exchange rate"; "the pillaging of raw materials"; "dependency"; "the failure of the green revolution"; "life-sustaining crops sacrificed for export crops"; "the International Monetary Fund is a starver of the Third World"; "the multinational corporations manipulate world commodity prices as they wish"—all rest, in the best instances, on theories too vague to be verified and, in the worst cases, on cynical untruths contradicted by verifiable experience. For the time being I have not examined the connective tissue that subtly binds sociology to ideology, knowledge to hallucination. I have simply cited several examples among particularly blatant scientific falsehoods.

The more precise and rigorous a science becomes, the more marginal is the role of scientific falsehood. On the other hand, the more conjectural a science is, the more all-invasive scientific falsehood can become. Certain domains, by their very nature and even though we possess precise knowledge about them, nevertheless favor the flowering of notions dictated above all by fancy, passion, and propaganda. For example, in discussions of the dangers of nuclear power stations, and even more of nuclear weapons, fiction is frequently added to reality in order to frighten the public further rather than to provide it with pertinent information. Scientists have sometimes made themselves the propagators of such factual distortions, deliberately exploiting their celebrity as "sages." Later we shall look at this phenomenon. But once again, it is not easy to decide, in the case of such abuses of trust, what is due to willful falsehood, what to ideological autosuggestion, and what to weakness of character in the face of diverse pressures. Usually the exploitation of scientific authority for purposes of nonscientific propaganda is less a consequence of simple lying than of complex mendacity.

On the other hand, the simple, willful, consciously fabricated lie, employed as a means of action, is current practice in politics—whether it emanates from governments, parties, labor unions, public services, or other centers of power. If it is banal to say that falsehood is an integral part of politics, that it constitutes a means of governing, as well as of opposing governments in power, that it is an instrument in international relations, that it becomes a right and even a duty when higher interests are at stake, and indeed a kind of professional obligation in cases where secrecy is called for, it is also true that our readiness to accept these "facts of life" ends up veiling the scope and influence of lying. The all-embracing and pervasive deceit that envelops mankind cannot but alter the perception it has of its own condition and circumstances, and of the factors determining them.

If we now consider the freedom to inform and the possibility of being informed—which is to say, the possibility that relatively accurate and varied items of information reach us every day as a matter of course and without our making a special effort to obtain them—then we can say that the world is divided into three sectors: the sector of organized, systematic state mendacity; the sector of free information; and the sector of underinformation. In the first, that of totalitarian regimes, the dominant forces are those of censorship—an essentially *passive* defense against undesirable information—and propaganda, an *active* technique designed to reconstruct and even to fabricate current news in order to have it conform with the general shape of events desired by the powers that be. In the free sector there is a great abundance of information, usually, in democratic countries, of fairly good quality, but with variations depending on the degree of influence or control that government, political parties, religious groups, corporations, and labor unions exercise over radio and television broadcasts. The third sector (the under-informed) is a mixture of the first two, with different blends of dictatorship and freedom, varying from country to country, but marked above all by a paucity of news. Censored or not, the flow of information is characterized above all by scarcity.

One might think that this third sector corresponds fairly neatly with what we call the Third World, but that would, in part, be an error. To begin with, a large portion of the Third World is, economically speaking, dominated by more or less communist, totalitarian systems. Second, other Third World countries and by no means the least important—one need think only of India, Brazil, and the Philippines—enjoy democratic institutions, recently installed, frail, and subject to eclipse though they may be. These countries have vigorous press and media networks, and offer news that is often more variegated, plentiful, and even more independent of state control than in certain economically developed countries. Finally, when dictatorships are installed in lands that have had a tradition of press freedom—in Chile since 1973, in Uruguay and Peru since the 1970s—the prevailing censorship does not always succeed in suppressing as much information as it would like. Such regimes are obliged to put up with certain long-established news organs, even though they persecute and finally ban them, because they are well known abroad and defended by obstinate journalists and owners. Nevertheless, taken as a whole and in view of the dominant political philosophy, the Third World, even there where information is or could be free to flow, is afflicted by a dearth of news, an anemia aggravated by the mind-numbing omnipotence of simplistic propaganda slogans.

In this rapid cutting up of the globe into three main sectors, it is noteworthy that the sector in which a free flow of information reigns is in numerical terms the smallest. This is also the case with democracy, itself a phenomenon that is anything but new. As I have pointed out in a previous book,* when we count up the world's democratic countries—which barely exceed a third of the members of the United Nations—we can easily lapse into excessive optimism. For among these countries are many that have relatively small populations—Switzerland, Belgium, Netherlands, Denmark, Norway, Luxembourg, and Austria, for example, or for that matter Canada and Australia, which though immense in physical size have only 25 million and 18 million inhabitants, respectively. If we take the number of human beings who enjoy real freedom of information and compare it to the overall population of the globe, we find that it amounts to an even smaller percentage.

Two elements of progress have, however, modified this sad impression of democracy and information. Since 1975 democracy has regained some ground in the world, and at the same time the transmitters of the free world have been making steady inroads into the totalitarian world and in Third World dictatorships, which have frequently complained about it. News agency dispatches, newspapers (though in driblets), radio broadcasts, and even television programs (in the immediate vicinity of frontiers and soon by satellite transmission) have been bringing to the various publics of the totalitarian and underdeveloped world news and commentaries their governments would prefer to deny them. However, we should not overlook movements in the opposite direction: increasingly, for example, the propaganda and propagandists of totalitarian countries penetrate without hindrance into the Free World, where they are often accorded a favorable reception.

Also worth noting in this brief roundup is the fact that political falsehood today is designed above all to deceive *public* opinion. Old-fashioned political mendacity was intended above all to fool other governments. Nowadays straightforward falsehood between the powers of this earth has lost much of its impact. Supplied with both public and secret information, every political leader has a fairly good idea of the other's means, resources, military might, and the internal solidity of its power. All, of course, can go on fooling one another reciprocally as to their *intentions,* but they succeed less and less in deceiving each other as to facts, and manage to do so only by resorting to subterfuge and

La Tentation totalitaire (Paris: Laffont, 1976); American edition, *The Totalitarian Temptation* (New York: Doubleday, 1977).

indirect methods, to the manufacture of lies, to which our age has given the name of "disinformation." This is a technique of willful deception aimed at poisoning the other party's sources of information by giving it the illusion that, thanks to the excellence of its secret services, it has picked up scraps of "information," which in fact have been deliberately fabricated and surreptitiously floated in the hope that they will be swallowed hook, line, and sinker. Furthermore, disinformation influences governments by modifying public opinion, which is often the main target in such campaigns. Carefully distorted facts are fed to newspapers, radio-TV media, experts, research institutes, churches—all of which condition public opinion while simultaneously advising and harassing political leaders with their admonitions.

It is thus first of all against public opinion—in other words, against humanity as a whole and not solely against governments—that modern mendacity, or the withholding of the truth, which is falsehood in its elementary form, is directed. Why? "The first and foremost of all forces is public opinion," Simón Bolívar once said. This is why those who have everything to fear if public opinion is too well informed are interested in seeing that the first and foremost of all the forces bearing down on it is falsehood.

In totalitarian systems falsehood is not merely one of the weapons of the political regime; it upholsters all sectors of public life. It provides the cement for masking the gap between a single party's exclusive domination and its manifest inability to manage society for the benefit of its citizens. Here falsehood is not simply an intermittent ruse, it is a persistent and permanent affirmation to the contrary of what everyone can see for himself. The authorization to say what everyone knows, to say out loud what everybody has long been whispering, is the real meaning of the Russian word *glasnost,* which Gorbachev has made fashionable. This word, wrongly translated in the West as "openness" or "transparency," is closer in meaning to "divulgation" or "bringing to public light." It is the action whereby one opens to discussion subjects notoriously familiar to the general public: alcoholism, factory or office absenteeism, bureaucratic corruption, the insufficiency or poor quality of consumer goods. Moments of "opening up" occur during periods of succession, when a new leader can hold his predecessor rather than himself or the system responsible for the catastrophic state of the economy. This was witnessed after Mao's death in China, just as it was after that of Brezhnev, of whom Gorbachev was the first truly valid successor, even though the ailing Yuri Andropov had already briefly outlined a *glasnost* operation, notably by declaring war on the discrepancy between genuine work and output and fictitious production. The reduction of this gap between fiction and reality, when it has become so wide and glaring that the very system is threatened by decomposition, was and is the aim of *glasnost,* which is designed primarily to denounce individual and bureaucratic failures. But to the extent that it does not attack the real, basic causes of failure—which is to say, the system itself—this process of "publicity" does not put an end to the fundamental falsehood on which such a society is based. Because a bad system can permit itself fewer errors than a good system—just as an anemic organism has far greater trouble recovering its strength after an illness, an abuse, or an accident than does a fine, healthy organism—totalitarian reformers track down backslidings and deceptions in the execution of tasks, just as they encourage the publication in the press of articles criticizing subordinate bunglers and the innumerable breakdowns of the machine, provided nobody proclaims the intolerable truth: that it is the machine itself that is bad and that it must be replaced by another that is entirely different. Even while attempting to be sincere, one must lie about essentials. The totalitarian falsehood is one of the most thoroughgoing history has ever known. Its aim is simultaneously to keep the regime's subjects from receiving information from outside and to keep the foreign world from knowing the truth about the real sentiments of the local population, in particular by making the work of foreign journalists on the spot extremely difficult. In international relations too, the use totalitarian states make of flagrant falsehoods exceeds the norm. All the authors who have described this immersion in falsehood—Orwell, Solzhenitsyn, Zinoviev (for it takes literary genius to bring home an experience that is almost uncommunicable in the cold, logical language of "experts")— all have insisted that falsehood is not simply an additive but an organic component of totalitarianism, a protective carapace without which it could not survive.

The citizens of democratic countries often praise a politician for his cunning, his artistry in fooling public opinion and outsmarting his rivals. It is almost as though the clients of a bank were to offer the manager a vote of confidence for his talents as a pickpocket. Democracy, however, cannot live without the truth; totalitarianism cannot live without falsehood. Democracy commits suicide if it lets itself be invaded by falsehood, totalitarianism if it lets itself be invaded by truth. With mankind now moving ever further into a civilization dominated by information, a civilization that would not be viable if it were nourished and sustained by regularly falsified information, I regard it as indispensable that democracy be universalized and, furthermore, improved. But present customs and habits being what they are, I think it more likely that falsehood will triumph, along with its political corollary, totalitarianism.

CHAPTER 4

The Great Taboo

Only in a democracy can one openly study the state of information in the contemporary world. A democratic regime alone permits an untrammeled observation of one's own system and the two others: the totalitarian system and the various hybrid systems in which censorship and freedom of expression are intermingled. Only in a democracy can a simple citizen undertake such an inquiry and make the results known for the edification of the public.

It is of course obvious that the leaders of totalitarian societies, thanks to detailed reports furnished by their secret services and embassies in foreign countries, are kept closely informed of what is written in Western newspapers and of what is publicly expressed in our radio and TV media, whose workings they understand so well. They themselves know better than anyone just how and why they monopolize the flow of information at home. But by the very nature of such systems, little or none of these data are made available to the general public, and no ordinary citizen is granted permission or the possibility to study the state of informational freedom in the world, still less to publish a book on this topic.

In a country with limited censorship, an intellectual may occasionally publish a book or an article severely criticizing the unfree flow of information in his country, but his declarations seldom arouse the public or open a major debate. An intellectual from a Third World country may have his findings published abroad—an occurrence that places him in an awkward position, exposed to the charge of treason. Similarly, an intellectual from a totalitarian country can express himself fully and openly only when he is in exile—which causes him to be condemned as a renegade in his homeland and often makes him look suspect to left-wingers in democratic countries. Generally speaking, Gorbachevian *glasnost* emanates from the top rather than from below. For all these reasons information about the state of information (both at home and abroad) is readily available only in democratic societies. Only there do people have the freedom and means to observe conditions in other, totalitarian or semitotalitarian, systems as well as their own, their vision necessarily being affected by the political hurly-burly of the democratic universe. The observer is accordingly subjected to all the pressures, agitations, distortions, and deformations inherent in democratic life. Information about the state of information is affected by the clashes of opinion in the legal civil war that never ceases to rage within democratic civilization and, more than anywhere else, in the midst of its system of cultural values. The obstacles to objectivity of information in a democracy are not censorship in any rigorous sense, but rather the prejudices, the partiality, the bitter hatreds dividing political parties and intellectual clans, which alter and adulterate judgments and even straightforward appraisals. Even more at times than rabid conviction, it is fear of an ideological "What will people say?" that tyrannizes and bridles freedom of expression. And what tyrannizes most of all, when censorship has ceased to exist, is the taboo.

The taboo, we should remember, is a ritual interdiction, what Roger Callois, in *L'Homme et le Sacré* ("Man and the Sacred"), aptly defines as a "negative categorical imperative."* He adds that the taboo always consists of a defensive interdiction, never of a positive prescription. But every prohibition implies a prescription. If you are forbidden to cross the field in front of you, you are in effect told to go around it or stay put. Now what, since World War II, has been the strongest taboo in contemporary democratic societies? To my mind, and particularly in

*Roger Callois, *L'Homme et le Sacré* (Paris: Gallimard, 1950).

Europe, it has been the taboo that keeps writers, journalists, and politicians from mentioning a violation of human rights, an abuse of power, or a run-of-the-mill economic setback, in short anything occurring in a country conventionally labeled "leftist," without immediately pointing to an equivalent imperfection in some right-wing dictatorship or democratic, capitalistic nation.

A friend to whom I showed the first pages of this book shortly after beginning to work on it remarked as he handed them back to me: "I heaved a sigh of relief when I read your condemnation of the Aryan myth. Even so, too many of the examples you have chosen are damaging to the Left. The reader will immediately think, 'There he is, lapsing back into his old obsessions. He has promised us a book on information, but now he's giving us the familiar song and dance about totalitarianism.' Please limit yourself to philosophical generalities. Or else don't cite an example that is embarrassing for the Left without immediately producing one that is devastating for the Right and, if possible, two for every one."

During the twentieth century democratic societies have been threatened and in some cases overwhelmed by two totalitarian foes determined by doctrine and by interest to do them in: Nazism and communism. They managed to get rid of the first at the cost of a world war. The second remained, and from 1945 until fairly recently it never ceased to grow in strength and to expand its empire. Nevertheless, the Left successfully foisted upon us the bizarre myth that the two totalitarianisms were still equally active, equally present, equally dangerous, and that it is a duty not to attack or to criticize the one (communism) without assailing the other (Nazism or fascism). Even so, this evenhanded treatment and this rigorous equivalence between a totalitarianism that has virtually disappeared and one that is still present in a number of countries were regarded as betraying a certain penchant for the Right. They marked the extreme limit one could reach in one's hostility to communism before being accused of fascism or of sympathy for "right-wing totalitarianism."

In democratic countries the communists, for obvious reasons, and also the bulk of the noncommunist Left, for murkier motives, refuse—or refused for a long time—to consider communism a form of totalitarianism. This refusal still prevails in large areas of the Third World. According to this view of things, which has been dying out on a rational level but which still exerts great influence over subconscious attitudes, totalitarianism today exists only in its fascist version, sustained and favored by "imperialism," this necessarily being American. It is therefore the only totalitarianism that must be seriously combated, by maintaining an unflagging vigilance against the rebirth (considered to be immediate or imminent) of the Nazi peril in Western Europe. If, since 1975 or thereabouts, elements of the Left have resigned themselves to talking or letting others talk about the totalitarian communist threat, this tolerance has not been stretched to the point of authorizing the Right to do likewise. The latter is congenitally suspected of harping on communism in order the more easily to keep silent about neofascism. In this view, only the Left is endowed with sufficient moral standing to be allowed to deplore the horrors of communism. You have no right to speak unless you have previously reveled in praises of Mao, Castro, or the Khmer Rouge of Cambodia. No denunciation of communism coming from old-fashioned "liberals" will be able to slip through the ideological customs check of the Left unless it is accompanied by a countervailing denunciation of a fascist abuse. Piotr Rawicz, a Polish writer living in Paris, told me how in the mid-1970s he gave a local newspaper an article on several books dealing with communism and Nazism. He had concluded by writing: "In any case, Nazism in my eyes has a great advantage over communism: it disappeared in 1945." When he opened the newspaper to see the printed version, he discovered that this final sentence had been cut.

For many vigilant watchdogs in Europe, Nazism must not be allowed to disappear from the scene. The greatest victory the modern democracies have ever won has apparently yielded no appreciable result. That the free world should remain vigilant and intransigent toward any renascence or symptom of rebirth of an extreme antidemocratic Right in its bosom or its sphere of influence is quite natural; indeed, it is an obligation and an elementary precaution. That knowledge and awareness of the pathological totalitarian debauch of the 1930s should be perpetuated, encouraged, and spread by history and classroom education is indispensable to enable Man to understand himself better and to be more distrustful of certain of his own inclinations. But confronted by those hallucinatory resurrections of the Nazi danger, one has the impression that something quite different is involved and that everything must be done to make people believe that this danger still lurks and is again about to become what it was in 1933 or 1939—as though we had not effaced it at the cost of so much bloodshed and suffering; as though our civilization had not rejected that fatal poison from its organism with a belated (it is always thus with democracies!) but in the final analysis heroic and uncompromising lucidity; as though, after so many abominations we neither foresaw nor sought to prevent, we had not finally and at such enormous cost enabled the cause of Good to triumph. Nobody can doubt it for a moment: Fascism and Nazism formed two political and moral perversions of which Europe was guilty. This is why the peoples of Europe rose up against those regimes and why, with the help of the United States and members of the British Commonwealth and at the cost of a harsh expiation, we fought, destroyed, and eliminated them from the scene close to half a century ago, eliminated them, I think, from any plausible scenario for the immediate future. What more can one ask?

So what is the purpose of pretending we are faced by the same monsters as before World War II? What need is satisfied by this chronological reversion, this cult of the mummies of the past? The answer to this question is central to the theme of this book. It can help us to understand how a screen has been fashioned through which our contemporary age reads its filtered information.

The 1987 trial of Klaus Barbie in Lyon, the city where he had commanded the Gestapo during the Nazi occupation of France, aroused a resurgence of the troubled feelings the French have about this period of their history. And not only the French, for everywhere in Europe and throughout the American hemisphere newspapers and the media got terribly worked up over the affair. The inherent contradictions were soon glaringly apparent. On the one hand, the governments of France had always wanted Barbie to be extradited or abducted in order to have him tried. Yet from the moment he was in French hands and during the pretrial preparations, the same insistent fear was repeatedly expressed that Barbie was going to use the law court to "sully the Resistance." That is, he was going to divulge the names of French double agents and traitors, of Gestapo informers, of genuine resisters who had supposedly talked under torture—nothing of which had later come to light. This conflict between official volition and secret dread attested an incoherent attitude toward the kind of information the trial was likely to produce. On the one hand, the trial was justified on educational grounds rather than for repressive purposes—the aim being to shed as much light as possible on this somber period so that the younger generation should be reminded of its horrors and atrocities. This was a thoroughly wholesome aim. On the other hand, there was an implicit refusal to allow the search for the truth to be carried through to its bitter conclusion. But would it not be of immense moral benefit to have the young realize that human beings are, alas, only too prone to collaborate with the stronger party, and not only when their country is subjected to foreign occupation; that every totalitarian power secretes base villainy; and that it is consequently better to live in a democracy, under the sole authority of laws that force men to be more virtuous? Was this not the whole point of this trial, its pedagogical raison d'être?

Shortly before the opening trial session, the speaker of the French National Assembly, Jacques Chaban-Delmas, a former prime minister as well as an important member of the Resistance, appeared on television screens to say that, having examined certain confidential documents that were supposed to be explosive, he wanted to reassure the survivors of the Resistance and other persons who had been active (or inactive) during the Occupation that those wretched documents contained nothing that could worry them: no traitor, no double agent, not even a single agent had been able to escape the postwar purge of 1944. No one had anything to fear; nobody, absolutely no former collaborator of the German intelligence services, had been able to spend his final years in ease and luxury or, having managed to escape detection at the time of the Liberation, to make a brilliant career under the Fourth and Fifth Republics. Coming from a former prime minister, this categoric assertion that no Nazi sympathizers had slipped through the net was utterly implausible, closer to the verbal hocus-pocus indulged in by a political exorcist than the product of a genuine desire to increase the historical and political understanding of ordinary citizens. Granted, there was the risk that Barbie might lie, smearing innocent persons with calumnious accusations, sowing discord among resisters and raising grave doubts about them in the country; but what naïveté on the part of the instigators to have sought this trial so eagerly without weighing the risks involved! Once the risks had been accepted, the authors of the trial should have thought seriously of thwarting Barbie's tactics rather than relying on the childish myth of an immaculate France, or at least of a France in which no guilty person was supposed to have escaped judgment.

For their part, during the months before the trial, spokesmen for Jewish organizations and SOS Racisme declared at several press conferences and in numerous interviews that during the immediate postwar years the French authorities had not cracked down severely enough on leading collaborators.* In France the postwar purge, which was neither infallible nor exhaustive nor always equitable, was, however, severe. Ten

---

*Founded some years ago by Harlem Désir, SOS Racisme is a watchdog organization that combats all manifestations of racism in France.

thousand French men and women were shot, while hundreds of thousands of others were condemned to prison sentences or to "national indignity" (being stripped of their decorations, medals, etc.). Even after their prison terms were up, those who had suffered such sanctions were shadowed by the infamy of the charges made against them and found it difficult to return to normal life. Those who lived through this period of French history cannot easily forget the poisoned atmosphere, understandable enough after the horrors of the war, and the witch-hunt that was launched against the Nazis' accomplices and even against individuals who were simply sympathetic toward the Vichy regime. But why then should some declare that the purge had let no traitor go scot free, while others claimed it had not gone far enough? The reason is that the first affirmation permits people to elude the historical truth, while the second promotes a political fable—which is to say, that Nazism remains an ever-present danger, an active volcano which continues to erupt. For indeed, if the postwar purge was insufficient, this means that Nazis are still among us. Taken together, these two incompatible conceptions—the idyllic and the diabolic—amounted to claiming that during the German occupation Hitler was helped by a mere handful of French accomplices, but that today France is crawling with unpunished collaborators and neo-Nazis. What lovely logic! Though it might discourage historians from revealing the hidden face of the Resistance, it was essential that Klaus Barbie's trial be seized upon as a fine opportunity for mobilizing French public opinion against an omnipresent Nazism, an inexorably rising fascist tide.

Here is an example. On May 9, 1987, French TV viewers were treated to a long, insistent close-up of the inevitable three dozen neo-Nazis parading through Lyon in fancy uniforms. High time to react to this great, immediate peril! Warning cries were heard and debates were organized (with a zeal that would have been more opportune in 1933) against the "revisionists," those pseudohistorians who still claim the gas chambers never existed. Instead of being treated as a handful of ridiculous numbskulls, these neo-Nazis were given enormous publicity and made the targets of a well-orchestrated indignation—something that gave these lunatic-fringe types a notoriety they could not have hoped to achieve on their own. What should have been scornfully dismissed and rapidly forgotten instead aroused appeals for a massive mobilization of the people. Against what? A new invasion of Hitlerian tanks? The emergence of an embryonic Third Reich? Absurd though such prospects were, the need was felt to inflate the harebrained lucubrations of these so-called "revisionists" in order to stir up heat against an imaginary peril and thus to be relieved of the obligation of having to combat other very real, very present dangers. Lashing out against the ashes of a past that people are not really interested in knowing about is less fatiguing than facing up to totalitarian dangers that are very much alive.

Quite different were the preoccupations of Simone Veil, the former French minister of health and later president of the European Assembly at Strasbourg, who was once an inmate of Auschwitz. In her analysis of the wartime period she said she refused to accept the "banalization" of genocide. Although I approve of this refusal, I must confess that I don't clearly grasp the meaning of the term. If she meant that we must refuse to forget the genocide practiced during World War II or reject a tendency to depict it as less scandalous than it was, then I am in accord; but I detect scant signs of such indifference to the past, save among the previously mentioned revisionist fanatics. History books, scholarly investigations, published stories, novels by the score, newspaper articles by the thousands, films by the hundreds—all of which, whether as fiction or as documentaries, have grown ever more numerous the farther we move away from the period in question—seem to me, on the contrary, to have ceaselessly maintained and developed our historical knowledge of the Nazi nightmare in general and of the Holocaust in particular, and to have deepened our horror before the inconceivable, unacceptable, ineffaceable spectacle of what some men at the time were capable of doing to others. I can find no trace of retrospective indifference toward these crimes against humanity, nor retroactive indulgence, nor any dulling of our sensibilities when they are evoked.

If by "banalization," on the other hand, Mme. Veil means the casual tepidity with which we have viewed and still view recent examples of genocide, I am readier to share her anxiety. Indeed, the dulling of our sensibility in the face of recent massacres—in Tibet, in Cambodia, in Africa—would seem to prove that we have not learned the lessons inspired by our recollection of past genocides. Knowledge of past crimes is merely upsetting if it does not serve to indict present mass murders and to prevent future ones. Remembrance is, of course, first of all the homage we owe to the memory of the victims; but it should also be a source of increased vigilance against the *repetition* of mass murders, not simply in the same places and against the same kind of people, but *wherever it may be, against whomever it may be.* But if certain mass murders were made "banal" in the 1970s and 1980s, they are those of the present, not those of the past. What has become banal for us is not the genocide of World War II, it is rather, save for one or two exceptions, the mass murders of today's world, which hardly need be recalled by an act of memory since they are taking place almost before our lowered eyes. To treat the past as something real and the present as something past seems to me a poor way of preparing the future.*

The vigilance we maintain with reference to the Nazi past serves several purposes. One of them, absolutely indispensable, is not to let the remembrance of it fade, nor to forget its lessons. Another is the exact opposite: to bury certain aspects of it, since we are unwilling and unable to avow or assume them. The third, more subtle and in practice the most important, function is to relive this period in an imaginary, mock-heroic fashion by giving Nazism a status of present peril. By loading it with all sorts of contemporary connotations, we help to sustain the myth that at the end of the twentieth century mankind is saddled with not one, but two totalitarianisms of roughly equal weight.

This bogus equivalence serves to minimize the misdeeds of communism, to make it look less redoubtable and less condemnable, just as before 1945 a legitimate fear of communism was used quite absurdly as a justification for those who supported or excused Nazism. To reason this way was an error when two totalitarianisms existed; but to absolve or tolerate the one when the other has disappeared becomes an abysmal aberration, one that cannot be excused as a simple miscalculation.

Recalling Hitler's crimes should incite us to fight similar crimes or, if we cannot prevent them, to make us more severe in our judgment of their authors. The opposite, however, has been occurring. The Nazi genocide of the past is used as an attenuating argument to justify or minimize present-day mass murders or exterminations carried out by "revolutionaries" in Third World countries.

One must not think that this soft-pedaling of the contemporary misdeeds of communism by exploiting the Nazi past is indulged in solely by a blind or conniving Left. Writing in the right-wing newspaper *Le*

---

*Quite by chance, while listening to a radio broadcast in May 1987, I heard someone who had escaped an anti-Jewish roundup ordered by Klaus Barbie say: "I am looking forward to an exemplary condemnation. Not because of the man—Barbie is a thoroughly secondary figure. What must be condemned is the ideology that engendered him." I must confess that at the outset of the trial I was looking forward to exactly the opposite. I then felt a desire, perhaps not very noble, for vengeance for the victims; I craved the public humiliation of an individual for whom I felt a deep repulsion; I was hoping his nose would be rubbed in the blood and scum of his crimes. The ideology that engendered him seems to me to have been condemned unequivocally once and for all a couple of decades ago—fortunately for all of us. What I feared was to see the trial give rise to grandiloquent platitudes, which were only too likely to "trivialize" the horror. As for Barbie himself, he had already been condemned to death in absentia at the conclusion of two trials held several years after the war.

Figaro (May 6, 1987) at the time of the Barbie trial, André Frossard, a conservative journalist and also a former anti-Nazi resister known for the fervor of his Catholic faith, for the keenness of his intelligence, and for his hostility to communism, declared that, all things considered, one could not compare Soviet crimes and the Gulag, no matter how great the horror they inspire, with Nazi crimes because "there was not in Russia a system that planned the liquidation of every human being under the pretext that he did not conform to the norms." Nazi extermination, he wrote, was directed against people who "had committed no other fault than to be born."

This kind of historical error, committed by such an author, betrays what deserves to be called the subconscious "interiorization" of the ideological taboo—an affliction to which even adversaries of communist ideology can succumb. To be sure, one must not confuse repression, even when it is very bloody, nor internment and deportation, even when they cause hundreds of thousands of human beings to die, with the planned, premeditated extermination of an entire human category. Similarly, "war crimes" committed in the heat of battle are currently distinguished from "crimes against humanity" committed with a cold-blooded determination to destroy a specific group or class of human beings. But the history of international communism, contrary to André Frossard's affirmation, does offer examples of extermination decided upon cold-bloodedly against a social or socioprofessional category or against a certain well-defined population. There is, for example, the case of Romania, where from 1947 to 1951 between 150,000 and 300,000 persons, including most of the country's intellectuals, were rounded up and many of them worked to death building the Danube–Black Sea canal simply because they were members of the "reactionary" middle class. A similar calamity descended on Afghanistan when, after the communist putsch of April 1978, some 27,000 "notables"—again including most of the country's intellectuals—were rounded up and eventually gunned to death in the notorious concentration camp of Pol-é-Charkhî, near Kabul. And there is of course the by now well publicized "social genocide" of Katyn, where, in 1940, more than 4,000 captured Polish officers were shot and hastily buried, while another 11,000 simply vanished from the prison camps of Kozelsk and Starobielsk, never to be seen again.

The most devastating of these "social genocides"—the one that swept over the Ukraine in the early 1930s—can even be said to have had a racist overtone. As we now know, this genocide was due to a famine deliberately provoked and organized by Stalin.* The weapon of mass starvation was used to crush a population of independent peasants—the kulaks—who were dead set against the collectivization of their lands, but it was also used against a people who were Ukrainian and thus non-Russian. As many victims then perished in the Ukraine as a result of this political famine as later died throughout Europe as a result of the anti-Jewish Holocaust. (I trust the reader will not suppose that I am trying to make the Holocaust sound "banal"; I am simply trying to treat the Ukrainian genocide in the same serious fashion.)

Should one consider the mass execution of political opponents, whether real or invented, or of a class whose way of life contravenes the norm, as being different in essence from executions for purely racial motives? The Soviet citizens who were decimated during the great purge of 1937, the Cambodians who were massacred by Pol Pot's Khmer Rouge toward the end of the 1970s, the Tibetans who were killed or done to death by the Chinese from 1950 on (one million, or roughly half the total population)—all these men, women, and children died not because they sought to rebel but because they had made the mistake of being born into the "wrong" social, religious, or professional categories, supposed "objectively" to be obstacles to the emergence of the "new man" (which is, by the way, a racist notion). No foreign or civil war justified these mass exterminations, save in the case of Tibet; and even there the excuse was flimsy, for the "liquidation" of the Tibetans assumed especially massive proportions during China's "Cultural Revolution," long after the conquest, annexation, and "pacification" of this mountainous land. The Chinese punished with death any Tibetan caught praying or speaking Tibetan! The Tibetan religion, even the language, was thus to be effaced from the earth. These awful events—in Tibet, as in Cambodia—occurred, as everyone knows, long after World War II, and yet to the best of my knowledge all the pedagogy of the Holocaust has failed to ruffle the placid indifference of Westerners toward these crimes against humanity. Crimes that suffered from several grave defects, making it difficult for people to get worked up into a state of righteous indignation. They were taking place now, they were taking place before us, and they were "leftist" developments.

I must inform the reader that I am dealing here with the subject of an in-built taboo in order to justify the apparent imbalance in the examples

*See Robert Conquest, *The Harvest of Sorrow* (New York: Oxford University Press, 1986).

I will offer later on. For the moment I am not interested in establishing a balance between a genuine source of falsified information and a phantasm. The effectiveness of the genuine source is, in fact, partly derived from the phantasm, which creates a propitious terrain for false equivalences—for example, between the way the Soviet empire was run and South African apartheid. One can judge—and I do judge—the second phenomenon to be as odious, and indeed even more odious, for human dignity than the first. But apartheid differs completely by virtue of its causes, its nature, its acts, its possible evolution, and its future repercussions. To mention these two cases as being simply two facets of the same totalitarianism, as some do, is by itself false information, of the kind that can only lead to catastrophic policies. Then, too, the confusion benefits the Soviet system only, for while one often hears people saying, "You have no right to denounce the Soviet danger as long as you haven't dismantled apartheid," one never hears, nor does anyone dare say, the opposite.

The imbalance is thus created here, at the very root of the perception that begins by positing a "right-wing totalitarianism" as something which in our present-day world is supposed to be as weighty, threatening, homogeneous, and international as the "totalitarianism of the Left." Now, this alteration of perception is in part due to the fancied persistence of Nazism, though it may be equally true in certain cases that this imaginary resurrection is deliberately cultivated to maintain the semblance of equality between the two "totalitarian" dangers. This bogus parallelism obviously benefits communist totalitarianism, which is still the kind that most threatens the contemporary world. Since my aim in this book is to decide whether the truth is better known and more effectively employed than was previously the case, I must describe some of the absurdities that have been generated by the myth of an everlasting Nazism.

Here is an example—one of which I was at first the unwitting artisan and later the flabbergasted spectator, increasingly intrigued by the cyclone I had unleashed. On Saturday, November 4, 1978, the weekly magazine L'Express, of which I had become the editor in chief two months earlier, published a long interview with Louis Darquier de Pellepoix, who from May 1942 to February 1944 had served under the Vichy regime as general commissioner for Jewish affairs. A journalist had finally tracked him down, still alive in Spain, whither he had fled after the Liberation of France in 1944. Offering this interview to French readers seemed to me justified for several reasons. First of all, it was a historical document. The writing of history involves gathering testimonies from all the protagonists involved, not simply from those one happens to like. During the German occupation of France only two men had served as commissioner for Jewish affairs—Xavier Vallat, who died in 1972, and this Darquier, now an octogenarian and in poor health, who did not have much longer to live (he finally died in 1981).* Yet in thirty-four years not a single French historian had gone to see him!

In my opinion, the Darquier interview was also of definite psychological and philosophical interest; it afforded us a precious insight into the mental workings of a doctrinaire totalitarian. All human beings harbor some subjective opinions that are unbearably intransigent. What distinguishes a totalitarian conviction is that it seeks to translate ideas and prejudices into action and, if possible, to annihilate all those who do not share its conviction or whom it designates as enemies. How does such a mentality operate? How does such a conviction grip a human mind so powerfully as to make it feel that things like imprisonment, deportation, and the murder of one's fellow human beings are perfectly normal procedures? A modest shopkeeper from Cahors, Darquier (whose addition of the noble-sounding "de Pellepoix" was an arbitrary fancy) developed his vision of the world with the help of the same *idées fixes* as those professed by the French intellectual and literary champions of that period's anti-Semitism—writers like Céline, Drieu La Rochelle, Brasillach, Charles Maurras, and Lucien Rebatet. Culture, intelligence, even genius were powerless against this type of fanaticism, instead helping to stoke its fires with the fuel of ignorance and imbecility. Our age having been so ravaged by totalitarian ideologies, it did not seem to me a waste of effort to produce a specimen that would allow one to grasp the genesis of such a mentality and the resistance a fanatical mind can put up when confronted with damning facts. Darquier refused to disown his past or to admit that he had erred in any way. In this respect he was no different from other totalitarian criminals far more intelligent than he.†

All these reasons for publishing Darquier's interview seemed to me so obvious, the historical case so compelling, Darquier's own statements of abject self-justification of such a palpable falsity, that when I made my decision I did not have the feeling that we were providing the public

*In fact, there was also a third, Charles Mercier du Paty du Clam, who was appointed in February 1944. However, he was later able to prove that he had used his post to protect Jews, and after the Liberation he was accordingly acquitted by the law courts.

†Classic examples are the leaders of communist Poland's first Stalinist period. Brilliantly interviewed by Teresa Toranska, they described their various setbacks and misdeeds with a guileless candor in an edifying book entitled *Oni* ("Them"). All of them concluded that they had never made a mistake and proudly asserted they would act in the same way if they had to start all over again. See p. 359.

with a particularly novel document. I remember that on the Friday immediately preceding the appearance of *L'Express,* when asked by a radio journalist what this issue contained, I merely mentioned the Darquier interview in passing, regarding it primarily as of archeological value, and devoted more time to praising a cover story entitled, "The Future for Schoolteachers."

Over the weekend I began to hear the rumblings of the thunderstorm I had unintentionally unleashed. At first I dismissed as idiotic several radio commentaries made by speakers who seemed to think, inexplicably, that Darquier's monstrous statements reflected the interviewing journalist's own opinions, and even that Darquier was the name of the magazine's reporter! Such grotesque misunderstandings, I said to myself, were bound to be swept away when well-intentioned readers could read the full text. But on Monday morning my perplexity grew when I heard Simone Veil, during a much-listened-to radio program, talk about a subject that overnight became a matter of national discord. It was during this radio interview that, as far as I know, Simone Veil brandished the charge of the "banalization" of Nazism—a term I continue to regard as nonsensical in such a context. Shedding light on the actions and thoughts of political criminals keeps people from becoming blasé about totalitarian horrors, and it forestalls the tendency to treat them as run-of-the-mill occurrences. For how can one in the same breath proclaim the need to combat the risk that the younger generation might forget or not even know about the Holocaust and yet denounce as a trivialization the publishing of a document that revives this memory by showing exactly how such a diabolical design could sprout in human minds? The pedagogic and prophylatic value of the historical study of genocide is reduced to nothing if we fail to understand how anybody can become its author or accomplice. The spectacle of the past should not serve simply to give us a clear conscience based on a retrospective condemnation of evil, but rather heighten our wariness as regards our capacity for committing it. In each of us there slumbers a Darquier de Pellepoix. It is precisely for this reason that genocides continue to occur.

We are blind to the mad logic of aberration when it resides within ourselves. Thus the so-called MRAP—Movement Against Racism and for Amity among Peoples—a front organization of the French Communist Party which naturally took part in the campaign against *L'Express* in the Darquier affair, had as secretary-general a man who, though himself a Jew, had nevertheless as a disciplined communist approved of Stalin's anti-Semitic drive at the time of the "doctors' plot" of 1953. Or let us take Claude Lanzmann, author of that monument of cinematography and history, *Shoah;* in the monthly *Les Temps Modernes* he was still able, as late as February 1987, to question the responsibility of the Soviets in the Katyn Forest massacre of April 1940. Although historians and even Soviet scholars and prominent political and journalistic figures in the USSR have amply confirmed this responsibility, established as early as 1943 in a report drafted by the Red Cross, Lanzmann could speak with stubborn skepticism of crimes "imputed" to Stalin by "Nazi propaganda." Did he not realize that in so doing he allowed himself to be gripped by an obsession for denying that which displeases him, an obsession virtually identical to the mania that prompts Robert Faurisson and other French "revisionists" to doubt the proofs of the existence of Nazi death camps? What he chose to regard as "bogus" death camps, simply because they were Soviet, were those—Kozelsk, Starobielsk, and many others—to which, before June 1941, some 2 million Poles, Lithuanians, Latvians, and Estonians were deported, and in which at least half of them perished.*

While developing her (to my mind debatable though respectable) arguments about the perils of making Nazism "banal," Simone Veil, with characteristic honesty, admitted that no one could mistake the intentions of *L'Express* or doubt the sentiments of the journalist who had interviewed Darquier. Indeed, it was difficult to harbor any doubts on the subject after reading the initial questions and answers:

L'EXPRESS: Monsieur, just thirty-six years ago you turned 75,000 men, women, and children over to the Germans. You are the French Eichmann.
LOUIS DARQUIER DE PELLEPOIX: What on earth are these figures?
L'EXPRESS: They are known to everyone. They are official. They can also be found in this document. (*I hand him Serge Klarsfeld's* Mémorial de la déportation des Juifs de France, *opened to the pertinent page.*).

Throughout the rest of the interview we had inserted italicized data each time our reporter had not had time to detail aloud the information that refuted or crushed Darquier. Here is a sample of the method used:

L'EXPRESS: In the month of February 1943 you proposed to the Vichy government a number of measures the Germans themselves had not even thought about.

---

*Robert Faurisson is a French university professor who is known for his strident efforts (in books, articles, etc.) to "disprove" the existence of Nazi gas chambers during World War II.

[Inserted quotation: "Declaration of Louis Darquier de Pellepoix to *Le Petit Parisien,* February 1, 1943]
I propose to the government:
1. *To institute the compulsory wearing of the yellow star in the unoc-cupied zone.*
2. *To deny to the Jews, without any exception, access to and exercise of public office. No matter what, in fact, may be the intellectual value and the services rendered by a Jewish individual, he remains a Jew and for that reason he introduces into the organisms where he occupies a post not only a natural resistance to the operations of Aryanization, but also a spirit which in the long run profoundly modifies the worth of the entire French administration.*
3. *The withdrawal of French citizenship from all Jews who have ac-quired it since 1927 . . .*

L. DARQUIER: This story about a yellow star in the free zone is some-thing I don't recall. It must be one more case of your Jewish propa-ganda.
L'EXPRESS: Absolutely not. Here it is, black on white, in *Le Petit Parisien* of February 1, 1943.
L. DARQUIER: Maybe, maybe . . .

In another passage our reporter, Philippe Ganier-Raymond (whom Darquier at one point called an "agent of Tel Aviv"), read off this accusing text:

L. DARQUIER: The Germans were all the time making things difficult for me.
L'EXPRESS: Ah, indeed! Then what is the meaning of this note, sent by Roethke, Dannecker's successor, to Knochen on May 29, 1943:
"Several times Darquier has asked us to support his legislative pro-posals, for he has long since lost all hope of the French government's accepting a single one of his projects"?
L. DARQUIER: That's one more fake! A fake fabricated by the Jews after the event. Ah, those Jews, they're unbelievable!

These lines—others were even more violent—should immediately have pulverized any possibility of misinterpretation, as well as any malevolent or stupid attempt to suggest that *L'Express* was in cahoots with the former general commissioner for Jewish affairs.
Nevertheless, most French newspapers reacted as though we had

wanted to promote the rehabilitation of the anti-Semitism of those Vichy years. I sometimes attend lavishly financed conferences where my conscientious colleagues muse out loud about the mysteries of objectivity—that ideal they all claim to be pursuing with an inflexible ardor, but which, alas, to judge by their words, is as unattainable as divine perfection. At such times I can't help but smile when I recall this Darquier episode and so many others, when assorted media, while knowing better, pretended to have detected the very opposite of what they had clearly seen or heard. The inner enemy of informational objectivity is often more redoubtable than the external foe, the lure of falsehood more potent in the individual than threats of censorship.

How was it that we were reduced to defending ourselves as though, despite all the precautions in the presentation, *L'Express* in 1978 had suddenly endorsed the eructations of a repudiated fanatic of the 1940s, when the magazine's systematic support of the Jewish cause and the state of Israel was common knowledge, when the two publishers, Jean-Jacques Servan-Schreiber and then his successor, James Goldsmith, were both Jewish or half-Jewish, when the chairman of its editorial board was Raymond Aron?

Discounting those who in the heat of the controversy and less from malevolence than sheer foolishness honestly thought *L'Express* had espoused Darquier's ideas, I find four reasons that explain this crass misinterpretation.

The first is political. In France the Left had taken to hating *L'Express,* which was regarded as having "veered to the right" since 1972. The magazine's criticisms of the French socialists' pact with the communists, culminating in the Union de la Gauche (the so-called "Union of the Left") and its Common Program (of political, social, and economic action) had been neither forgotten nor forgiven. In 1974 we had been the first of all French news organs to publish extracts from Solzhenitsyn's *Gulag Archipelago.* Later, in January 1976, Jean-Jacques Servan-Schreiber had decided to devote an entire issue, with the print order raised to a million copies, to the publication of extracts from my book *La Tentation totalitaire**—a move the Left had looked upon as an aggression. Whence the hatred and thirst for vengeance that alone can explain how a journalist as clever as Pierre Viansson-Ponté could write a front-page article in *Le Monde* (November 7, 1978) in which he pretended to wring his hands and to bewail *L'Express*'s conversion to the cause of anti-Semitism and "collaboration."

---

*In English, *The Totalitarian Temptation* (New York: Doubleday, 1977).

This was just one of many cases in which we saw the noncommunist Left, which claims to be intellectually autonomous, sink to the level of the most uncouth Stalinism as soon as it is engaged in a polemical row. But the sheer joy of feeling "This time we've got them!" was by no means unknown to right-wingers either. Their rancor went all the way back to our battles on behalf of the independence of Algeria (which they had ferociously opposed) and had been rekindled by our opposition to most of the political and economic measures of presidents de Gaulle and Pompidou and also, most recently, by our lukewarm support for Valéry Giscard d'Estaing.

A second reason, less anecdotal and more respectable, was the panic aroused among Jewish organizations, which were and remain ever fearful that evocations of past anti-Semitism, even when intended to pillory the guilty, could revive this vice rather than killing it off. The wish to recall the past out of pious remembrance of the victims is contradicted by an urge to repress it for fear of provoking an uproar that could boomerang against the Jews. Every time a Jew in France produces an essay, a work of history, a film that too precisely describes anti-Semitic ideologies and persecutions, other Jews immediately rise up and blame the author for reviving anti-Jewish passions by indulging in unhealthy exaggerations. This is what happened with Raymond Aron; after approving the publication of the Darquier interview and cosigning (with me) an indignant refutation of Viansson-Ponté's unacceptable allegations, he began to waver, and after being approached by eminent friends from the Jewish community he even ended up writing an ambiguous editorial in *L'Express* in which his solidarity with the magazine was anything but strikingly expressed.*

Interestingly enough, recent Jewish immigrants and those who had been naturalized shortly before or after World War II, almost all of them from Central Europe, never for a moment doubted our good intentions. They (or their descendants) always supported me in the debates several Jewish associations invited me to attend. It seemed glaringly obvious to them that exposure of the pitiful, nauseous ratiocinations of a sanguinary fanatic could only be intended to arouse a feeling

*About the publication of the Darquier interview, Aron wrote: "Absent from Paris at the moment the decision was taken, I had no advance knowledge of the text, and the editorial committee was unable to debate it" (*L'Express,* November 11, 1978). This sentence is at variance with my own recollections. While it is true that Aron did not read the interview, I told him that I had it in my possession and meant to publish it. He offered no prior objection and left on a trip. In fact, neither he nor I imagined the storms that sheer foolishness and ill will were going to unleash.

of disgust in the public. They were historically unaffected by the troubled sentiments that older Jews, along with other Frenchmen, felt about their country's fascist past—a past that was at once reproved and absolved, spurned and stifled, conjured away and usually minimized and which, though of course condemned, was above all filed away like a "closed book" and supposed to remain that way through a tacit pact of forgetfulness.

This leads us to the third reason why the French go through the phony motions of horrified surprise when an unsavory fragment of their history is thrust under their noses (and not only the French, but all Europeans, since with the exception of the British, the Swedes, and the Swiss, all the peoples of Europe contributed their stone to the construction of the totalitarian edifice which finally collapsed in 1945). The Darquier interview jolted the "purest" Frenchmen by disagreeably reminding them that there had existed a Nazism of purely French origin. The Nazism that ravaged our country was not due entirely to the 1940 defeat and the German occupation. The shopkeeper from Cahors, who had been triumphantly elected to the Paris municipal council as far back as 1935 on a program that had but one article—anti-Semitism—had neither been imported from abroad nor imposed by the invaders. What many persons feared in the furor unleashed by *L'Express* was what was later feared during the trial of Klaus Barbie—that people were going to start delving into the past of collaborators and resisters. Inevitably and unpleasantly, this is exactly what happened. As certain files were reopened, up cropped the names of active and highly placed persons who had been partisans of Vichy or even a bit more. Their panic added to the flood of protests. These persons had excellent professional and social contacts. I realized this one day when the magazine's owner, Jimmy Goldsmith, burst into my office during an editorial meeting and, sinking into an armchair with a hand raised to his forehead, said in a tragic tone: "We don't want bloodshed! We don't want bloodshed!"

Heavens! When had we craved bloodshed? We looked at each other, dumbfounded. What blood had we or could we have shed? In reality, what was involved was not a matter of life and death but one of civic comfort for several of Jimmy's acquaintances, persons who, though they had been granted amnesty long before, had files that were not empty. Just as Aron had been worked on and "brought around" by certain Jewish organizations, misled by a shallow analysis of what had been published, so Jimmy had been softened up by former collaborators who were now comfortably integrated in the business establishment of which he himself was a part. Or rather, each had been subjected to similar pressures. When it was a question of being lectured to by partisans of Vichy, Aron had his close friend, Alfred Fabre-Luce, a former apologist of collaboration with the Germans who had later repented and whose past Aron had chosen to "forget" even though he had not spared him in his paper, *La France Libre,* during his wartime years in London. Not long thereafter, at a reception given in Aron's home, Fabre-Luce drew me aside and took me to task, shaking his head for emphasis as he berated me: "Ah, what a nice mess you've made! Now we're going to have a new purge. You've opened the door to civil strife."

The fourth reason for the curious reactions aroused among the French by the Darquier interview is the most interesting of all, as it reveals an irrational behavior fraught with the most fateful consequences. It is based on our need to imitate the battle against anti-Semitism, against the Holocaust, against collaboration with the occupying forces, Nazism and Fascism, *as though these were present-day battles.* To begin with, this mimicry offers us a symbolic satisfaction and an oneiric revenge; by waging the heroic battle many failed to fight in 1940. Furthermore, in this battle against ghosts, victory is assured. The outcome is certain: Darquier is defeated in advance. To the clear conscience of those who place themselves in the camp of the righteous is added the pleasure of doing so without risk. Finally, in assailing an enemy that no longer exists, we can reassure ourselves that we have done our duty as defenders of liberty—something that frees us from the burden of doing so in the face of the genuine, concrete, present-day threats that imperil liberty but which are obviously more difficult to counter.

In the galvanization of national energies provoked by the Darquier "scandal," even French magistrates and judges felt it behooved them to display against the Vichy regime the courage many had so deplorably lacked thirty-five years before. One day in early November, as we were lunching, Robert Badinter, the future minister of justice, who was then the lawyer for *L'Express,* told me that the previous evening he had found the *parquet* (the area of the Palace of Justice reserved for prosecutors and judges when they are not in court) "seething and buzzing" with rage over the Darquier affair. I should, he said, prepare myself for judicial prosecution. According to the strict letter of the law, the simple fact that statements like Darquier's had been printed, even though they were energetically disapproved of, amounted to the crime of inciting racial hatred. What then was one to do if one wished to publish the utterances of some historical figure who expressed opinions that are perilous to human rights? In theory, each time one reprints the page from Aristotle justifying slavery or Gobineau's *Essay on the Inequality of Human Races,* one exposes oneself to the rigors of the law, which considers only the materiality of the crime and not the publisher's intent. At any rate, the weighing of intention is left entirely to the discretion of the judges. Now if the intention of *L'Express* was clear, so too was that of the *parquet.* Its members wanted to work up a phony row by pretending to believe not that what the magazine had offered its readers was a document relating to events now four decades old, presented without a trace of equivocation in its moral judgment, but that instead it had concocted an anti-Semitic manifesto of its own. Rumors were spread that cast doubt on the genuineness of the interview, as though we had faked both the person and his statements for purposes of pro-Nazi propaganda. I was called upon to produce the tape recording. Now, there is no law specifying that all interviews must be taped. Thousands of interviews were written up before the invention of the tape recorder. And since the appearance of this invention, not all of those who are interviewed will accept the presence of an instrument that sometimes disturbs them. I twice interviewed Valéry Giscard d'Estaing during his presidency, and once I interviewed the king of Spain—in each case without a recorder. Their remarks were nonetheless faithfully transcribed. Many other journalists also prefer to work by taking notes.

Nor was this all. Darquier's utterances were well known. Some of them had even appeared in *Le Monde* a couple of months before without, oddly enough, arousing a hurricane, or even a faint breeze. The judicial situation was surreal, but, as Alain Peyrefitte, then minister of justice, said to me in an amused, offhand tone, "It would have been inconceivable that the judiciary should not have been aroused and taken to the road." The road, however, turned out to be a dead end. In the presence of an examining magistrate, who was as courteous as he was baffled, I offered a detailed account of what had happened—and thereafter I heard nothing more.

I should add that while preparing the interview for publication, I had taken the precaution on August 27, 1978, of phoning the Chancellery in order to find out what had happened to Darquier's judicial file. I was informed that Darquier had been condemned to death in absentia on December 10, 1947, that the sentence had been commuted in 1968, and that the only stricture maintained against him was an interdiction against his returning to France. The ideological masquerade that had sought to saddle *L'Express* with the criminal's own grotesque theories—theories we had sharply challenged—ran out of steam very quickly, save for an absurd epilogue involving the Ligue des Droits de l'Homme (an old and exceedingly left-wing French human rights group), which showed itself a good bit fussier in this case than it had during the Moscow show trials of 1937. Henri Noguères, its president, demanded a "right of reply" of the same length as the objected-to interview. I was kind enough to grant him this right, against all juridical rationality— and I am still waiting for the text.

The real epilogue (and the one positive result) of all this agitation was the decision made by Antenne 2, France's second television channel, to show *Holocaust*, a four-part series describing the nightmarish sufferings of a German-Jewish family during the rise of anti-Semitism in the early years of the Third Reich and its martyrdom during the years of the "final solution." With their customary absence of logic, the French, while ceaselessly proclaiming their desire to combat forgetfulness, had refused to allow the three state-controlled television networks to buy *Holocaust*, which had been presented not long before at an international festival and the rights to which had been acquired by the world's major TV networks, including one in West Germany. The president of TF1, France's first TV network, had explained his refusal by invoking artistic reservations, the American film series being considered of poor quality and unworthy of our TV screens. This scornful excommunication could only inspire mirth. The French television networks, in offering works of fiction, had shown themselves incapable of tackling major contemporary subjects and treating them in a simple, direct manner, in a style at once popular and carefully conceived, serious and true. Our TV fiction oscillated between wretched time fillers and a shoddy bunch of supposedly avant-garde works exhibiting a precious estheticism which pleased no one except their authors. Our best achievements were in the field of the historical TV film, usually based on some classical novel, provided that the subject was at least a hundred years old and uncontroversial. The aim was to entertain without teaching.

Holocaust was the exact opposite of such conventional productions. The producers had had the courage to choose one of the most painful themes of our age, a shame for mankind, a scenario that was unsettling and disturbing. The historical skein was solid, the characters were strongly delineated and interpreted by fine actors, the dramatization was fictionalized without phony embellishments or excessive simplicity. Raymond Aron, who had spent some time in Berlin as a scholar in the 1930s and who thus had a firsthand acquaintance with the place and period, told me how struck he had been by the psychological truthfulness of certain characters, of whom he had known the real-life equivalents. One he had known had been astonishingly similar to the great Jewish doctor whose ancestors in the film had never been anything but German and whose patriotism, public services, sensibilities, culture, and tastes were so totally German that he could not get himself to accept the likelihood of the incipient persecutions, and who was accordingly unable to be on his guard against them.

That the character delineations and situations needed for a TV series could here and there skirt the bounds of melodrama was not surprising. But the point must be made. Those who never cease to talk about popular art and mass culture must accept the simplifications that are inseparable from them, and which, after all, characterized a large part of popular fiction during the nineteenth century. Otherwise, it would be better to stick to straightforward documentaries, which, though they can be superior in historical accuracy, will never have the same impact on the great mass of TV viewers. Claude Lanzmann, who was then working on *Shoah,* made strenuous efforts to stop the showing of *Holocaust* in France, fearing that it would undercut him and spoil the subject. Not only did this attitude betray a scant respect for the public's freedom of choice, it was based on an erroneous diagnosis. *Shoah* was vastly superior in quality to the American TV series, but it was a work of another kind. The two do not appeal to the same kind of curiosity or emotion. There was no more reason for one to exclude the other than there would have been to prohibit the publication of *Quo Vadis?* to assure the continuing success of *The History of the Decline and Fall of the Roman Empire.* Sinkiewicz had tens of millions of readers (and eventually an even greater number of movie and TV viewers who have seen one or more of the many films adapted from his novel), but I doubt that he took one reader from Gibbon.

Thus I was frankly scandalized that a country capable of reacting so violently to an article-interview referring (in 1978) back to events that had taken place in 1943, a country furthermore anxious to perpetuate the memory of the Jewish genocide, should be the only one not to show the first televised narrative of quality and scope made about those tragic events. Accordingly I undertook in *L'Express* to alert the public to what was happening, in an effort to persuade the authorities to change their minds. I was then taken to task during a press conference by the president of TF1, who accused me of having made myself a traveling salesman for *Holocaust* because my publisher, Robert Laffont, had brought out the scenario in book form (something I was not even aware of). Once again we can admire the moral level on which ideas are debated in

France, notably the sense of professional ethics the head of a state-owned enterprise displayed in making this calumnious charge. Was he obeying instructions from "on high"? I do not know. Was it because President Valéry Giscard d'Estaing did not wish to see pro-Israeli sympathies aroused? Or because he did not wish to offend the Germans? This would have been naïve on his part, but politicians are often naïve. Anyway, from then on I addressed our pleas on behalf of *Holocaust* to Antenne 2. They let me know that they wanted to show the film but that they lacked the necessary funds to buy the rights. I immediately had the magazine announce the launching of a subscription drive to "come to the rescue of poverty-stricken French television," and the gifts poured in. For after several weeks devoted to the "Darquier affair," public opinion had swung around to support *L'Express*—so blatant was the inanity of the charges leveled against us and the nastiness of the intentions that had inspired them. I knew perfectly well that a state-controlled organism has no right to receive gifts. Our subscription drive was simply a way of maintaining public pressure. Once we had won the battle, the subscribers were reimbursed. For in the end the president of Antenne 2, Maurice Ulrich, a man of marked subtlety and flair, phoned me to say that he had just bought the rights to *Holocaust.* Given the success of this TV series and the enormous commotion it aroused, he did not, I believe, have reason to regret his decision.

Ten years after this extraordinary hullabaloo, something similar occurred in the Federal Republic of Germany, though on a far vaster scale and at an incomparably higher political level. However, the stone wall of dishonesty and imbecility which a simple attempt at historical clarification ran into, on this occasion, in Germany and elsewhere, was exactly the same. I am referring to the hurricane unleashed by the speech Philipp Jenninger, the Christian Democratic speaker of the Bundestag, delivered in Bonn on November 10, 1988. His speech was made to commemorate the fiftieth anniversary of the dreadful *Kristallnacht* (the "Night of Broken Glass") during which, in many German cities, SS storm troopers and Nazi goon squads had attacked Jews, ransacked their apartments, looted their shops, set fire to synagogues, and roughed up, arrested, and imprisoned thousands of persons. How was it that the majority of the German people had managed to remain indifferent to this horror, perpetrated against their fellow countrymen? More generally, what social and psychological factors can help us to comprehend the 1933–38 period, during which Nazism installed itself in one of the most cultured nations of the world, hitherto a paradise for philosophy, music, science, historiography, sociology, and what the Germans call

Geisteswissenschaften (liberal arts or humanities), a nation that boasted an advanced system of public education as well as a galaxy of venerable and prestigious universities?

Such was the challenging question Jenninger set himself to answer. He could have contented himself by getting off a few shamefaced but indignant expostulations, he could in an emotional, trembling voice have condemned racism, anti-Semitism, and the "exclusion" of the Jews, and he could have wound up with a vibrant, demagogic peroration, exhorting his listeners to increase their vigilance over and against a Nazi threat forever being reborn in us. He would then have scored a huge success, he would have won over all the virtuous simpletons and hypocritical *arrivistes* of our planet, precisely those who are too incapable or lacking in curiosity to prevent new exterminations from occurring, or even of discerning them when they take place, never having properly analyzed the real causes of the previous ones. In this way Jenninger would have notably advanced his political career. Instead, by choosing probity, by undertaking a thoughtful analysis of the social and psychological factors that made the triumph of the Nazis possible, he destroyed his political future.

A first barrage of wire service dispatches and articles lashed the Bundestag president's speech as tantamount to a justification, to a rehabilitation of Nazism, and in any case to an absolution. The hideous specter of "revisionist" history was portrayed as making its solemn entry into the Bonn parliament via the speaker's rostrum! It was this incredible, indeed unspeakable interpretation of his speech that unleashed an onslaught on Jenninger of such irresistible violence that he was obliged to resign within the next twenty-four hours, on November 11. A particularly revealing symptom of the times in which we live was the potent role played by television in this "scandal." Screens all over the world flashed sequences of the same pictures, provided by a West German TV network, which showed some Bundestag deputies hiding their faces in their hands in an overt display of affliction while other deputies pointedly walked out of the chamber. The overall impression was one of universal consternation and disapproval. It so happens that the Bundestag numbers 520 deputies; however, in accordance with usual practice, the TV cameras concentrated on two or three dozen deputies, less than 10 percent of the whole, who adopted unusual attitudes, that is, those who did not understand or *did not want to understand* the speech. This is not, of course, the fault of television; it films whatever moves. No TV cameraman or crew director is going to focus on immobile heads, even when they are 90 percent of those present. Thus televiewers saw what they took to be almost all of the parliamentarians leaving the assembly hall.

This first wave of largely visual opprobrium was followed by a second wave of commentaries and editorials. These helped to rectify the first, hastily spread impression. Jenninger, one was now given to understand, had not really glorified Nazism. On the contrary, he seems to have condemned it. (It was very kind to note this, but the benefit of the doubt came too late to help the unfortunate deputy.) However, his error, the commentators went on, in seeking a *historical* explanation of the phenomenon, was to have presented Nazi racism in overly neutral terms; it was to have appeared to admit it, in a word—and here the inevitable, nauseating cliché cropped up again—to have made it "banal."

In an editorial published by the Italian newspaper *La Repubblica* on November 15, 1988, Alberto Cavallari trotted out precisely this kind of cliché when he wrote: "Thanks to this flurry of speculation-justifications, history itself risks being abolished." Heavens! How can one abolish history by practicing it, and on the contrary serve it by turning one's back on it? This apologia in favor of obscurantism is a direct consequence of the "taboo" mentioned earlier on. It amounts to saying that there are things that are unintelligible and for which anathema alone is fitting. One thus ends up adopting an attitude of flight from the truth—into anathema, the interdiction of knowledge—for the sole sake of vulgar polemics. It presents a grave danger, as I have pointed out; in rejecting a dispassionate study of those human and social motivations that expose all individuals and all peoples to the totalitarian temptation, one always leaves open the possibility that they may succumb to it. For an anathema, like a curse, does not teach, nor does it cure. Understanding alone teaches, forestalls, cures. The totalitarian peril cannot be reduced by preferring indignation based on ignorance to a cure through intelligent appraisal.

During a third phase of the Jenninger affair, the truth finally triumphed. With an exceedingly rare moral nobility and professional rigor, Turin's *La Stampa*—after, like most other newspapers, it had written on November 11 that Jenninger had delivered an apologia for Nazism—admitted and rectified its error. "There is something positively flabbergasting," Barbara Spinelli wrote on the sixteenth, "in the disdain that Philipp Jenninger continues to arouse here in Italy, as everywhere among the German and European Left. Neither elucidations nor exact quotations, it seems, are of any avail. Of no avail either is the fact that certain authoritative persons, like Simon Wiesenthal, an experienced Nazi hunter, should nevertheless have defended Jenninger, should have approved of his portrayal of Hitlerian Germany, and should have termed his resignation a 'great tragedy.' " And in *La Stampa* of November 18, Galli della Loggia explained: "This newspaper has been the only one in our country which—confronted by the objective enormity of a news dispatch according to which the president of the German parliament had made a public apologia of Nazism . . . later wished to verify and to understand exactly what had happened by getting hold of the text and publishing it. Readers of *La Stampa* were thus able to discover with their own eyes that this piece of news, judged according to factual standards, was absolutely false."

The truth is so disgraceful that it seems hard to believe. Close to a week had passed since the event had occurred, newspapers everywhere had poured out millions of words of pompous commentary and virtuous homilies, and yet outside of the German-speaking world not a single European or American daily had, prior to the *La Stampa* issues of November 16 and 17, thought of accomplishing this elementary act of genuine information: publishing the text of Jenninger's speech.

In the examples I have analyzed, the prevailing attitudes mix a refusal to acquaint oneself with history with a need to relive it in a theatrically bogus manner. Willful ignorance of the past engenders falsification of the present. Such is the function of the taboo.

CHAPTER 5

The Function of the Taboo

The Left, and above all the noncommunist Left, needs to maintain the fiction that there exists in the world a rightist totalitarianism that is as imposing as it was in 1935 or 1940, in order to whitewash the abuses of communist totalitarianism. To be sure, violations of human rights, tyrannies, repression, exterminations, and even genocide are rife outside the communist sectors of our planet. This is only too evident, and such practices were widespread long before communism made its appearance. That it is necessary to combat such scourges and to strive to create a kind of democratic world order is something that every honest person is convinced of. Yet this is precisely what we are not doing. For we refuse to understand and thus to treat the specific ills we claim to be attacking when we lump them all together and regard realities as disparate as South African apartheid, General Pinochet's dictatorship in Chile, the Seoul government's repression of student demonstrations, or even, in a democracy, the forcible return to their homeland of clandestine immigrants lacking proper entry permits, as manifestations of a supposedly single, undifferentiated totalitarianism of Nazistic inspiration.

It is essential to combat all forms of injustice in the world, and at the same time to have a good knowledge of the Nazi past. In fact, however, most of us cannot be bothered to acquire a truly accurate knowledge of the Nazi past; instead, we prefer to use highly charged terms like "Nazi" and "fascist" to project a uniform coloration on contemporary infringements of human dignity—which, thanks to the confusion thus engendered, we cannot fully understand, explain, or extirpate. The result is a double rejection of accurate information—first as regards the realities of Nazism, and second with respect to existing abuses of human rights.

Even before the Darquier uproar, I had seen this fear of knowledge manifest itself when, in 1968, the Paris publisher Jean-Jacques Pauvert brought out a new edition of Edouard Drumont's *La France juive* ("Jewish France"). A writer named Jean-François Held, wrongly supposing that this new edition was part of a book series of which I was then the editor—like too many journalists, he hadn't bothered to verify a piece of "information" to which he attached great importance—accused me in the weekly *Le Nouvel Observateur* of behaving like a propaganda agent for the anti-Semitic Drumont. In fact, I had refused to include this book in the series I was editing because a certain Society of Drumont's Friends, which was entitled by law to oversee the publication of his works, was also entitled to force the publisher to include, as a preface, a long rehabilitation of Drumont written by the extreme right-wing historian, Etienne Beau de Loménie. Much as I approved of the idea of allowing my contemporaries to form their own opinion of Drumont, I heartily disapproved of having this particular work praised. I made the point in an article published in *L'Express,* in which I severely criticized Beau de Loménie's apologia and invited readers to ask themselves why Drumont's crazy but murderous theories had enjoyed such mysterious success during the final decades of the nineteenth century. *Le Nouvel Observateur* nevertheless continued its attack, even *after* the appearance of my article, which it pretended to know nothing about. I was thus obliged to reply a second time, this time in the pages of *Le Nouvel Observateur.*

Since *La France juive* had first been published in 1866, there must have been powerful motives for wishing to conceal this 102-year-old text. Wouldn't it have been better to ask oneself how such stupid, vulgar gibberish could have exercised such ideological sway over French culture right up until 1939? But perhaps this fact was too humiliating for our national pride. People had apparently forgotten that in 1931 Georges Bernanos, the prophet of a left-wing Christianity, had himself published an anti-Semitic pamphlet—"La Grande Peur des bien-pensants" ("The Great Fear of the Righteous")—which paid homage to the memory and exalted the glory of Edouard Drumont. This convenient amnesia was but one more symptom of the two-faced behavior I have sought to describe in the cases of Barbie and Darquier: the tireless brandishing of the scarecrow of right-wing totalitarianism, accompanied by a veto on the publication of documents that could permit the public to know what right-wing totalitarianism really is.

"Why not publish *Mein Kampf*?" Held objected. "Why not?" I countered. "Indeed, it is something that is absolutely needed." I went on:

It is absolutely necessary that as many persons as possible gain a thorough knowledge of a book whose author came close to killing Europe, who gave our civilization a taste for blood and corruption, who scarred the history of the world, and who shook our epoch to its foundations. Or must we always start again from scratch? Must we always confront new right-wing assaults with empty heads and hands? Wouldn't it be better to realize that such phenomena can recur?

To "demystify," in my opinion, is not to reach conclusions for readers, but rather to permit them to reach their own. It is not to make judgments for them, but to provide them with material enabling them to judge for themselves.

Our illusion is constantly to imagine that the Right, in its most virulent form, is a buried monster, and always to be surprised and caught off guard when it reappears. Even worse is failing to recognize, in its present manifestations, the repetition of past acts and doctrines. When I was twenty, I fancied that after the lessons of World War II we would never again see concentration camps, yet they have never ceased to exist; that never again would we witness genocide, but it continues without interruption; that never again would we see racism in action, when we see it all around us; that never again would we see strikes or peaceful demonstrations quelled by force, when such things happen almost daily; that never again would we see freedom of information contested, suppressed, or curtailed, whereas in fact almost nowhere is it tolerated by governments; that never again would we see military coups d'état, when there is hardly a year that does not bring us a new one; that never again would there be dictatorships, yet no matter where I look, I see dictatorships; that guarantees for the individual against police forces and the judicial apparatus would become untouchable, whereas you can count on the fingers of one hand those countries where such guarantees are more or less respected.

Is it, then, wise to regard past expressions of reactionary thinking as being no more than prehistoric curiosities, which have been refuted by facts and are therefore unworthy of being mentioned? Is it logical to add immediately afterwards that people must be kept from reading such texts, since it might harm them? Rather, is it not that we want to draw a curtain of silence over a past we are ashamed of?

I am afraid that we stand to lose a great deal if we treat our fellow citizens as children incapable of thinking for themselves and weighing the evidence, and I am worried by the thought that in wanting to depict the past in rosy hues we are once again preparing for them a vitriolic future.

As can be seen, at the time there was a certain naiveté in the way I posed the question. How can you claim to teach young minds to identify and to repel the Nazi temptation if you forbid them to become acquainted with the ideological sources of yesterday's Nazism? I did not yet realize with sufficient clarity that spreading accurate knowledge of Nazism was not at all, either then or later, the sought-after goal. The goal was double. It was, on the one hand, to apply the "Nazi" label to all sorts of forms of behavior that may be thoroughly reprehensible but which have nothing to do with Nazism as a historical phenomenon; on the other hand, it was to keep people from realizing that genuine Nazism no longer exists and that since the defeat of Nazism the main totalitarian threat has come from communism. The greatest possible ignorance of the past is thus the surest guarantee of the greatest possible deception in the present.

The cases I have referred to might lead one to think that my thesis is applicable above all to France and to those countries that were occupied by Nazis or Fascists. Such countries do indeed have a troubled relationship with their past, due to their desire to condemn and at the same time to deny acts of collaboration with the totalitarian occupier. This relationship with the past can become even more morbid in countries that were themselves the cradles of Nazism and fascism. More disconcerting, however, has been the mania for seeing fascism everywhere at work, decades after its death, even in countries that were never fascist nor occupied. In the United States the very excesses of McCarthyism in the early 1950s were later exploited to forge a deterrent weapon, used to deflect any criticism aimed at the Left or even at totalitarian communism. Any intellectual who is worried by the ideological vulnerability of the West to communist propaganda still runs the risk of being accused of wanting to "revive McCarthyism" or of indulging in a "witch-hunt." Even in Great Britain some persons are now called "fascists" simply because they have chosen to vote Conservative or have refused to swallow unilateral disarmement. Thus, during the election campaign of the spring of 1987, *The Guardian* compared Margaret Thatcher to a "Nazi general." Dennis Healey, a former Labour defense minister and chancellor of the Exchequer, declared to a crowd that Mrs. Thatcher's government was composed of "this lady's slaves, silent survivors of her personal holocaust."* Given the connotations of the word "holocaust," such hyperbole can only be attributed to shameless dishonesty or complete irresponsibility. The "trivialization" of this supreme insult, however, would not be tolerated for a moment in the opposite case; there would have been a *storm* of protests, for example, if Mrs. Thatcher had thought of calling Mr. Healey a "Chekist" or a "friend of the Gulag" because he expressed his admiration for the Soviet Union or recommended renationalizing enterprises she had privatized.

Electoral frenzy is not the only explanation for such excesses. It has long suited the Left to denounce as "fascist" ideas differing from its own, just as it has often felt the imperious need to inflate "fascist" perils to distract attention from communist threats. Hopelessly outdated "precedents" from the prewar or World War II period are thus dredged up to magnify the marginal political phenomena of the present. Early in 1985, for example, I was startled to receive an invitation from the European Parliament to come to Brussels as an "expert" in order to testify on the "rise of fascism and racism in Europe." Since the last fascist dictatorships—those of Greece, Spain, and Portugal—had disappeared from Europe ten years earlier, and since no party capable of taking power had laid claim to their doctrines, and since nothing comparable to the powerful prewar "leagues" now seemed able to subvert the democracies, I might have thought that a serious breakdown in postal deliveries had occurred and that now at last I was receiving a letter sent to me half a century before. But no European Parliament existed in 1935. Unbelievable though it seemed to me, there could be no doubt about it. In September 1984 the European Parliament, acting on a motion presented by the socialist group, had undertaken to set up a committee of inquiry into the "Rise of Fascism and Racism in Europe." This same parliament, moreover, feeling itself invested with a universal mission, had exhorted the committee of inquiry to pursue the fascist blight beyond the borders of the European Community. First, however, Europe had to be cleaned up. Thus, at a moment when Soviet imperialism was continuing relentlessly to spread the net of its ingenious strategy over the West and the world in general, when terrorism of Middle

*Quoted by *Il Giornale* (Milan), May 22, 1987.

Eastern origin was assailing our liberal societies, when we were suffering from a chronic sluggishness of employment, when our lagging economies and technologies were being upset by the commercial competition of Japan and of new industrialized states, when post-Brezhnevian totalitarianism was being perpetuated in the colonized "satellites" of Central Europe—that is, in a neighboring and kindred area, linked to us by history and culture—the number-one priority question for the European Parliament, the one to which it had decided to devote its time and the taxpayers' money, was the rise of fascism. And this in one of the rare regions of the planet in which democracy seemed solidly enough entrenched to be able to exclude any possible return of fascism, at least for the politically foreseeable future. Yet the "rise" of fascist "perils" was also considered to be a top-priority issue by eighteen of the twenty-four "experts" who had been invited to come to Brussels, all expenses paid, from January to March 1985, to testify before the committee. I was one of a minority of six who felt that, compared to the mass Fascist movements of the prewar period, the existing right-wing extremist groups were distinctly residual phenomena.*

The very theme proposed for the committee's inquiry was enough to make one fear that the aim pursued was not information but the furtherance of an ideological objective. The use of the term "fascism" made possible an operation of verbal alchemy, designed to fuse disparate elements. There do indeed exist in various parts of Europe extreme right-wing groups or grouplets, either very small or very heterogeneous in their membership, among which several dozen maniacal editorialists are to be found who are possessed of a nostalgia for Nazi imagery. They include faithful followers of the traditional Right, some of them royalists or Catholic "integrists"; groups of thinkers without direct political affiliations—such as the new "intellectual Right" in France, which is to say the theorists of publications like *Éléments* and *Nouvelle École,* which are anti-Christian, anti-American, and anticapitalist; and terrorist groups calling themselves "black" whose real inspirers and wire pullers are difficult to identify—indeed, in the Federal Republic of Germany, as a specialist on terrorism has written, "all, we repeat *all,*

---

*The other "minority" members included professors Raoul Girardet and Olivier Passelecq, both from the Institute of Political Studies in Paris; Professor Erwin Scheuch, of the Federal Republic of Germany; the French writer André Glucksmann; and the Soviet dissident and exile Mikhail Voslensky. The twenty-four "testimonies" were reproduced *in toto* in the final report, a copy of which I have before me as I write these lines. But a far greater number of persons from all over Europe—deputies, labor union leaders, presidents of different associations—had also been invited to enlighten the parliamentary committee.

neo-Nazi groups have been launched, infiltrated, and manipulated by East Germany."*

Except for the National Front in France—an extremely diverse, ultra-nationalist and anti-Arab-immigrant party rather than an avowedly neo-Nazi formation (I shall have much more to say about it later on)—not one of these groups has so far managed to assemble enough voters to be able to send more than one deputy to a national parliament. The only neofascist organization that was able to obtain parliamentary representation within a country for any length of time is the MSI (Movimento Sociale Italiano) which, thanks to proportional representation and a 5 to 6 percent share of the vote, regularly wins several seats. However, being excluded from what the Italians call the "constitutional arc"—which means that it is treated by the Chamber as though it did not exist—this party, having no newspaper and being automatically excluded from the backstage negotiations leading to ministerial reshufflings, in practice exercises no influence on government whatsoever. Besides, breaking with prewar Fascist doctrine, the MSI has in theory accepted democratic principles and turned its back on the putsch as a method of seizing power—a method which, given the MSI's weakness, would do no more than make it a laughingstock and land its leaders in prison were it ever to be tried.

The formulators of the question concerning the "rise of fascism" in Europe were thus perpetrating a double fraud. They were associating today's sporadic fringe groups with prewar fascism and uniting these disparate groups into a bogus, monolithic whole. This was the second alchemical fusion, one making it possible to distill the magic potion in its essence: the pressing need to deal with a global fascist danger. To compare the skeletal fringe groups of the extreme Right that exist in the final years of this century with the mighty mass movements that dominated the European political stage between the two world wars is to flout credibility. To make this assimilation look at all serious, one has to bestow on the extreme Right a certain consistence, unity, and coordination. Taken by itself, each of these tiny groups is a mosquito; lumped together as a whole, they can be made to look like an army of elephants.

*Xavier Raufer, *Terrorisme* (Paris: J.-J. Pauvert, 1984). The author cites certain facts to substantiate his thesis. "On Christmas Eve of 1959 the synagogues in many large German cities were smeared with swastikas. There was an immense outcry all over the world. The federal government was forced to apologize. *Pravda,* in particular, raved against the 'revanchists.' Two of the paint smearers were arrested, and they gave the name of their boss: Bernhard Schlottmann, an agent of the East German Intelligence Service who had been operating under the orders of his superiors."

On June 4, 1987, the left-wing Paris weekly *L'Événement du Jeudi* splashed this huge headline over its cover page: L'INTERNATIONALE NEO-NAZIE. Here too we note an inversion in the perception of the perils that threaten us. At a time when a truly living, truly real, and gigantic "International" existed—which was maintained by Moscow and whose omnipresence and leading role in world affairs could not be denied—our leftists expended feverish bursts of imagination to assemble a few scraps of paleontological rightism caught in the interstices of our amply democratic societies, so as to be able to shout, "Don't be fooled! Stop looking toward the East! Look at what's happening right here! Take a look at the neo-Nazi International! That's where the real danger lies." And so a Paris weekly ran this scary headline just when Gorbachev was outwitting the leaders of Western Europe by promoting his plan for the denuclearization of our continent—an ancient Soviet ambition aimed at encouraging the withdrawal of U.S. forces and the dismemberment of the security system set up forty years ago, at the time of the signing of the North Atlantic Treaty. But, the headline suggested, enough of such trifles! Let's instead talk a bit of really serious perils, and, if necessary, let's invent them!

This attitude could be interpreted as betraying the secret resignation of a civilization which, realizing it was too weak to resist the force that was dominating it bit by bit, made up for it by waging a theatrical war against a foe that was fictitious, or which had in any case been grossly inflated. To highlight the bogus unity of a new international fascism, not to say a Fascist International, the standard recipe was pulled out and into the same stew were tossed the hotheads of muscular neo-Nazism, the dangerous criminals of "black" terrorist movements, and even scientific researchers who make the mistake of choosing sociobiology as their academic discipline. In London both *The Guardian* and *The Times Literary Supplement* have gone as far as to confuse or pretend to confuse French neoliberals—disciples of Locke, Montesquieu, and Tocqueville—with the so-called New Right, the intellectual heirs of Gobineau and of the superpatriotic advocate of a monarchical restoration, Charles Maurras.* Incompetence? Insincerity? The two often assist each other. The first stage in the concoction of this witch's brew consists of artifi-

*On February 6, 1986, *The Guardian* attacked the French review *Commentaire,* founded by Raymond Aron and edited by one of his most faithful and remarkable intellectual heirs, Jean-Claude Casanova, decreeing that, like myself, he was part of the *nouvelle droite* ("New Right"). I had already received the same treatment in *The Times Literary Supplement* because of my book *Le Rejet de l'État* ("The Rejection of the State"), which came out in 1984. In fact, the French New Right has nothing to do with economic and political liberalism, which it hates.

cially unifying and amalgamating the scattered shock troops of fascism in various European countries, the second of adding representatives of the democratic Right—conservatives, advocates of economic liberalism, adversaries of nationalization and collectivism. In the end everyone becomes a fascist—except, of course, socialists and communists.

This practice of what deserves to be called "totalitarian tar brushing" is, however, only one aspect of the question we are analyzing—as was made quite clear by the very terms of the invitation I received, early in 1985, to go to Brussels to testify on the alarming condition of contemporary Europe. To the disturbing "rise" of fascism to be submitted to the august consideration of the European Assembly, the authors of the inquiry had added the growth of racism. We must now examine the political function of this notion in the taboo.

CHAPTER 6

The Political Function of Racism

Thus, as we have seen, the function of the great taboo has been to legitimize the totalitarianism of what is still known as "the Left." In theory the guardians of the taboo have sought to assure a fair balance in the distribution of the judgments made about the two totalitarianisms. In practice, however, this apparent impartiality has been based on the fabrication of a rightist totalitarianism which, in the political context of the second half of the twentieth century, has been purely and simply a figment, a creation of the mind, what in ancient philosophy used to be called a "being of reason." What was meant by this term was not that this so-called "being" was rational or reasonable, but simply that it was a product of our cognitive faculty, a concept to which no real object corresponded.

Admittedly, not all modern noncommunist regimes can be regarded as democratic. But these nondemocratic noncommunist regimes do not constitute a single homogeneous political and strategic power built according to the same principles, possessing the same power structure, and inspired by the same ideology. In other words, in the year 1991 there does not exist a worldwide Nazi movement that could be regarded as the antithetical twin or sibling of a worldwide communist movement. Up until recently the ostensibly evenhanded treatment accorded to the two actually benefited communism. Thanks to this artifice, the latter was absolved or at least given a suspended sentence on the grounds that we had no moral right to declare it the enemy of the human race so long as international fascism had not been extirpated. Since, however, international fascism did not exist, it ran little risk of being extirpated anytime soon—something that gave the immunity enjoyed by communism a virtually eternal lease on life.

Furthermore, on a purely formal, verbal plane the purported evenhandedness of treatment was not in fact respected. We did not castigate the crimes against humanity committed in Afghanistan with one thousandth of the vigor we expended in our daily diatribes against South African apartheid. In the economic sphere, Western firms have been leaving South Africa, whereas they have been multiplying their efforts to do business with the Soviet Union. No leader of a democratic country would dream of receiving General Pinochet or of visiting him, even though he has allowed a free presidential election to take place in Chile. On the other hand, the president of the French Republic and the prime minister of Italy felt it quite natural to receive General Jaruzelski at a time when Poland was still a Soviet "satellite," and the prime minister of Spain (and many other celebrities) visited Fidel Castro in Havana. The former Greek prime minister, Andreas Papandreou (a socialist, like the other three gentlemen), showed himself in the 1980s to be even more categorically favorable to international communism and terrorism each time the opportunity arose. Thus not only in theory, but also in everyday practice, the equality or immediacy of the two totalitarian dangers was for a long time a myth contrived so as to benefit communism.

I have elsewhere written of this "absolving" behavior, calling it in French the *renvoi dos à dos* (the evenhanded, back-to-back rejection of disparate phenomena).* If I return to the subject here, it is to examine this mental disposition from the point of view of information. Up until recently, when the symptoms of economic weakness became too glaringly evident to be denied any longer, the process of "evenhanded rejection" tended to favor communist regimes. The paramount desire to avoid any unilateral condemnation of communism—"so long as fascist regimes exist"—led to massive censorship or, at the very least, to a

*In *How Democracies Perish,* Chap. 24.

notable dilution of information about the communist world and its official or unofficial allies, along with a tacit acceptance of the chronic nature of human rights violations inherent in the communist system. One can say all sorts of things about the authoritarian regimes of Chile since 1973, of the Philippines before 1986, of South Korea until 1987, and of South Africa today—but one cannot say that information about them was lacking. Nobody could suspect the media in the West of drawing a veil of silence over the crimes and misdeeds of those governments, or of underestimating the magnitude of the popular protests and demonstrations they had to cope with. When such regimes launch salutary reforms, our media rarely deign to inform us, except halfheartedly and usually to emphasize their inadequacy. On the other hand, when a liberal reform is announced in a communist country, it is warmly and confidently hailed, given detailed coverage, and endlessly discussed. The reform, whether genuine or bogus, is not allowed to pass unnoticed. The mere announcement that a "reformist leadership" is planning this or that is taken on trust, as tantamount to realization, and to doubt that the program has been effectively realized is considered a sign of ill will. Thus, in the case of the Soviet Union, the mere announcement by Mikhail Gorbachev that he was pursuing a policy of *glasnost* was regarded as a guarantee that a genuinely free press had suddenly materialized all over the country. And the mere enunciation of a policy of *perestroika* was treated as a kind of wish fulfillment, as though a miracle could be accomplished overnight. Hence the perplexed astonishment of so many persons in the West when they began to realize, five years after its official launching, that the policy of "restructuring" had basically altered nothing and that the economic plight of the Soviet Union was more critical than ever.

In dealing with Western statesmen a journalist is expected to display a critical sense and not to confuse declarations of intent with acts. But in dealing with Soviet statesmen such wariness is regarded as tendentious and biased behavior. According to the *Neue Zürcher Zeitung,* several times during the year 1987 the editors of a number of leading West German newspapers berated their Moscow correspondents, taking them to task for displaying too much skepticism and lukewarmness toward Gorbachev's reform program. They were asked to treat them henceforth in a more "constructive" spirit and with more enthusiasm and faith in the future.

It is for reasons such as these that in posing the question as to whether our contemporaries effectively use and really *want* to use all of the information available to them, I have reached the conclusion that it is most frequently in the communist camp, and more generally among left-wingers, that I have encountered instances of flagrant dissimulation or willful neglect of the truth. For a long time intellectual dishonesty was to be found on the Right, or at least it was fairly equally distributed between Right and Left. But since 1945 this apparently essential element of human happiness has been selfishly monopolized by the Left. Between the two world wars Hitler's and Stalin's followers could compete on equal terms in deception, knowingly and cynically practicing it for the benefit of democratic-minded dolts, who in their eyes were so easily hoodwinked. But since the disappearance of Nazism, and above all since European socialists and assorted American "liberals" have taken to copying communist methods in their handling of public debates, intellectual dishonesty has by and large become a province of the Left. It is not that the Right no longer wishes to employ it; it is simply that it has lost the talent for doing so. It no longer possesses the necessary philosophical resources or dialectical virtuosity. Even when extreme right-wingers tell the truth, no one believes them anymore. As for the "liberals," they fall into the trap laid for them by leftists by accepting their postulates, not realizing that those postulates are rigged in such a way that they contain the seeds of their own inevitable damnation.

A good example of these poisoned postulates is the notion of "racism" as it is employed today—a notion so vast and so vague that no democrat, no matter how sincere and scrupulous, can avoid being accused of it.

The first step in using racism for the construction of the great taboo is to reduce a multiple reality to one phenomenon—that is, to reduce diverse forms of behavior which, though reprehensible, are of varying gravity, harmfulness, and above all origins, to a single, fundamental concept: that of "racism." The second step is to assimilate this monolithic denominator, which has been obtained by the artificial fusion of myriad forms of discriminatory and scornful behavior, with the ideological, doctrinaire, pseudoscientific racism of Third Reich theorists. Finally, in a third stage, any measure aimed at selecting human beings and at distinguishing them from one another, even for purely practical, scholastic, hygienic, or disciplinary reasons, is termed "discriminatory." For example, imposing selective examinations for admission to a university may be a sound measure or a bad one. It can be discussed from a pedagogical or social point of view. But during the *lycée* (high school) student demonstrations against selection that took place in France in November and December 1986 and slightly later in Spain, technical considerations played no role whatsoever in the discussions. The rhetoric of the protesters was based on antiracist metaphysics. It condemned the very principle of examination as being a *comportement d'exclusion* (behavior of exclusion). The dominant slogan was "No to Discrimination!" In other words, a candidate for admission to a university whose degree of knowledge was to be tested was likened to a South African black or a Jew persecuted by Hitler. The conservative Chirac government, which had proposed selective standards for university admission, was accordingly branded as "fascist," since selective admission, judged in terms of the racist paradigm, could only imply separation, exclusion, discrimination, and—who knows?—perhaps deportation as well.

Every totalitarian system is driven by an ideology designed to justify a plan of general domination, which it seeks to realize, among other things, by the elimination, physical if need be, of hostile or troublesome groups. In communist ideology the groups are social; in Nazi ideology they are racial. Founded on the dogma of the biological inequality of human races, of the superiority of certain races over others, and on the supposed right of "superior" races to enslave, even to exterminate, so-called "inferior," impure, or harmful races, the racist metaphysics of Nazism, as is well known, inspired a program of extermination of European Jews and gypsies and subjugation of Latins and Slavs. What made and makes this theory particularly absurd is the fact, well known to anthropologists, that there is no Jewish "race." Judaism and Judeity (this latter term coined by Albert Memmi to designate the feeling of belonging to a custom-based cultural tradition of nonreligious Jews) are to be found in almost all human races.* To be sure, a contradiction in terms is virtually an intrinsic requirement of ideological sectarianism. What Marxist stops to think that during the twentieth century social injustices have been reduced in capitalist societies and aggravated in socialist societies?

Nazi racism was a clearly defined monstrosity, precisely located in time and space, an ideological classification founded on an obsessive fear of the pure and impure, which is not so different, according to other criteria, from the segregative communist mentality, with its "viscous rats," "lubricious vipers," its "jackals" and "hyenas," who can be mastered only by "liquidating" them and through "struggles." In the same way, at the time of the French Revolution and during the civil war of the Vendée, the Convention proclaimed its firm determination to "exterminate the brigands of Vendée," including the civilian population, in order "entirely to purge the soil of Liberty of this accursed race." One

---

*Albert Memmi, *Portrait d'un Juif* (Paris: Gallimard, 1961). English translation, *Portrait of a Jew*, trans. Elizabeth Abbott (New York: Orion Press, 1962).

marvels at the logic of a form of reasoning that advocates genocide in the name of liberty. The "behavior of exclusion," in its varied forms, allied to a totalitarian ideology, leads in effect to such "logic."

Does it follow from this that *all* forms of xenophobic behavior, even when limited to a certain condescending distrust of foreigners, such as one encounters in all countries, are offshoots of Nazi ideology or lead in the same direction? If so, then mankind in its entirety has always been Nazi-inspired and continues to be so. In that case mankind would be incurable, and the sole solution would be to exterminate it. However, distrust or fear of or contempt for an individual who comes from a different community, speaks a different language, practices a different religion, and has a different physical appearance are ancient and universal sentiments. They give rise to standard forms of exclusiveness—in the better cases, to the establishment of personal distinctions, in the worst, to forms of segregation. These are, alas, spontaneous, popular modes of conduct that human beings display toward one another. This is not a reasoned choice, it is an anthropological fact. To surmount these sentiments and to correct such behavior, each of us requires education and a political philosophy—fruits of a long participation in democratic civilization, of a long impregnation of minds by a humanistic and universalist morality. "It is racism that is natural, and antiracism that is not," wrote Memmi. "The latter can only be a long, difficult conquest, forever threatened, as is any cultural acquisition."*

Getting everyone to possess this cultural acquisition is not a result that is easy to obtain rapidly and everywhere, and it will certainly not be obtained if every individual whose soul still harbors traces of xenophobic or racist prejudices, and who does not entertain desirably courteous or fraternal relations with his North African or black neighbor, is condemned out of hand as a Nazi butcher. In France the association SOS Racisme has often launched campaigns the principal thrust of which has been less a moral obligation to improve mutual understanding between Frenchmen and Africans than the excommunication of Frenchmen, who are regarded as abject racists worthy only of service in Hitlerian shock troop units. Such insulting generalizations can only infuriate all sorts of persons who do not feel at all racist and have no intention of becoming so. They cannot but hamper the group's avowed aim, assuming that it is to improve relations between groups of different origins and not to envenom them in order to exploit them politically.

A particularly nefarious mistake, I would even say a criminal error

*Albert Memmi, *Le Racisme (description, définition, traitement)* (Paris: Gallimard, 1982).

when committed willfully, is to equate attitudes of rejection provoked by major influxes of immigrant workers with ideological and exterminatory racism. Such negative attitudes are clearly undesirable and everything should be done to make them disappear, but this can be achieved only through education, explanation, and persuasion, and above all by improving the specific conditions that generate clashes between new arrivals and old residents. It is not by insulting the latter and calling them fascists that one can hope to encourage the growth of friendly sentiments toward immigrants, who, from the old residents' point of view, are invaders. Tolerance cannot be taught by preaching intolerance. How indeed can you imbue your society with a respect for the human dignity of immigrants if you act with scorn when speaking to your compatriots? The same persons who denounce a "behavior of exclusion" with respect to immigrants or people suffering from AIDS are guilty of the same unbridled ostracism when they consign their fellow citizens to the nether regions of Nazi racism, when they seek to impose political anathema on those who happen to be hostile to immigrants.

In poor urban districts, in particular, large concentrations of human beings engender intercommunity frictions which owe less to racism than to the difficulties of daily living. The clearest proof is that such frictions arise, for example, in the United States between "Hispanics" and blacks and between American and Haitian blacks; in India between the Bengalis residing in Bengal and the Bengalis flooding in from Bangladesh; in Italy, in the early 1960s, between the southern Italians who had flocked northward to Lombardy and Piedmont to take advantage of jobs created by an industrial boom and northern Italians, who often treated their southern countrymen far worse than the French have treated North Africans, West Germans the Turks, or even Norwegians the Pakistanis. Since the early 1980s Felipe González's socialist government in Spain, wishing to combat unemployment, has constantly erected barriers against immigrants from Latin America, even though these immigrants do not differ from the Spaniards of the peninsula in language, religion, or race (pure American Indians never seek to emigrate to Europe). It is worth noting that Felipe González justified his policy with the same reasons used by Jean-Marie Le Pen in France: the immigrants would do the locals out of their jobs. It has been amply proved that this calculation is almost always false in developed countries, where a high degree of unemployment can coexist with a need for manpower. It is true that in certain cases the local worker risks having the job he wants given to an immigrant, but this is because the immigrant is *more highly qualified;* in other words, what is involved is immigration from a more highly developed to a less highly developed country. The refusal of residency permits and the many bureaucratic harassments and expulsions that Hispano-Americans have had to endure in Spain since 1982—and this from a socialist government—have been particularly shocking, inasmuch as millions of Spaniards found and continue to find jobs in Latin America, whither they flocked in droves after the Spanish Civil War and where many of them have since been able to settle and make a go of it. In wishing to protect the interests of Spanish workers, Felipe González, in my opinion, nonetheless committed an economic mistake as well as displaying moral shabbiness. But does this give others the right to call him a follower of Eichmann?

In France, when racial tensions due to immigration began to swell the ranks of Jean-Marie Le Pen's National Front, the leftists who were then in power made no attempt to deal with the deep-rooted causes of those tensions. They regarded Le Pen's ascension as a political windfall. On the one hand, they sought to put over the idea that Le Pen's National Front was the reemergence of the extreme totalitarian Right of prewar France; on the other hand, they modified the French electoral system in such a way as to permit this extreme Right to obtain seats in the parliament and thus a measure of legitimacy. Finally, they accused French conservatives of complicity with the National Front and thus, by a kind of historical extrapolation, of complicity with fascism and racism. The infernal wheel had now come full circle. The European Assembly's committee of inquiry was thus offered "proof" of the thesis it wanted to establish: that the National Front was nothing less than a reincarnation of Hitler's National Socialist Party, and the conservative French Right was not essentially different from the National Front nor, on the European plane, from fascist or racist currents of opinion. Thus was manifested an ancient obsession, one particularly dear to socialists (one that does not, however, keep them from proclaiming themselves the champions of toleration and pluralism). Whoever is not socialist cannot be a true democrat!

The most striking thing about this fashionable comparison between the "Le Pen phenomenon" and the birth of the Hitlerian movement in the 1920s and 1930s was the shoddiness of the analysis and the sloppiness in the study of the data. When the future premier, Michel Rocard, solemnly declared, "Hitler too had his beginning, and he had only a small part of the electorate behind him," he was right only to the extent of thinking that it is better to try to cure an illness in its early stages than later on. But he was also committing a gross error of logic; for while it is true that everything that becomes great starts out by being small, not everything that is small is destined to become great. Every schoolboy knows, or at any rate knew in the Middle Ages (but we seem to have regressed since then in our use of formal logic), that a single quality shared by two distinct entities does not make all of their other qualities common. While it is true that Louis Renault was no more than a humble garage mechanic before becoming one of the great automobile manufacturers of the twentieth century, it doesn't follow that all humble garage mechanics become great car constructors. If Van Gogh, who was a genius, sold no paintings during his brief career, it doesn't follow from this that a painter who doesn't sell any canvases is a genius.

Much as I deplore it, I must admit that the French Left, and the liberals who have been terrorized by the Left, have done all they could to build up the image of the National Front. But I am by no means sure that their gift for transforming vexations into catastrophes will suffice to raise the NF to the level of power Adolf Hitler's National Socialist German Workers' Party enjoyed in its heyday. Instead of concentrating on the real causes of Le Pen's electoral progression from 1983 on in order to discover what was novel in it and what specific remedies should be applied, we rushed to embrace some ridiculous historical analogies, which, to make matters worse, were flattering to Le Pen! For if Hitler is for us the incarnation of evil genius, he was nonetheless a genius. To compare Le Pen to Hitler is to place him on the same level as a man who was able to make himself the absolute master of a nation that was composed of 80 million inhabitants and which was the foremost industrial power in Europe, a man who hoodwinked the subtlest diplomats and the leading politicians of his age, who in just ten years built up the finest, most modern army in the world, and who in less than a year conquered almost all of the Old World with the cooperation—obtained at the decisive moment with a flabbergasting virtuosity—of the Soviet Union. In terms of sheer force—and sheer force, alas, exercises a great fascination on human beings!—Le Pen was lavishly honored in being placed as a historical figure in the same league with the chancellor of the Third Reich. I would even say that putting him there was a signal blunder and a rare piece of foolishness. What an "image" he was offered, and gratis too! Le Pen, judged capable of upsetting the course of world history, even to the detriment of humanity—what a promotion!

Of what earthly use, one wonders, are all the new instruments of knowledge at our disposal—public opinion polls, sociological studies, economic statistics, psychological explorations of the human mind, and so on—when they permit such wild exaggerations? The National Front has been thoroughly and scientifically scrutinized as to its origins, its electoral recruiting, its social basis. In 1984, for example, a scientific survey showed quite clearly that the increase in Le Pen's electoral following was largely due to negative responses to immigration, employment, juvenile delinquency, and crime, but that public opinion as a whole continued to reject the racist *ideology,* remained very firm in its theoretical antiracism, and, save for a tiny minority, approved of judicial punishment for racist misdemeanors.* Instead of insulting their fellow citizens and indulging in wild and stupid historical speculations, our political elite should have felt duty-bound to find out *why* "the presence of immigrants is felt to be a threat," what the conditions of life and the collective forms of behavior are, among immigrants as well as among the already established population, that give rise to this sentiment, and finally, how these attitudes, on both sides, can be improved in order to dissipate mutual distrust. A few hours, even a few minutes of not particularly tiring intellectual labor could have sufficed for our political helmsmen and moralizing orators to realize, by simply glancing at this and other surveys, that hostility to immigration has little to do with ideology, political convictions, or socioprofessional status, and that it diminishes with the *level of education.*

Nothing has contributed more to obscuring the real nature of "Le Pen-ism" than the continued insistence on terming it a "right-wing" movement. In reality, in recent years the National Front's electoral support has increasingly been drawn from traditionally left-wing strata of society. In 1987, after analyzing several public opinion polls, Jérôme Jaffré, director of the SOFRES political surveys, concluded that Le Pen's electorate comprised more and more voters from low- and medium-income categories—workers, employees, middle-level professionals—and the young, and that they were being attracted in proportionately higher numbers than toward other parties. Le Pen's electorate included as many voters who had opted for the socialist challenger, Mitterrand, in 1981 as who had opted for the conservative president, Giscard d'Estaing. The number of Le Pen followers who had come over from the liberal parties of the center and the center right barely totaled 12 percent. This refuted one of the Left's favorite propaganda and polemical themes: the idea that the Le Pen movement is simply an extension of, and represents a "hardening" of, the French

*Muriel Humbertjean, "Les Français et les .nmigrés," Chap. 5 of an annual *SOFRES—Opinion publique* (Paris: Gallimard, 1985).

conservative center. In fact, as Jaffré noted, Le Pen's electorate "has steadily separated itself from the classic Right."*

The National Front, it is also worth noting, is equally separate and quite distinct from the fascist movements of the first half of the twentieth century. The French men and women who have joined it have been little inclined to look for political guidance in the pages of *Mein Kampf*, which only a handful of them have ever bothered to read. However, being constantly portrayed as the champions of gas chambers, they may eventually be tempted by curiosity to find out just what the National Socialist *Weltanschauung*, which is so regularly attributed to them, actually consisted of. In reality, as Michel Winock, a most competent historian of such political currents, has noted, the Le Pen movement adheres far more to the old tradition of "national populism"—which is not, as it happens, an exclusively French phenomenon, but whose prototype was the "Boulangism"† of the late nineteenth century, which fizzled out quickly enough. National populism draws its recruits from relatively humble social strata (poor whites and blue-collar workers in the United States, for example); its adherents tend unquestionably to be racist and xenophobic, but are prompted by thoughtless prejudices, not by a clearly argued ideology; and in Europe at any rate it represents or once represented a threat to democratic institutions. The bitter lessons of World War II have forever disqualified the programs of the traditionalist Right, as of the prewar revolutionary Right, both of which openly favored the establishment of authoritarian regimes and were oriented toward the destruction of democracy. These right-wing movements effected a work of historical and theoretic argumentation which was at least equal in scope to Marxist literature, and which, in addition, was headed in the same direction on certain points—notably its condemnation of capitalism, liberalism, parliamentary rule, and universal suffrage as a way of choosing governments. Fifty years later neither Jean-Marie Le Pen nor anyone else in France, even if they wished to, could permit themselves to include the destruction of democracy in their political

*Jérôme Jaffré, *op. cit.*, Chap. 10, and "Ne pas se tromper sur M. Le Pen," *Le Monde*, May 26, 1987. In a model of good reporting undertaken for the weekly *Le Point* (July 20, 1987), Christian Jelen showed how, thanks to the influx of immigrants, two city quarters in Aix-en-Provence that had long voted for a communist majority had, between 1981 and 1986, become electoral fiefs of the National Front.

†Named after General Georges Boulanger (1837–91), who for a while was very popular and whom the antirepublican Right of the early Third Republic thought to be capable of overthrowing the Republic and installing a new regime. A classic paradox; for Boulanger was a "creature" of Georges Clemenceau, who at the time was the leader of the extreme Left in the French parliament.

programs without running the risk of being disowned and politically destroyed—which fact, however, according to the previously mentioned public opinion polls, does not keep a majority of Frenchmen from considering Le Pen "a danger for democracy." This—a reassuring sign—indicates that their wariness remains alert, even if the NF abstains from explicit antidemocratic rhetoric.

As for elementary racism with its "discriminatory behavior"— whether openly declared, latent, or even murderous—and which is in general severely rejected by most of the population, it is a typical racism born of conflicts created by immigration. It is not a hostility toward immigrants due to a preestablished philosophy. It is a derivative, not a doctrinaire, racism, which can be explained as being due to poor relations with immigrants. But from the moment people refused to face up to the reality of such conflicts—a social reality that has existed since time immemorial—from the moment that anyone daring to point out that a large-scale influx of immigrants into an urban community was bound to ignite misunderstandings was accused of being a "reactionary," and from the moment that it was forbidden to envisage the possibility that the wrongs committed and the tactlessness were not invariably to be found among the local population, then it became quite clear that those who acted thus were simply running away from the human, economic, social, political, scholastic, cultural, and religious problems posed by immigration. These persons were no longer rulers; they were simply demagogues whose sole interest was in viewing the situation from the angle of the polemical advantage it could afford them in blasting away at their adversaries. In so acting they were quite naturally paving the way for other demagogues, who had only to stoop to reap the benefits of the incompetence and cowardice of our political and religious authorities in the face of historical reality. When one lacks the courage and honesty to tackle a thorny problem, when one's sole concern is to use it as raw material for the delivery of self-righteous speeches, then one transforms the difficulty into a stinking corpse, and from then on one loses the moral right to stop up one's nostrils when the cadaver begins to stink and attract vultures.

One day in a Marseille suburb I heard a schoolteacher tell some parents in thinly veiled terms that they were "racists" because they were worried to find that their children were enrolled in classes where almost half the pupils did not speak French properly! The idea of setting up special cram courses for the children of immigrants who speak French badly or not at all is, it seems, a form of "discriminatory behavior." To my way of thinking, *not* setting up such classes is what is truly discriminatory. The pedagogic art should conceive of education in terms of the student's needs, and by that I mean of his or her need for *progress;* it does not consist of adapting oneself to the student's present state of ignorance. Like his political mentors, this opinionated schoolteacher probably thought that, thanks to himself, *le fascisme ne passera pas* ("Fascism will not triumph").* In fact, however, he had just created two more voters for Le Pen's National Front.

Years ago, when the so-called *nouvelle droite* ("New Right") first appeared on the scene, the sociologists did not bother to analyze it seriously; they simply exploited it in order to accuse middle-of-the-road liberals of complicity with it. Unlike the National Front, which accumulated voters without having much to offer in the way of ideas, the New Right was teeming with ideas but had few voters. Above all, as Raymond Aron wrote in 1979 in an editorial published in *L'Express,* it deliberately refused to "emit a judgment about the democratic system." And Aron went on: "Its antiegalitarianism orients it toward the right, but it is a Right that does not in the slightest resemble that of Georges Pompidou, still less that of Giscard d'Estaing. In its eyes, the democratic-liberal Right is no more than a watered-down version of egalitarian socialism and an attenuated version of American mercantilism." I would go even further: thanks to its cultural anti-Americanism, the New Right was closer to the socialists—to Jack Lang, the minister of culture, and Régis Debray, for example—than to middle-of-the-road liberals. Needless to say, none of these considerations kept the leaders of the Left from "amalgamating" liberals and members of the New Right, just as they did later with conservative liberals and Le Pen's National Front.†

On February 21, 1985, during an evening meeting to denounce racism, held at the Mutualité hall on Paris's Left Bank, the prosocialist audience booed and hissed the speakers of the liberal opposition before they had even reached the rostrum. Antiracism is based on a universal moral claim; it affirms the absolute value of the human being. To let it degenerate into a campaign theme for local elections is no way to respect the universality of the moral law. Awareness of the Good and the Bad does not belong solely to left-wing party cardholders. Even from the point of view of political dodges, it is not easy to see just what benefit accrues from such outrageous behavior. When the former prime minister, Laurent Fabius, undertakes to claim that he can no longer discern any

---

*This was the famous left-wing slogan of the 1930s, comparable to the *"No pasarán!"* cry of the Republicans during the Spanish Civil War.

†I must remind the reader that in France a "liberal," being someone who believes in the free enterprise system, is usually a conservative and not a left-wing radical.

appreciable difference between the Right and the extreme Right, does he measure the enormity of his statement? For if he were correct, it would mean that 60 to 65 percent of the French would, according to socialist terminology, be "fascists." Either the statement is false, in which case one cannot excuse this irresponsible remark, or it is true, in which case France is in a truly desperate state, one for which the socialists, who have been governing it, should be held to account.

The impression one therefore gets is that the Left, suddenly deprived of ideology and programs, has been using the "fascist peril" to reconstruct the Manichean universe it needs to feel at ease. Whether in the fields of economics, social guarantees, industrial modernization, freedom of the press, or education, all of the socialist parties in power in Europe today have in practice been veering toward neoliberalism or simple realism. The issues of defense, of foreign policy, of the Third World, particularly in France, no longer see liberals and socialists pitted against one another along clearly defined lines.

To what, then, can the Left still pin its identity? The Communist Party is still hibernating in its ideological ice block, hoping to survive into the third millenium in this embryonically congealed condition. Accordingly, the Socialist Party is girding its loins for the struggle against the "brown pest."

But alas, as we have seen, the "Le Pen phenomenon" does not fit well with a Manichean interpretation of French politics.* The wolf is rampant and roaming through the sheepfolds. A public opinion poll undertaken by IFOP (Institut Français d'Opinion Publique) and published in the weekly *Le Point* magazine on April 29, 1985, showed that antipathy toward Arabs was most pronounced among workers and least among industrialists and major wholesalers and retailers, and in the liberal professions. Racist prejudices transcend social class and party lines. They cannot therefore be exploited in a battle in which the Good Guys and the Bad Guys can be docilely aligned according to hoped-for electoral contours. It is only fair to add that the pre-1981 governments of Jacques Chirac and Raymond Barre, as well as the right-wing town councils, bear their share of responsibility, having channeled immigrants toward poorer urban areas already plagued by wretched housing conditions.

Xenophobia alone does not explain the rise of the National Front. In a survey published on March 28, 1985, the newspaper *Sud-Ouest* (edited in Bordeaux) made mincemeat of the usual clichés by comparing charts

*Eric Roussel, *Le Cas Le Pen* (Paris: J.-C. Lattès, 1985).

showing rises in the unemployment rate with the drop in left-wing voting strength since 1981. In eleven out of twenty-six departments in which the extreme Right won more than 9 percent of the vote in the local elections, the level of unemployment was found to have increased by 70 percent or more. In the Loire, a department with an old working-class tradition, which was economically hard hit though it had absorbed few immigrants, the Le Pen movement had already attained 10.7 percent of the vote by 1984. The presidential majority (composed of socialists, communists, and members of the relatively small MRG—Mouvement des Radicaux de Gauche) fell from 52.8 percent to 33.9 percent. Le Pen made the same sort of breakthrough in Lorraine and Alsace, where the number of immigrants was lower than in southern France.

Why are such "smear tactics" and alleged affinities so odious and dangerous? First, French society is held responsible for anti-Semitic assaults committed by international terrorist groups.* Secondly, every effort is made to get us to believe that tensions born of cohabitation, due to the immigration of foreign workers, indicate a resurgence of ideological and totalitarian racism—in a word, of Nazism—such as it was in its early years with its systematized, pseudoscientific doctrine of the inequality of human races. Here we are confronted by a challenge at once less serious but more difficult to cope with. The worst eventuality, it is true, always has its partisans. False tragedies serve as an excuse for those who are unable to solve real problems.

Thus, instead of looking for remedies suited to practical difficulties and to the psychological upheavals that are engendered by any strong concentration of immigrants in an urban context, French leftists have concentrated their energies on explaining such phenomena as linked to the revival of a vast fascist and racist conspiracy. They then proceeded to link the wave of anti-Semitic bomb blasts that hit Europe after 1980 to this theory. After having allowed local resentments due to immigration to degenerate into xenophobia, they concocted a witches' brew of anti-Semitism and bygone fascism in order once again to impute this glorious

*The two most murderous anti-Semitic assaults perpetrated in Paris over the past decade were a bomb blast outside a synagogue on the rue Copernic (October 3, 1980) and a submachine gun assault on a Jewish restaurant on the rue des Rosiers (August 9, 1982). Readers curious to know more about the propaganda operation mounted by the Left in an effort to blame French liberals for terrorist actions planned in the Middle East would do well to read the preface to another book of mine, *Le Terrorisme contre la démocratie* (Paris: Pluriel, 1987), particularly pp. ix–xiii. Do French socialists realize that this kind of calumny is exactly what Hitler used in order to get rid of his opponents?

mixture to middle-of-the-road liberals! So pleased were they with this ingenious "find" that they did not bother to busy themselves seriously with the causes of plebeian neoracism and international terrorism. "The multiplication of bomb attacks of Fascist or neo-Nazi inspiration in Western Europe obliges us to wonder about certain convergences that seem less and less fortuitous," declared an editorial in the October 5–6, 1980, edition of *Le Monde,* whose front page was dominated by a single headline: BOMB BLAST AGAINST THE RUE COPERNIC SYNAGOGUE. On the front page of the same issue, in an article entitled "The State Bereft of Honor," Philippe Boucher denounced the "active tolerance" and the "passive complicity of the police, of the authorities, of the state" toward the extreme Right. Jacques Fauvet, the newspaper's editor in chief, wrote on this same first page: "Obsessed by its rearguard battles against the thousand and one variations of Marxism, whose death it nonetheless ceaselessly celebrates, an entire intellectual class, now dominant in new clubs and in the media, has forgotten to riposte and even to pay attention to articles and works that have been peddling a fundamentally authoritarian, elitist, and racist doctrine."

In its October 3–4, 1982, issue, under the headline COPERNIC—TWO YEARS LATER, *Le Monde* wrote: "There can be no question anymore of accusing the neo-Nazi Right, and of suggesting Spanish, Cypriot, or Libyan origins [for the bomb blast against the synagogue]. . . . No! The police are now sure of the conclusion they reached quite rapidly. The bomb blast in the rue Copernic was committed by a marginal Palestinian group." I doff my hat to this meritorious act of contrition. But I must add that this particular Palestinian group was in no way marginal, that it enjoyed both Libyan and Syrian support, and that in their 1980 articles Philippe Boucher and Jacques Fauvet had not simply incriminated "the extreme neo-Nazi Right"; they had blamed the liberal government of President Giscard d'Estaing and of Premier Raymond Barre (1976–81), as well as "an entire intellectual class"—by which were meant the "new philosophers," the "new economists," the neoliberals, and in general the adversaries of totalitarianism, who, they claimed, were guilty of carrying on "rearguard battles against Marxism." Fauvet was obviously poorly informed about the orientation taken by the "sense of history," for during those years it was particularly Marxism that was waging "rearguard battles."

When calumnious imputation reaches this pitch, one is no longer in a democratic system. In a democracy the political struggle perhaps allows for (I don't care for it, but I am resigned) a certain dose of falsification of facts for polemical purposes, but it cannot tolerate an absolute falsification. For this is precisely what characterizes totalitarian regimes. Yet it is worth noting that French socialists of the so-called "democratic" brand quietly adopted this habit during the 1970s. On June 28, 1987, at a meeting of the French Socialist Party, Jean-Pierre Chevènement, who after serving as minister of industry and then of education, was now minister of defense, lived up to his reputation as the party's notorious "ideologist" by reviving the deadly equation: Racism equals Fascism, which equals liberalism. What did his demonstration consist of? Very simple. The liberals, he claimed, had ridiculed the socialist measures which in 1982 had been aimed at reducing the importation of Japanese tape recorders; thus they are in favor of the free circulation of goods. But the moment they were back in power, in 1986, they expelled a hundred clandestine African immigrants who did not have proper visas and so on. (Placed on a charter flight, these Malians were flown back to their homeland at French government expense.) Chevènement's conclusion thus was: For liberals, goods have greater value than human rights.

Obviously, if it is with such elevated thoughts and a probity of this stamp that the socialists intend to face the challenges of our age, there is little for us left to do but to hide our faces and keep quiet. But there is one point I shall point up in this macaronic tirade, because it denotes a new extension in the list of forms of behavior that are defined as racist or fascist. If, so as not to violate human rights, a country must decide that all foreigners from all the continents of the earth are entitled to cross its borders in undetermined numbers, to reside on its territory without prior authorization, without work permits, without definite means of livelihood, without any control or time limitation, then I wonder what countries in the world can escape the charge of being fascist and racist? In any case not those from which most of the immigrants to France have come.

In reality, the governments of Third World countries (as any traveler knows from experience) usually gird themselves with very strict and troublesome regulations regarding visas, frontier controls, and residence permits. I might add that one must be particularly brainless to advocate the suppression in Western countries, and only in Western countries, of any control of identity papers and the banning of expulsions of foreigners who have broken immigration laws, at a time when the democracies are precisely those countries that are the most infested with terrorist bands of all kinds. Once the liberals followed the left-wingers onto this slippery ground, everything could and did become "racism" and "Hitlerism": isolating a contagious invalid, flunking a student after an exam, sending clandestine immigrants back to their respective homelands.

It is in this sense that we can properly speak of the "banalization" of Nazism. When Simone Veil popularized this term in 1978, she committed a slight lapse of language by excess of zeal. What she wanted to thwart was the *justification* of Nazism or, better still, the *normalization* of Nazism—that is, of presenting genocide as something "normal." But "banalization"—in the proper sense of the word, meaning "rendering banal" or "rendering innocuous"—is what we are witnessing now when the maniacs of exclusion find traces of "Hitlerism" everywhere and paste this historical and ideological concept onto the most insignificant facts and gestures that happen to displease them. What abhorrence can "Nazism" inspire in young people when they are solemnly told that the frontier policeman who verifies a traveler's identity card is a Nazi?

At the height of the uproar created by the expulsion on a charter flight of a hundred Malians, the "rightist" minister of the interior, Charles Pasqua, declared that he had not been particularly keen on offering a plane to these clandestine immigrants and that he would have been quite happy to have packed them into a train. To this intolerable "provocation" the president of SOS Racisme, Harlem Désir, responded by shouting that Pasqua was a new Klaus Barbie, since the former Lyon Gestapo chief had also in 1943 packed trains full of Nazi victims and had dispatched them to the death camps!*

During the trial of Régis Schleicher, a member of the Action Directe terrorist group that had gunned down two Paris policemen and then finished them off as they lay bleeding on the ground, one of the accused shouted to the court: "We are here in front of Vichy's Special Sections!" Why not? Had he not been affected by a "behavior of exclusion" in being brought to trial for murder? Did not everything he had recently read and heard indicate that to win public sympathy, one must brand those who demand the application of the law, or who are simply of a different opinion, as being Vichyists, Fascists, or Nazis?

Gradually French liberals, paralyzed by the remonstrances of the Leftists, ended up confusing, under the same dreadful appelation of "discriminatory behavior," simple applications of the law or democratic regulations with real racist vexations, brutalities, and crimes. On the

---

*SOS Racisme, which has been partly financed by France's socialist government, has made a specialty of organizing noisy concerts of pop music and hard rock. Afforded lavish TV coverage, these dithyrambic spectaculars have probably done more to fan racist xenophobia in France than to deflate it.

other hand, when a North African committed a crime, many journalists said nothing about his nationality for fear of being termed "racists"—something that increased the irritation of French residents in mixed urban districts and brought more votes to Le Pen. Impotent virtue being a more accessible luxury than active intelligence, our left-wingers thought they had done their duty by uttering the execrated words "Dachau!" or "Treblinka!" and by stigmatizing the "leniency" of liberals who wanted to reduce the National Front's electorate through political action based on real conditions of social life. The mental debility of the general public reached hitherto unexplored heights on the day when left-wingers and intimidated liberals rushed forward (while continuing to exchange insults) and fell straight into the latest of the snares contrived by the Jean-Marie Le Pen workshop: his proposal that all the *"sidaïques"* (victims of AIDS) be locked up in *"sidatoriums."** The Nazis having interned homosexuals in concentration camps and having murdered handicapped individuals, it was with terms borrowed from the Barbie trial that AIDS henceforth had to be combated!

This AIDS storm, alas, confirms the rule that human beings are often less interested in reliable information than in its possible repercussions on their beliefs and cravings. Pierre Bayle, the first Frenchman to have set out (in the seventeenth century) to compile a critical dictionary of historical and philosophical terms, noted this most aptly: "Obstacles to sound scrutiny do not spring so much from the mind's being devoid of science as from its being full of prejudices." Even in scientific and medical matters it is precisely scientific and medical considerations that carry the least weight in our debates. Left-wingers and liberals are both afraid that a collective fear of the epidemic will favor discriminatory modes of behavior toward homosexuals, drug addicts, and foreigners. Xenophobia due to AIDS, furthermore, is rampant everywhere: in the Far East against Europeans, in India against Africans, in Italy against the Swiss, in England against the Scots. Extreme right-wing demagogy takes advantage of the panic to demand measures of banishment. It thus provokes (by way of reaction) the opposite tendency, which leads people to exaggerate the dangers of exclusion and to minimize those of the virus.

How can one fail to see that by entering into this game of furious denunciations, accompanied by soporific diagnoses, one is contributing to the victory of the demagogues? From the moment when in questions

*In French, AIDS is called "SIDA"—*Syndrome d'insuffisance dans la défense anti-immunitaire.*

of *dépistage* (preliminary tracking), hospital care, and preventive measures to limit the contagion our remarks are guided above all by a fear
of being associated with Jean-Marie Le Pen, he has already won.

The striking thing about this polemical uproar was the way in which
the arguments gradually shifted from strictly medical, scientific, and
therapeutic considerations. French bishops even felt the need to certify
that AIDS was not a form of divine punishment! Whereas a sober
assessment of the problem should help to elaborate a definite policy, it
is the political "cleavages" that serve as criteria for analyzing the problem. Must we, on the pretext that universal testing (which would be both
unrealistic and unrealizable) would risk infringing individual human
rights, renounce all forms of systematic tracking? This is something that
has never previously been seen in the history of epidemics.

It seems contradictory to want to combat a malady while heeding a
doctrine that decrees it immoral to ascertain its full extent in the population. There is not and should not be any antagonism between the medical and moral aspects of the struggle against this curse. The two aspects
are indissolubly linked and have, in medical practice, always been so.
Left-wing demagogues, who cripple the medical approach in the name
of morality, are every bit as dangerous as right-wing demagogues who
deny the moral aspect in the name of medical efficiency.

Above all, what scientists should disregard are the political and ideological pressures that are brought to bear. That they are now influencing
the debate became strikingly apparent during the Third International
Conference on AIDS, which was held in Washington, D.C., in early
June 1987, and at the colloqium organized a few days later (June 20–21)
by the Mérieux Foundation near Annecy on the theme of "Epidemics
and Society." That the battle against AIDS cannot be launched without
the participation of politicians is self-evident, if only because of the
gigantic costs involved. But political action is one thing, prejudices and
political passion quite another, and furthermore harmful to any action
decided on. And so it was quite simply flabbergasting, during the
lengthy discussions of this new malady, to hear certain sociologists place
the blame exclusively on "the violence society exercises against its members" or proclaim that "the real danger is fear"—as though the HIV
virus did not exist, that it was a pure invention of adversaries of the
sexual revolution or, at worst, a disagreeable detail in the general portrayal of human relations.

For we should not forget that at the moment when such remarks were
being made, AIDS was a mortal malady for which no truly effective
medical treatment yet existed, and an epidemic to boot. At the Annecy

conference Madame Michèle Barzach, the French minister of health, insisted that the term "epidemic" did not fit AIDS. It was merely, she claimed, an *endémie* (an endemic disease). For the general public the word *endémie* has a less frightening connotation than epidemic. But the historians of illness who were present all politely pointed out that an *endémie* is a lasting epidemic. In the sixteenth century, after having been imported from the New World, syphilis was at first an epidemic, but from the next century on it became endemic, and thus a "native malady." As Professor Luc Montagnier explained in his paper, the diffusion of the virus today, like those of yesterday, is above all due to the intermingling of populations.

Most of the great epidemics of the past aroused irrational reactions because human knowledge had not yet reached a stage where it could identify the cause of the malady, discover its mode of transmission, and hope to find a way of treating it. Now, in the final stretch of this century, we should be able to avoid such irrational reactions, since we know the nature of the virus, as well as how it is transmitted, and have good reason to believe that ways will be found to neutralize it. But the solution will come from scientific research and preventive therapy, and from nothing else. It will come not from starry-eyed optimism, nor from tirades on the respect due to the individual, nor from frenzied anathemas against "impure" persons. To sweep aside these dregs of subthinking, scientists must not let themselves be terrorized; they must impose a scientific attitude with greater forcefulness and intervene earlier in the debate each time a new manipulation of known facts is observed, no matter where it comes from.

It is curious to note how certain phantasms—for example, the Hitlerian phantasm, linked to AIDS—seem to be equally shared by totally opposed ideological families. At the Washington conference a "Union Against Capitalism and Imperialism" had leaflets distributed denouncing AIDS as a "racist offensive of the U.S. government against gays and blacks." In Paris the "gay" movement put on a demonstration on June 20, 1987, openly sporting a rose-colored triangle—a clear reference to the Nazis' persecution of homosexuals. Some of the demonstrators even dressed up as World War II deportees, donning the sinister prison garb of the inmates of Nazi concentration camps.

I have no idea if the HIV virus is Hitlerian, fascist, Stalinist, Trotskyist, deviationist, or social traitorist, if it sports the pink triangle or the swastika, and I imagine that the virus itself doesn't know. I find these hallucinations and pompous prophecies profoundly disturbing. At the time of the Great Plague of the fourteenth century, all of Europe's doctors were arguing among themselves as to whether this "Black Death" was transmitted by touch or by miasma in the air. Wishing to know which in order to be able to take preventive measures on behalf of his people, the king of France decided to consult the loftiest minds of the Sorbonne. After having duly deliberated, these eminent representatives of the country's intellectual elite delivered their solemn verdict. The malady came neither from atmospheric miasma nor from personal contacts; it was the result of a certain astrological conjunction of the planets!

Although our means of acquiring information today are vastly superior, I wonder if, in dealing with AIDS, we are much more intelligent.

Behind the enormously exaggerated to-do over a racist and fascist danger in Europe comparable to what existed before World War II, there lurks in truth a persistent refusal, in the purest Leninist tradition, to recognize the genuineness of liberal, pluralist democracy. No matter how stubbornly they may seek to deny it, European socialists, like American "liberals"—if not all of them, at any rate many of them—consider that the dividing line between the defenders and the enemies of democracy and human rights passes between them and the liberals (in the European sense; "conservatives" in the American sense) and not between democrats as a whole and communists. In other words, the real totalitarians remain in their eyes the partisans of capitalism and the open society, and curiously enough, they are even more persuaded of it today than they were in the past. Since 1975 this has been the case with most of the parties that belong to the Socialist International—in particular British Labour Party members, and the West German SPD after Helmut Schmidt lost the chancellorship. This is even truer, of course, of all those who are to the left of the socialists—the German "Greens," American "radicals," the champions of the Campaign for Nuclear Disarmament in the United Kingdom. They too always demonstrate against NATO, the United States, the West—never against the Soviet Union, the Sandinista dictators of Nicaragua, or the Stalinists of Addis Ababa who have been decimating the unfortunate peasants of Ethiopia. They shout for free elections in South Korea without perceiving that they have already taken place there, but never in Angola or Mozambique or Vietnam. The myth of the rebirth in Europe of a racist or fascist movement, of which middle-of-the-road conservatives are supposed to be the objective accomplices, not to say the inspirers, responds to this need felt by left-wingers, in the face of periodic conversions moving in the opposite direction, to redraw the old separation of the world into two absolute camps: partisans and adversaries of liberal capitalism.

Dimitrios Evrigenis, author of the final report summing up the work of the European Assembly's committee of inquiry, finally recognized with much common sense and honesty that the anxieties that had motivated the inquiry on the "fascist threat" were childish. He concluded that there was no real rise of fascism in Europe, that no significant challenge to the democratic system had been found. On the other hand—and here he was unquestionably right—he noted an accentuation of xenophobic tendencies in the context of badly managed immigration, a political exploitation of these tendencies, and a certain indulgence toward this exploitation; something he wisely denounced with devastating linguistic humor as the "appearance of a new species: the *xenophobophile.*" Combating "xenophobophilia" is thus a duty for the democrat, and fortunately a task quite within his reach. "Xenophobophilia" is in effect a patent or latent ill in every society, an ill to be watched and constantly neutralized. It is not the final cataclysm for democracy. Nor is it a cardinal sin that will condemn our liberal civilization to permanent indignity, as the Left would have us believe.

CHAPTER 7

The International Function of Antiracism

Our political vocabulary is so lacking in rigor that one ends up wondering if ambiguities and obscurity have not been deliberately cultivated in this particular field. It is indeed amazing that where so much confusion reigns, so little effort has been made to introduce a minimum of clarity in the use of words. Thus on one side of the Atlantic the terms "liberal" and "liberalism" signify the exact opposite of what they mean on the other. Similarly, in South America they mean the opposite of what they mean in North America. In Europe and Latin America a "liberal" is someone who reveres political democracy—by that I mean a system that imposes limits on state power, not one that favors the omnipotence of the state over the people it rules. In the economic field a liberal is someone who believes in free enterprise and the market—in a word, who believes in capitalism. Finally, a liberal is a defender of the rights of the individual, one who believes in the cultural superiority of "open" and tolerant societies.

In the United States the term "liberal" has come to mean something

quite different. A North American liberal supports the massive intervention of the state in the economy and in the authoritarian redistribution
of wealth. He (or she) feels more sympathy for socialist than for capitalist regimes, particularly in Third World countries. An American "liberal" tends to agree with the Marxist theory that political liberties are
illusory unless accompanied by economic equality. The American "radical," for his part, is the emulator of violent revolutionaries, and not at
all of our European or Argentinian "radicals," who are persons of
negotiation and compromise.* An American radical is a "liberal" who
becomes an advocate of violence. For years American "liberals," particularly in the universities, closed their eyes to violations of the most
rudimentary human rights in Fidel Castro's Cuba, and later in the
Sandinistas' Nicaragua. They are close to Europe's Marxist Left, to the
extremists of the British Labour Party, and to the pro-Soviet, albeit
anti-Stalinist sectors of the Socialist International of the 1970s and 1980s,
which were swayed by the influence of men like Willy Brandt, Olof
Palme, and Andreas Papandreou. Like them, the American "liberal"
dislikes his own civilization and much of Western culture, and among
the cardinal sins he classes "imperialism"—which, as far as he is concerned, means any attempt, no matter how timid or abortive, to keep
this civilization and culture alive.

On the other hand, in North American parlance a "conservative" is
strikingly similar to what is meant by the term "liberal" in Europe and
Latin America—where a "conservative," as the word's etymology sug-
gests, is somebody who wants to keep everything frozen in its existing
state. However, inasmuch as liberalism, be it economic, political, or
cultural, has been unable to develop in Europe and Latin America
without upheavals—simply because those continents for decades and
even centuries were shaped and fashioned politically by various forms
of state control, administrative *dirigisme,* socialism, and corporatism,
both in practice and in ideology—the liberals have never been conservatives in any literal, static sense, but rather, reformers; they upset traditional ideas and deeply anchored habits. In a sense they are closer to
being revolutionaries.

The adjective "revolutionary" has in reality no absolute meaning, but
only a relative one, since it qualifies a change in relation to a given
situation. This given state of affairs or status quo is not the same every-

*In France the so-called Radical Socialists were one of the most important political parties
of the center during the last two decades of the Third Republic (1919–40) and the fourteen years
of the Fourth Republic (1944–1958). There is still a socialist faction calling itself the MRG—
Mouvement des Radicaux de Gauche.

where, nor does it last forever. Nothing in itself is revolutionary. In China and Cuba the "revolution" has come to be synonymous with the established order, with the regime in power—which power likes to think of itself as immutable and seeks to maintain itself in a perfect state of "conservation." Consequently, the term "conservative" too has no fixed, permanent content; it offers no fixed catalogue of solutions, since what is to be conserved or rejected is never the same as one moves from one society to another, and from one historical moment to the next. How discouraging it is to realize that, notwithstanding the thousands of courses of "politology" and "political science" taught all over our planet, despite millions of words of political commentary written and uttered every day, we have not been able to introduce a minimum of order in the most elementary political vocabulary. For my part, as the reader may have noticed, I have adopted the expedient of using "liberal," "liberalism," and "conservatism" in quotation marks when used in the North American sense, and without quotation marks in the European or Latin American sense.

If anything, the semantic fog in which the notion of socialism has come to be enveloped is even thicker and more confusing. Later, I will list the half-dozen meanings of the word "socialism"—each of them incompatible with the others—which we employ all the time as though they were interchangeable, something that renders the term unintelligible. For the time being I will limit myself to noting that every socialist with whom you discuss the matter will generally refuse to subscribe explicitly to any specific definition of socialism, and will even deny the validity of all the concrete examples of socialism you may ask him to pass judgment on. For such conversational partners, socialism is always that which *is not,* something that is "neither this nor that." It is *not* represented by the diverse and, alas, imperfect regimes that claim to be socialist; it is not reducible to one or another of the definitions that are to be found in the works of "respectable" authors or in innumerable political programs.

Why then this flight into the mists of indefinability? It stems from the contradiction that any definition of socialism embodies, if one tries to make it too precise. Inasmuch as the socialist ideal was founded on the desire to juxtapose incompatible advantages, it can survive intellectually only in a tolerated confusion of contraries. This is why its champions beat a hasty retreat as soon as too harsh a light is trained on the subject, and why they accuse you of not playing fair if you suggest that they should choose between several versions of socialism. In 1981 French socialists claimed that nationalizations (of banks, etc.) were good because they did away with profits; then, in 1983, that they were good because they permitted profits. In the interim their moral doctrine on the question of profits had changed. But they did not seem to feel that only *one* of the two propositions could be true, and only one of the two authentically socialist. They had not, they thought, corrected an error; they had simply "deepened," enlarged, refined the analysis. Using Sartrian phraseology, I would say that their "fundamental choice" is not to choose, and that they exist "in the mode of denial." As Laurent Fabius, the former socialist prime minister, has put it: "Socialism *is not* a landscape that is easy to describe and which can be discovered all of a sudden from a hilltop."* No doubt. The idea that the consequences of a political program could preexist before its enactment and assume the form of a panorama is absurd. But then, what is socialism? Socialism, says Monsieur Fabius, "is a direction." But which direction? Therein lies the mystery.

In much the same mysterious way Burma, in most newspapers and TV broadcasts, suddenly ceased to be socialist when the people rose in revolt against the rulers and when, in August 1988, we learned the extent of the economic catastrophe and political oppression due to the regime. The latter was referred to as a "military dictatorship" or, sometimes ironically, as the "Burmese road to socialism"—which suggested that it was not "true" socialism.

Those who specialize in predictions of the future happily repeat, like Jacques Lesourne: "We are progressively entering into an informational society." Are they not being a trifle overoptimistic? Communication? Transmission? Yes. But information?

Yet there is one word, it seems, about which today there exists no doubt at all—a word that is employed in the same sense, it is thought, by all parties, in all doctrines, in all latitudes: the term "racism." What could be more felicitous and opportune than this apparent unanimity? The struggle against racism, the notion of racism, its extension even to fields that have nothing to do with races or ethnic groups (today people speak of antihomosexual, or antiyouth, or anti-old-age "racism"), antiracist disapproval (as vehement as it is universal), the subordination of almost all other slogans to this imperative priority and the reduction of almost all human rights violations to "racism"—these have conferred on this

*Le Monde, July 19–20, 1987. (Italics mine.)

problem an overwhelming emotional and ideological power in the final decades of the twentieth century. Racism, in fact, has relegated almost all other human causes to second place.

If one admits that respect for the human being and the duty to treat the individual "always as an end and never as a means" can furnish the basis for universal morality and, in politics, for an international principle, than one can reasonably consider the struggle against racism as being essential to the defense of human rights. But the tendency that prevails in our age is to regard human rights violations as being serious only when they include some racist component. But there exist many cases of affronts to human dignity, of persecutions, even of exterminations, that have causes quite distinct from racism—that stem, for example, from religious fanaticism, as in the Iran of Khomeini's "Islamic revolution," the China of the "Cultural Revolution," the Cambodia of the Khmer Rouge. Whereas modern slavery, in both North and South America, was nourished by the black African slave trade, slavery in the Arabic world, on the African continent itself, in Greco-Roman antiquity, later in the serfdom of the Middle Ages, and right down to the middle of the nineteenth century in Russia offered few or no racist features. In many countries and in different epochs, slaves and serfs have usually belonged to the same races as their lords and masters. Were they any better off? Aristotle considered the slave to be inferior, by essence, to the free man, even though both were usually Greek—or at least, if the slave came from some conquered people, he was no different from the Greek, his master, in the color of his skin. But does Aristotle's thesis merit our indulgence? Does the relegation of the slave to the level of subhuman become acceptable as soon as it is not effected according to a racist criterion? If the enslavement of black Africans during the period of the slave trade was doubly odious because of its racist character, it was nonetheless the state of servitude itself that was the essence of the crime committed against human dignity. If the whites had limited themselves to despising the blacks in an abstract way while remaining at home and leaving the blacks in their homelands, the harm done to Africans, while existing on a moral plane, would, we must admit, have been less serious in practice and easier to remedy later on. Even if racism constitutes a violation of human rights, all violations of human rights cannot be traced back to racist causes.

Why is it that today the only infringements of freedom and dignity that count and, it seems, are deemed abominable are those that are or can be ascribed to racist behavior? Since the early 1980s South Africa has thus come to be the most stigmatized of all nations and, it could almost be said, the sole truly guilty party in the contemporary world.* During the summit meeting of the world's seven most industrialized states held in Venice in June 1987, the head of the Canadian delegation declared that apartheid is the "most important human rights issue of our time." Now while it is indeed a very serious problem, an inexcusable form of harsh treatment, other forms can be cited that are just as harsh, indeed, more so. For example: the 600,000 "boat people" from Vietnam who have perished since 1980, of whom 40 percent were children. Yet the industrialized nations of the free world apply economic sanctions to South Africa while providing economic aid and credit to Vietnam! What value can a human rights philosophy have if it is not universal, if it is applicable to certain human beings but not to others? Doesn't it, too, slide back into the sin of racial discrimination, so vigorously condemned in other instances?

Why has apartheid become the supreme contemporary sin—to such an extent that it often crops up, quite illogically, in discussions that have absolutely nothing to do with it? For example, on the evening of the British general election of June 11, 1987, a black Englishman, a member of the Labour Party who had just been elected a member of parliament for the constituency of Brent, commented on his victory by declaring to the BBC: "Brent will never be free so long as South Africa is not free." What did South Africa have to do with the British elections? If this member of parliament meant that Mrs. Thatcher was wrong to oppose the imposition of economic sanctions against South Africa, he should have sought to prove his thesis. But even if he could convince us of its validity, he would not at the same time have proved that the United Kingdom is not free. Does his ringing affirmation mean anything at all, given the fact that there have always been peoples who are free and others who are not—which fact does not keep the former from being free? But even if we admit the validity of this assertion in the highly metaphysical sense that no man is truly free so long as all are not free, why is South Africa the only land that is cited as being deprived of liberty? A number of other contemporary examples of slave societies come to mind. Why, then, does the name of South Africa, though the country is not without rivals in the art of oppression, crop up with such repetitive, obsessive frequency in the ideological oratory of our time?

For this privileged status there are both a general and a particular

---

*This chapter was written before Iraq's invasion of Kuwait.

cause. The particular cause concerns the exceptional economic importance and geostrategic situation of South Africa. Since 1975, when South Africa became a major African power, the Soviet Union has been seeking to promote the conquest of power by the blacks of South Africa in such a way as to exclusively benefit the African National Congress (ANC), which has always been pro-Soviet, as has the South-West African People's Organization (SWAPO) in Namibia. In a future People's Republic of South Africa the ANC could play the same role as Colonel Mengistu's DERG in Ethiopia. Aided by many conscious and unconscious allies, the USSR has been carrying on a work of worldwide propaganda concerning South Africa which for it is simple routine, the kind of work it has long been accustomed to doing and in which it has experienced few setbacks. The purpose of this propaganda is to concentrate all of the planet's available indignation on apartheid, portrayed as the absolute evil, the major curse of the contemporary world and such an incurable ill that no one should dare to defy the bounds of decency by raising the question of the kind of regime that is to succeed the present one. Will it be democratic or totalitarian? If the Soviet Union succeeds in this objective, the result is certain to be a totalitarian regime, in which human rights will be violated even more than under apartheid. But by the time we perceive what has happened, the regime will have been solidly established. Left-wingers and "liberals" will then recognize with consternation the new regime's totalitarian character. They have a long experience of such climaxes and will surely recover from the shock. Their ardor in clamoring for, not to say provoking, such dénouements is equaled only by their promptness in forgetting, when the time comes to evaluate the dire consequences of attitudes assumed in the past. In Africa itself apartheid is almost the only subject on which the African states manage to agree each time an Organization of African Unity (OAU) summit meeting takes place.

Even so, the Kremlin's desire to keep the international spotlight trained on South African apartheid could never have become so potent internationally had it not been able to draw on a vaster, more general source of strength, which gave it a prodigious momentum: the fact that we tend to reduce almost all human rights violations to racism, and, furthermore, to reduce all forms of racism to that practiced by whites against other races or ethnic groups.

Let us continue for a moment with the specific case of Africa. Here, since 1960—which marked the beginning of the independence process— the human rights violations, persecutions, and even exterminations perpetrated by blacks against other blacks have caused far more deaths and inflicted infinitely greater sufferings than those caused by the misdeeds of white oppressors in South Africa. Almost all these black misdeeds have been due to what in Europe and the United States we would without hesitation call "racism"—since these crimes were for the most part committed against a dominated ethnic group by a dominant one. In effect, our customary political and ideological explanations, borrowed from Western rhetoric, mask and provide a surface coating concealing deep-seated conflicts between hostile tribes. For righteous-thinking left-wingers—those who are ever prone to idealize the Third World—tribal realities constitute a factor of history they don't like to be reminded of. For daring to remind my listeners of these realities during a public debate on "Democracy and Development" in 1985, which was attended by Jean-Pierre Cot, the former socialist minister of cooperation, Bernard Kouchner, founder of Médecins sans Frontières and president of Médecins du Monde, and a number of specialists in African affairs, I was booed and hissed by the overwhelmingly Third World audience. I had taken the trouble to consult a number of recent sociological treatises in both English and French, and I found that they no longer contained a single chapter devoted to the notion of tribe as such. Similarly, encyclopedic dictionaries now usually limit themselves to vague definitions and airy generalizations, without providing any of the numerous historical and contemporary examples that might help the reader to understand the underlying forces that have plunged so many emancipated black African countries into destructive civil wars and massacres.

The war in Biafra, which, toward the end of the 1960s, caused a million deaths in Nigeria, was aimed at smashing the power of the Ibos. This ethnic people wanted to break away from the central power. The delineation of the country's constituent states in the recently independent Nigeria had been calculated and carried out by the dominant tribes in such a way as to keep the Ibos from profiting from the country's oil revenues. Nigeria, the most populous and richest country in black Africa, has since then more than once distinguished itself by racist actions. In 1983, for example, its government acted with extraordinary brutality in suddenly expelling some two million foreign workers who had immigrated illegally and who were forced to trudge back on foot to Ghana, Benin, Chad, Niger, or Cameroon. Several thousands of these unfortunates perished of exhaustion on the way. When one compares the protests that the occasional expulsion of a few dozen illegal immigrants provokes in any European country, one can only wonder if a love of human rights is their principal inspiration. How can we believe it when we see the authors of such protests suddenly become mute when rough treatment on an infinitely vaster and more barbarous scale is meted out by blacks to other blacks?

The same question springs to mind when one considers the case of Burundi, a country of five million inhabitants regulated by a system of intertribal relationships that cannot be otherwise defined than as a form of black apartheid. Here the members of the Tutsi tribe, who make up 10 to 15 percent of the population, lord it over the downtrodden Hutus, even though the latter are five to six times more numerous. The levers of central political power are solidly held by the Tutsis. The regime is a dictatorship and could not conceivably be regarded as anything else. In 1987 thirteen out of fifteen of the provincial governors were Tutsis, as well as virtually everyone in the army (96 percent).* On all major roads soldiers (Tutsis, naturally) check the identity papers of all peasants (Hutus, naturally) who may be moving around, but who do not have the right to leave their particular "residence zone." The authorities in Burundi thus act even more harshly than those in the Republic of South Africa, where the famous "pass" or "circulation permit" was abolished in 1985.

In 1972 the Hutus tried to revolt. Their insurrection was crushed by the Tutsis, and 100,000 Hutus were killed. Inasmuch as there are five times as many blacks in South Africa as there are Hutus in Burundi, we can easily imagine the international outcry there would have been if, applying the same ratio, South African whites had in less than one year killed 500,000 blacks. But in the case of Burundi silence prevailed, broken only by a few dry news dispatches presented without comment. Not only that, conscience-stricken leaders in the West subsequently fell all over themselves in their haste to display marks of friendship and offer economic aid to the Tutsis. President François Mitterrand chose, not once but twice, to honor these merchants of genocide with his august presence—the first time in 1982, the second time in 1984, during an African summit meeting at Bujumbura. Indeed, two years later, when the so-called Carrefour du Développement scandal broke out in Paris, it looked very much as though this meeting had been used to divert huge sums of public money not to downtrodden Hutu peasants but to French officials of the Ministry of Cooperation in Paris and to the electoral

*Blaine Harden, "Burundi Tempers Its Black Apartheid," *The Washington Post,* July 1987, reprinted in the *International Herald Tribune.*

treasure chests of certain French socialists. Third Worldism *oblige*
. . . one must accordingly begin by helping oneself.*

From Western countries the Tutsis now receive more than $150 mil-
lion in economic aid each year (in 1986 dollar values). Burundi even
figures among the favorites of the World Bank and of several industrial states, notwithstanding its troubled past and its more than curious present, of which the donors and the international functionaries
never speak. It would be disobliging. They prefer to insist on the "economic efficiency" of the Tutsis, who are, it seems, "good managers"—a quality, be it noted in passing, that can even less be denied to
South African whites, but that does not suffice to grant the latter absolution. The Catholic Church, which had championed the cause of the
wretched Hutus in Burundi as an elementary respect for Christian
charity commanded it to do, was accordingly shunned and banned by
the Tutsi regime. The government proceeded to assail the clergy as the
henchmen of . . . Belgian imperialism! As a matter of historical fact, it
was the Belgian Church, during the colonization period which began
in 1919, that had sent out most of the missionaries. Today, however,
the official government radio station launches daily diatribes against
the Catholic Church, accusing it of having, with its "racist white
god," destroyed "Burundian culture." (Here we see the blessings of
such countries' "cultural identity.") Priests are regularly imprisoned,
but I have yet to see many petitions distributed on their behalf by
theological circles in the West. The Burundian authorities have con-
fiscated and nationalized Christian schools. No Mass can be celebrated
during weekdays, for the Hutus are denied the right to assemble. Sunday Masses, the only services authorized, are conducted under military surveillance. I have never heard one of our pro–Third World
bishops, whether European or American, protest this persecution,
aimed at Catholic clergymen who have come out courageously on behalf of the victims of a bloody oppression carried out according to
patently racist criteria. Why is Bishop Desmond Tutu's noble struggle
against South African apartheid regarded as eminently Christian, why
has it won him worldwide glory as a champion of human rights, further consecrated by a well-earned Nobel Peace Prize, whereas a
shroud of silence has enveloped the clergy of Burundi, who have also
been combating a local form of apartheid, and who have, furthermore,

*In France the so-called Ministry of Cooperation is entrusted with the task of providing
aid to underdeveloped countries. The Carrefour du Développement was one of its operating
agencies.

been trying to avert the chance outbreak—always possible with the Tutsis—of a second genocide?*

Oh, have no doubt about it—our crusaders of antiracism would be able to digest this new genocide just as euphorically as they did that of 1972 and the other acts of discrimination perpetrated by the Burundian regime. On the other hand, their delicate stomachs can tolerate nothing, not even fish, imported from South Africa. This I discovered one day after reading an item in *Ouest-France* (August 4, 1987)—an anathema fulminating against "the tuna fish of apartheid." The Buddha, it is said, was so sensitive to the moral properties of the food he ate that one day his digestive tract was shaken by nauseous fits after he had eaten some fruit which, unknown to him, had been obtained through theft. I also learned from *Ouest-France* that a certain Yves L'Helgoualc'h, a follower of the ascetic saint and president of Concarneau's Comité du Thon Blanc (White Tuna Committee), had in August 1987 sent a letter to the State Secretariat for the Sea asking it to "impose an embargo on imports coming from South Africa." Such a measure, the virtuous fisherman argued, "would adhere to French declarations hostile to apartheid." Apart from that, it "adheres" very well to the irksome fact that South African tuna is cheaper than the French—which is why French canning companies prefer to buy it. At Concarneau, as at the Carrefour du Développement, fraternity and the pocketbook make excellent bedmates.

During the summer of 1988 the massacres in Burundi were resumed on a massive scale, claiming the lives of tens of thousands of victims. At the time I was in Italy, and every morning I read the leading Italian dailies, as well as the *International Herald Tribune* and *Le Monde*. I also listened to the BBC and watched Italian TV news roundups. Once again I was struck by the extraordinary detachment with which, without exception, the journalists reported this new bloodbath. They spoke of it as though it were some natural catastrophe. A single death—what am I saying?—a single incarceration in South Africa would have unleashed a planetary storm and twenty pop music concerts. If the extent of the killings was not concealed, never once was the word "racism" used. *Le Monde* headlined one of its articles ETHNIC CONFRONTATIONS IN BURUNDI. What a lovely euphemism! The headline RACIST CARNAGE! would more accurately have reflected the contents of the article. A

*In early September 1987 the ruling dictator of Burundi was overthrown by a coup d'état while he was adding the luster of his presence to a "Francophone" summit meeting in Montreal. He was immediately replaced by another dictator, likewise a Tutsi, to be sure, but less anticlerical, it seems.

"confrontation" neither implies nor indicates murder. Confrontations take place in parliamentary assemblies, on sports grounds, in philosophical debates, without genocide. If such a term is to be used, one might just as well say that the Holocaust of World War II was basically no more than an "ethnic confrontation" between Germans and Jews.

The moderate terms used by the press on this occasion strikingly confirmed this elementary prejudice: that racism, for us Westerners, can be only of European or American origin. When African students are persecuted at the University of Nanking, when they are beaten, persecuted, humiliated, and even tortured by Chinese students and police, as happened in December 1988, was this not racism, since it took place in the Third World? The "progressives" usually give this reply: the bad conscience of the former colonial powers inhibits them when they have to criticize decolonized countries. But it was not a process of colonization that provoked the Nanking upheavals or created the tribal system, the root cause of the massacres in Burundi. On the contrary, throughout Africa the European colonial authorities sought to weaken this tribal system—something for which they were taken severely to task by anthropologists and others.

In October 1988 the argument based on the bad conscience of the postcolonial French was again revived to justify the silence of left-wing intellectuals when the Algerian army killed several hundred rioting students, most of them adolescents fed up with a regime that had brought them nothing but food shortages and police repression. The indignation of the "progressives" was slow to heat up at the sight of an army firing heavy machine guns on children who were simply demanding "bread and freedom." The indignation of the socialist president of the French Republic, François Mitterrand, normally a great dispenser of resounding, ready-made phrases about human rights, was particularly inaudible. When he finally said something, it was a word of compassion . . . to succor the oppressors. He offered "the economic aid of France" to the Algerian government. To give money to thieves because the people demand they be given back what has been taken from them—such is the quintessence of Third Worldism!

However, the moral conscience of France's intellectual class, thrown off balance even more by the referendum with which General Pinochet was preparing a transition toward democracy, finally began to stir and the repression in Algeria was belatedly condemned. But the real scandal, in my opinion, was not the delay of several days; it was that this belated awareness of what was going on on the other side of the Mediterranean was several years overdue. For the previous ten or fifteen years the situation in Algeria, with its economic débâcle, the rottenness of a corrupt *nomenklatura,* a totalitarian terror exercised by a socialo-Islamic police force, were well known, but nothing was said about them because of the taboo that keeps left-wing journalists from describing things as they really are in "progressive" Third World countries. As for the intellectuals' "postcolonial guilt complex," the excuse was almost comic. Is there any sense in expiating the evils of colonialism by offering aid to and making oneself the accomplice of venal brutes who for well-nigh thirty years have inflicted on the unhappy Algerian people the three constitutive failings—or *f*'s—of Third World socialism: *famine,* dictatorial *force,* and administrative *fraud*?

The indifference of international opinion to crimes against humanity when they are committed by Africans at the expense of other Africans explains the astonishing esteem long enjoyed in Europe by one of the twentieth century's most sinister tyrants: Sékou Touré, the dictator of Guinea, a land he reduced to starvation and terrorized from 1959 until his death in 1984. The number of people he arranged to have tortured, executed, or condemned to life imprisonment runs into the thousands. One of them was the archbishop of Conakry, a native of Gabon and a French citizen, who was eliminated in 1970. Considering the relatively small size of Guinea's population, Sékou Touré's purges can be flatteringly compared in percentage terms to Joseph Stalin's in the USSR. It was not wise to be one of Sékou Touré's ministers. Most of the individuals to whom this honor was offered prudently chose preventive exile when they still could do so, in preference to acceptance, which usually brought with it a gory end. For the Guinean leader's collaborators were rounded up by truckloads and tortured, hanged, shot, or incarcerated in prison camps until they died. The Guinean jails and prison camps, whose extent and atrocities newspapers and TV networks belatedly described *after* the death of the "president," were not a whit inferior to Heinrich Himmler's choicest realizations. Sékou Touré, who, like most of the members of his successive governments, belonged to the Malinké tribe, harbored a particular hatred for the Peuls, a desert-dwelling people. He had several thousand of them tortured and massacred in periodic pogroms. Unless I am mistaken, this brutal behavior bears some resemblance to racism. Nevertheless, Sékou Touré received a visit from François Mitterrand at a time when the leader of the French Left was still in the opposition. Later having become president of the Republic, Mitterrand in his turn received the Guinean chief of state with all the honors due to his exploits, on the occasion of an African summit meeting held in 1982, a summit of hypocrisy.

This virtue being by no means the sole prerogative of the Left, it is only fair to add that already in 1978 President Valéry Giscard d'Estaing had seen fit to make an official trip to Conakry. Raymond Aron then published in *L'Express* what for him was an exceptionally stinging editorial in order to stress the degree to which this visit, a source of consternation from a moral point of view, could not even be justified in terms of realpolitik. Knowing that Guinea's economy was in a state of total catalepsy, Giscard doubtless reckoned that the moment had come to tear this country away from Soviet influence and to bring it back into the bosom of France's sacrosanct "African policy." This is an example of the errors so habitually committed by certain liberals, who understand next to nothing of the workings of international communism. For when a communist country is in desperate straits, the Soviets hasten to advise it to obtain as much money as it can from the capitalists. They rely on the naiveté of good-natured simpletons who think they have won a victory due to their personal charm, when all they are being asked to do is to provide the funds.

The USSR, it is interesting to note, has retained its political and strategic influence in Guinea. Lenin was the first to explain and apply this method with great ability.* Not only did the Soviets not leave Guinea in 1978, in 1990 they were still there. They continue to exploit the country's bauxite mines, which are among the richest in the world and provide the country's chief raw material export. They exercise a right of indefinite exploitation, as part of the reimbursement they insist is due to them for past "economic aid." This costly and onerous economic aid consisted of the delivery of thousands of tons of scrap iron, so-called agricultural machines, among which figured the famous snow-plows whose notorious inapplicability in an equatorial climate became the laughingstock of the world. The favorable treatment lavished on the Guinean dictator by the two French heads of state had but one result: Sékou Touré, simultaneously courted by communist and democratic leaders, found his power reinforced by a kind of ecumenical mandate enabling him to continue victimizing his people. Not only were the two French presidents unafraid to shake hands with this repugnant individual—whereas they would never have dreamed of receiving a South African deputy state secretary—they did so without the slightest benefit, even from the viewpoint of the most elementary Machiavellianism.

The Guinean murderer was also honored with noisy praise from the director-general of UNESCO, Amadou Mahtar M'Bow, who hailed him

---

*I quoted this text in Chapter 18 of *How Democracies Perish.*

as a great humanitarian democrat and Third World progressive. This fatuous flattery could come as no surprise to those who were aware of the extent to which, in the 1970s and 1980s under Mr. M'Bow's manage- ment, UNESCO became a pro-Soviet sounding board. This was a betrayal of UNESCO's mission, and indeed of the UN's mission, and one that should not have been tolerated. Florence Nightingale is usually credited with the admirably commonsense remark that "Whatever else they do, hospitals must not spread disease." But in fact international organizations whose mission supposedly is to eliminate misery and barbarism, end up spreading the very ills they are designed to cure. The financial aid they distribute serves less to succor poor populations than to enrich the dictators who starve and subjugate them. Whether as a result of political passion or out of fear of being called "racists," many international functionaries become the accomplices of the tyrants' conspiracies against their own peoples. What sense is there in inveighing against so-called "revisionist" historians who dare to assert that the Hitlerian genocide never took place, while at the same time finding it perfectly normal that the director-general of UNESCO should officially heap praise on a *contemporary* practitioner of genocide such as Sékou Touré or, for that matter, the Ethiopian dictator Mengistu, to whose statesmanly virtues Mr. M'Bow also once paid official homage?

Let's say you are the head of a totalitarian Third World country and you need money and shipments of various supplies to meet your military expenses and pursue the realization of the "revolution." The "fraternal" countries are not in a giving mood, while your credit with capitalist countries is at rock bottom. What do you do?

The answer is that you wait for a good famine to come along— something which, given the sterilizing effect of your agricultural policy, is bound to happen, particularly if the sun cooperates by holding back the rainfall. Three quarters of socialism mixed with one quarter of drought will suffice. Once the famine really sets in, you hide it from the rest of the world for a year or two—something you can easily do since you control the movements of all foreigners on your territory. You let the famine grow, develop, and erupt until it attains a scope and horror capable of shaking international opinion.

At this point you pull off a bold stroke. You offer a scoop to a foreign TV team. The team films a bunch of fleshless children whom you have carefully brought together. Broadcast during prime time by the BBC, CBS, or some other major network, this harrowing documentary plunges capitalist television viewers into a state of horror-stricken compassion. Simultaneously—and this is a key element in the planning of this operation—you vehemently accuse capitalist governments of having willfully refused or delayed help, because they were unwilling to help a "progressive" state. This indictment is immediately taken up and repeated by left-wing organizations in democratic countries and by the Churches. Overnight Western governments find themselves transformed into culprits, the ones really responsible for the famine you have provoked and aggravated. Money and gifts, public as well as private, flow in from all over the world.

A new phase of the operation now begins; for everything must be done to keep the aid from reaching the victims. You need too much of it for yourself, for your army, for your *nomenklatura,* to reimburse debts incurred with "fraternal" countries, and above all to accelerate agricultural collectivization and the Revolution, to eliminate your adversaries, and to consolidate your power. The trucks sent to distribute rice, grain, and flour will transport soldiers or, even better, displace peasants from their homesteads to distant collective farms, where they will die far from indiscreet eyes. Visitors who prove to be too curious and "nosy"— usually members of nongovernmental organizations, doctors, and other hotheads—will be neutralized, accused of having diverted the foreign aid themselves. Treat them like thieves, like spies! Since your calumnies against these witnesses will eagerly be taken up by the Third Worlders of their own countries, you need only expel them to have them scoffed at and criticized by their virtuous compatriots.

After which, having made a small fortune at the expense of 1,200,000 Ethiopians dead of starvation, Colonel Mengistu Haile Mariam—for it was obviously his exploits I was just describing—needed only to receive the ovations of the Non-Aligned Movement, of the Socialist International, of "liberation" theologians, and of the World Council of Churches, ovations augmented by several thousand cases of Scotch whisky, bought with hard currency to enable the Party dignitaries to celebrate the tenth anniversary of their Revolution in proper style—as happened in 1984. In 1973 Emperor Haile Selassie lost his throne as a result of a famine which had claimed 200,000 lives. The progress accomplished since then allows us to gauge the superiority of socialism over feudalism.

In fact, Colonel Mengistu did no more than follow a recipe concocted by Lenin during the great famine of 1921 in the Soviet Union—one often adopted since then, particularly by the Hanoi regime in Cambodia. But if Mengistu did not invent the recipe, he probably surpassed everyone else in its execution.

One is seized by nausea at the deliberate blindness that international charitable organizations, United Nations functionaries (but this is no surprise), and the bureaucrats of the European Community in Brussels displayed toward the crimes of the college of dictators of Addis Ababa. The cries of indignation voiced in Paris by Médecins sans Frontières* garnered them more opprobrium than was earned by those responsible for the exterminations. Two taboos joined forces to create the joint silence shared by naïve simpletons, "useful idiots," and cynical accomplices: the sempiternal fear of being taken for a reactionary in criticizing a so-called "progressive" (but in reality totalitarian) state, and that of seeming to be a racist if one condemns the massacre of Africans by other Africans.

All over the planet, humanitarian aid is now diverted by the rulers of despotic states to the detriment of the populations they are oppressing. A doctor who personally witnessed this gigantic racket on several continents did not hesitate to call it the "humanitarian pitfall."† His book makes harrowing reading. It is an inventory of "useful catastrophes," sometimes even imaginary ones, that are based on skillfully spread rumors but are fruitful operations nonetheless. The author tells how the regimes or political parties wishing to acquire or reinforce control over the masses operate, how they interpose themselves between humanitarian organizations and local populations, how they intercept aid in order to use it for their own ends. He cites the example of the Sandinistas who, after the fall of Somoza, in order to eliminate other political parties and to monopolize power without elections, resorted to the most brutal methods in laying hands on the international assistance offered to Nicaragua, in particular aid from the United States. (It is worth recalling that during its first two years the United States helped the new Nicaraguan regime.) Despite this aid, the impoverishment of Nicaragua began *after* the consolidation of the Sandinista dictatorship. Thus totalitarianism extends its grip thanks to money provided by the democracies. Truly, hunger is for socialism the "most precious capital."

If the Ethiopian nightmare benefited from almost universal indulgence and silence, it was because of what Glucksmann and Wolton have called "revolutionary immunity."‡ But even the rare beings whom it does not paralyze and who have taken the trouble to ascertain the facts do not know what conclusion to reach—or else they draw a contradictory conclusion. Like Bob Geldof, the generous and naïve rock-and-roll

---

*Médecins sans Frontières is a privately financed group of French doctors who volunteer to tend the sick, set up hospitals, and train medical apprentices in underdeveloped countries.

†Jean-Christophe Rufin, *Le Piège* (Paris: J.-C. Lattès, 1985)

‡André Glucksmann and Thierry Wolton, *Silence, on tue* (Paris: Grasset, 1986).

star who, thanks to the concerts he organized, collected billions for the starving inhabitants of Ethiopia which the "progressive" officers of Addis Ababa then diverted to war purposes. Fed up and disillusioned when informed of the mass transfer southward of Ethiopian peasants, which was enough to finish off the dying, Geldof nevertheless felt that he and others must continue, no matter what. "I would have worked, even at Auschwitz!" he exclaimed. But with whom exactly? Many harsh things, some of them unjust, have been said about Bob Geldof's organization, Band Aid. This organization did indeed try—and more strenuously than was generally reported—to keep its aid from being diverted by the Ethiopian dictators. But the latter were smarter and had little trouble fooling the "good whites" and using the aid for their own cynical ends.

In August 1987 the communist regime in Ethiopia began once again to deny the existence of a new famine—yet one more!—the first signs of which had appeared in the northeast of the country. The UN's first alarming reports on the appearance of famine conditions were rejected as inaccurate by Mengistu, who claimed that all was well. Now, a famine—and this is something that is still not generally realized—presents certain early warning signs that make it possible to take remedial action at the outset. It is at that moment that one should appeal for international help, which then has some chance of being effective. Once this stage is passed and the famine has been allowed to degenerate into a widespread catastrophe, the distribution of emergency supplies encounters almost insurmountable difficulties (to say nothing of loss through theft or diversions); for to be effective the aid has to be both more massive and more rapid. With each passing day the starving multiply and are increasingly weakened through lack of food. The more urgent the need for help, the harder it becomes to deliver the food in time and the greater the waste due to inadequate means of transportation, while the number of dead and dying advances at a gallop.

Leaders who, for political reasons, deliberately allow the development of a famine—one that ends up claiming tens and sometimes hundreds of thousands of lives—can rightly be regarded as guilty of crimes against humanity. But what political motives can inspire such a policy? First of all, there is a reluctance to proclaim the failure of a regime and a system by ingloriously admitting that such shortages of food are a recurring phenomenon. It so happens that the three African countries that were most affected by food shortages for much of the 1980s were the three most communist and sovietized countries of the continent: Ethiopia, Angola, and Mozambique. They obviously offered adverse propaganda for those who wanted to see communism extended to other countries—notably Namibia and South Africa. Furthermore, the governments forcibly imposed on those three countries and maintained with foreign help have had to deal with internal guerrilla movements. In allowing incipient famines to become catastrophes, to the detriment of their populations, those governments arouse a wave of international sympathy—something that invests them with the trappings of legitimacy. The instinctive reaction of international opinion is to say: when children are dying of hunger we're not going to argue about the nature of the regime in power. (This argument holds only, of course, for cases where the starver regime is communist or cryptosocialist.) At the same time, taking advantage of a universal feeling of compassion, combined with inattention, the authors of the famine place the blame on the guerrilla forces that have been combating them: in Mozambique, on the RENAMO movement; in Angola, on UNITA. This explanation is all the more palatable to the Western press and human rights groups since both of these movements receive military help from South Africa. The conclusion they draw is that these "rebel" movements would not exist but for this foreign help; in other words, the resistance to the regime in power has no real roots in the country—exactly the thesis the communists would like to see credited.

There is no denying that a civil war harms a country's economic activity, its agriculture in particular. But there are numerous examples that illustrate the now notorious propensity of communist regimes to create artificial food shortages when no civil war is raging. Throughout the 1960s and 1970s Angola and Mozambique were the theater of a very long, tough internal war of decolonization. Yet never, during this period, did either sink as low as it now has under a communist regime. Despite the war of independence and Portuguese oppression, never did they experience a total economic collapse and the complete disappearance of all the basic commodities that communism was supposed to provide.

But so what! Western newspapers are usually quite willing to accept the communists' explanation each time a famine occurs. For example, on December 31, 1984, *The New York Times* ran this headline: ANGOLA'S CIVIL WAR REDUCES A FERTILE DISTRICT TO HUNGER.* This kind of reasoning absolves the regime of responsibility. Two and a half years

*Article by James Brooke. At present there is no civil war in Vietnam, but in 1988 the desperate authorities in Hanoi announced that seven million people were threatened by starvation (not to mention the million who had fled in boats).

later, in describing a new famine—or rather the same one, which in the meantime had become endemic, *The Washington Post* sounded the same alarm by headlining: ANGOLA, ADMITTING HUNGER CRISIS, ASKS URGENT AID.* After declaring that a million inhabitants of the capital city of Luanda no longer had anything to eat, the *Post*'s correspondent wrote: "The farmers refuse to sell their food for Angolan currency"— simply because the local currency is worthless. They want to exchange their foodstuffs for clothes, soap, and so forth, articles the city dwellers likewise lack! It was thus clear that foodstuffs *did* exist, and that the civil war had *not* destroyed agricultural output. But the reporter was not interested in drawing the logical conclusion. He preferred to stress the point that the famine in Angola was due to a fall in the price of petroleum (pumped from the Cabinda enclave), this being an accessory to the destructive guerrilla operations of UNITA. It was indeed astonishing to see how ready he was to adopt the viewpoint of the authorities in Luanda. One gets the impression that the critical capacity of American journalists is exercised exclusively against their own government. The less prone they are to believe what the White House or the Pentagon tells them, the readier they are to swallow what they are told in Luanda or Maputo. In Europe's noncommunist press, *The Guardian* alone surpasses them in gullibility.

Early in 1987 the U.S. ambassador in Mozambique sent a report to his government (which immediately dispatched some emergency aid), warning that a gigantic famine was imminent. When, shortly afterward, rumors of this new peril began circulating in Europe, there was an immediate reaction: the sole cause was RENAMO (the anticommunist guerrilla movement). The BBC, in a broadcast made at 1610 (universal time) on May 10, 1987, declared categorically: "This famine is *exclusively* due to RENAMO!" This trust placed in Mozambican socialism must have made many people laugh in East Africa, where the BBC's World Service has many listeners, but where, from 1967 on, a year after Samora Machel's takeover (aided by an impressive cohort of North Koreans and East Germans)—which is to say, long before the appearance of RENAMO—everyone knew there was nothing to eat in Mozambique. Socialist miracles are sometimes rapid.

Why, then, this willful blindness? Because under no circumstances must one reproach Africans for having deliberately allowed other Africans to perish. That would be "racism." Mass killings and famines must therefore be explained either by external interventions or by bad weather

*By Blaine Harden, reprinted in the *International Herald Tribune,* August 15–16, 1987.

conditions.* Such pseudoexplanations are in truth the most racist of all, for they cause people to lose interest in the fate of millions of Africans who are abandoned to the whims of cruel and incompetent despots.

The tragic history of Uganda offers at least one example of why such explanations are insufficient. Uganda was once one of the most fertile regions of Africa. Trade flourished thanks to a large Indian population, which had settled there long before. Then along came Idi Amin Dada, who in a few years exterminated hundreds of thousands of Ugandans, expelled the Indian merchants and shopkeepers (without the slightest trace of racism, needless to say), ruined both agriculture and commerce, and transformed this land of milk and honey into a museum of horrors. Even with the most acute guilt complex in the world, it is impossible for a Westerner to see in this work of African self-destruction anything but a strictly aboriginal drama—particularly since for a long time other African lands displayed an abject complaisance toward, and even a certain admiration for, Amin. How, indeed, could the governments of the continent have *elected* Amin president of the Organization of African Unity at a time when people had long known about the atrocities he had committed in Uganda? And what moral right do they retain, after such a decision, to appoint themselves the defenders of South African blacks? One is even led to wonder if those wretched South African blacks are not now enjoying their happiest years under a waning system of apartheid, at a time when the entire world is up in arms on their behalf; whereas, a little later under a "progressive" regime, anything might happen without anyone lifting a finger to help them. Those who then display any misgivings will be dismissed as "fascists"! Did not the "progressive" Gaddhafi help Amin militarily right up to the very last moment?

As for this last moment, it may be recalled that it was provoked or hastened by the intervention of the Tanzanian army. At the outset this was an operation of humanitarian salubrity, accordingly applauded in the West. But thereafter? Thereafter the Tanzanian army transformed itself into an army of occupation, pillaging, ransoming, starving what was left of the Ugandans. Tanzania behaved like a conqueror. Here too, what was involved was a purely Africano-African rampage. The cause of famine in Uganda was not economic backwardness but political criminality.

*Up until very recently, the communist authorities in Maputo consistently dismissed RENAMO as being made up of "bandits" trained, armed, and financed by South Africa. The Angolan government in Luanda has maintained the same propaganda line with regard to UNITA.

Europe, whose suicidal struggles have inflicted two world wars on the planet, certainly has no lessons to hand out. This is not what I am suggesting. The point I wish to make is that conferences devoted to the Third World will continue to be pointless exercises as long as people are solely concerned by the economic causes of underdevelopment, while ignoring the often more decisive political causes: despotism, administrative and managerial incompetence, waste, rapacious plundering, corruption. For, as Bechir Ben Yahmed exclaimed courageously in an editorial published in 1976 in *Jeune Afrique:* "The underdeveloped are not the local populations!" They are the leaders.

It is easy to understand why certain Third World leaders are so favorably disposed to the thesis that their underdevelopment is of purely external origin. This enables them to heap all the blame for their setbacks and failures onto the developed nations, to distract attention from their own incompetence and rapacity, and to obtain new credits permitting them to carry on as usual.

I am not in any sense advocating a return to what once was called "Cartierism"—the trenchant thesis propounded by the French journalist Raymond Cartier, who advocated a suspension of aid to poor countries.* The industrialized world must face its responsibilities, but only its own. Foreign aid, let there be no doubt about it, should be maintained, increased, diversified. But it should also be made effective. For this it is essential that the problems of areas to be developed be dealt with as problems in other parts of the world are tackled. When one speaks of inflation and unemployment in industrialized countries, the debate focuses on the responsibility and the managerial efficacy of the governments of the countries involved. It is not concentrated primarily on natural catastrophes or economic fatalities. When, in a Western country, a given sector of the economy is in a state of crisis, the blindness of entrepreneurs or the lack of foresight of the state is assailed. In speaking of the economic débâcle of communist societies, we do not hesitate to raise the question of governmental incompetence and dishonest administration. Why, then, must questions of competence and political honesty not be raised as soon as one tackles the problems of the Third World?

Why, for example, have we been so slow to challenge the principle of those sacrosanct "agrarian reforms," which always consist not of distributing land to the peasants, but of combining it into cooperatives

---

*A thesis later propounded, with far better arguments, by the British economist Peter Bauer.

under the control of ignorant, venal urban bureaucrats—something that so discourages the peasants and engenders such a drop in productivity that countries that once were agriculturally vigorous are now reduced to importing food from other countries? Why is so little mention made of the dire consequences of corruption?* Corruption is rife at the very summit of innumerable regimes (and the most "progressive" are not those where the bosses help themselves the least to the "goodies" available). Why then is it not more openly denounced? Because one is a friend of the Third World?

A friend of the Third World, or a friend of Third World tyrants? It is odd that the sufferings of poor peoples arouse indignation only when they can be imputed to the West. Former colonies were freed from foreign domination only to succumb to that of their own people, whose cruelties and rapacious plunderings seem to have been legitimized by independence. If Third World governments are increasingly free from the political supremacy of developed countries, the peoples of the Third World are more and more subjugated by their own governments, most of them installed by forceful coups. Political egalitarianism between sovereign states has above all favored autocrats, whom nobody, for reasons of postcolonial propriety, dares call to account. They even manage, with the help of UNESCO, to keep light from being shed on their devious operations, making sure that the "imperialist" information thus dispensed is censured and rigged in their favor.

In Uganda the genocidal tally for Amin's regime can be fixed at a figure of roughly 200,000 dead. A little later, after Amin's departure and between 1980 and 1985, the figures, according to different estimates, run from 300,000 to 500,000 deaths. According to Elliot Abrams, who was then assistant secretary of state for human rights in Washington, between 100,000 and 200,000 Ugandans were killed during the three years that followed Amin's departure: a truly stunning number, since

*The subject, it must be admitted, has become less "off limits" and taboo-stricken, as corruption has caused ever greater and more obvious damage. While covering a meeting of the Organization of African Unity in Addis Ababa, Jacques de Barrin wrote in *Le Monde* (July 21, 1987) these lines, which could not possibly have appeared several years earlier in an avowedly left-wing newspaper: "If the ruling African elite behaved in a responsible way, one could harbor hopes for Africa. Who knows if the total amount of pilfered funds is not on the same order as the continent's external debt, now estimated at around $200 billion?" To this sacrilegious question the heads of the African states replied at a subsequent meeting of UNCTAD (United Nations Conference on Trade and Development) by demanding . . . economic sanctions against South Africa (*International Herald Tribune*, August 3, 1987). On the subject of agrarian reform, see Guy Hermet, *Sociologie de la construction démocratique* (Paris: Economica, 1986, pp. 100ff).

Uganda's population totals—or rather used to total—about 15 million inhabitants.

Notwithstanding his authoritarian talents, Robert Mugabe, in Zimbabwe, managed in February 1983 to exterminate only 3,000 Ndebeles—from the tribe of his political rival, Joshua Nkomo. I have no idea if Mugabe was assisted in this task by the six hundred North Korean instructors whom "Big Brother" had most fraternally made available to him in 1981. But when I think of the profusion of televised news roundups in the 1960s and 1970s that assailed the whites of Rhodesia, showing them to be rifle-carrying bandits, ready on their farms to shoot down anyone who might attack them, I am amazed by the indolence of these same media ten years later and the lack of zeal they display for filming present-day conditions in Zimbabwe. We were not exactly deafened after the massacre of the Ndebeles by protests against Mugabe uttered by the usual defenders of human rights. But neither the extermination of those Ndebeles, nor his racist dictatorship, nor the presence of North Koreans could keep Mugabe from scoring a personal triumph as the host of the summit meeting of "nonaligned" countries in his capital, Harare, in 1986. However, did not this "summit" accomplish its essential duty in condemning for the umpteenth time the West's complicity in the regime of apartheid?

I have no intention of prolonging this survey of African necrology. But it would be unfair of me to omit all mention of Rwanda, a serious competitor to Burundi in the business of mass killings, or the public executions of different ministers in Liberia in 1980, or the slayings of petty thieves in Nigeria almost every week. And how, finally, could I fail to render the homage due to the phenomenal Francisco Macias Nguema, who, as the boss of Equatorial Guinea, managed from 1968 to 1979 (when he himself was finished off) to kill 50,000 of his fellow citizens and to drive 150,000 others into exile? Of the 300,000 inhabitants tiny Equatorial Guinea boasted in 1968, only 100,000 remained at the end of Macias's reign! Not content with slaying or driving into exile two thirds of his compatriots, he also had several thousand immigrant Nigerian workers massacred while they were on Guinean soil. This elegant scenario took place under the complacent eyes of Soviet "advisers," for Macias Nguema had likewise placed his country in the Soviet camp. This is a fact it is necessary to recall, or rather to state (for I doubt that many newspapers or television stations in democratic countries have provided this information).

To be sure, a democratic country like France was also wrong in protecting a tyrant like Jean Bédel Bokassa in the Central African

Republic. But without trying to excuse France, it must be said that it also organized the coup d'état that overthrew him, once the sanguinary folly of its "charge" had become too patent. Above all, the clumsy support offered by France to Bokassa for years drew down upon it a tempest of well-deserved vituperation. But I cannot recall ever having heard the African or international community addressing the mildest reproach to the Soviet Union for its support of Macias—nor, for that matter, for its later support of the tyrant of Madagascar, a fine example too of virtuosity in the art of promoting hunger and shedding blood.

One could, as I have said, enrich this necrological survey by adding other African examples. But the samples I have presented here seem to me sufficient to suggest some solid conclusions regarding the pertinence of certain claims made on behalf of human rights and the international role of "antiracism."

During the thirty years that separate 1960 from 1990, the total number of black African victims of crimes against humanity committed by other black Africans far exceeded the number of victims of apartheid. The two cannot even be compared, so staggeringly different are the figures and so different in degrees of horror are the facts.

This realization, it may be objected, does not excuse apartheid. Of course not, and that is precisely what I mean. For the opposite is also true: Apartheid is no excuse for the rest. But particularly since 1970, this is the use to which apartheid has been put. I, too, have a horror of apartheid. But people who defend human rights in one case and not in another disqualify themselves by this very process of discrimination. Either human rights are universal, or they are nothing at all. To invoke them in one case and to ignore them in others proves that one basically doesn't care a rap for them and is simply using them as political weapons for purposes that are actually totally different. Anyone who denounces apartheid *and nothing else* actually approves of apartheid. The only way of fighting effectively for human rights in South Africa is to fight for these rights in *all* of Africa, and in the world at large. What right have the leaders of African states to demand political rights for everyone in the Republic of South Africa when they themselves accord them to no one in their own countries? And when, furthermore, there is hardly one among them who holds power thanks to an election, or at least an election that was any more than a grim farce?

What they are attacking, therefore, are not violations of human rights, nor even the particular violation known as "racism"; it is for the most part the racism of whites against blacks or Arabs. Or, to be more precise, what is involved is a desire to attribute to racism—and thus to prohibit—every aspiration of developed societies, be they white or possibly Asian, to defend their interests in a normal fashion, if this defense leads them to oppose blacks or Arabs, even for reasons that have nothing to do with racism. To want to regulate immigration, to control the use of economic aid, to thwart the hostile acts of some Middle Eastern or African state—all of these normal political activities, they would have us believe, stem from racism. It is here that the notion of apartheid, in itself indefensible, is used in an equally indefensible manner as a weapon of international propaganda. All Western forms of behavior that do not happen to conform to Third World wishes can thus be attributed to "racism" and accordingly discredited.

The truth is that the struggle against apartheid and racism was long ago diverted from its true intent and end. In the West it is sometimes used for purposes of domestic politics that have absolutely nothing to do with any action in favor of South African blacks. Here is an example, culled from the recent political history of my own country. Referring to the student demonstrations of December 1986, Lionel Jospin, the first secretary of the French Socialist Party, challenged the Chirac government in these terms: "Do we want to catch up with South Africa, world record holder for imprisonments?"* Now, while it is true that one French student died as a result of inadmissible police brutality, not a single French student was given a prison sentence in 1986, while South Africa, no matter how somber its record, is, when it comes to incarcerations and, even more, to summary executions, way behind most of the "progressive" African states with which Monsieur Jospin's party maintains such fraternal relations. As can be seen, the term apartheid has become a magic formula, a multipurpose political projectile. For the oppressed blacks of South Africa, the utility of this "banalization" is strictly nil.

Of course—and this must be repeated—racism is not, alas, the only crime in the world. Entire populations—one has only to think of Cambodia, Indonesia, and the Philippines—have been decimated for reasons having nothing to do with racism. No matter how intolerable racism may be, the fact remains that to suffer a lack of respect, to be subjected to insulting treatment by a racist in a law-abiding society, is for me, as an individual, a less unpardonable crime than to be assassinated by a despot, even if the color of his skin is the same as mine. All things considered, I prefer discrimination without murder to murder without discrimination. The former can be corrected by time and education, the

*Le Monde, December 4, 1986.

second can never be. Or should the murderer from now on have the right to clamor: "I killed him, yes, but not because of racism. You cannot therefore hold anything against me!" If the only crime today that is considered to be inexpiable is racism, does it follow and are we entitled to conclude that all crimes against humanity are permitted, provided that they are not inspired by racism? Or, more precisely, by white racism—the only variety that is usually talked about? And, to be even more precise on this subject, white racism is truly reprehensible only when it comes from a capitalist or democratic society. The massacre of Asiatics or Africans by socialist Europeans is authorized, just as is discrimination against the blacks of Cuba. The only true racism, in the final analysis, is white, capitalist racism.

This selective antiracism is applied even to the past. Thus the only slave trade on which the historical memory is concentrated, with a feeling of retrospective revulsion, is the deportation of blacks to the Americas and the Caribbean islands. We happily disregard another "scene of the crime": the slavery that exists throughout the Arabic world, the fifteen million black Africans who were uprooted from their villages and forcibly transported to the Moslem lands, whether in North Africa or the Middle East, between the seventh and twentieth centuries. We forget that in Zanzibar around the year 1860 there were some 200,000 black slaves for a population of 300,000 inhabitants. We forget that slavery was not officially banned in Saudi Arabia until 1962, and in Mauritania not until 1981! I say "officially," for in practice, for example in Mauritania, it still exists.* In 1987 it was reported to be making a comeback in the Sudan. On August 21, 1987, an Agence France-Presse dispatch (published by *Le Monde*) brought us the news that the Sudanese army had just massacred between 250 and 600 civilians in the southern part of the country. We were simultaneously informed that, according to the president of the International Catholic Mission, Monsi-

---

*See Murray Gordon, *Slavery in the Arab World* (New York: New Amsterdam, 1989). In the same way, social injustices and economic inequalities are condemned only when they are observed in Western societies or stem from white oppression. As Jacques de Barrin noted quite correctly in the previously cited article (*Le Monde,* July 21, 1987): "There is perhaps on this continent, with the sole exception of South Africa, no more inegalitarian society than Zambia's." Yet this unjust situation, which anyone who wants to can discover for himself, has never kept Zambia's permanent boss, the ineffable Kenneth Kaunda—the only African leader I know of who can weep copiously at will—from making himself a reputation as a Third World hero, because he is a past master in the art of blaming the World Bank and multinational enterprises for the damage caused by his own incapability. This was equally true of Julius Nyerere of Tanzania, where for twenty years his calamitous rule was more systematically applied, and who was even better organized in the methodical concoction of both short- and long-term disasters.

gnor Bernd Kraut, who had just returned to Khartoum, Moslem Arabic militias were involved in the slave trade. (What a bonanza for the TV networks—if only this information had come from South Africa!) This slave trade, according to Monsignor Kraut (as quoted by AFP), involved "hundreds, indeed thousands of victims, inhabitants of the south and for the most part children from eight to fifteen years of age, whose parents had been killed in battles or during raids staged by the police militias of the Rizagat tribe." The prelate added that these children "are sold in the north for the sum of 600 pounds for a boy and 400 pounds for a girl." (One U.S. dollar equals 2.5 Sudanese pounds.)*

This, then, is the lesson to be drawn from this comparative survey, which has been almost exclusively and deliberately limited to Africa. When wholesale violations of human rights are considered important only when occurring in a "racist" context, one is bound to end up with a stunted and distorted vision of the political and social realities underlying those violations. No exhaustive or even approximative information about those realities has been able to affect our Western contemporaries' conception of the world. For this reason it has proved incapable of influencing public debates and steering governmental policies in a constructive direction capable of creating real improvements—not simply the simple substitution of one tyranny by another, which is presently what we see happening most of the time.

It was only with the advent of ancient Greek civilization, followed by those of Rome and modern Europe, that there was born within a specific culture, if not a certain modesty, at least a self-critical point of view. With Montaigne, for example, and even more with Montesquieu there gradually developed an awareness of the relativity of cultural values. We do not have the right to decree that a custom is inferior to our own simply because it is different, and we should make a determined effort to appraise our own habits and institutions as though we were viewing them from outside.

However, for Plato, Aristotle, and the philosophers of the eighteenth-century Enlightenment (who include the Founding Fathers of the American Republic), this relativistic principle did not mean that all customs are of equal value, simply that all should be impartially judged, including one's own. We should not, they felt, be more indulgent toward ourselves than toward others; nor, however, should we be more indul-

*Whereas *Le Monde* thought this news item important enough to figure on the front page, the *International Herald Tribune* accorded it a tiny space on page 2 (making no mention of the slave trade), while the paper's front-page headline was devoted to Ronald Reagan's links with South Africa.

gent toward others than toward ourselves. The great, original achievement of Western culture is to have established a tribunal of human
values, of human rights, and of rational criteria, before which all civilizations should be judged. It is not to proclaim that all are equivalent—
that would be tantamount to no longer believing in any values
whatsoever. The fact that, as Allan Bloom has reminded us, different
opinions have existed at different times about the Good and the Bad does
not for a moment prove that not one of those opinions is true or superior
to the others.* For some time now the radically different idea has
prevailed that we should forbid ourselves to judge, and even more to
condemn, any civilization *except our own.* Bloom, for example, asked
his students to answer this question of practical morality: "You are a
British administrator in the Indian Civil Service around the year 1860,
and you are informed that a widow is going to be burned alive with her
deceased husband. What do you do?" As Bloom discovered, "either
they remain silent or reply that the British should never have been there
in the first place." Although this point can be argued, the answer does
not reply to the question, and it betrays above all a desire not to have
to condemn a non-Western crime.

Since, furthermore, there has been no letup in the severity with which
Western civilization is judged by us and by others, and since this civilization remains a legitimate target for every virtuous soul, it is the only one
today that receives more than its fair share of critical arrows. Thus today
the only crime that is regarded as inexpiable is white racism. And so it
should be, provided that one does not draw the corollary and claim that
a crime ceases to be serious when perpetrated by members of another
community. Why should it be moral to shoot homosexuals when this
happens in Iran? Why do American "liberals" remain silent when Jesse
Jackson calls New York "Hymie Town"? Because he is black. Can a
candidate for the U.S. presidency permit himself to be anti-Semitic
simply because he is not white? What an uproar there would have been
in France if the blond-haired, blue-eyed Jean-Marie Le Pen had called
Paris *"Youpi-Ville"*!

When with vibrant virulence Montaigne stigmatized the crimes committed by Europeans during the conquest of the New World, he did so
in the name of a universal morality, from whose commandments, in his
eyes, the Indians themselves were not exonerated. Our civilization invented self-criticism in the name of a body of principles that is valid for
all human beings, and which, therefore, all civilizations should respect,

*Allan Bloom, *The Closing of the American Mind* (New York: Simon & Schuster, 1987).

in genuine equality. It loses its raison d'être if it abandons this point of view. Herodotus's Persians thought everyone except themselves was wrong; we modern Westerners are not far from thinking that everyone except ourselves is right. This is not a development of the critical spirit, something that is always desirable; it is, quite simply, its total abandonment.

CHAPTER 8

On Complex Lies

f one were to draw up an inventory of falsehoods, it would be materially impossible to achieve a rigorous balance between "right-wing" mendacity and "left-wing" mendacity. There is simply a far greater supply of this merchandise on one side than the other. Expressed in strictly arithmetical terms, any attempt at evenhanded impartiality would degenerate into moral partiality, for in the contemporary world the falsehood of the Left is present in far greater quantity than the falsehood of the Right.

To begin with, the term "Left" itself is bogus. Originally devised to designate those who defend freedom, law, happiness, and peace, it is now flaunted by the majority of despotic, repressive, and imperialist regimes, in which those who do not belong to the ruling class live in poverty, and often abject misery. Nevertheless, the idea still persists that the Left, far from being that conglomerate of totalitarian mastodons and dwarfs which presently encumber our planet, is no more than a feeble, flickering, tiny flame of justice, holding out against the chloroforming cone of a gigantic, omnipresent, omnipotent Right. This is why "right-wing" lies are denounced far more often than those of the Left, since they are supposed to constitute the sole real danger and the sole form of scandalous deception.

Let us by all means continue to criticize, with all the severity they merit and for as long as they are with us, South African apartheid and General Pinochet, but let's not pretend they are subjects that no one talks about and which benefit from a silence of complicity or a guilty indulgence on the part of the media. The average TV viewer is kept informed, not once but half a dozen times a day, of South African and Chilean misdeeds. But the fact that Afghanistan had seventeen million inhabitants in 1978 and no more than ten to eleven million in 1988 is something one is likely to learn only by chance. The horror of the Holocaust, perpetrated by the Nazis, can never be too strongly stressed, but no one can claim that it is unknown or condoned—save by a handful of perverse imbeciles whom the Left, instead of ridiculing, have brought into the limelight. On the other hand, how many persons realize and above all have had it dinned into them daily that the Ukrainian genocide of the early 1930s also claimed five to six million lives? The past atrocities of the colonial powers have been detailed quite rightly, and far more often than the recent atrocities of the "progressive" regimes that took over as a result of decolonization. The entire world was informed of the massacres of villagers by Americans during the Vietnam War (if only because their authors were, fortunately, brought to trial and condemned by *U.S.* military courts). But how many television networks and news-papers showed as much insistence on reporting that, once Vietnam had become completely communist in 1975, some 60,000 persons were shot during the first three months following the conquest of the South by Hanoi's armies, that 20,000 more were executed not long afterward, and that 300,000 died during the next few years as the result of harsh treatment in concentration camps? I know of Western newspapermen, and even photographers, who roamed Vietnam in 1975 and 1976, and all they saw—O, noble souls!—was "happy people." Of reeducation camps, needless to say, they saw nothing.

For years after the annexation of the South by the North and the Vietnamese invasion of Cambodia, the French television team that en-joyed a virtual monopoly in covering Indochina was directed by Roger Pic, a faithful friend of Hanoi. To be sure, this exclusive privilege was due partly to the fact that until recently the standard practice of commu-nist countries was to admit only teams that were ready in advance to serve their propaganda. But that was not the only reason. The ideologi-

cal preferences or the passive incompetence of editorial staffs in Paris
also explains the preponderance, in the documentary roundups of all the
TV channels, of grossly falsified and tendentious reporting—which, I
might add, the noncommunist left-wing press never criticized. But this
is something it should have done, if it had really wanted to apply its
supposedly new model of equity to all forms of dishonesty, no matter
whence they come.

The systematic mention of crimes committed by left-wing regimes is
possible only in certain specialized magazines, as well as in confidential
round-table discussions whose participants are immediately labeled as
"ultra-rightist." This is not something I can change. Falsification or
insuffiency of information favors the Left more than the Right, and both
are more successful when practiced by the Left than by the Right. On
the Left one finds—I won't say necessarily and always—more malpractice, but certainly more *hidden* or attenuated malpractice, which benefits from a certain protection against information gathering. When I say
"of the Left," please note that I do not believe that the authors of those
lies and omissions are from the Left. I am content to label them as they
label themselves. My personal opinion is that they have usurped the
qualification of "the Left" and that they are imposters. This is why it
is no exaggeration to say that left-wing lies are "necessarily" more
abundant than those of the Right. When as a practical matter one
continuously and massively violates the morality one likes to profess in
theory, one is bound to accumulate mendacious versions of facts, far
more so than when one is simply cynical. Falsehood then becomes a
permanent life jacket, while the truth becomes the main foe and those
who reveal it the most dangerous and hated of adversaries.

In the preceding chapters I offered a number of examples in order to
unmask the deceitful "parity" of left-wing and right-wing mendacity.
However, for a left-winger, simply acknowledging such a parity is in
itself a concession, designed more to prove his sincerity than to express
his deepest thinking. But there it is: it is in this feigned symmetry that
the most deceptive stratagem resides. In reality, as we have seen, during
the first half of the twentieth century democracy conquered and an-
nihilated the great totalitarianisms of the Right. And the real key to the
understanding of the history of the second part of the twentieth century
has been the variety and success of the means whereby an ostensible
struggle on behalf of the Left has served as a spearhead for the promotion of tyrannies. Right-wing ideology emerged from World War II
thoroughly discredited, whereas the ideology of the Left was enveloped
in an immunity that made it virtually invulnerable, no matter how

monstrous its failures and its crimes. The old-fashioned Right, the one that proudly asserted the right of an elite to govern all society in an authoritarian manner and for its sole benefit, has been reincarnated in the ruling classes of socialist countries. There has been no dearth of Fascist-type dictators, both military and civilian, of the Latin American, Korean, Greek, or Filipino kind; but nobody can plausibly claim that they enjoyed the slightest prestige in public opinion or were kindly treated by the media in the West. Politically, they were quarantined far more severely than socialist totalitarianism. As for the classic "Right" of the democracies, the so-called "conservatives"—I mean the redoubtable Right, which wielded power only when the voters granted it—it has almost everywhere applied or annexed social democratic programs. To speak of a powerful recrudescence of right-wing ideology, because of the rebirth of economic liberalism that has taken place since 1980, is to brandish a crude political slogan. This neoliberalism stems not from an ideological battle or a preconceived conspiracy, but from a humdrum and reluctant facing of the facts: these being the failure of command economies, the patent harmfulness of an excess of administrative *dirigisme,* and the financial dead end to which the provider-state invariably leads.

If the falsification of information is today above all a left-wing phenomenon, it is because the vision of the world that is common to the Left can survive only in the shadows. For the human beings who are sustained morally or politically, materially or intellectually, by this vision of the world, to accept the harsh light of reality—that is, to accept the gathering and analysis of facts—would amount to damming up the very source of their beliefs and influence. This is why in the political, journalistic, and literary history of the Left, we are offered the spectacle of a periodic return of an indefensible but inevitable inconsistency. What does it consist of? The socialists (like American "liberals") frequently pay lip service to the cult of democratic virtues and the constitutive values of open societies, to tolerance, respect for the adversary, and pluralism. They are ready, they say, to forswear once and for all the unnatural union of the Left and totalitarianism. They have understood, they solemnly vow, the need forever to separate an authentic Left from those Stalinist practices that so harmed their reputations. Even communists occasionally harness themselves to the task of remaking a communist party without communism, purged as though by magic of the vices without which it would not even have been founded. These ephemeral health cures usually wear away quite quickly in the noncommunist Left, where the solemn oath of repudiating all totalitarian barbarism resurfaces in a cyclical fashion. This pledge always serves as a new fundamental and unbreakable law. It goes without saying, it seems, that for this "renovated" Left no pious untruths will any longer be placed at the service of its ideology, no semiofficial falsehoods placed at the service of its party, no vicious lies concocted to harm its foes. Truth, probity, dignity henceforth raise their impregnable ramparts between the regenerated Left and that sectarian temptation—the cult of falsehood.

Here it is important to distinguish the evolution of political *parties* from the persistence of an ideology—a cultural phenomenon that is more than simply political. For example, in Spain the Communist Party has practically disappeared (except among the labor unions), and the Socialist Party, which has officially repudiated Marxism, is pursuing a liberal economic policy. But many intellectuals and journalists—notably those working for television channels and the influential daily *El País*—continue to peddle an antiliberal ideology worthy of the 1960s: anticapitalistic, Third Worldist, anti-American, pro-Castro. Right up until 1985 they stubbornly dismissed as "reactionary" all denunciations of the failure of the communist system—which, thanks to *glasnost,* turned out to be even more apocalyptic than anything the most virulent anticommunists (Gorbachev obviously included) had depicted. Everywhere the cultural "Left" has fallen behind the political Left.

This shift has been even more evident in Italy, where the Italian Communist Party has pursued its evolution toward the acceptance of a market economy and Western-style democracy. It is the very prototype of a "communist party without communism," just as the Spanish Socialist Party is now a "socialist party without socialism." During *L'Unità*'s annual fête, staged in September 1988 in Florence, the nationally distributed Communist Party daily published a major study prepared by one of the party's main leaders, Achille Ochetto. The author argued that the hour had struck for all communists, who would have to accept liberal capitalism. To mark this change with a spectacular symbolic gesture, he even proposed to abandon the hammer-and-sickle emblem! Nor was this all. On September 11 this same *L'Unità* continued to vituperate against the baleful consequences of the state's intervention in the Italian economy!

Italy offers us another striking example of this anti-ideological drift. Ever since Bettino Craxi took over, the Italian Socialist Party (PSI) has become the most outspokenly anticommunist member of the Socialist International, at any rate far more so than the Christian Democrats in Italy. Admittedly, the Italian Communist Party remains the strongest in Western Europe. However, in ten years it lost ten percentage points and by 1989 the PSI had almost caught up with it in public opinion polls. Above all, the Italian Communist Party has unambiguously been excluded from Italy's parliamentary majority, from which, on the national level, it is now separated by a veritable iron curtain. The trend has been so marked that it has even given rise to occasional comic spectacles. Thus, during the traditional Friendship Fête staged by the Christian Democrats in Verona in September 1988, the socialists vehemently upbraided the Christian Democrats for their "impure alliances" with the communists in certain municipal councils, sarcastically dubbed "abnormal councils" *(giunte anomali).*

But in Italy too the communications industry, culture, the press, the media, what I would call the "vegetative" realm of thought and the basic ideological metabolism, remains quagmired in left-wing conformism. This is particularly true of two newspapers that account for more than half the circulation of all national newspapers: the veteran *Corriere della Sera* (at least when it was edited by Piero Ottone and Alberto Cavallari) and the recent *La Repubblica,* which since 1970 has become the Italian press's most commercially successful newspaper. These newspapers sometimes give one the impression of pursuing the Cold War; for we should not forget that the Cold War was marked as much by the systematic anti-Americanism of the Marxists as by the anti-Sovietism of European liberals.

Nevertheless, in Italy too the upper intelligentsia, in contrast to the lower clergy of culture and the media, has freed itself from the totalitarian temptation and has effected its ideological mutation. As an example, let me cite this declaration made by Renzo de Felice, the great historian of Fascism and himself a socialist, speaking of Hitlerism and communism: "To conclude, the truth is that they were identical phenomena. Totalitarianism characterized and defined Nazism, as it did Stalinism, without any real difference between them. I may perhaps have expressed myself in extreme terms; I may have said it brutally; but I think that the moment has come to stick to facts and to shatter false and useless myths."

In principle, noncommunist leftists no longer support totalitarian regimes in the name of a future socialism or of an abstract duty of solidarity toward all left-wing parties; they no longer close their eyes to human rights abuses committed by those regimes; they have noted and, they say, have drawn definite conclusions regarding the perpetual failures of collectivist economies. But in practice—and in propaganda—it is quite a different story. If one looks at the decade of the 1980s, one finds the same leftist complaisance toward newly born Marxist-Leninist regimes as toward their predecessors. Leftists are no more demanding now than they were before in insisting that these new states be economically successful, and respect democratic legitimacy, human rights, even the simple right to life. To protect and justify these regimes, left-wingers have, as they once did with the USSR and China, continued to deny facts, willfully altered information, and refused to answer certain arguments in any fundamental sense, and consequently have resorted to personal, calumnious, and defamatory attacks against those who think differently.

For example, according to European left-wingers and North American "liberals," the communist team that seized power in Angola toward the end of 1975 and which is now installed in the capital city of Luanda is Angola's legitimate government. Its adversaries—the guerrilla fighters commanded by Jonas Savimbi—can thus only be henchmen of South Africa and the CIA. During the 1980s, when Savimbi occasionally made trips to Europe, European political leaders, particularly the socialist ones, aped by many liberals who were afraid of being called "fascists," refrained from meeting him, except secretly. What reasons had they for behaving in this tendentious fashion? After the fall of the Salazar regime, the new Portuguese government, which was resolved at last to give Angola its independence, arranged a meeting at Alvor, in the Algarve, of the leaders of the three organizations that had maintained the anti-colonial struggle for fifteen years. The three organizations that were thus brought together in January 1975 were Roberto Holden's FNLA (National Front for the Liberation of Angola), Jonas Savimbi's UNITA (National Union for the Liberation of Angola), and Agostinho Neto's MPLA (Popular Movement for the Liberation of Angola). This last organization was openly communist and pro-Soviet. Neto and his lieutenants had made many trips to and attended many courses in Moscow. They made no secret of their wish to make Angola the "Cuba of Africa." At the time their influence seemed to be limited to the capital. It was almost certainly less great than that of UNITA in the country as a whole. The best way of finding out would have been to let the Angolans vote. This was foreseen by the Alvor accords, which quite logically granted independence on the understanding and the pledge made by the signatories that the three parties would take part in elections under the control of Portuguese observers, by November 1975 at the latest.

Those elections were never held (just as there were no free elections in Poland from 1945 until 1989). In February 1975 Cuban "advisers" began arriving in Luanda, followed later in the spring by airborne Cuban troops, which were obviously transported there in Soviet aircraft, since Cuba lacked the logistical infrastructure to undertake an operation of this magnitude over such vast distances. This confiscation of power by the communists in Luanda was greatly facilitated by the preference felt for the MPLA by the new leaders in Lisbon. Indeed, the Armed Forces Movement, which was then the seat of power in Portugal, was dominated by communists. The then prime minister, General Vasco Gonçalves, and other ministers, such as Admiral Rosa Coutinho, had secretly or openly long been members of the Communist Party or, like Melo Antunes, were supporters of the Soviet Union. They arranged to have weapons turned over to the MPLA during the so-called "transition period"—which resulted in a transition toward nothing . . . save dictatorship, starvation, and bloodshed. Finally, on November 11, 1975, with the help of Fidel Castro and a conniving Portuguese government, Agostinho Neto violated the Alvor accords by unilaterally proclaiming the establishment of a People's Republic of Angola, for the sole benefit of the communists. The elections were postponed to an indefinite later date, doubtless (in Neto's mind) pending the subsequent conclusion of the world revolution. Fidel Castro, a competent mentor, had doubtless given him sound advice, having used exactly the same tactics in Cuba in 1959.

Shortly before that, it is true, on October 22, 1975, a South African military column had penetrated into Angolan territory in a vain and belated endeavor to check the Soviet takeover of Angola. This lackluster effort had received the tacit approval of the U.S. secretary of state, Henry Kissinger, who, however, was unable to offer any concrete help; for neither then nor later was any U.S. help authorized for Savimbi by a Congress that had precipitated the fall of Saigon and the invasion of South Vietnam by the armies of Hanoi (in total violation, here too, of the Paris accords of 1973). The South African foray ended in a shameful fiasco, but it permitted the cheerleaders of international communism to claim that the military presence of the Cubans was simply a "response" to the aggression of the South Africans, although in fact tens of thousands of Cuban soldiers had reached the country several months before.

Gabriel García Márquez, the 1982 Nobel Prize winner for Literature and a smart successor of those great friends and literary allies of totalitarianism Romain Rolland, Henri Barbusse, Louis Aragon, Pablo Neruda, and Jean-Paul Sartre, then proceeded to write a series of reportorial articles describing the humanitarian arrival of the Cubans, who had rushed there *in extremis* to save Angolan democracy and socialism.

It would, as a matter of fact, be most instructive to total up the number of authors of whom it can be said without exaggeration that their pen nibs dripped with blood and who nevertheless received the Nobel Prize for Literature—the prize that was refused to Jorge Luis Borges on the pretext that he had backed the generals of Argentina during the 1974–84 period. Now there was a magnificent calumny! What the Left could not forgive Borges for was not to have approved "progressive" terrorism—which was precisely what had *provoked* the intervention and subsequent dictatorship of the Argentinian generals. Though far removed from outright approval of the generals, his lucid stance was enough to make Borges a "rightist" author and thus un-Nobelizable. I might add, parenthetically, that this is a fine sample of left-wing logic. If Borges, without taking the slightest personal risk, had applauded the work of left-wing terrorists in Argentina and had then castigated the generals by signing petitions and articles composed in various palatial hotels in Europe, he could have obtained the Nobel Prize.

Even a brief résumé of the events of 1975 and their order of succession is enough to demolish the deceitful propaganda put out by García Márquez—or rather, it *should have* sufficed. But the legend according to which UNITA was in reality no more than an instrument of the "apartheid regime" of South Africa fulfilled too many hopes and wishes in the heart of the worldwide Left. In early October 1987 I could still hear this historical lie repeated by a British "university professor," a "specialist in African affairs," during the well-known BBC news feature called "The World Today"—this at a moment when a major battle was about to begin between the Sovieto-Cubans and UNITA, this time with the openly declared assistance of the South Africans. After 1980 Savimbi had been forced to rely on South African help, given the fact that the Western democracies had offered him either no help or insufficient assistance, leaving him and his partisans no choice except suicide or cooperation with South Africa.

For its part, the international Left regarded these Angolans as unworthy of existing, they who had chosen not to die and who had reluctantly agreed to receive South African support. It is easy to practise journalistic virtue in the comfort and security of a Paris, London, or New York news-dispensing office. From that moment on was projected the image so badly needed by the Left. In Angola a "progressive" regime, which was working for economic progress and social justice, and trying to discover an "original road" toward democratization, was being set upon by a destabilizing conspiracy conducted by "hideous" mercenaries without popular support and armed by the forces of apartheid and the CIA. Thus the old malady one had thought the Left to be cured of—that is, the tendency to regard a dictatorship as legitimate the moment it is part of the Soviet bloc and its adversaries as fascists and bourgeois reactionaries because they demand free elections—this old malady had by no means disappeared; it had simply shifted to the Third World.

Nicaragua was another example. Clinging to the schemas of the past, the Left could still not grasp the fact that its standard scenario of a "young people's republic of the Third World setting out on the road to socialism" was part of another, far vaster scenario: that of the extension of the Soviet empire. It had learned nothing from the economic, political, and human failures of "progressive" states that had gained their independence, above all in Africa. All the knowledge accumulated about the débâcle of communist systems and of Third World socialism had served no purpose whatsoever. All the contrary evidence had simply had no impact on left-wing prejudices. Intermittently, no doubt, the damning evidence upset the established rhythm, but then the dogmatic machine resumed its usual tempo, for even if it sometimes stalls, it never stops completely.

We were offered new proof of this on October 10, 1987, when, during a state visit to Argentina and Uruguay, François Mitterrand declared with studied emphasis at Montevideo: "Democracy is nothing without development." To be sure, I realized long ago that for François Mitterrand an idea has no value as regards intrinsic content and as a statement of something known; rather, it is like an arrow, the chief interest of which is to be found in the position from which it is fired and the target at which it is aimed. For every individual—and in particular for every politician, we must hasten to admit—the interest possessed by an idea is divided in varying proportions between its truth-containing and its utilitarian function, between its content of information and its polemical power. But in few individuals more than in François Mitterrand have I seen such a complete effacement of the function of truth to the benefit of the function of utility. It is not, or not solely, a form of insincerity. It is simply the natural and total triumph of the tactical over the conceptual dimension.

This disposition of the presidential mind confers a particular significance on the aphorism of Montevideo. If the French president chose to deliver such a statement, it was because it was intended to calm the doubts and torments of the Left after ten years of sharp criticisms of Third Worldism by economists and historians. It can only have been out of kindness, from a sense of concern and the need to comfort the demoralized flocks of believers, and not because he regarded it as true, that such an intelligent man could have appropriated such a stupid cliché.

In reality, if democracy without development was meaningless, then neither the French or the American revolution nor the British reform movement should have been undertaken. At the time those happenings took place, all three nations displayed acute symptoms of what today would be called underdevelopment. Switzerland in the nineteenth century was a very poor country. Nonetheless, for centuries it had been practicing a form of direct democracy on the level of the canton, very much in advance of the rest of Europe. Should this have been halted so long as the country was not rich? I was under the impression that freedom was good in itself, independent of the standard of living of the population. And I thought that the Left had understood it. But the Montevideo adage proves that this is not the case, and that swift can be the relapse into the most shopworn platitudes in the gallery of ideological wrecks—i.e., that personal and political liberties have no real existence as long as economic and social rights have not been satisfied. But, we may ask, which rights? At what level of development can a society be regarded as ripe for democracy, and how is this to be determined? For everything is relative. Any society, according to the criterion adopted, can be considered as underdeveloped or developed. Brazil is at once overdeveloped and underdeveloped. Spain with its Andalucía, Italy with its *mezzogiorno,* Great Britain with its North of England—do all of them, because of these pockets of poverty, practice a democracy which, if Mitterrand is to be believed, is "nothing"? In 1944 France itself was profoundly underdeveloped, suffering from shortages of food, clothing, housing, electricity and heating, public and private transportation, with an annual per capita income that was less than that of 1900. Should freedom for this reason have been deferred and the Vichy regime prolonged until the country's economic development reached its plenitude? And who would be qualified to fix the degree of development above which a democracy ceases to be "nothing" and becomes a "something"?

It is easy to see what prompted Mitterrand to try to clean the mildewed façade of Third World ideology. The avalanche of written works and the vigor of the intellectual currents which, all over the world, once more attribute a leading role to the market economy and free enterprise in the development of political democracy are enough to irritate a socialist. Someone had to stake out a contrary position and call a halt to liberal pranks. Unfortunately, the record of collectivized Third World economies speaks for itself, and a public speech cannot modify it. The record is devastating. It is probably no accident that leaders of developing countries now swear by the market economy with the somewhat naïve zeal of neophytes.

By an ironic coincidence, on the very day the French president was launching his appeal in Montevideo, two of the toughest fossils of the socialist fauna—General Jaruzelski in Poland and the ineffable Ne Win, the inspired creator of the Burmese "model"—declared themselves bankrupt, handed over the keys of the shop, which was collapsing all around them, and warned their fellow citizens that from now on, in order to survive, they would have to rely solely on their personal ingenuity. For Mitterrand, in such a context, to unearth the old saw of economic development, regarded as the antithesis of private enterprise and as independent of democracy, was to display a singular deafness to the language of plain facts. Furthermore, as articulated in Argentina and in Uruguay, this thesis was flagrantly at variance with history, which Mitterrand so often likes to cite. Could he possibly not have known (for I can only believe that his ignorance was feigned) something that is an indispensable element in any serious reflection on the subject of development? I mean that Argentina and Uruguay are *formerly developed countries that collapsed into a state of underdevelopment as a result of crises of political democracy.* From 1938 to 1955 or thereabouts, these two countries on the southern horn of Latin America rivaled Great Britain and France in terms of living standards and social security benefits. Their prosperity was destroyed—in Argentina by Juan Perón's *justicialismo* (a kind of anticapitalistic, authoritarian, income-redistributing labor movement) and later in both countries by the "revolutionary" terrorism of the Tupamaros, inspired by Fidel Castro's and Che Guevara's Marxism. Heads of state are supposed to possess vastly superior means of gaining information than are available to the common run of mortals. If only they would make use of them more often! However, uttered by the lips of the socialist president of France, the apothegm of the pampa betrayed a desire not to face but to wish away reality, thanks to the incantatory declamation of a dogmatic obsession, a form of "thinking" so degraded that it is closer to immunology than to ideology.

For even from the ideological point of view Mitterrand's formula was rash, one threatening to hasten the demolition of the cause it was supposed to uphold. Even a child could see that indirectly it offers an argument in favor of the uncontestable successes of nondemocratic capitalism in certain "newly industrialized countries"—such as Taiwan and South Korea (before it had begun to democratize itself), which have achieved superb levels of growth under the authoritarian leadership of more or less enlightened despots, or Singapore, a "muscular," albeit not dictatorial, regime. In Africa the Republic of South Africa is the only country that can fly the banner of economic development, and while the blacks suffer a segregation that is unacceptable from the moral point of view, their standard of living, though much lower than that of their white compatriots, exceeds that of the blacks of every other country of the continent. Even General Pinochet's Chile has been developing more steadily and is now better off than its neighbors, Bolivia or Peru, though it has had to weather crises, albeit less terrible than those provoked by the regime of Salvador Allende. It was during the last fifteen years of Franco's dictatorship that contemporary Spain began to take off economically, completely overhauling its aging industrial plant and giving birth to a well-to-do middle class. All things considered, even though the "classic" developed countries have for the past two centuries managed to progress mainly because of the almost constant union of capitalism and democracy, there exist certain cases where countries have "taken off" without democracy, at least for a while, whereas this has never happened without capitalism. In short, what Mitterrand revealed with his Uruguayan maxim is that when all conceivable and variable combinations are taken into account, there is one ingredient that has revealed itself in practice to be absolutely incompatible with development: socialism.

From where, then, comes this refusal or incapacity to take into account and assimilate the less-than-mysterious teachings of the world's postwar economic history? Here too, in questions of economy as in its attitude toward "progressive" totalitarian regimes, we had for a moment the impression that the noncommunist Left had taken a major step in trying to break with the dogmatism of the past and had at least agreed to assimilate the most elementary lessons of experience. But I fear nothing of the sort occurred. Thus in 1987 François Mitterrand, decreeing in advance that the fairly conducted elections in New Caledonia were bereft of all democratic value since they were vitiated by the relations existing between the colonizers and the colonized, denounced what he called the "unjust force of the law." In so doing, all he did was to repeat a vaguely Marxist stereotype. The law, wrote Lenin in 1917 to warn the Bolsheviks against the democratic temptation, is "the organization of violence aimed at crushing a certain class." How, seventy years later, can one say any progress has been made? How can such a declaration, made by the president of the Republic, be taken to signify an intellectual "renewal" among French socialists?

To be sure, today, when they govern or hope to govern, the socialists abandon most of their dogmas, one after the other, under the pressure of facts. From 1981 to 1983 the French Socialist Party was the last to include a "break with capitalism" in its political program for a developed country—a country that was made to pay through the nose for this privilege. But the "propositions" it put forward in 1987, in anticipation of the presidential elections of 1988, carefully eliminated all the threats of a "change of society" and other "radical reforms of structure" that had brightened its 1980 "project." As the journalist Alain Duhamel wrote in October 1987: "During the next seven-year presidential term, France may perhaps again have a socialist as president; but she will no longer have a socialist president."*

With the exception of Britain's Labour Party, which still includes a large number of the dying species of Europe's messianic Left and which has paid heavily for their stubbornness with repeated electoral defeats, the socialist parties, including some in the Third World, have in practice since 1980 adopted a kind of watered-down liberalism, even though they have sought to save face by baptizing it "pragmatic socialism." Generalizing this kind of rhetoric, one could hail as "navigation" the setting out in boats that regularly sink a few lengths out to sea and describe staying behind on land as "pragmatic navigation." But if the socialists' "pragmatic" action has enabled them to move closer to reality, their vision of the world, as though to compensate, has grown even more distant from it. It is as though they have been stepping up the pace in the field of ideology in order to compensate for the privations they have reluctantly been forced to inflict on themselves in the sphere of management.

Now, ideology is the principal source of informational disruption because it reposes on a systematic, global falsehood, not simply on an occasional one. In order to remain intact it must ceaselessly defend itself against the testimony of the senses and the mind, as well as against reality itself. This exhausting struggle forces the ideologues to increase the daily dose of falsehood needed to cope with the hard evidence that emanates from the inexorably real. Thus it is precisely at a moment when Marxism-Leninism is losing all credit with its adepts as a principle for managing human societies that, like the light from dead suns that expired millions of years ago, whose source is extinguished but which keeps reaching us, it shines most brightly in the ideological sphere. Hence the Left's superiority in the fabrication of falsehood. It cannot content itself with ordinary falsehood, that which the Right practices in politics with equal generosity—Machiavellian, tactical, circumstantial,

*Le Point, October 12, 1987.

opportunistic, interested, professional mendacity. These forms the Left also practises readily and assiduously, but it adds an infinitely more demanding falsehood, since ideology forces one ceaselessly to modify one's image of the world in terms of the vision one would like to have of it.

A "liberal" government may be wrong in displaying too much indulgence toward apartheid; but it won't go as far as to deny its existence.* On the other hand, for a long time the Left simply denied the existence of Soviet concentration camps, Vietnamese "reeducation camps," torture in Cuba, famine in China. The Right may have displayed excessive indulgence toward Franco for economic and military reasons; but never did it claim that he had conducted regular, free, pluralist elections. On the other hand, *The Observer,* a left-wing London weekly, could write on August 23, 1987, that it was a shameful thing that the Reagan administration should stubbornly continue trying to "overthrow the elected government of Nicaragua." No matter how favorable he might be toward the Sandinistas, a serious journalist who has done his homework properly could not honestly assert that the conditions in which the elections of October–November 1984 were held could allow one to consider that the government in Managua had been "democratically elected." What wouldn't people say of the conservative *Sunday Telegraph* if it dared to speak of General Pinochet's "democratically elected government" on the grounds that he too had held an election? Finally, it is worth noting that Ronald Reagan did not set out specifically to "overthrow" the Sandinistas; all he asked was that they agree to free elections, and he decided to aid the Contras as long as regular elections were not held in the country. One could disapprove of such a policy, but one could not claim that it was hostile to democracy, since on the contrary it aimed to reestablish it.

Never did so many massive socialist famines take place in the Third World as in the 1980s. Yet leftists in the Western world did all they could to prove that these disasters were due to everything except the totalitarian form of government and the socialist management of the economy. The noncommunist Left has supposedly "detotalitarianized" itself. But curiously, its system of excuses for totalitarian failures remains unchanged.

Let us return, for example, to the scenario of the "explosion of famine

*The attempt by so-called "revisionist" historians to deny the existence of Nazi gas chambers is hardly worth recalling. The influence wielded by a handful of mentally deranged fanatics simply cannot be compared with the massive, daily distillation of Marxist ideology through millions of different channels all over the world.

in Mozambique," such as we left it in February 1987. The U.S. ambassador in Maputo had just sent the State Department a report pointing out that three and a half million Mozambicans were threatened by an immediate and serious famine, even more devastating in scope than the Ethiopian famine of 1984. Washington immediately decided to dispatch several million dollars' worth of emergency aid and to mobilize other countries, international organizations, and nongovernmental agencies.

On February 7 a BBC commentator explained that this famine was due to the conjunction of two factors: drought and the guerrilla war being waged against the Maputo regime by RENAMO or the RNP (National Resistance Opposition of Mozambique), supported by South Africa. Thus, once again the world was offered the ritualized response: when a famine breaks out in a Marxist-Leninist country, it is *never* the consequence of governmental action or inaction, or of the economic system itself. It can be due only to climatic disasters and sabotage fomented from outside by hostile powers.

This explanation is similar to that which communist leaders, ever since 1917 and wherever they have seized power, have given in order to disclaim responsibility for starvation or for the scarcity of consumer goods, which have been the almost permanent hallmarks of their regimes. Why, then, do Western analysts accept such excuses in a less critical spirit than that sometimes displayed by communist leaders themselves?

In reality, Mozambique had been a socialist state since 1975, the year in which it acquired its independence. For twelve years a single party— FRELIMO (Mozambican Liberation Front)—had ruled the country singlehandedly, supported and indeed controlled by a swarm of Soviet and East German advisers. The revolution craved by "progressives" all over the world could thus develop without hindrance.

However, after a mere two or three years disaster loomed. And so in 1980, having begun to doubt the extent of the financial assistance provided by the Soviet protector, FRELIMO's leader, Samora Machel, made overtures to the United States, Europe, and even South Africa in order to obtain loans, but without altering the country's economic system. The economic situation failed to improve. Although guerrilla forces continued to consume the crops, or what was left of them, and to disrupt transportation, they were not the main causes of the shortages. For why had such shortages not reached such a critical point during the fifteen years of the war of liberation against the Portuguese army that had preceded independence? A war that was just as harmful to agricultural output and to the distribution of foodstuffs as the insurrection that followed! Furthermore, though South Africa undoubtedly aided RENAMO, it cannot be regarded as solely responsible for its existence. We might do well to ask ourselves, when considering anticommunist guerrilla wars, what the deeper causes are for their springing up, independent of the foreign assistance they may receive.

The Mozambicans did not and do not need to be influenced by Pretoria to want to do away with a police dictatorship that has done nothing but create starvation. As for drought conditions, they can persist for one or two years, but not eternally, and above all they become truly catastrophic only when they are added to already endemic shortages. In Chapter 12 we shall see how here, as in the case of the USSR and Vietnam, ideology has been the root cause of famine in Mozambique. Everywhere socialism boasts its aim of constructing a "new man." This notion can be found cropping up time and again from the very start of the history of communism. The idea was first propounded by the Jacobins of France in 1793. The State becomes the owner of individuals. The great merit of collective farms is above all that they destroy individual liberties. It so happens that they also destroy agriculture, but their prime objective is not agricultural. When a famine threatens a human mass as gigantic as three and a half million people, it is because the government responsible has let it increase without letting its existence be known, for fear of losing face or for reasons of propaganda. A simple crisis of foodstuffs is apt to be harshly judged by international opinion; the tragedy of mass starvation, however, arouses pity and unleashes an avalanche of foreign help, a good part of which is diverted by the government and the army to ensure their own political survival.

What we thus witnessed was a repetition of the Ethiopian scenario. And although the United States was the first country to have alerted the world to Mozambique's plight, it was a foregone conclusion that it would be blamed for having let things reach this pass.

It is truly disconcerting to observe to what extent the explanatory system employed by noncommunist politicians and newspapermen in free-world countries so often coincides with that employed by the governments of Maputo, Luanda, Addis Ababa, and Hanoi in order to explain away the famines that reign in their countries. What, one may ask, has happened to the elaborate intellectual studies done on the famines and food shortages that have marked seventy years of communist regimes? Of what use is the mass of documentary evidence that has accumulated and which shows that the roots of such shortages are largely to be found in the socialist organization of the economy—data that could be of use to commentators lucky enough to possess this mass of information? These data have been analyzed and confirmed, and thanks to them there are now more people at the end of this century who are persuaded of the sterility of socialism than there were at its beginning. And yet, when it comes to judging a *particular* case, this mass of information is virtually worthless. But this is what really matters, for it is with respect to particular cases and while there is still time to act that it is vitally important not to make and remake the same mistakes. Yet they are repeated.

Personally, I find nothing to suggest that leftists have managed to overcome the prejudice that grants to theoretically "progressive" regimes a social immunity whereby they are simultaneously absolved of responsibility for any absence of democracy, disregard for human rights, and lack of food for their citizens. Nor have I noticed the disappearance of the complementary prejudice, according to which anyone who is a liberal or a "conservative" in a democratic civilization is regarded as being virtually or totally a "rightist." Noncommunist leftists claim to have understood that the market economy, buttressed by all the necessary corrections, has proved to be the only way forward. And yet in each specific case all their reflexes impel them in a direction opposite to this claimed conviction. They behave like a doctor who, having sworn to high heaven that he fully understands that arsenic tends to be harmful to the human organism, nevertheless goes on prescribing massive doses to each new patient, while accusing those who would like to stop him of being public poisoners. They are willing on the theoretical level to blame socialism for being repressive and famine-inducing, while the democracies, regardless of their imperfections, are praised for having created the richest, least unjust societies in human history. But in the reality of individual, concrete diagnoses, it is the elected leaders of prosperous democratic societies whom the Left brands as "reactionaries," and the totalitarian tyrants whom it stubbornly continues to regard as progressive philanthropists.

In 1986, for example, I was both outraged and amused (by the silly spectacle offered) to read an account of the International PEN Club's Forty-eighth Congress, held in New York on January 14 (as reported by the *International Herald Tribune,* reprinting an article previously published by *The New York Times*). The next day the same paper reported the diatribe Günter Grass had launched against Saul Bellow, who had ventured to declare that the United States was not a totally reactionary country. That authors or literary managers should get up and walk out of the hall simply because the U.S. secretary of state, George Shultz, had been invited to speak—as though he were a cabinet minister of a totalitarian country—can only, I think, be explained as due to a mixture of political incompetence and intellectual dishonesty; above all, when the same audience listened respectfully to Amadou Mahtar M'Bow, the gravedigger of UNESCO. That sixty-six writers, apparently voicing the opinion of many other participants, should in an "open letter" have termed the invitation addressed to Shultz, the representative of a democratic state, as "inappropriate," and this in a country where power is granted *by the citizens,* strikes me as being a piece of arrant foolishness when one considers the general situation of the world today. "Your administration," wrote the signatories of this letter, "upholds governments that silence, imprison, and even torture their citizens because of their convictions." Which governments? South Africa. In 1986 this was obviously the most burning case. But could it honestly be said that the U.S. administration was "upholding" Botha and defending apartheid? Like many European governments, Washington would like to see apartheid done away with, while avoiding the economic collapse of South Africa thanks to the imposition of African-style "socialism"—the evils of which in the rest of the continent were described in the previous chapter.

Quite a few of the signatories of this letter—including several well-known American writers, such as Norman Mailer and William Styron—had accepted the invitation extended to them in 1983 by Jack Lang, then minister of culture, and François Mitterrand to take part in a cultural jamboree at the Sorbonne. At that time France's socialist government had resumed the sale of arms and nuclear power plants to South Africa. This had not kept these American writers from acclaiming the president of the Republic in Paris, whither, it is true, they had been transported in a Concorde supersonic jet and where they were lodged at the Ritz Hotel—all of it at the French taxpayers' expense, a consideration obviously making for indulgence. But what other "torturing" governments was the U.S. administration supporting at the time of the PEN Club conference in New York? That of Chile? Certainly not. Pinochet did not enjoy U.S. support. Since 1983, furthermore, Latin America as a whole has been more democratic than at any time during the last quarter of a century. El Salvador? But Napoleón Duarte was a left-wing Christian Democrat, democratically elected despite all the efforts made by the guerrillas, who knew they were in a minority, to sabotage the elections. Turkey? To be sure, this was no model democracy; but would it have been wise to let Turkey fall under Soviet control by expelling it from NATO? On the contrary, it could have been considered indispensable to keep it in the NATO system without rejoicing over the fact that it had strayed from the democratic path. It is, furthermore, worth recalling that Turkey had not been expelled from the Council of Europe, and consequently the governments of Western Europe observed an attitude toward it that was every bit as ambiguous or embarrassed as the Reagan administration's. Did the American writers get up and march out of the main amphitheater of the Sorbonne when François Mitterrand made his solemn entry in 1983? Not at all. Besides, in December 1983 Turkey returned to the democratic fold—which is more than can be said for any of the "progressive" countries usually so cherished by American "liberals."

As for Mr. M'Bow, he proved himself to be one of the greatest adversaries of freedom of expression and creativity ever to have headed an international organization. From 1976 onward he made several attempts to have UNESCO adopt the notorious "International Order of Information," the real aim of which was to establish a system of generalized censorship benefiting the worst dictators of the Third World. Considering the state of information on our planet, it was truly ridiculous to see the PEN Club, at this New York congress, seriously propose an inquiry into a mythical "censorship" in the United States and at the same time pay homage to Mr. M'Bow, whose endeavors tirelessly promoted the search for a form of planetary censorship.

The insulting terms used by Günter Grass in his attack on the United States betray the same inversion of facts and values. For, after all, an elementary sense of shame should have reminded Grass that it was we Europeans who invented Nazism, Fascism, Stalinism, Francoism, Pétainism, and anti-Semitism. As for the McCarran-Walter Act of 1952, which was assailed at this PEN Club congress, its abrogation could perfectly well have been demanded while at the same time recalling that the United States is not the only democracy that reserves the right to withhold visas to propagandists who, rightly or wrongly, seem dangerous to its institutions. Besides, the McCarran-Walter Act has never kept Gheorghi Arbatov and other Soviet or communist spokesmen from publishing books and articles or making lecture tours in the United States. Finally, this particular act was abrogated in 1987, the event being passed over in almost total silence.

If there was one place in the United States where, in 1986, one should have looked for a manifestation of the totalitarian spirit, it was, I fear, not in the Washington administration but in the U.S. PEN Club—to judge, at any rate, from the public statements made at this congress. The theme of this congress was, unless I am mistaken, "alienation." And indeed, it perfectly illustrated the alienation of a good part of the United

States' intellectual class from its own people and from a majority of the democratic world. The intolerance and sectarianism which dominated its sessions made it the incarnation of the very opposite of the values it was claiming to defend.

What is the point of rejoicing over the electoral decline of communist parties in the West if their cult of error and terror, their intolerance, and their scorn for human individuality have infected large areas of the noncommunist Left? And how are we to explain the fact that this Left, while claiming to be nontotalitarian, went on stubbornly defending totalitarian regimes (notwithstanding all disclaimers) throughout the 1980s? For the principle of arithmetical equity—between rightist and leftist totalitarianisms—of which I have already shown the intrinsically phony character, was not even truly applied. Thus, in April 1986, at the Hôtel Lutétia in Paris, a conference was held at which a number of former political prisoners from Cuba testified about the tortures and the brutal hardships they had been made to endure. The "judges" seated on the podium—they included the actor-singer Yves Montand, the Spanish writer Jorge Semprun, the French intellectual Bernard-Henri Lévy, and myself—simply asked questions of the witnesses, men and women who were introduced by the poet Armando Valladares, who had organized the conference on behalf of Resistance International. This particular formula had been borrowed from the "Sakharov Tribunal," itself inspired by the "Russell Tribunal" of the 1960s. In the hall there were, I would estimate, about two hundred persons, some of whom also raised pertinent questions. There were also about a dozen journalists on hand—from wire services, newspapers, and radio and TV media. But one could well ask what on earth they were doing there, for most of the Paris press chose to ignore this conference.

The eyewitness reports heard at this conference were devoid of ideology; they consisted of accounts of personal experiences and descriptions of precise facts. If members of the press had wanted to contest the truthfulness of the witnesses, they had every opportunity to do so by subjecting them to counterinterrogation. But they did nothing of the sort. In this case the journalists were in no hurry to use the "sacred right to information" that they brandish with such insistence when other matters are being discussed. Indeed, it is easy to imagine what a wealth of articles would have blossomed forth in the pages of French and foreign newspapers if the political prisoners and the victims of tortures invited to testify at the conference had been victims of the South African police. All of which proves once again that the noncommunist Left has in no wise corrected its partiality in favor of totalitarian Marxist regimes. Its unilateral silence can doubtless be explained as being due more to a kind of intellectual paralysis than to a deliberate choice. Reluctantly, to remain credible, it must recognize certain indisputable realities. But it has not changed its opinion on fundamentals, nor as regards the positioning of the dividing line separating "reactionaries" from "progressives." For such leftists, if only through mental inertia, Castro remains on the good side of the dividing line, while Valladares had placed himself on the bad side, even if his only crime was to have been thrown into prison by the Cuban dictator.*

I am not being fair when I say that there was no reaction to this conference. One did occur—in the form of a campaign of defamation and calumnies launched against Valladares. Phony documents forged by the Cuban and Soviet secret services were circulated in the West, aimed at "proving" that the poet had once worked as a police agent for the dictator Batista (whom Castro overthrew in 1959). Valladares' extremely young age during the 1950s made this charge utterly implausible, as implausible as the bogus "police card" which contained several grotesque errors committed by the "organs" of state security. The card was adorned with a much too recent photo, and the height of the "agent" (Valladares) was given in meters and centimeters, whereas in Batista's day Cuba still used feet and inches!

The anti-Valladares campaign was put into circulation in Greece, thanks to the left-wing publication *Pontiki,* a weekly that has sought to make a specialty of "investigative journalism"—a label that once suggested a high level of journalistic precision, but which more recently has all too often served as a form of accreditation for mendacious reporting. *Pontiki*'s "investigative reporting" and its "duty to inform" amounted to treating Valladares as a "fascist, an assassin, a torturer, a humanoid [sic!], a phony poet fabricated out of nothing by the CIA."

Armando Valladares had to reply to this barrage of "investigative" insults by suing the Greek weekly. At the trial a minister from Andreas Papandreou's socialist government came to testify *in favor* of the insulting and defaming weekly. Valladares lost his lawsuit, the court considering that the author of the article had not been motivated by "any personal animosity against the plaintiff and that he had not had any intention of offending him"! This strange manifestation of "justice," which was given considerable play by the wire services, did not, so far

---

The Guardian (February 6, 1986) referred scornfully to Resistance International as a "strongly anti-communist organisation." As its founders—Vladimir Bukovsky, Armando Valladares, and others—had been former Gulag inmates, it was indeed asking a lot of them to be procommunist.

as I know, arouse the indignation of the left-wing press in Western Europe.

Admittedly, Valladares was at the time vice president of Resistance International, which sponsored the Paris conference and which was regarded by the Left as reactionary. Why so? One no longer knows what one must do and which viewpoint one must adopt to be able to criticize communist totalitarianism without being labeled a "reactionary." It is not true that all the noncommunist Left requires is that one criticize totalitarianism from a democratic point of view. For even when this is done, it is not enough. What it demands is that communist totalitarianism not be criticized, or at least that it be criticized for *past* offenses, it being understood that that particular page has been turned, a new chapter has been opened, and the present offers nothing but bright hopes of improvement. This partiality may be due less to willful choice than to a psychological block; but for those who are victims the result is the same.

In the particular case of this conference—one example among thousands—what governed the behavior of most of the information professionals was not information at all. The possibility of acquiring or completing a precise knowledge of Cuba's repressive police and prison system, if need be by challenging the former prisoners' accounts, played a completely marginal role in the journalistic welcome accorded to the conference at the Hôtel Lutétia. For the leftist press the only questions that mattered were who the organizers were and whose cause the various eyewitness accounts would benefit. This last point was, as it has always been, the most important. It greatly transcends any preoccupation with the truth or falsity of the imparted information. The awful, inquisitorial expression once commonly heard in French left-wing circles—"What *place* are you talking about?," an expression of atrocious vulgarity compounded by its veneer of cryptic elegance, has always been a way of declaring that the truth is less important than one's "collusions" and that one should prefer one's alliances to one's information. The technique of the "amalgam," as is well known, is a procedure that consists of accusing you of approving the totality of the acts or ideas of a particularly detested individual or party simply because your opinions happen to coincide with theirs on some specific point. Hitler having nationalized large sectors of German industry, I am indulging in an amalgam if, for example, I say that François Mitterrand, given his 1981 program of massive nationalizations, was basically an adept of Nazism. But in that case the amalgam is damaging only in one sense. If, for example, you say nasty things about Castro, you find yourself lumped

together with Pinochet, who also says the same sort of things, and so
you are discredited. But to find yourself placed on Castro's side because
you have spoken ill of Pinochet does not dishonor you at all. Yet the
two dictators have an equal quantity of blood on their hands. No matter
how much it would like us to believe the contrary, the noncommunist
Left has been shameless in its constant use of the amalgam; that is, it
replaces the intellectual discussion of arguments by the moral extermination of persons.

It does not occur to the present-day Left that the perfect society it would
like to see constructed and, in the meantime, the mediocre democracy
which, thank Heaven, we still enjoy in certain respects in spite of the
Left, cannot exist without a minimum of sincerity, probity, and respect
for the truth. It refuses to understand that freedom of expression destroys democracy when it becomes an oft-used freedom to lie and to
defame. It remains faithful to the old principle of fanaticism: that a just
cause—and what cause is not just in the eyes of its partisans?—justifies
unjust proceedings. Does it not understand, will it never understand,
that democracy is the regime where there is no single just *cause,* only
just *methods*?

Is it fair, for example, to headline an article on Peru VARGAS LLOSA,
CHAMPION OF THE NEW RIGHT'S CAMPAIGN? In France the appellation
"New Right" carries with it specific connotations, as I have pointed out
in an earlier chapter. In thus headlining the article filed by its correspondent in Lima, *Le Monde* was suggesting that Vargas Llosa was tending
to adopt a neofascist stance.* The newspaper was seeking to suggest to
its readership, which is not just French but European and Latin American as well, that the novelist would eventually be supporting authoritarian solutions tending to favor the rich, and in any case of a "reactionary"
character.

What exactly was involved in this matter? In September 1987, wishing
to rid himself of an onerous foreign debt in one fell swoop, Peruvian
President Alan García announced his intention to nationalize all of the
country's banks. Now, you can perfectly well oppose a measure of this
kind without being a fascist and even because you are a democrat. In
Latin America, nationalizations have never redressed ailing economies
or benefited the poorest strata of society, whether they have been undertaken by military or Marxist dictatorships. In Peru, in particular, a

*Le Monde, September 30, 1987.

dictatorship that was both Marxist *and* military undertook a sweeping program of nationalizations over a period of eleven years (1969–80), leaving a bitter taste in the mouths of most citizens, since during that period the standard of living sank by half—inflicting, as always happens in such cases, great hardships on the poor.

Equally damaging were the consequences of Mexican experimentation in this field—something that should logically give pause to any rational Latin American. President José López Portillo's nationalization of the banks in 1982 proved to be a disaster for the country's economy and for the standard of living of its poorest citizens. Furthermore, if, overlooking all economic considerations, one wishes to preserve a fragile democracy, one should naturally be wary of overexpanding the state-controlled sector, above all in Latin America, where there is a well-entrenched tradition of corruption and where the dominant political class is a past master in the art of manipulating the economy for its own benefit and of falsifying democratic procedures in the process. The history of Mexico's PRI—the "Revolutionary" Institutional Party—which has held power nonstop since 1929, offers abundant proof. Even the recent history of Peru, ruined by the voracious nationalizations effected by its Marxist officers, was not enough to keep *Le Monde*'s correspondent from writing: "If the state has broadened its sphere of action over the past twenty years, it has been precisely to try to correct the unjust distribution of incomes." But to try is not necessarily to succeed, and the "broadening of the state's field of action" in this case did nothing but further impoverish the needy. Instead of studying the facts and conscientiously reporting them, Nicole Bonnet (for such was her name) simply recited the most shopworn "progressive" catechism.

Another thing she failed to tell us was that a great many of those opposing the proposed nationalizations were persons who had voted for Alan García in the presidential elections. And to what party did Alan García belong? To APRA—the Alianza Popular Revolucionaria Americana. And what exactly is the APRA? It is a group of Latin American parties founded in 1924 by a Peruvian, Raúl Haya de La Torre (1895–1979), an alliance roughly corresponding to what in Europe is called social democracy. In other words, the APRA was born from the refusal of a powerful current of socialists to adhere to the Third International, a refusal and a break with Moscow that was similar to those that had marked the Congrès de Tours four years earlier in France, and which other socialist parties all over the world were to imitate. This particular current of socialist democracy can thus boast a long tradition of hostility to communist collectivism. In the matter of the nationalization of

Peruvian banks, one can quite properly regard Vargas Llosa as being faithful to the tradition of democratic socialism in Latin America, whereas Alan García had been abandoning it.

But alas, not one of these economic, political, or historical details was brought to the attention of *Le Monde*'s readers. Provided with some historical perspective, they would most likely have begun seriously to doubt the supposedly "New Right fascism" of Mario Vargas Llosa. Why then this act of deception? Because the purpose of the article was to denigrate the Peruvian novelist by making it seem that he had purely and simply joined the ranks of the "reactionaries." For years, along with Mexico's Octavio Paz, Mario Vargas Llosa has been the anti-Castro, anticommunist, anti–Third Worldist, the anti–García Márquez advocate of political democracy in Latin America. Hence the need to expel him toward the Right, and even better toward the "New" Right. In Latin America one doesn't have the right to be a democrat if one is not a Marxist—such is the logic behind this kind of "banishment." What makes this example particularly absurd is the fact that elsewhere during this same period *Le Monde* had seemed to be acclaiming the return of democracy in Argentina, Brazil, and Bolivia, all of which gave themselves governments determined to denationalize their economies. If one were to ask the newspaper's editor in chief or the foreign news editor whether, given the orientation of most of the articles they publish about Latin America, they logically favor the return of Castrista or Allende-type policies, they would immediately and vigorously protest that such was absolutely not the case. Many left-wing newspapers—and this is true in many countries—keep attacking liberalism in biting terms, but, save for certain exceptional cases, they do not at all wish for the victory of socialism. At the same time they go on insidiously demolishing its critics.

Thus *Le Monde*'s correspondent in Lima also wrote: "The New Right is represented by the Liberty and Democracy Institute, founded seven years ago [in fact in 1979] by Mario Vargas Llosa. His philosophy has been summed up by the economist Hernando de Soto in his book entitled *The Other Path,* an essay on the informal economy." As an example of the journalist's "duty to inform," this paragraph is a gem. To begin with, it was not Vargas Llosa who founded the Liberty and Democracy Institute. It was in fact Hernando de Soto, of whom Vargas Llosa is both a friend and a supporter. Vargas Llosa simply wrote the preface to de Soto's book, written in 1986. Next, the institute does not in any way adhere to the ideology of the "New Right." The French right-wingers who write for *Éléments, Nouvelle École,* or GRECE (Groupement de

Recherche et d'Étude pour la Civilization Européenne) have never, to the best of my knowledge, been invited to Peru. The Liberty and Democracy Institute intends to adhere to the traditions of Tocqueville, Montesquieu, John Locke, Adam Smith, von Mises, Schumpeter, Aron, and Hayek—something which, let us hope, has never constituted a presumption of sympathy for fascism. I don't think that Latin America has suffered from any excess in that liberal and tolerant tradition, nor that the intellectuals who support it deserve to be defamed. *Le Monde*'s correspondent admittedly had every right to criticize those intellectuals' ideas. But this was not what she did. She gave them ideas that are not theirs. Furthermore, she carefully refrained from describing the actual contents of Hernando de Soto's book, *The Other Path.* * Since it had not been translated into French, only a few readers could know what this work of sociological investigation (and not of "philosophy") contained, and exactly what the journalist meant by "informal" economy. Above all, her readers could have no idea that the work of inquiry directed and signed by Hernando de Soto concerned the economic situation of the poorest Peruvians, describing how they manage to survive despite a system of state control organized for the benefit of the wealthy, and furthermore less for the benefit of industrial entrepreneurs than of the members of the ruling political, bureaucratic, and labor union elite—as is almost always the case in Latin America.

Anyone who reads *The Other Path* is likely to be dumbfounded by a first casual glance at the principal figures and statistics it contains. For the "informal" sector in this enormous country does not simply comprise those whom in Europe we refer to as "little jobsmen" or workers in the so-called "black" economy (i.e., those who do part-time work and don't declare their earnings to the fiscal authorities). The Peruvian "informals" don't simply unblock kitchen sinks or repaint ceilings on Sundays. They are much more than hawkers or street vendors. The total turnover of their commercial activities exceeds that of all the country's chain and department stores combined. In the capital city of Lima this "informal" commerce, involving 439,000 individuals, accounts for 83 percent of all market activities, whether indoors or outdoors. Peru's "informal" industry turns out just about every kind of manufactured product: furniture, TV sets, washing machines, clothes, kitchen utensils, bricks, cement, electrical equipment, shoes, tools of all kinds. Nor is this all. The "informals" dominate the construction industry and public

El Otro Sendero (Lima: Editorial El Barranco, 1986). GRECE, which was founded in 1969, is a cultural organization that shares the general tendencies of the New Right in France.

transportation. They have built entire neighborhoods, hundreds of thousands of houses and apartments, first of all for themselves and then for others. And I don't mean shantytowns, but normal housing developments. Half of Lima's population lives in houses built by the "informals." As for public transportation—everything from the collective taxi to the buses—if Lima suddenly had to rely on official municipal transport facilities, nine tenths (more precisely, 95 percent) of the inhabitants would have to walk! All in all, about 60 percent of all work hours are performed in the "informal" sector. And let no one try to compare this thriving sector with clandestine workshops in which a ruthless watchdog boss exploits an underpaid proletariat. Here it is the poor folk of the Third World who have themselves built up this "informal" economy, for it is the only way in which they can survive.

Hernando de Soto and his team provided a graphic demonstration of how and why this vital sector exists by resorting to experimental verification. They asked a modest citizen, representing the poor social stratum, to file a regular request for official authorization to open a clothes-making workshop according to the legal norms. To obtain his authorization this man had to present his request and follow it up through eleven successive ministerial or municipal departments. Ten out of eleven of the functionaries involved extorted a bribe—known in Peru as a *mordida,* which is to say a passing "bite." The postulant was instructed by his mentors not to cough up, to see how long the delay occasioned by each refusal would be. In two cases, however, he was forced to pay the bribe, for otherwise his file would have been buried forever. In the end the would-be tailor needed 289 full-time workdays to carry out the necessary formalities, and, adding up the various expenses involved and the resultant loss of income, he found himself the loser to the tune of $1,231. This sum, representing all of those lost workdays, was thirty-two times higher than the minimum wage in Peru in 1986; so it is easy to understand why for the vast majority of the country's active population there is simply no way of creating an artisanal enterprise under legal conditions. But this did not keep Madame Bonnet from praising "the broadening of the state's field of action in order to correct an unjust distribution of income."

Other tests of the same kind confirmed this first experiment. Forty-three days of petitioning and an outlay of $590.56 were needed to obtain official permission to set up a humble fruit-and-vegetable stall in a Lima street. The prize discovery was this: six years and eleven months of petitioning, needed to obtain an official authorization for a number of families who wanted to build houses on a vacant lot. Hence the irresistible growth of "wildcat" enterprises and an "informal" market.

What this also proves is the vanity of theoretical babblings. Free enterprise "liberalism" is, first of all, a spontaneous mode of behavior—which does not mean it is a guarantee of success in every case. But far from being some kind of visionary myth, it is the natural reaction in society of the human being in dealing with immediate problems. It is a basic economic *modus operandi.* All sorts of ways of intervening can subsequently be imagined to improve this behavior. Sometimes they improve it; far more frequently they hamper it; never in any case can they replace it.

The facts bear this out. Contrary to the vapid pontifications that so often have been made on this subject, freedom to initiate and to help oneself is perhaps the primary defense the small have against the big, the weak against the strong. Conversely, the state, which claims to be the corrector of injustices, ends up most of the time weighing down on the small and the weak in order to protect the big and the strong: the political establishment, the bureaucracy, the leading firms, an inflated army, powerful labor unions. To circumvent these ramparts, the have-nots can make a go of it only in the "parallel" or underground economy, which is to say in the real one.

This is true of the Third World, but not only of the Third World. Let us take a close look at what happens in developed countries. The importance of the underground Italian economy is well known; it has even been tabulated and charted in the periodic reports put out by CENSIS (Centro Studi Investimenti Sociali). The case of Spain is no less enlightening. In 1986 Felipe González's government had a report drafted that was based on investigations made at its request by five private social and economic research institutes. This inquiry necessitated 64,000 separate interviews. What they revealed was that in Spain there are no less than 300,000 small clandestine enterprises, whose annual turnover can be estimated as worth three trillion pesetas—which is to say, a quarter of the gross national product. In certain regions—in Andalucía and Levante—the "informal" economy accounts for 40 percent of the total production. These figures indicate that the real level of unemployment is fortunately lower than the 21.5 percent recorded in the official statistics. Furthermore, inasmuch as the informal sector accounts for 25 percent of Spain's GNP and between 60 and 70 percent in Third World countries, fiscal fraud and the desire to escape the burdens of social security payments can no longer be attributed exclusively to the maneuvers of fat capitalists and of a handful of smart tax evaders. It is sheer intellectual, journalistic, and political irresponsibility not to bother to study the deep-rooted causes of this "parallel" phenomenon and the positive benefits derived from it by the poorest citizens, whom the state neglects.

Admittedly, the subterranean Spanish economy should in theory pay out billions of pesetas every year to the fiscal authorities. This is consequently a terrible loss for the country's internal revenue service. But, as the report intimates, in Spain (and this is just as true for Italy or Peru), if the fragile enterprises of the "underground" sector were taxed normally, they would not pay anyway; they would simply disappear. Neither the fiscal authorities nor the social security system would gain a penny, and Spanish society as a whole would be the loser on a tragic scale. Accordingly, the real question that legislators should be asking themselves is why there are laws and regulations of such a kind that a sizable proportion of national output would be condemned to death if they were applied. What in such a situation is bad, and what should be changed—reality, or the law?

Why, then, are calumnious observations against a disinterested writer to be found in an article by a newspaper correspondent who is neither an editorialist nor a propagandist nor a prominent politician, an article that contains everything except genuine information about Peru? Why this rejection of the truth? Is it due to a desire to defend the myth according to which free enterprise liberalism is "rightist," whereas socialism is "leftist"? Anyone who has read the classic works of liberalism and taken the trouble to study the historical evidence is forced to reconsider such oversimplified equivalences. Doubtless this is why socialists would rather not face the facts. It pains them to think that socialism might aggravate poverty, inequalities, and arbitrary state control. The argument used by socialists to defend their cause amounts to asserting that liberalism abolishes all social solidarity. But this is patent nonsense. What societies, if not liberal societies, invented the sophisticated and costly methods of social protection we enjoy today? In addition to which, socialists make this distinction: they say "yes" to political liberalism but "no" to economic liberalism.

At this point their reasoning is not only off course. All one has to do is to read Marx to understand why. For how can one withdraw all, or at any rate the greater part, of economic power from civil society in order to give it to the State, and yet hope that the thus enfeebled citizens will be able resist the abuses of political power? What means would they have for doing so, once they have been dislodged from the economic strongholds of their autonomy? For this reason liberal authors have always maintained—is this perchance the shameful secret that socialists would like to conceal at almost any price?—that the real frontier between Left and Right passes between systems in which property-owning citizens retain the main part of economic decision making in their hands and systems in which they lose it. Economic interventionism always reduces political freedoms, be they no more than the simple "franchises" of France's Ancien Régime.

In his book *The Omnipotent Government,* Ludwig von Mises, one of the great Viennese who were forced to emigrate because of the Nazis, amused himself by comparing the ten urgent measures prescribed by Marx in the Communist Manifesto of 1847 with Hitler's economic program. "Eight of those ten points," von Mises noted ironically, "were carried out by the Nazis with a radicalism that would have delighted Karl Marx."*

In the case of Vargas Llosa and Alan García of Peru, it is well to remember that the central control of credit in the hands of the state is an absolute arm that has been cherished as much by the socialists as it was by Hitler and Mussolini. Nazis and Fascists, we should not forget, were, almost as much as Stalinists, zealous nationalizers. It may well be with such sinister precedents in mind that Vargas Llosa felt it his duty in 1987 to warn that the total concentration of the banking and financial system in the hands of the state, and particularly (as in this case) of a corruption-ridden state, was a peril for democracy and in any case a brake on economic expansion. And yet, as the case of Madame Bonnet shows, a journalist during the last few years of this waning twentieth century can, in one of the world's best newspapers (*Le Monde*), write an article without paying any heed to information, whether it be provided by contemporary events or through knowledge of the past.

There would be nothing odd about this situation; it would even be logical if *Le Monde* or any other quality newspaper (it could be *The Guardian, The New York Times, El País,* or *La Repubblica*), were an organ of combat in the service of totalitarian collectivism. But this is not the case. If one were to argue the matter to its logical conclusion with the chief editors of *Le Monde,* they too would probably declare themselves hostile to the principle of collectivizing all banks. Why then should they tar somebody with the brush of the New Right who is as

---

*Ludwig von Mises' book was first published in the United States in 1944 (during World War II) under the complete title *The Omnipotent Government: The Rise of the Total State and the Total War* (Spring Hills, Pennsylvania: Libertarian Press, 1985).

much opposed to such measures as they are? Why make a travesty of Vargas Llosa's arguments and denigrate his person if one does not believe in the cause for which one is doing it? Such inconsistency, illustrating the complexities of falsehood, is doubtless due to what could be called the residual afterglow of declining ideology. One no longer believes in socialism, but one continues to besmirch the partisans of capitalism as though one still had something coherent to oppose them with.

This persistence of a phenomenon after the disappearance of its cause is one of the sources of ideological falsehood. Liberalism is well known to have nothing in common with fascism. Indeed, the Fascists hated traditional liberals with even greater ferocity than they did communists; yet people go on claiming that socialism is the only true antagonist of fascism. Thus Jean Daniel, editor in chief of the left-wing Paris weekly *Le Nouvel Observateur,* could carry on a polemical debate with the editor of the monthly *L'Esprit* (Jean-Marie Domenach), who was once very close to Marxism but has since been completely purged of this ideology, and who because of this "highly suspect" shift was promptly accused of complicity with the extreme Right of Jean-Marie Le Pen. Replying to Domenach's protests, Jean Daniel wrote, among other things: "The liberal Right has clearly understood it: Le Pen is part of its family album, just as Italian terrorists are part of the family album of the Marxist Left."* This amalgam was not lacking in ingenuity, since it allowed the author to simulate impartiality. It was the classic hocus-pocus of dual rejection. But the comparison disintegrates as soon as it is judged by any standards of rudimentary historical and political knowledge. The expression "the family album of the communist party" was employed in Italy during the 1970s by Rossana Rossanda, the moving spirit behind the leftist intellectual movement Il Manifesto. The argument had some substance. It reminded the communists that, while their party had gone over to parliamentary "legalism" and "formal" democracy, basic Marxist-Leninist doctrine had not changed in decreeing that bourgeois democracy was a sham and a snare, and that the proletarian revolution could be carried out only through violence. Consequently, she argued, it was the Red Brigades that had remained faithful to the basic doctrine, and not the *embourgeoisés* politicians of the Italian Communist Party's leadership. The latter, in any case, should do

Le Nouvel Observateur, October 16, 1987.

a bit of soul searching and admit that one cannot with impunity teach a Bolshevik doctrine of the seizure of power by force and then decline all responsibility when certain persons apply it. In short, Rossana Rossanda asserted, the Red Brigades had simply limited themselves to interpreting Marxism-Leninism literally.

Nothing of the sort is to be found in the tradition of liberal doctrine. Where, in *The Federalist Papers* or in Tocqueville, can one find even an embryonic justification of extreme right-wing violence? The *bête noire* of Charles Maurras, of Mussolini (I assume Jean Daniel is familiar with the work of Renzo de Felice, the great historian of Fascism), of Hitler, was liberalism; it was "rotten" parliamentary democracy, in which all parties were damned. They hated liberals far more fiercely than they did communists, of whom Maurras used to say (correctly from his point of view): "They are not the worst; they are at least not republicans." The target of the terrorists of the Organization de l'Armée Secrète in France, and of Le Pen's partisans during the Algerian war, were the Gaullists. It was de Gaulle whom they tried to assassinate several times, never Maurice Thorez or Guy Mollet, leaders, respectively, of the Communist and Socialist parties. How, then, can a political writer like Jean Daniel, who is notoriously well acquainted with all these facts, deliberately commit such a gross piece of historical misinterpretation, if not for reasons of amalgamation? And why does he thus violate morality for the greater glory of a political philosophy he no longer even believes in, if not because the last remaining objection he can still brandish against the liberals consists of spuriously claiming that at the outset they were indistinguishable from the Fascists? Still half blinded by "ideological afterglow," he is reduced to forging this myth; and in so doing he is obliged to ignore all the elements of information furnished by his memory and to propound an absurdity. For if liberalism and fascism were one and the same, and if consequently in our times there had existed only fascist and socialist regimes, it is difficult to see where liberty, in this twentieth century of ours, could have found a safe perch. That in spite of everything it managed to survive was due to the existence of regimes that were neither socialist nor fascist and which, in truth, are those mankind has the least reason to be ashamed of.

We find ourselves confronted here by despairing ideologists who no longer believe in their own ideological message. But let us not imagine that for this reason they have grown less intolerant. Quite the contrary. A school of thought that knows it is in a state of decline struggles even more fiercely to preserve its identity. Aware of the weakness of their position, the ideologists of the Left are even more crabbed and crooked in defending it. They are reduced to extremities, all the more so since they flee from the field of information and logical argumentation, where they know in advance they are beaten. All that is left them is a junk shop full of intellectual bric-a-brac, but they cling to it with a savagery augmented by their loss of sincerity. In articles of general analysis one now often reads socialist texts that the most touchy of liberals could happily sign. But the abandonment of theoretical dogmas makes it all the more imperative for socialists to exterminate the adversary, since he cannot be refuted. As Jacques Julliard, who like Jean Daniel is an editorial writer for *Le Nouvel Observateur,* wrote in an excellent book, "The [French] Left won its [1981] victory at a moment when it was already in a state of ideological débâcle." And farther on: "The social utility of the nationalizations was discovered to be just about nil."* Rare are the liberals who permit themselves such harsh judgments. Politicians of the Left in their turn vie with intellectuals to contest old principles. From 1982 or 1983 on it was hard to open a newspaper without reading items like these: ARGENTINA: PRESIDENT ALFONSIN ATTACKS THE PUBLIC SECTOR† or MR. RAJIV GANDHI DELIVERS A VIOLENT DIATRIBE AGAINST FORTY YEARS OF SOCIALIST MANAGEMENT.‡ Or the head of Spain's socialist government, Felipe González, declares: "The appelations of liberal, socialist, and conservative are empty of meaning."§ Remarks of this kind abound, in the United States as elsewhere. They kindle hopes of a dialogue that might at last be civilized.

But such hopes are vain! It is precisely because events have ruined their doctrine that European socialists and American "liberals" are so obdurate in defending their cultural identity. In France this rearguard action consists of relegating all citizens who remain impervious to left-wing "sensibility" to a kind of extreme right-wing limbo. This is why—particularly since the Klaus Barbie trial—the period of the Occupation (1940–44) has become such an obligatory touchstone. All those who do not share the ideas of the Left or at least its propaganda themes are thus placed "beyond the pale." Yet the majority of citizens in all the countries of Europe in which elections were held in 1986, 1987, and 1988 voted against the Left, or, as in France and Spain, for a Left that was more

---

*Jacques Julliard, *La Faute à Rousseau* (Paris: Seuil, 1985). The nationalizations involved seven key industrial sectors and thirty-eight private banks.

†*Le Monde,* November 30, 1986.

‡*Le Monde,* November 1, 1986.

§"Los apelativos de liberal, socialista y conservador están carentes de contenido" (*Diario 16,* March 25, 1987).

liberal than socialist. That really adds up to a lot of neo-Nazis in Europe—in fact, between one half and two thirds of all its inhabitants! But this huge absurdity doesn't bother the propagandists. Could it be that everything that is not socialist is perforce Nazi?

"Jacques Chirac's is the most reactionary government France has known since Vichy," cried Pierre Mauroy, the former socialist premier, in December 1986, at a moment when students were staging massive demonstrations against the principle of selective admission to universities. Serge Klarsfeld, the lawyer who did so much to establish the historical truth about the deportations to Germany of French Jews and Jews living in France, appealed to the committee of the so-called "wise men," which had been given the task of preparing a report aimed at eventually reforming the Nationality Code.* He reminded the "sages" that in 1941 "Xavier Vallat, the high commissioner for Jewish questions in the Vichy government, refused to recognize Jewish children born of foreign parents in France as French—a decision that led to the deportation and death of most of them in 1942." The intimation is clear. If, forty-five or fifty years later, anyone should dare to revise the French Code of Nationality, he or she will become an accomplice of the crimes against humanity committed in 1942.

In fact, the two situations have absolutely nothing in common. No roundup, followed by a cattlelike dispatch to death camps, now menaces North Africans and blacks in France. Nobody has ever thought of refusing French citizenship to their children born in France. On the contrary, it has been suggested, in order to put an end to occasional mix-ups, that, on reaching adulthood, the interested adolescent ratify his adherence to French nationality. The suggestion aroused objections (which is why a commission of "sages" was set up). But how can one reasonably deny that the influx of immigrants, who come and go frequently, was bound during this second half of the twentieth century to lead to new difficulties, in particular with their countries of origin? How, in this new context, when millions of human beings can move around with hitherto unknown ease, can a government be forbidden to reexamine the norms for the granting of citizenship? Does such a government deserve to be compared to the Nazis and to French collaborators? Even if it makes mistakes, even if it gropes to find some middle way between gullible acquiescence and discrimination, should it be tarred with the supreme insult, which from sheer overuse finally degenerates into a paradoxical triviality? For that is what "banalization" really is. The

*Le Monde, October 27, 1987.

work accomplished in the past by Serge Klarsfeld merits the esteem of all, but it should not serve as an excuse for the mindless bandying about of insults and blackmail threats, nor of historical amalgams that are totally lacking in serious substance.

In short, the situation is simple. We have all "got the message." If, from 1985 to 1990 in France, one happens to disagree on some point with a "leftist," then one is a Nazi. Outside of socialism—and, furthermore, a socialism that no longer knows how to define itself—there is no path other than Hitlerism, today rechristened as "indulgence for Le Pen."*

It is curious to see people who vehemently condemn the "behavior of exclusion" indulge in it brutally themselves in order to dispatch to the hellfire of the damned anyone who ventures to contradict them. How would Régis Debray react if his support for the (communist) *Frente Farabundo Marti* of El Salvador were enough to get him compared by his adversaries to Lavrentii Beria, Stalin's cold-blooded police chief? The entire Left would consider such a step repugnant, imbecilic, grotesque. But when the same methods are employed by the Left, all is well. And, I again insist, on the part of the *noncommunist* Left, the one that periodically claims to have abjured all Stalinist aberrations.

In 1985, when he came out with his book *Les Empires contre l'Europe,* Régis Debray did not arouse the slightest whimper of reprobation among his fellow socialists because he compared certain authors, too anti-Soviet for his taste, to . . . Marcel Déat. The latter, a notorious collaborator at the time of the Nazi occupation, was condemned to death after the Liberation for intelligence with the enemy. Now, what resemblance can there be between a man who championed collaboration with the totalitarian power that had occupied France and contemporary intellectuals who above all wanted to keep France from being occupied by another totalitarian power, the Soviet Union? On the ethical plane, at any rate, the analogy is self-destroying. But it is here that ideology— by which I mean a dogmatic system of political beliefs—makes its miraculous intervention, all the more imperiously thanks to its supreme disdain for facts. Unable and unwilling to discuss these facts or to reply to arguments, Debray resorts to analogy in order to besmirch those he is powerless to refute.

*On July 21, 1988, the communist daily, *L'Humanité,* called the Constitutional Council "Pétainist" because it had taken a decision displeasing to the French Communist Party.

In addition to blurring one's perception of the real world, ideology suspends the exercise of moral awareness. More precisely, it is ideology that serves as the criterion for distinguishing good from evil. Under its sway a base calumny, an abject insult, becomes lawful, if employed to strike down a recalcitrant resister. The ideologist does not wish to know the truth; he is interested only in protecting his own system of beliefs and in destroying, if only intellectually, all those who do not think as he does. Ideology reposes on a communion in falsehood, implying the automatic ostracism of anyone refusing to partake. This is why it implies the simultaneous suspension of mental faculties and moral sensibility.

Quite aside from its infamous character, Régis Debray's reference to Marcel Déat is quite simply idiotic. Now, Debray is no idiot. His intelligence must therefore have been blocked. The pretext for this analogy is obvious. Marcel Déat justified collaboration with the occupying Nazis (after June 1941) in the name of an "anti-Bolshevik crusade." Ergo: all those who are anti-Soviet are pro-Nazi. Here again we encounter our old friend, the paralogism which fastens on one point in order to establish a category, even though this common denominator is not upheld for the same reasons by those who adopt it. Régis Debray having at one time been a student of philosophy at the higher university level, he cannot consciously have committed such a gross error of logic. He erred, I think, as a result of an ideological "stroke," which is even more common than a heart attack. Even a modest dose of historical knowledge, no doubt present early on but later suddenly vanished from his memory, should have made him beware of this comparison, in reality perilous for his thesis. For Marcel Déat was a socialist and never ceased proclaiming himself a socialist, and, like many socialists between the two world wars, he was above all else a pacifist. It was pacifism that gradually led him to collaborate with the Germans, after it had prompted him in March 1936, when he was French minister for air, to oppose a military intervention against Hitler, who had just ordered the reoccupation of the Rhineland. Like Debray, a doctor of philosophy as well as a socialist, Déat offers a classic case of a man of great intellectual gifts and excellent intentions who is led by a concatenation of abstract arguments, which are more and more divorced from practical experience, to espouse a policy that is the very negation of his first objectives. As a victim of ideological deviation, his is a singularly instructive case. If Déat, an irresponsible harbinger of totalitarianism and the promoter of one tyranny as a rampart against another, can be regarded as a precursor of a political current in the 1980s, it is the one represented by the West

German "Greens" or the French signatories of the "Appel des Cent."* Which does not mean that I amalgamate them with Déat.

Ideology functions as a machine for destroying information on the basis of assertions that are totally contrary to the evidence. For example, when Régis Debray declared in 1979 that "the word Gulag was *imposed* by imperialism"† (my italics) ("imperialism" meaning for him, of course, *American* imperialism), the future diplomatic adviser of the president of the French Republic was indulging in a brazen inversion of facts, a process typical of ideological thinking. He transformed the effect into the cause. If, according to Debray, there is such a thing as the Gulag, it is not because Lenin and Stalin created it, it is because "imperialism" employed the word—a truly grotesque claim since, in fact, those five letters are derived from the initials of the USSR's prison and concentration camp administration!

Many Western ideologists defend the principle of socialism with far greater ardor than do communist leaders themselves. Khrushchev, Gorbachev, and Deng Xiaoping have all criticized the thousand and one things wrong with their economies with a critical cruelty that has sometimes exceeded the most withering epigrams coined by "reactionaries" in the West. Mikhail Gorbachev's book *Perestroika,* which was published in the West toward the end of 1987, is in places one of the most biting indictments ever made of the ridiculous sterility of the Soviet economy. On his angrier days Fidel Castro has often painted a gloomy picture of Cuba's poverty and "revolutionary" inefficiency. On the other hand, during the summer of 1987 I heard the archbishop of Toronto, along with other good apostles, depict Cuba as an El Dorado, a Switzerland of the Caribbean. These discordances are due to the fact that communist leaders have to grapple with realities, no matter how much they might like to avoid them, whereas the ideologists, whether men of the cloth or not, move airily on a cloud of empty words and in the weightless realm of unreality. To be sure, communist leaders lie, and indeed their entire system rests on falsehood. For decades they waged war on information. But then one day, they themselves are obliged to admit publicly what everybody (except for Western ideologists) has known for years. Such is the meaning of the word *glasnost:* to say openly what everybody knows. These leaders resign themselves to this "can-

*The "Appeal of the Hundred" was a manifesto signed by one hundred left-wing French intellectuals and politicians which in the spring of 1982 denounced the installation of Pershing II missiles on the continent of Europe. One of the signatories was the present French foreign minister, Roland Dumas.

†Jeannine Verdès-Leroux, *Le Réveil des somnambules* (Paris: Fayard-Minuit, 1987).

dor" when the only choice left them is between frankness and collapse. In 1987 Felipe González was quite right to use irony in dealing with the sectarian Marxists of the Spanish Communist Party, who had been berating him for his excessively liberal policy, and to have retorted that this policy, whether they liked it or not, had been "endorsed" by Gorbachev and Deng Xiaoping.* Needless to say, the latter are plagued by an internal contradiction, since they wish to cure the ills of their economies while perpetuating the political system that caused them. Still, this very contradiction is a fact of life. The ideologists, on the other hand, deal only with their own abstractions, which encounter no resistance save in the realm of accurate information. This they accordingly abolish thanks to intellectual hocus-pocus, what Molière wittily called the "marvellous power of the magic virtue."†

In developed countries this "magic virtue" prompts people to continue praising a socialist *doctrine* which no practicing socialist in the social or economic field explicitly proposes to apply. In this case ideological falsehood consists of delivering the old diatribes against capitalism while knowing full well, ever since the full inanity of socialism became glaringly apparent, that one has nothing to replace it with. "To deal a death blow to capitalism"—once the rallying cry of François Mitterand—has today a singularly hollow ring and almost no adepts.

In the case of the Third World, the ideological destruction of information is even more patent, for it involves the deliberate falsification or neglect of pertinent statistics that are generally known or can be obtained without difficulty. How would the press react if, in the course of a public debate, a cabinet minister, a bishop, or a leading intellectual were to assert that France has five million inhabitants, that the average annual per capita income in the United States is less than $1,000, or that the living standard in Germany has never ceased to decline since 1945? Yet every day in the West idiocies of this kind are proferred about Third World countries. Such monstrous enormities are all too placidly and literally accepted by the professionals of information, who, when they are not themselves the authors, do not bother to contest them.

Let us take an example that is no laughing matter: that of the number of persons who die of starvation every year. Having failed in communist societies and having never been tried in democratic lands without irreparable harm or costly damage that takes years to repair, Marxist socialism today has ceased to be of any use save as a rhetorical battering ram

*Cambio 16, November 1, 1987.
†From L'Étourdi ("The Blunderer").

against capitalism in Third World countries. Yet the Third Worldists would have us believe that capitalism is permanently responsible for a planetary genocide. We who live in developed regions are making grave-yards of poor countries, which we plunder and starve—all these massive, silent, and daily "executions" being the dire consequences and the condition of our own enrichment. The Swiss sociologist Jean Ziegler has been hammering away at this theme in countless books for years. It is this particular ideology's last life raft. For if, alas, it becomes evident that socialism saves nobody, there remains the consoling thought that capitalism kills the world—which for the ideologist is what is essential. We have lost paradise; let us at least keep hell.

In this macabre system of accounting, the extravagance of the figures is on a par with the credulity with which they are accepted. During a Club de la Presse broadcast in 1981, Louis Mermaz, who is one of the French Socialist Party's leading figures and who served from 1981 to 1986 as president of the National Assembly before becoming a minister in Michel Rocard's government in 1988, exhorted the press to "denounce this monstrosity of the *capitalist system*—world hunger—which claims fifty million lives every year, thirty million of them children."* In January 1982 Terre des Hommes, a nongovernmental "welfare" organization which also serves as a vehicle for international propaganda, teamed up with Antenne 2 to produce a week-long series of features devoted to illustrating this slogan: "Fifty Million Human Beings Die of Hunger Every Year." In 1984 *Le Nouvel Observateur* devoted a vast "inquiry" to the subject of worldwide hunger, which began with this sentence: "The last war resulted in 45 million deaths in five years; today just as many men, women, and children die *each year* of starvation."†

I have taken these quotations from the French media, but I have often heard similar figures tossed around during Third World debates in the United States, South America, and Scandinavia. This arithmetic is frequently used too as a kind of dissuasive argument in order to stifle debate on other subjects. During a TV program dealing with books about AIDS and epidemics in general, the participants were trying to estimate the number of persons affected by AIDS when a doctor brusquely interrupted them by declaring: "In any case, it's not a very big figure, compared to this other one. Just think—all over the world

*Statement made on July 5, 1981. This French "Press Club" program is a much-listened-to weekly feature of Radio Europe No. 1. Every Sunday evening fifteen to twenty journalists interrogate a political figure for one hour.

†November 23, 1984. The figure given here is on the low side. The number of victims usually cited is sixty million.

40,000 people die of hunger every day!" Jean Delumeau, a professor at the Collège de France and an eminent French historian who had been quoting from one of his books to illustrate the problem of epidemics across the ages, nodded in obviously troubled agreement, followed by the silent, compassionate acquiescence of the assembled company. This particular doctor* was less greedy than Mermaz or Terre des Hommes, for 40,000 deaths per day add up only, if I may so express it, to 14,600,000 dead per year—a sharp reduction from the forty-five million to sixty million often claimed.

This was very kind of him, but unfortunately insufficient. As any qualified demographer can point out to curious souls, every year about fifty million human beings die in various parts of the planet. All cannot die of hunger, nor can 60 percent of them be children, nor do they belong exclusively to the Third World. At the time these glib statements were made, there were about 4,700,000,000 human beings on this planet, the average mortality rate from all causes, in all regions, and of all ages being 11 percent of the total. In this total the number of deaths due directly to food shortages varied, according to the year, from one million to two million. During the 1980–90 decade almost all of these victims were located in Africa, particularly in countries equipped with or afflicted by a Marxist regime: Ethiopia, Madagascar, Angola, Mozambique—to which must be added the Sudan, which is not Marxist.

Contrary to what so many ideologists claim, the most murderous famines of our age have taken place in communist countries and cannot therefore be blamed on capitalism. In fact, the *great famine maker of the twentieth century has been socialism.* The main causes of contemporary famines have been political. Among the most famous of these political causes are the collectivization of farmlands in the Soviet Union in the 1930s (five million to six million dead in the Ukraine alone), Mao Tse-tung's "Great Leap Forward" (several tens of millions dead), and the recent forced transfers of populations in Ethiopia. Almost always, when one encounters some of these astronomical figures so readily brandished by hypocrites or naïve dolts, the famine turns out to have been *due to the initiative of a communist regime.* In most noncommunist countries, including India, which around 1970 was considered a hopeless case, the most serious famines have bit by bit been reduced by increasing agricultural productivity, accumulating reserve stocks, developing transport, and offsetting climatic irregularities, and only in communist

*Dr. Willy Rozenbaum, head of the AIDS department at the Claude-Bernard Hospital in Paris.

lands or in countries close to Marxist socialism do food catastrophes still occur on a medieval scale.

Curiously lame and hobbled is the old war-horse that socialist and Third World ideologists like to drag out to overawe us, since, to begin with, the number of deaths in the world due to lack of food amounts in reality to about 2 to 4 percent of what they claim; and since this still excessive and scandalous percentage must be imputed not to a supposedly indicted capitalism, but to socialism! Let us be clear on this point. The problem of "world hunger" concerns far more human beings than those who die directly of starvation. Chronically insufficient food and malnutrition affect enormous numbers of human beings, including many in the Soviet Union (to judge by what Mikhail Gorbachev has told us, and I am willing to take his word for it); they increase vulnerability to various diseases that shorten human life. But this is not what the ideologists want to talk about, particularly since life expectancy (something they do not, apparently, know, true though it is) has increased over the past quarter of a century in the world (except in the Soviet Union—I regret to appear to be bearing down on the USSR, but what can I do?). What they particularly want to talk about, and what they do indeed talk about, is not the lack of foodstuffs but the fifty millions who supposedly *die* of hunger every year—an utterly absurd figure but one packed with ideological dynamite.

This example, culled from among hundreds like it, illustrates the mystery posed by the seeming fruitlessness or outright rejection of information. A man like Louis Mermaz is both practically and intellectually perfectly equipped to be well informed, since, on the one hand, he has a Ph.D. in history, and since, on the other hand, as president of the National Assembly at the time he made those remarks, he had many aides capable of preparing files for him on the subject. How, then, can he get off such wild untruths? And even supposing that he deliberately exaggerated the figures for the purposes of propaganda, how is it that not one of the fifteen or twenty journalists taking part in the Club de la Presse program sought to contradict him by quoting the rudimentary statistics his profession makes him duty-bound to possess? Can it be that a professor from the prestigious Collège de France, an eminent historian and specialist in the history of diseases, and thus of famines, could not have had the required information in some corner of his head, in order to rectify the glib remark of the doctor, who was himself misled not by any incapacity or inability to know but by simple lightheadedness or ideological bias? And how can one explain the carelessness with which a major TV channel neglects to check the false figures provided to it by the Terre des Hommes group and blindly transmits them to millions of TV viewers without, furthermore, arousing the protests that should have been heard from some members of the public—and this in a country that is supposed to have one of the highest educational levels in the world?

Doubtless it will be objected that it is not the job of the media to provide a "magisterial lecture" supported by "boring" figures, but rather to arouse the pity and thus the generous response of the watching masses. But this argument is fallacious, for the artificial inflation of figures can easily provoke discouragement instead. Why should the citizens of wealthy countries go on aiding the Third World if it is repeatedly dinned into them that the standard of living in Third World countries has been declining ceaselessly? In fact, from 1960 to 1984 the improvement in real income per inhabitant was on the order of 22 percent in Africa, 122 percent in Asia, and 162 percent in Latin America.* Yet throughout those years the slogans that triumphed were those that would have us believe that the "gap" (between rich and poor) is constantly "widening" and that "poverty is increasing" with each passing hour.

A sense of human solidarity is best aroused by the feeling that generosity has some chance of being effective. When confronted with only a few famine areas in which one or two million of our human brothers and sisters are threatened by death, the public in rich countries is likely to conclude that averting the worst is not impossible, that it can even be accomplished without too much difficulty, and that providing aid is all the more urgent as a duty since it can help those who dispense it to achieve concrete results. But if one begins by brandishing the specter of *fifty million* annual deaths and by speaking of a menacing, ever-mounting tidal wave, people simply feel overwhelmed. A disaster on such a cosmic scale defies the imagination and leaves us with a feeling of helpless impotence. These statistical phantasmagoria, far from inciting people to action, have the unpardonable effect of demobilizing energies by making any eventual assistance look as ridiculously small as a piece of bread floating on a sea of corpses. The aim of such ideologists, of course, is not to succor the unfortunates, it is to damn capitalism. Myths, far better than reality, serve this ideal.

*The OECD Observer, no. 143, November 1986 (Paris: Organization of European Cooperation and Development).

Thus, in dealing with the Third World as well as with developed countries, we encounter the malady I described earlier: ideologists who no longer believe in their ideology but who fight even more hotly to defend it. The Leftists know socialism has failed, but they are all the more determined to condemn liberals as being "reactionaries." Why? The socialists have become "pragmatic" liberals, they are now trespassing on the liberals' "hunting ground," but they don't want to confirm their own conversion. They must thus find a way of denoting their differences, by proclaiming that the liberals have become rightists, and that they alone, the socialists, have discovered liberalism "with a human face." Thus "recentered," the socialists maintain the illusion of their cultural identity by pushing the centrists over to the right.

The astonishing prosperity and apparent invulnerability of ideological falsehood, above all when it concerns raw facts rather than complex interpretations, raises a question that is not without significance. To what practical consequences can the activity of human beings lead, and what control can public opinion exercise over this activity, if both are inspired by notions so far removed from reality? And why should this be the case at a time when realistic assessments and solid information are, in almost all domains, so readily available?

CHAPTER 9

The Need for Ideology

What is an ideology? It is a triple form of dispensation: intellectual, practical, and moral.

The intellectual dispensation consists of retaining only facts favorable to the thesis one is defending, even, if necessary, inventing them, and of denying, omitting, or forgetting others to keep them from becoming known.

The practical dispensation suppresses the criterion of effectiveness in judging policies, depriving setbacks and failures of all refutational value. One of the functions of ideology is also to fabricate explanations that absolve it. Sometimes the explanation is no more than a mere affirmation, an act of faith: "It is not to socialism that one should impute the difficulties encountered in their development by socialist countries," wrote Mikhail Gorbachev in *Perestroika*. Reduced to its logical armature, this sentence amounts to saying "It is not to water that one should impute the problems of humidity that afflict flooded countries."

Finally, for the ideological protagonists the moral dispensation abolishes all notion of good and evil; or rather, for them it is the service due to ideology that replaces morality. What is a crime or a vice for the common run of mortals is not one for them. The ideological absolution of murder and genocide has been dealt with at length by historians. The point is less often made that ideology sanctifies bribery, nepotism, corruption. So lofty is the idea that socialists have of their own morality that, listening to them, one is almost ready to believe they make corruption honest by indulging in it and that their virtue is untarnished when they succumb.

Since it exempts one from the sway of truth, honesty, and efficacy and accordingly offers such great conveniences, it is hardly surprising that ideology, cropping up under a variety of other names, should have enjoyed the favor of human beings from time immemorial. It is not easy to live without an ideology, for one is then confronted by an existence that comprises nothing but particular cases; each demands an appropriate knowledge of specific facts, with the attendant risks of trial and error in action, possible serious consequences for oneself, dangers of suffering and injustice for other human beings, and the likelihood that the person who has to decide for himself what to do, being unprotected by any ideological carapace, will subsequently be overcome by remorse. There are no such problems for the ideologist, who soars above goodness and truth, who is himself the source of the True and the Good.

Let us take, for example, the case of a cabinet minister well known for his uprightness, his devotion to human rights, his love of liberty. Yet he would not hesitate to bring pressure to bear on an administration and to resort to threats to have his wife, in defiance of normal procedures, appointed professor in a leading university and to have the incumbent removed. Such a despotic abuse of power giving rise to rank family favoritism—which he would bitterly denounce if he saw it practiced by somebody outside his own camp—ceases to seem shameful when it emanates from himself. This is not individual complacency, a banal psychological mechanism. Rather, it is because this man is not isolated, he is accompanied and upheld by the sacred substance of his ideology, which cushions his conscience and leads him to think that, himself being the source of all virtue, he is capable only of good actions. "In order to understand how it can be that a man should be at once zealous in his religion yet greatly debauched," Pierre Bayle once wrote, "one need but consider that in most men the love of religion is no different from other human passions. . . . They love their passions as others love nobility or their homeland. . . . To think, therefore, that the religion in which one has been raised is exceedingly good, and to practice all the vices it forbids, are extremely compatible things."* In its early stages an ideology is a crucible of beliefs that, though devastating, can nobly inflame minds. In its final stages, it degenerates into a syndicate of personal interests.

Although ideology possesses no immediate efficacy in the sense that it does not solve any concrete problems (since it is not derived from an analysis of facts), it is conceived with a view to action. It tranforms reality, indeed far more powerfully than exact knowledge does. This, in fact, is the very subject matter of this book. Ideology is ineffective in the sense that it does not provide the solutions announced in its program. Thus the collectivization of land brings not abundance but poverty. It nevertheless has a prodigious capacity for affecting the real world since it can impose an economic aberration that is fatal to agriculture on hundreds of millions of human beings. In other words, collectivization is not an agricultural truth; it is an ideological reality that, though destructive to sound agriculture, has been far more concretely disseminated during the twentieth century than simple agricultural notions have. If to the USSR, China, Vietnam, and Cuba we add the many Third World countries in which experiments with collective farms, bureaucratic norms, and state control have ruined traditional agriculture without replacing it with a truly modern agriculture, we discover that in our times ideological delirium has had at least as great a run as rural pragmatism.

During the final third of the twentieth century, productive agriculture—one capable of producing large annual surpluses—has been concentrated in a mere handful of regions of the globe: North America, Western Europe, Australia, New Zealand, Argentina. These areas, which have a "capitalist" agriculture, constitute the planet's agricultural reserve, the breadbasket of the world, while at the same time assuring many of their farmers of a high standard of living. Almost everywhere else (with a few rare exceptions—Brazil and India among others) experiments have been made more or less systematically with collective or cooperative formulas that have provoked the collapse of production, accompanied by poverty, hunger, and famines. This devastating balance sheet, which can be read at a glance, has not kept the ideologists, even those who do not explicitly profess Marxism, from continuing to advocate the same "agrarian reforms" of a bureaucratic, centralized-management type each time they examine the case of a Third World country.

*Pensées diverses, CLV.

Ideology is a classic example of one of those familiar notions whose seeming clarity vanishes as soon as we try to define it with precision. Coined around 1800, the term first designated the study of the formation of ideas, in the simple sense of mental representations, and was later extended to embrace the philosophical school of Destutt de Tracy and Condillac. It was, however, Marx and Engels who, fifty years later, gave the concept of "ideology" the meaning which, at once rich and confused, it has basically preserved to the present day.

Ideology, according to their theory, was the constellation of notions and values that are destined to justify the domination of one social class by another. Ideology, according to them, cannot be regarded simply as falsehood—it does not exclude sincerity, since the social class benefiting from it believes in this falsehood. This is what Engels called "false consciousness." The prevailing falsehood can, however, also seem true to the exploited class, a form of aberration that was baptised with a term which likewise became famous—"alienation."

Ideology seems to have been born under the star of contradiction. How, if it is illusion and falsehood, can it be effective? Even though ideology, by virtue of some of its characteristics, can be termed irrational, it should be noted that many ideologists have claimed, not always unjustly, that they were supported by scientific argumentation. To be sure, they refuse to heed displeasing arguments and facts—something that is the very negation of the scientific spirit. Most of them end up with the kind of irrational ratiocination and verbal mystification that we normally refer to as "double-talk." Still, every ideologist believes and gets others to believe that he possesses a global system of explanation, founded on "objective" proofs. Marx finally managed to integrate this particular aspect into his general theory. But what of it? Many sociologists as eminent as Talcott Parsons, Raymond Aron, and Edward Shils have retorted: in no case does ideology depend on the distinction between true and false. It is an indissoluble mixture of observations of fragmentary facts selected for partial purposes, and of passionate value judgments, which are manifestations of fanaticism, not of knowledge. For Shils the influence exercised by the ideologist is akin to that of the prophet or religious reformer, not to that of the scientist, no matter how misguided the latter might be.

An obvious objection springs to mind: Should religions not be distinguished from ideologies? Of course; but there exist religious reformers, such as Savonarola and Khomeini, who extend their religion into a political and social ideology, the totalitarian nature of which serves to legitimize the exercise of absolute power. In much the same way we can consider the revocation of the Edict of Nantes in 1685 and Louis XIV's subsequent persecution of French Protestants as having been as much an ideological as a religious act; since the notion of the divine right of kings to rule conferred on Catholicism the function of legitimizing absolutism. When prophets indulge in ideology, they become men of action and political leaders.

However, the criterion of fanaticism is not enough to elucidate just what an ideology is nor how, in practice, it is able to operate. We must therefore go back to our starting point and recognize that an ideology always includes an element which, if not rational, is at least "comprehensible" (as Max Weber used to say), along with a dose of effectiveness. This is all the more necessary since ideology—and this is one of its main components—acts on masses and renders them active. Sometimes it shapes an entire civilization, or at least a social or cultural segment thereof: intellectuals, cadres, workers, students. One can only begin to talk of an ideology with respect to collective beliefs. The solitary ideologist is relatively inoffensive. For Lenin ideology was—as it remains for his successors—a weapon of combat in a war of classes for the world-wide triumph of the revolution. It is thus far more militant than the mere prejudice, the consoling illusion, the humdrum error, the absolving excuse, the soft mania, or the conventional platitude, although it includes and feeds off all of these. A conventional notion can be passive, whereas ideology is always active and at the same time collective.

Sometimes among moralists and novelists one finds the mystery of ideological crystallization portrayed in all of its awesome plenitude. It is hardly necessary to mention certain well-known classic works on the subject—the story of the Grand Inquisitor in Dostoevsky's *Brothers Karamazov,* or *The Possessed.* There are also some precious insights to be found in the "Genealogy of Fanaticism" in Emile Cioran's *Précis de décomposition* and in his *Histoire et Utopie.* Or again, in Mario Vargas Llosa's *The Story of Mayta,* the superb, stifling portrayal of the birth and growth of a terrorist ideology in a certain group. The novelist makes us relive from within a concrete case of a delirious and at the same time carefully reasoned vision, experienced and above all translated into acts by specific individuals. It could be the story of the founders of the Peruvian "Shining Path" movement, those professors of Maoist philosophy who (like the Khmer Rouge of Cambodia) are persuaded that they have the right to kill all those who oppose their plans.

For ideology is a mixture of strong emotions and simple ideas, linked to a certain mode of behavior. It is at once intolerant and contradictory. Intolerant, because it is incapable of acknowledging that anything outside itself exists. Contradictory, because it is gifted with a strange faculty for acting in a manner opposed to its own principles, without, however, having the impression of betraying them. Repeated failures, furthermore, never lead to a challenging of these principles; all they do is to incite believers to be more radical in their implementation.

In his book *L'Idéologie* (1986) the sociologist Raymond Boudon produced some illuminating studies of historical and contemporary cases of ideology. He analyzed *L'Esprit du jacobinisme,* as viewed by Augustin Cochin; Third Worldism and the "theory of dependence"; and the Lysenko affair in the USSR. With respect to the last, it seems to me that he underestimates two traits of ideological behavior. The first is an abstract fidelity to orthodoxy, even if "praxis" has to be sacrificed. "For it is exceedingly true," as Jacques Monod wrote, "that the fundamental basis of classical genetics is incompatible with both the spirit and the letter of the dialectic of nature, as propounded by Engels." The other somewhat overlooked aspect is the fact that the practical implementation of Lysenko's theories was one of the causes of the backwardness of Soviet agriculture—a fine example of the indifference ideologists show to the setbacks reality inflicts on them. How is one to explain the "rationality" of a suicidal ideology? Above all Raymond Boudon excels when he portrays the ravages of ideology in his own field of sociology, and in the philosophy of science. His analysis of certain books that enjoyed enormous prestige during the previous quarter of a century permits one to realize once again how strong, in intellectual circles, are the impulses "that confer the authority of science on conventional ideas." The furious, dogmatic reaction of the ideologists of antipsychiatry to the discoveries made as to the organic causes of schizophrenia—a subject I will return to later—well illustrate this "derivation," as Pareto would have said, no less than the erudite charlatanism of the first racist theories toward the end of the nineteenth century.

Marx and Engels popularized the term "ideology" by incorporating it into the socialist vocabulary in their work *German Ideology,* which was finished in 1846, and the word has since been used above all in a political sense and context. Even before socialist thinking had become a major intellectual current in the early nineteenth century, the French Revolution and the "enlightened" philosophers of the eighteenth century who paved its way had reduced all ideologies to political ideologies. Since then—and this has been particularly true of the twentieth century—when we speak of "ideological struggles" or desire a possible "end of ideologies," it is understood that political doctrines are involved. For the average reader or listener, this goes without saying. Even Islamic fundamentalism has less impact in the purely religious domain than it does as a political movement clothed in religious justifications. It is in this respect that it affects us, manifesting itself above all as the hatred felt by part of the Third World for the democratic civilization of the West and their wish to destroy it. Tocqueville had already shown us "how the French Revolution was a political revolution which proceeded to act in the manner of religious revolutions."* It was not destined to be the last. However, certain religious revolutions have evolved like political revolutions. This is no new curse. The crusades of the Middle Ages and the sixteenth century's wars of religion were as much political as religious. Religions have often served as ideological vehicles for wars of conquest and colonization, forcibly imposing on the vanquished a radical metamorphosis of society—as Islam did in the Maghreb and Christianity did in the New World. It is quite normal that in our day we should be reminded of political examples when we think of ideology, just as before the eighteenth century people were always reminded of religious examples.

Even today, however, nonpolitical ideologies flourish. They can be found in philosophy, ethics, art, even science. If the principal characteristic of an ideology can perhaps be regarded as being its impermeability to "alien" information in order to protect an interpretative system, then it becomes clear that ideological "enrobing" immunizes entire constellations of convictions against assaults of reality in almost all spheres of thought and human activity. Ideology is political when it tends toward the conquest or conservation of power. But not all ideologies are primarily aimed at wielding power, even though not one of them is entirely uninterested in this. To the craving for intellectual domination is added the desire to preserve the influence of a coterie, or of one's ability to apportion university posts, material resources, honorific satisfactions. The barriers erected against the dissemination of a new scientific theory are often the result of the all-too-human resistance of a generation or group of scientists whose careers, academic posts, and prestige depend entirely on the authority conferred on them by the theory that is in the process of being dethroned. Albert Einstein made the point himself. A discovery hardly imposes itself at all by forcing the intellectual conviction of the scientific community through demonstrations and proofs; it establishes its ascendancy far more through the gradual disappearance of the adherents of the old theory and their replacement in influential posts by a new generation of researchers. But no matter how influential

*Alexis de Tocqueville, *L'Ancien Régime et la Révolution,* Book I, Chap. 3

human weaknesses, vanity, hatred, rivalries, personal interests, and even intellectual blindness may be in quarrels that divide scientists, and no matter how much they may try to delay the diffusion or acceptance of new knowledge, it nonetheless remains true that in the field of science it is objective criteria and the accuracy of information that ultimately decide the debate.

Such is anything but the case for the immense tribe of doctrines that mix science and ideology or, more precisely, which consist of an ideology based on science, constructed out of elements that are borrowed from scientific disciplines and language. Marxism is the best known of these mixtures, but many others exist, and I would even say that it is this type of doctrine that above all generates and perpetuates human disputes, for the simple reason that they are neither totally verifiable nor totally refutable. They are thus admirably designed to keep passions running at fever pitch, and they usually disappear thanks to the weariness of the adversaries involved and to the lassitude of the public without any final proof having been provided to put an end to the discussions. But these hybrid mixtures occupy a far larger place in what is called "cultural life"; they take up far more time, result in the blackening of a far greater amount of paper, and arouse a far greater uproar on radio broadcasts and TV programs than "knowledge" *sensu strictu.* To understand, if not to be able to explain, this, we must admit that these hybrids satisfy an intellectual need: the need for ideology. Human beings experience all sorts of needs for intellectual activity other than the need to know. The *libido sciendi* is not, contrary to what Pascal said, the principal motor of the human mind. It is only an accessory inspirer, and only among a small number of us. The average human being seeks the truth only after having exhausted all other possibilities.

Terms like "rationalism," "positivism," and "structuralism" designate first of all a working method, then a hypothesis as to the nature of reality, and finally a global ideological vision. To be sure, behind all stages of scientific research there looms the theoretical image of the idiom in which a generation of intellects formulates its preferred apprehension of reality: mechanism or vitalism, "fixism" or evolutionism, functionalism or structuralism, atomism or gestaltism. Since the development of molecular biology, it is the vocabulary and representation of phenomena drawn from the worlds of computers and linguistics that have left their imprint on scientific sensibility, which expresses itself by means of "programs," "codes," and "messages." Michel Foucault used to call these partly conventional images "discursive formations." But Foucault maintained that they were entirely ideological, and he thereby sought to efface all distinction between science and ideology. Which amounted to saying that as far as he was concerned, there was no such thing as real knowledge, only different ways of viewing reality.

Foucault wanted to abolish the distinction between science, on the one hand, and a scientifically thematic ideology on the other, because this suppression is characteristic of this kind of ideology, in which he himself excelled. What characterizes the ideologist who propounds a scientific thesis is that he lays claim to being upheld by scientific demonstrations and experiments, while refusing any confrontation with objective knowledge, except on terms that suit him and on his specially chosen ground. His use of information simply mimics the scientific approach, which he does not regard as binding, and it possesses demonstrative value only for someone who has first embraced his ideology without prior questioning. To confront a scientific ideologist by objecting to the inexactitude of his findings or to the extravagance of his inductions is to be guilty of poor taste; it is a sign of malevolence, since the intrinsic thrust of ideological thinking is to make the value of the argumentation depend on the thesis that has to be established, rather than vice versa; or—expressed slightly differently—the value of the thesis does not depend on the solidity of the argumentation. The general public, during the period when a scientific ideology enjoys its favor, remains unaffected by refutations based on the checking of facts and the reasoning involved, simply because it does not demand any precise knowledge from this "discursive formation" but merely a certain gratification, which is both affective and dialectic.

Who can recall the dominion enjoyed between 1955 and 1965 over the minds of Europeans and Americans by the work of Father Teilhard de Chardin? It was difficult to escape its sway, difficult indeed to open a newspaper or book without coming across some reference to this work. Teilhard satisfied a strong ideological need, because he seemed to have conciliated Christianity and Darwinian evolutionism, human paleontology and cosmic spiritism. His works, marked by verbose grandiloquence and hermetic prolixity, became best-sellers. He delighted the Left no less than the Right (save for Christian fundamentalists), he was the intellectual inspirer of the Second Vatican Council, and for a whole decade he was virtually unassailable in liberal and moderate publications, as well as in the Marxist press, which, notwithstanding the thick fog of language, saw in him a magician capable of effecting the marriage of Marxism and Christianity. So bewitching indeed was the spell cast over intellectuals by Teilhardism that the only ones who, in the midst of this euphoric ecstasy, were not allowed a hearing were the biologists—at any rate the real ones, those who had retained enough lucidity to escape the prevailing ideological thrall and who were sufficiently intrepid to admit their doubts. Needless to say, the defense mechanisms of this particular ideology functioned day and night; thanks to a curiously spontaneous consensus in the vigilant intellectual community, they harshly repulsed, before they could be printed, any scraps of information capable of damaging Teilhard's lucubrations.

I was personally able to verify the effectiveness of this defense by trying for a long time and in vain to find a French publisher for an anti-Teilhard article that had been written by the English biologist Peter Medawar, a 1960 Nobel Prize winner for medicine. In 1962, during a trip to Oxford, I had come across this article while leafing through the philosophical journal *Mind*. Several Oxford friends who were either biologists or philosophers told me that this article had put an abrupt halt to the penetration of Teilhardism in Great Britain, because without polemical fuss it had simply pointed a finger at the weaknesses of the biological and paleontological information which had served as a springboard for Teilhard's lofty verbiage. I recrossed the Channel with a copy of *Mind* under my arm, confident that I could easily interest the editor of one or another of the French newspapers I then wrote for or with whom I was on friendly terms. But to my astonishment I encountered a strange resistance amounting almost to a brush-off. The article was too long, it was too technical, it was too English! In fact, it was written clearly, certainly far more so than Teilhard's diffuse gobbledygook. Technically, it was quite within the scope of any reader accustomed to reading scientific news items and commentaries in good newspapers. I obtained Medawar's permission to condense the text for the French version, retaining only the most striking examples of bogus biological and paleontological evidence. Nothing doing. I then realized I was up against a case in which science is powerless to thwart ideology. The ideological use of biology, like the later ideological use of psychiatry or linguistics by Michel Foucault and Roland Barthes, apparently exempts such adepts from having to appear before the tribunal of exactitude; they reject its competence, esteeming that it does not behoove them to have to furnish explanations to any narrow-minded "scientism."

The function of ideologies clothed in scientific vestments is to put the prestige of science at the service of ideology; it is not to subject ideology to the control of scientific method. The success of Teilhardism was due to the fact that it "reconciled the Catholic Church and modernity"—in the sense that it provided a verbal concoction and a metaphysical potion rendering Christian dogma compatible with the evolution of the human species and human paleontoltogy. All that was asked was that it fulfill this ideological mission. Obviously no one had read Teilhard's work with a view primarily to increasing one's knowledge of the sciences of biology and human life. But—and therein lay the ambivalence of this ideology—everyone had to *pretend* to have read it for this purpose, while resolutely abstaining from any truly critical examination of the work's "scientific" basis.

Medawar was accordingly regarded as the Devil incarnate, one who at all costs had to be silenced or discredited as being dull and devoid of imagination—even though, it is worth recalling, no political issue was involved. Hence the brush-off I received from my journalistic friends. Not that they were fierce adorers of the reverend Father. I would be more inclined to say that they didn't care two hoots about Teilhardism. But, being professionally alert and receptive to the circumambient atmosphere, they sensed that they had nothing to gain by printing Medawar; on the contrary, they risked being taken to task for "retrograde scientism" and for being insensitive to "boldness" and "modernity"—this last quality, curiously enough, usually being attributed to laborious patchings-up of archaic doctrines.

During a dinner with a friend, the historian Pierre Nora, I was delighted to hear François Jacob (who was to win the Nobel Prize for medicine in 1965) tell the editor in chief of an important weekly how interesting Peter Medawar's article was and what a good thing it would be if it were published in France. To my bitter surprise, the great biologist was no more successful than I had been in his efforts of persuasion, his incomparable authority notwithstanding.

Intrigued by the repeated rebuffs, I one day described them in detail to a highly cultivated gentleman who, after resigning as the cultural editor of an important magazine, was looking around for money with which to launch his own literary and philosophical publication. He was vastly amused by the ideological opportunism and the craven submission to current intellectual fads displayed by those "opinion makers" whose crass conformism I had just described. "All right," I said, "I'll take you at your word, and the day you launch your own newspaper, promise me you'll publish the Medawar piece in one of your first issues." He swore he would do so.

He kept his promise, but in the following manner. When the great day came, I opened the newly born paper with joyous expectation, only to receive a shock. Half of the front page was taken up by Medawar's article, the other half by a dithyramb in Teilhard's honor, which had been especially commissioned and written by one of the famous Jesuit's most assiduous promoters. It was thus no longer a case of at last allowing science to speak out against an ideological imposture; instead, two "opinions," announced as being strictly equivalent, were juxtaposed, one being "for," the other "against." The demonstrable argument and the pseudoscientific mishmash became two eminently estimable "viewpoints." The truth was still not strong enough to be allowed to stand on its own legs.

The crowning touch was inadvertently provided by the layout editor or his assistants, who had transposed the titles "For" and "Against." A large "FOR" in block capitals had been placed over Medawar's critical article, and a no less strident "AGAINST" majestically crowned the homily of Teilhard's extoller. This, as one can well imagine, further illuminated the debate for the general public! Three years later Teilhard de Chardin was no longer talked about. He had been replaced by another expert mixer of metaphysics and pseudoscience, with this time not Christianity but Marxism as the basic ingredient: the "philosopher" and political theorist Louis Althusser.

Althusser's ideological mixture, albeit similar to Teilhard's, was far more political. It was an offshoot as much as an affluent of politics, and thus an illustration of the most current kind of ideology. By its very nature, too, it catered to a need at once intellectual and emotional: the rejuvenation of Marxist doctrine at a moment when its explanatory power as a theory was crumbling into dust. Althusser's "seasoning" retarded this process of putrefaction by a full decade, and in certain places by two decades; for in 1987 when I was in the Philippines, I was still able to meet someone who was an Althusserian. The originality of the author of *Reading "Das Kapital"* consisted first of all of injecting into a moribund doctrine a few hormones drawn from what were then the liveliest disciplines: structuralism, Lacan-style psychoanalysis, linguistics, and the philosophy of "discourse."* This form of assistance is standard procedure in all operating rooms for ideological reanimation. But Althusser's originality consisted above all in not trying to save Marxism by "humanizing" it, as had repeatedly and naïvely been tried before. He understood that humanism, human rights, and democracy would lead communism into an impasse. An ideology cannot be reinvigorated by copying, or pretending to copy, its opposite. To put it on its feet again, one must add force and prestige to what is in it that is

---

*Jacques Lacan (1901–1981) was the most influential of modern French psychoanalysts. The psychoanalytical fashion he succeeded in launching in France is discussed in Chapter 12 (see pp. 379–80).

unique, to what in the time of its splendor constituted its supreme attraction for its genuine adherents. The irreplaceable essence of Marxism is not the notion of the class struggle, nor the equal sharing of goods, nor the elimination of harsh working conditions—all of them ideas developed before Marx by several historians, notably by Augustin Thierry and François Guizot, as well as the Utopians; it is the dictatorship of the proletariat and its practical historical application—which is to say, Stalinism. The sophisticated justification Althusser sought to provide for Stalinism—wherein, through a superbly provocative irony, the only reproaches he could make were, all things considered, certain unfortunate "bourgeois tendencies"—allowed Marxism to expire with a flourish, at any rate as a philosophy.

It is not merely our ability to consult documents and to think clearly in the scientific, historical, or philosophical domain that is inhibited and suspended by the need for ideology; it is even our capacity to observe commonplace facts as they are perceived by our visual, tactile, and auditory faculties. Even overlooking intentional liars, just think how many great intellectuals and journalists there have been during the twentieth century who perceived only abundance and prosperity in countries where entire populations were dying of hunger. These ideological hallucinations are anything but new. One of the purest examples from the past was the discovery of the South Pacific toward the end of the eighteenth century—by which I mean the way in which it was related in Europe.*

The "Tahitian lie" in effect was born from the encounter of the Europe of the Enlightenment, which had been nourished on fanciful notions about the "noble savage," with a local reality which those first observers studied in a most careless fashion and whose originality interested them but little. And yet—one could almost say unfortunately—the expeditions dispatched to Tahiti were deliberately composed of eminent, handpicked intellectuals, of scientists and fervent readers of *L'Encyclopédie*. This choice of observers provided excellent results in matters of botanical and astronomical observations. On the other hand, the moment the question of looking at social mores and customs came up, the "philosopher-navigators," as they have been called—the Britons

*On this subject, see the excellent book (containing an anthology of texts, a historical account, a bibliography, and commentaries) by Eric Vibart, *Tahiti—naissance d'un paradis au siècle des Lumières, 1767–1797* (Brussels: Editions Complexe, 1987).

Samuel Wallis and James Cook, the Frenchman Louis Antoine de Bougainville—seem all too often to have been incapable of seeing what was going on before their very eyes. Having embarked on the search for an existing Utopia, for a "new Cytherea," they made their dreams the raw material of their observations.

What they needed was an honest "noble savage." Accordingly, they said not a word about or else did no more than vaguely mention the incessant petty thefts of which they were the victims. The "noble savage" should be peace-loving; so regretfully and without harping too much on them did they take cognizance of the tribal wars that ceaselessly devastated the islands during the periods of their expeditions. When European vessels were attacked and sailors massacred, the European chroniclers more often than not effaced these unpleasant episodes from their accounts, preferring to stress periods of reconciliation and friendship with the Tahitians. Such moments, admittedly, were filled with pleasures, if only because of the sexual freedom reigning on the islands and the total absence of a guilt complex linked to erotic pleasure, the main topic of the moral reflections of contemporaries. Diderot particularly dwelled on this in his *Supplément au voyage de Bougainville.* But reading between the lines of these descriptions of voyages, one discovers that the exquisite Tahitian girls did not yield without receiving something in exchange, and that the price paid for their love, carefully reckoned according to their youth and beauty, was fixed in advance by virtue of a common accord. A practice, in other words, that was not so different from that which used to be indulged in in the gardens of the Palais Royal and other Paris pleasure spots, where Bougainville, a cultivated and worldly libertine, was a notorious and much-appreciated habitué.

Should not the "noble savage" be an adherent of liberty? Of course. For that reason these philosopher-navigators never willingly perceived the rigorous division of Tahitian society into four highly stratified social classes. Unaffected by any superstition, the Oceanian, we are told, reveres no idol—which shows what poor eyesight these navigators had. The Polynesian, they inform us, is vaguely deist. No doubt he has read Voltaire's *Dictionnaire philosophique,* and he adores the "supreme being." So here he is, a precursor of Robespierre!

Only reluctantly did these enlightened gentlemen, who came from a realm of civilized cruelty to contemplate the Natural Goodness of the Savage, nevertheless concede that the Tahitians, notwithstanding their philanthropic penchants, indulged in human sacrifices and infanticide. Another regrettable failing: many of the Oceanic peoples were cannibals. Furthermore, Cook, who, all things considered, was the most lucid of the explorers of this time, was shorn of all his illusions on this subject thanks to a final ethnographic observation. He ended his career most ingloriously inside the stomachs of several natives of the Hawaiian Islands. In short, writes Eric Vibart, "the Tahitian was never presented such as he was, but only as he was supposed to be in order to accord with the essence of the dream." And that is why, today as yesterday, it is so difficult to struggle against falsity and its everlasting sources, most of which are within ourselves.

On the basis of this particular slice of our cultural history, we might be tempted to infer—paradoxically enough—that the worst foe of information is the eyewitness. At least this is the case—and, alas, all too frequently—when the eyewitness reaches the scene stuffed with prejudices and is irresistibly inclined to flatter those members of the public to whom he will later report. The example of Polynesia and eighteenth-century literature is far from being an isolated case. From time immemorial, human beings have projected their political dreams onto distant lands, or have brought them with them.

Falsehood, as well as involuntary or semiconscious blindness, springs from the fact that we use external or distant realities as basic elements in the ideological battle waged in our own civilization, even sometimes in the most trivial and ephemeral political debates in whatever country happens to be ours. In 1975 French socialists denied the existence of any totalitarian plot in Portugal, for fear that admitting that there were signs that Lisbon was threatened by a communist takeover, which was clearly perilous for the country's newly born democracy, might reflect unfavorably on the reputation of the (socialist-communist) Union of the Left in France. Any journalist who unflatteringly described what he saw going on in Lisbon was immediately accused of wanting to harm the Union de la Gauche in France. Portugal had no right to an autonomous existence! Its contemporary history had to furnish arguments for or against the socialist-communist Common Program of the French. Thus, instead of an increase of information based on firsthand experience being used to guide action, it was a preprogrammed action that served to regiment information. In the same way, during the prerevolutionary period of the eighteenth-century philosopher-navigators, the common belief in the "noble savage," whose natural goodness was thought to have escaped the corrupting influence of civilization, despotism, and "superstitions," was in Europe a key element in the ideological framework of the century of the Enlightenment. To have brought back from the Pacific observations establishing that the state of nature, or what passed for it, offered traits that were sometimes far more inhumane than our own meant taking the risk of shaking this particular structure to its foundations; it amounted to saying that Hobbes was right and Rousseau wrong. As almost always happens, the fear of provoking a domestic uproar superseded people's concern for universal truth.

The scientific mind—unless a powerful constraint bears down upon it, as in physics and biology—can also fall prey to ideology, notably when one is dealing with sociobiology, sociology, anthropology, and history. I am not referring here to the ineluctable relativity of the observer's point of view in the human sciences—the theory of which Raymond Aron, following in Max Weber's footsteps, elaborated in his *Introduction to the Philosophy of History.* This relativity, which is inherent in the very conditions of historical awareness, presupposes the elimination of the *subjective* factors that distort information. Without attaining an almost inconceivable objectivity—which is to say, a complete concordance between concept and object—it can at least tend toward impartiality. It is, however, this impartiality that ideology sometimes harms when the very nature of the scientific discipline offers a measure of imprecision to observation and in practice withdraws the observer from the control of the scientific community. For example, Claude Lévi-Strauss, in *Le Cru et le Cuit* (The Raw and the Cooked), virulently denigrates the *Bororo Encyclopedia,* put out by the missionary fathers of the Order of Saint François de Sales. He is pitiless in contesting the exactitude and even the veracity of the observations recorded in the encyclopedia, which is devoted to Bororo society. Given the fact that these Brazilian Indians have been studied by nobody except the Salesian Fathers and Lévi-Strauss, one develops a certain anxiety in discovering that these scientists, though a mere handful, cannot agree—not on an interpretation, but even on the basic facts of the life of a tribe comprising hardly more members than their own small circle of Indian-studying anthropologists in Brazil.

Lévi-Strauss's ire is due to the fact that the Salesian Fathers are not "structuralists" and that certain facts they have recorded undermine his structuralist interpretation. The ideological deformation—if such there be, for it is impossible for an "outsider" to settle the question—is in this case purely epistemological. There is nothing political about it. A scientist clings to his interpretational frame of reference and rejects rebellious facts and those who dare record them. This is a fairly frequent cause of information rejection, and in a way it is inherent in science. However, many other causes of this kind of rejection may be external to science as such, and are derived from moral, religious, political, or cultural prejudices having nothing to do with the subject being researched.

One may recall the polemical debate aroused by the work of Margaret Mead four years after her death in 1978. Her critics claimed that in two major works that for decades had been regarded as basic textbooks for all students of anthropology—*Coming of Age in Samoa* (1928) and *Sex and Temperament in Three Primitive Societies* (1935)—Mead had embellished the mores of the Oceanic islanders who were the objects of her investigations. In reality, it was said, their habits were far less "soft" than she had depicted them, and she was accused of having deliberately omitted mentioning certain neurotic traits, depressions, repressive cruelty, and the rapacity characterizing many aspects of behavior in those societies. A disciple of Franz Boas and faithful to his "culturalist" school, Mead was alleged to have revived the "left-wing" ideology of the eighteenth-century philosopher-navigators and to have been influenced by "Third World" prejudices (even before the term had been coined); that is, she had apparently idealized the "cultural identity" of primitive societies in order to contrast them to the hypocrisy, the selfishness, and the rapacious violence of the industrial capitalist societies the white man had produced.

This idealization of non-Western societies sometimes exposes "liberals" to surprises, or prompts them to measure the morality of distant societies according to criteria that are completely opposed to those they use to judge their own. I remember how dismayed and dumbfounded a German Protestant clergyman in Windhoek, Namibia, once was when the sermon he was delivering to a congregation of Protestants, almost all of them black, was suddenly interrupted by roars of laughter after he had uttered the virtuous words: "Let's not forget—the Bochimans are human beings, like any other!" This well-intentioned clergyman had just discovered that blacks, too, have their "inferior races."

More righteous and above all more illogical was the correspondent of *The Washington Post,* the quintessence of the American "liberal," who showed himself without pity for his own society as well as of a limitless indulgence for the customs of Saudi Arabia, the Third World country he had singled out in order to bestow on it the balm of his understanding solicitude. On January 19, 1987, *The Washington Post* published an article entitled "Saudi Justice Looks Savage to Us, but It Works," over the byline of David Lamb, the newspaper's former Middle East correspondent. There was something not a little surprising about this article, written by a "liberal" who was convinced of the pointlessness of an excess of penal deterrence for the United States and published in a newspaper as rightly preoccupied by human rights in Western democracies as *The Washington Post.* The journalist began by admitting that the punishments prescribed by law and often applied, furthermore in public, by Saudi justice—whipping, amputation of the hand, decapitation, stoning—"may seem" brutal according to "Western standards." But this is precisely the point, he wrote; we should rid ourselves of ethnocentric criteria and understand that this system of justice derives from the Sharia, Islamic law, which, being of sacred origin, allows for no softening of sentences due to the indulgence of judges or the evolution of local mores. Even the presence of a lawyer, when a suspect is forced to make a confession, is a Western custom we have no right to ask an Islamic country to adopt without gravely offending the Moslem mentality through incomprehension and disrespect. Above all, this mode of justice—to us so seemingly barbaric—presents a marked advantage: it is efficient! The proof? According to 1982 statistics, David Lamb goes on, 14,000 crimes and petty offenses were committed in Saudi Arabia for a total population variously reckoned at between six and eleven million inhabitants according to estimates which, if I may be pardoned for insolently pointing this out, make one marvel at the precision of Saudi statistics. Now in that same year of 1982 half a million crimes and petty offenses were committed in the city of Los Angeles, which has a population of seven million inhabitants. In other words, forty times as many! Eloquent figures, indeed! And so the journalist concluded by quoting approvingly these words uttered by a U.S. university professor, a wise man and a specialist of the Sharia whom he had met in Riyadh: "Well, in this country it is true. So they cut off a few hands of guilty people and avoid horrors like rape and murder. Can you really say that makes them barbaric and us civilized?"*

This eminent Islamic scholar glossed over the fact that rape and murder are punished not by the amputation of a hand but by whipping, which is often carried out until the victim is dead, or by beheading. Petty thieves are punished by amputation. And how does Mr. Lamb, who is surely a partisan of the sexual revolution and of women's liberation in the United States, justify the punishment reserved in Saudi Arabia for adultery, in particular for the adultery of *the wife only,* which consists of burying her under a heap of stones in a public lapidation? True, this

---

*The remarkable thing is that such opinions should be professed by intellectuals who at home consider police checks of individual identities—admittedly of a non-"cultural" identity—to be violations of human rights.

type of execution has been modernized since biblical times; no longer does a vile, sadistic mob throw stones at the adulterous woman. In today's Saudi Arabia a heavy truck filled with stones is driven onto the square and they are unloaded at one time onto the unfortunate female, who is knocked senseless and buried under the resultant avalanche.

Notwithstanding this technical and humanitarian progress, this particular journalist was gripped by a sudden fear: that his praise for Saudi "penal law" might provide unhealthy arguments to advocates of the death penalty *in America* and of more repressive justice *in the West.* He then indulged in a confused and laborious effort at rectification, going as far as to imagine that Saudi crime statistics might be lacking in reliability and to suggest that, if Arabs commit so few crimes, it is less because of the deterrent influence of repression than because they form a "society that believes in the sanctity of the family, a religious, moral people."

How can one explain this chaotic mixture of veneration of atrocious customs and ludicrous recantations? First of all, through the well-known taboo concerning absolute respect for the "cultural identity" (of foreign peoples), which prohibits Mr. Lamb from judging and condemning a non-Western civilization. In this surprising case the all-powerful taboo seems invested with a positively miraculous power, considering that Saudi Arabia, in the eyes of a liberal, can only be regarded as a reactionary land. No progressive parameter capable of providing him with an excuse can here be applied. Second, Iran's Islamic revolution and Moslem fundamentalism have created a current in the Left that is favorable to Moslem fundamentalism wherever it is to be found, as well as to the moral, spiritual, and political virtues of Islam—which are doubtless great, though perhaps not those of its manifestations described and so prized by *The Washington Post.* Third, praise for the Sharia above all serves the sacred mission of denigrating Western civilization, but in a way that leads to the height of ideological absurdity, since the *Post*'s worthy journalist forbids us to imitate the model he lauds for fear of falling prey to repressive perversion.

In elaborating the notion of ideology in its modern sense, Marx and Engels unquestionably illuminated one of man's sovereign psychic properties. That our convictions, our vision of the world, our opinions on Good and Evil do not for the most part stem from inherently intellectual motivations and cannot therefore be refuted or modified by thought alone, are things that La Rochefoucauld, Pascal, La Bruyère, and

Chamfort had already clearly formulated and illustrated with a subtlety of detail far richer and more varied than that of the two founders of communism. But the latter had the merit of formulating a precise and global theory, one showing how our errors, to the extent that they emanate from causes external to thought, cannot be corrected solely by the effects of critical reflection, argumentation, and information. Up until then all philosophical treatises on the subject of error supposed it to be due to technical faults, defects of reasoning, insufficiencies of method, and a lack of rigor in verification procedures. The moralists, and they alone, had the intuition that the human appetite for falsehood, the desire to be wrong, the thirst for lying to oneself, and the need to believe that it is in the name of Good that one does Bad doubtless play an even more powerful role in the genesis of error than do strictly intellectual failings—contrary to what the philosophers had proclaimed. These forms of behavior may even, in human beings, have constituted a primitive form of adaptation to reality. From the moment Man began to think, he felt frightened by knowledge. Man's ability to construct almost any theory in his mind, to "prove" it, and to believe it is limitless. It is equaled only by his capacity for resisting evidence that refutes it and his virtuosity in changing it—not by taking into account new elements of information that were hitherto unknown to him, but by responding to new practical or emotional exigencies.

Marx and Engels, with their theory of ideology—in their eyes sharply differentiated from "scientific truth"—were not propounding a simple return to pragmatism in judging social events. Pragmatism consists of maintaining that our concepts, although lacking in hard-and-fast theoretical objectivity, possess a practical objectivity as intellectual tools fashioned for and by action, with resulting dividends (what William James called the "cash value" of ideas). In the Marxist theory of ideology, on the other hand, concepts—such, for example, as the divine right of kings—are simply misleading and illusory justifications of a supposedly immutable social order, and thus mystifications that retard rather than promote the cause of human progress. At once subjective and collective, such ideological constructs separate us from concrete reality as much as from historical truth.

In matters of description Marx and Engels on the whole were right. But when it came to explanation, they were shallow in the extreme. Their hypothesis was applicable only to a limited proportion of ideological production. It was their contention that the sole source of ideology is the social class, the fact of belonging to a class, and the class struggle. The only ideology that exists is one of class.

The first weakness of this explanation is that it implies an oversimplified sociology of classes. Classes, according to Marx and Engels, are supposed to be homogeneous and surrounded by hermetic borders and to display no evolution, no overlappings, no osmosis, no mobility or progression, save through the revolutionary surgery brought about by the dictatorship of the proletariat. But the history of modern societies since the middle of the nineteenth century belies this summary schema. If the sole source of ideology were to be found in particular class interests, how simple everything would become! A rational treatment could then be applied to a rational cause. It would be easy to know just what to do. But nothing authorizes seeking solace in such a rudimentary analysis. Marx was not altogether unaware of this, since he forged the notion of "alienation" to designate the process whereby we often adopt the ideology of the class that dominates us. This paradox is based on a sociology that can still be considered rational, since it admits that the dominant class controls the means of communication, culture, and education and can exert a religious, political, and moral indoctrination which enables it to mold the mentality and beliefs of the dominated classes. Unfortunately, far less rational, although just as manifest, is the inverse alienation—that of dominant classes that adhere to an ideology contrary to their interests, indeed that of an entire civilization subscribing to intellectual constructions that aim to justify its destruction. Furthermore, it is possible to impose on the dominated class convictions that are at once hostile to the governing class and totally false. Finally, ideology presents a complexity that vastly exceeds the childish alternative of a dominating "superstructure" superimposed on a suicidal "alienation." Ideology, being more than a vulgar travesty of social relationships—which most of the time it expresses very poorly indeed and with which it often has no contact at all—can easily take the form of banal hypocrisy and seems more mysteriously to satisfy a highly spiritual need for falsehood.

The deformation of science through ideology stems from this need, which has no materialistic ingredient. Political prejudice, too, can exercise an influence on science, but more as a passion of the mind than as a literal transcription of the class struggle, more still by intellectual terror and its natural corollaries—conformity and fear. Bernard Lewis, a leading specialist in Islamic studies, has denounced the recent trend, now so fashionable in the United States and Great Britain and on the

European continent, to limit the recruiting of Middle East scholars to partisans of Islamic fundamentalism and Palestinian militantism.* This, we are told in "scholarly" Western journals that are openly subsidized by Colonel Gaddhafi's Libya, is an indispensable guarantee of "objectivity." The most astounding thing is that this definition of "objectivity" should be upheld by eminent English, American, and French "Orientalists." If the Greeks alone had the right to write about Greek thought, we would have to burn the works of Zeller, Gomperz, Werner Jaeger, Rodier, Brichard, and Guthrie. According to this extraordinary "logic," even for teaching posts in Western universities, Middle East specialists should preferably be chosen from among Arabs, in any case from among Moslems, and in no case from among Jews, to which this profession should be forbidden. Bernard Lewis cites a Pakistani journal which rejected the moral competence of the great Islamic and Arabic scholar Évariste Lévi-Provençal (1894–1956), author of *History of the Moslems in Spain.*

The idea that to be able to work on Islamic civilization, even on that of medieval times, it is necessary to sympathize with present-day Islamic radicalism and fundamentalism has already begun to spill over into other disciplines. A high proportion of the Hispanic scholars who have taught in U.S. universities since 1960 have been sympathizers of Fidel Castro. This kind of servility can perhaps be explained, if not excused, on the part of Soviet or Chinese scholars who are afraid of no longer being able to obtain the visas to enter China or the USSR needed to pursue their research. But is it absolutely necessary, in order to maintain one's competence in the history of Hispanic civilization, to be assured of access to Cuba, which is simply a tiny fragment of the Hispanic world, an interesting one, no doubt, but not indispensable? Here the distortion of the scientific spirit can only be explained as due to ideological prejudice and conformism. One day I heard the editor of a famous French encyclopedia declare, during a TV program, that it was best to have a Castrista write the article on Castro, and to have a Marxist write the article on Marx. In this way, he told his audience, we would be assured of complete "objectivity."

According to one curious conception of science, it seems that to specialize in a culture one must admire the political leaders of the moment in the country one is studying. This requirement, of course, is valid only for communist and Third World countries. Must students of

---

*Bernard Lewis, "The State of Middle Eastern Studies," in *The American Scholar,* Summer 1979, and "The Question of Orientalism," *The New York Review of Books,* June 24, 1982.

English culture and civilization join or applaud the Conservative Party when Margaret Thatcher is in power? John K. Fairbank, director of Harvard University's prestigious Center of East Asian Studies (a center that bears his name), in reviewing Simon Leys's *The Burning Forest* in *The New York Times* in 1987, wrote that Leys' indignation over the massive destruction of classic works of Chinese art that took place under Mao reflect an "elitist" point of view.* Thus a great China specialist so adores Mao that he can without batting an eyelash accept the destruction of half of the cultural patrimony to which he has dedicated his career! Let us suppose that the Djuma mosque at Isfahan, that of the Omeyyades at Damascus, the Medersa of Fès, and the Alhambra of Granada were all destroyed, and that an Islamic scholar of international repute should declare that it was "elitist" to shed a tear over these lost works of art. What an uproar that would cause! But as soon as it involves Mao Tse-tung, iconoclasm becomes respectable. I am waiting for the Italian scholar who, to illustrate the grandeur of the scientific spirit, will have the courage to inform us that if the Uffizi Palace in Florence, Saint Peter's in Rome, and perhaps the Palace of the Doges in Venice were burned to the ground, it would not be a great loss, save to a small elite—inasmuch as, to repeat Mr. Fairbank's formula, the artists to whom we owe those works of art "did not live in an egalitarian society." But quite *entre nous,* it seems to me that this eminent sinologist does not thoroughly know his subject if he imagines that communist China, or for that matter any communist country, is an "egalitarian society." Thus we see how ideology, pushed to its delirious extreme, can prompt genuine scientists, whose function it is to study and to know, to express smug satisfaction over the annihilation of their sources of knowledge.

When they change their minds, it is because the political leadership in the countries of which they are specialists has itself changed. Sovietologists who used to dismiss grim pictures of the Soviet economy and society in the 1970s as polemical and tendentious suddenly became of a merciless lucidity toward the Brezhnev era once Gorbachev began criticizing the "stagnation" of his predecessor. One wonders what role the "intellectual's mission against the powers that be" (to trot out the familiar cliché) or the "sacred independence of the researcher" play in such pitiable about-faces. In the same way Jonathan Chaves, one of the rare U.S. sinologists who did not prostrate himself before Mao Tse-tung's frozen feet, has pointed out—now that the Chinese Communist

*Simon Leys, *The Burning Forest: Essays on Chinese Culture and Politics* (New York: Holt, Rinehart and Winston, 1987).

Party has itself admitted the atrocities that were committed during the period of the Cultural Revolution (1966–76), it might have been expected that the "China experts" would indulge in a bit of self-criticism and admit they were wrong.* Not at all. They now admit that the Cultural Revolution—the "Ten-year Holocaust," as it is called in China—was a monstrous aberration, but they admit this not because they have understood the phenomenon but simply because they have continued to follow the Peking party line!

So the basic question, once again, is to determine of just what use this faculty of ours for thinking, this machine for receiving, storing, classifying, combining, and interpreting information is. In 1970 I devoted several pages of my book *Without Marx or Jesus* to analyzing *The Little Red Book* and other works by Mao Tse-tung, stressing the intellectual poverty, even the burlesque cretinism, of the Peking despot's apothegms. I was greatly relieved the next year when Simon Leys's liberating work *Les Habits neufs du président Mao* ("President Mao's New Clothes") appeared and I realized I was no longer alone in my opinion. But who will ever explain to us how millions of intellectuals all over the world, students and professors making up the elite of the world of higher education in democratic societies, could for five or six years have treated this tissue of pretentious nonsense as worthy of serious meditation? How could they have admired it except by switching off their intelligence and their cultural awareness? Those who did so were Free World intellectuals who were not forced to indulge in such an abdication of the mind. Theirs was both a willful and a disinterested stupidity in the manner of their egregious predecessors of the Stalinist period, they too having often been superior intellects—if we overlook their Stalinism. "What is one to say of a Romain Rolland, a Langevin, a Malraux, who admire and approve the so-called Soviet regime without being forced to do so by hunger or some degree of torture?" Boris Souvarine wrote in 1937. And Souvarine noted that the editorial board of the French Communist Party daily, *L'Humanité*, "is every bit the equal of *Pravda* in servility and meanness, without the excuse of being caught in the vicelike grip of a totalitarian dictatorship."†

In his *Chronicles* article Jonathan Chaves told how he personally knew of specialists of Chinese civilization who would have nothing further to do with a colleague if he had said something favorable about

*Chronicles, July 1987.
†In an article later published in an essay collection, *L'Observateur des deux mondes* (Paris: Éditions de la Différence, 1982).

Simon Leys's *Chinese Shadows.* * This is one more sample of the paradoxical phenomenon—professionals of intellectual life who are swayed
in their judgments and behavior by all sorts of forces except that of
intelligence. Like some sinologists, many sovietologists also commit the
shortsighted error of professing that in order to be worthy of studying
a country, one must approve of its leaders and all its customs. Once
again this curious criterion! Only convinced advocates of slavery should
be authorized to study Greek or Roman history, only pro-Nazis should
be allowed to study Hitler's history, only arsonists and the burners of
books and paintings should be deemed worthy of tackling the biography
of Savonarola. In the United States many sovietologists—though not all
of them, fortunately—were such worshipers of their subject matter that,
like Stephen Cohen, they had the dubious honor of seeing their books
translated into Russian and distributed in the Soviet Union, so closely
did these works coincide with the official theses of pre-*glasnost* Russia.

As a symptom of the annihilation of the scientific spirit through
passion, let me simply quote a phrase of Moshe Lewin's in the introduction to his *The Making of the Soviet System,* in which he denounced
what he irritably termed "the recent anti-Soviet fad in the French intelligentsia."† Lewin scornfully dismisses this anti-Soviet phenomenon with
a wave of the hand as a passing Parisian storm cloud, a futile, snobbish
craze. This is an example of how a historian, blinded by ideology, ceases
to behave like a historian and refuses to recognize the validity of a
cultural event which, contrary to his claims, is of the greatest importance. Since 1917 French intellectuals have been bogged down in arguments over Marxism-Leninism and the Soviet Union, in quarrels
concerning Stalinism, "socialism with a human face," the Marxist theory of knowledge, and dialectical materialism. Favorable or hostile, all
were "situated" with respect to this complex of theories and realities.
But after seventy years the debate has lost its substance and significance,
the Soviet question is closed, at any rate in the sense of its former acuity,
and there is general agreement among French intellectuals that Marxism is no longer of any interest, save as a philosophical doctrine like any
other. This is a significant historical shift, as significant as the last gasp
of medieval scholasticism was in earlier centuries. Yet one who claims
to be a historian refuses to understand this!

Ideological pressure was brought to bear and forcibly applied to

Ombres chinoises—first published by Robert Laffont in 1974, with new and amplified
editions in 1976 and 1978.
†Moshe Lewin, *The Making of the Soviet System* (New York: Pantheon Books, 1985).

science in the age of Copernicus, Giordano Bruno, and Galileo. But in our times this is no longer possible save in the historical sciences and sociology, far less—or almost not at all—in the more rigorous mathematical, physical, and biological sciences. Nevertheless, physicists do not hesitate to abuse their prestige as scientists to wage ideological battles outside the field of their competence or over questions that have no more than an ostensible link with their particular fields. This was and still often is the case with physicists who, being hostile to their country's nuclear armament for political reasons or because they are attached to the cause of unilateral pacifism, exploit their prestige as scientists to impress the public and, in the name of science, to bludgeon it with categorical judgments, which in reality are dictated by nonscientific motives.

Unlike most other intellectuals, scientific researchers—at least those who deal with specific sciences whose methods and aims make unverifiable affirmations difficult or impossible—are subjected to the demonstrational constraints inherent in their disciplines. But outside the sphere of their particular disciplines they can free themselves of such constraints if prompted by personal temperament or ideological bias. However, the intellectual rigor to which they are subjected by the strict standards of their scientific specialty—without which it simply could not exist—cannot be transposed outside the specific field of research. Some of the greatest scientists cease to be scientists as soon as they move away from their specialized fields. They are then capable of making incoherent pronouncements and uttering the silliest exaggerations. In other words, their intelligence, when applied to a general topic, can all too easily lack the built-in safeguards that scientific work, by virtue of its constitutive laws or *modus operandi,* imposes on them when they are actively engaged in research. While doing such research they have no choice. The issue is cut and dried. Either one proceeds according to the rules, or one is forced to quit. But outside the strictly scientific sphere the craziest impulses can take revenge. Partisan dishonesty, weak reasoning, and the arbitrary rejection or even falsification of facts, as well as a complex of personal resentments, can impair the healthy functioning of minds which, within the "sheepfold" of science, are among the finest in the world.

The false, odious, mendacious declarations made at one time or another by a Frédéric Joliot-Curie, an Albert Einstein, or a Bertrand Russell when venturing beyond the sphere of physics or mathematical logic constitute an anthology from which I shall draw on later. Nobody, of course, would dream of denying these great men, any more than scientists as a group, the right to profess any opinion they might have on any subject that interests them, without being confined to their particular specialty. They enjoy the same freedom to do so as other human beings. But intellectual imposture begins when they impose the hallmark of their scientific prestige on attitudes that seem to be derived from their particular competence, when in reality they are not. When a scientist proclaims his sympathies for this or that political party, he indulges in a venial propaganda operation, as do writers, actors, painters, all those who place a famous name at the service of a cause, even though the cause might call for qualities of judgment having nothing to do with those that make them excel in their main activity. This slight abuse of confidence, however, assumes an unpardonable gravity when the offender claims that there exists an internal and strictly scientific link between his knowledge as a scientist and his political or moral stance, the reality of which the general public obviously has no means of verifying. Such was the case in the early 1950s when Joliot-Curie exploited his prestige as a Nobel Prize winner in Physics in order to denounce the U.S. atomic bomb as harmful and praise the Soviet atomic bomb as eminently salutary to mankind. One can perfectly well be a genuine atomic scientist and yet formulate irresponsible affirmations on certain aspects of nuclear problems that have nothing to do with basic research—for example, problems of nuclear strategy. By a simple process of association, the public will readily believe that the opinions of a nuclear physicist on issues of nuclear strategy are more solidly based than those of a shopkeeper or a farmer. But this is not necessarily so. The latter discipline (nuclear strategy) is as distinct from the former (nuclear physics) as the management of an industrial enterprise is from macroeconomic theory. A Nobel Prize winner for Economics would not necessarily make a good president of a multinational corporation or even a good grocer.

As General Pierre Gallois has remarked, "Since its foundation (shortly after the end of World War II), the *Bulletin of the Atomic Scientists* has never let a month go by without announcing the imminence of a nuclear catastrophe."* The reason for this endlessly repeated error is that one can have a thorough knowledge of the structure of the atom and know various ways of liberating intra-atomic energy, and yet be an ignoramus in questions of strategy. If an atomic physicist wants to evaluate the risks of nuclear, or even conventional, conflict, whether

*Pierre Gallois, *Le Guerre de cent secondes* (Paris: Fayard, 1985). General Gallois is one of France's leading authorities on questions of nuclear strategy and deterrence.

or not he is a Nobel Prize winner, he must fulfill the same conditions as the ordinary citizen; he must study the balance of political, military, economic, and ideological forces between the great powers concerned, their alliance systems, their perceptions of looming threats, the level and nature of existing tensions in bilateral relations, as well as the multilateral implications of these relationships in regional conflicts and in indirect confrontations via Third World countries. Competence in geostrategy is not derived from competence one may have in theoretical physics—any more than a thousand years ago a blacksmith was more qualified than a shepherd to judge politics and strategy on the grounds that warfare was then fought with swords and that he was one who made them.

A first-class airplane manufacturer has *ipso facto* no prior claim to becoming an air force chief of staff or a minister of defense, any more than an automobile engineer has to becoming a crack race car driver. However, the *Bulletin of the Atomic Scientists* sees fit, under the authority of science, to publish any number of purely political articles. I was made personally aware of this in 1972 when an excellent physicist named Rabinovitch wrote a critical review in the *Bulletin* of my book *Without Marx or Jesus.* What had particularly irked him and motivated a violent attack was my thesis that the United States was neither a fascist society nor a society that was headed for fascism. At the time this thesis had astounded not only the Left in Europe but U.S. "liberals," who were particularly numerous in the country's scientific community. Because of the Vietnam War and—this goes without saying—without the slightest perception of the totalitarian danger posed to Southeast Asia by Hanoi, it was then a postulate of many U.S. intellectuals that the United States was entering a pre-Nazi period. I recall having been invited to or, to put it more graphically, flayed alive during a debate in New York in November 1971, at a kind of intellectual gathering—a "bureau of minds" (as Voltaire would have called it) called the "Theater for Ideas." The hall was packed with professors from the major universities of the Eastern Seaboard. The officiating panel was composed of John Kenneth Galbraith, who acted as moderator, Wassily Leontief (a future Nobel Prize winner for Economic Science), and Eugene McCarthy, who was still aureoled with his newfound glory as the "destroyer" of President Lyndon Johnson—first, because of his stubborn opposition in the Senate to the Vietnam War and second, because of his remarkable success in several primaries during the early part of the 1968 presidential campaign. In particular, the unexpectedly high number of votes cast for Eugene McCarthy during the New Hampshire primary, which is fa-

mous for being a positive or negative weather vane of the eventual
outcome of an election, demoralized Johnson and was a major factor in
persuading him not to run for office again. I might add, parenthetically,
that Senator McCarthy's exploit in New Hampshire is a classic example
of how false notions are formed and subsequently acquire an indestructible hold on the popular imagination. The "liberal" press played up the
result as a victory for McCarthy. It was without any doubt a significant
moral and political triumph. But arithmetically the senator arrived in
second place behind Johnson, who thus actually won. The surprise was
due to a less-than-expected gap between the two Democratic candidates
in an electoral system in which a president seeking a second term
traditionally faces little opposition within his own party. But the papers
gave the New Hampshire primary such a buildup that it soon came to
be accepted that McCarthy had "defeated" Johnson during this early
runoff. Everyone spoke of it as a historic fact, and I myself believed it.
Indeed, it was Eugene McCarthy himself who set me right during this
encounter at the Theater for Ideas.

It was, as it happened, the only interesting revelation he had to offer,
at any rate in the domain of facts. For I was granted more than enough
in the field of hallucinations. Briefly stated, Eugene McCarthy—and in
this he was backed by most of the audience and by all members of the
panel, including the moderator, who did very little moderating—accused me of having committed an evil deed in spreading the fable that
the United States was not headed toward totalitarianism. At this time
the prevailing slogan, one that had been coined by Dr. Benjamin
Spock—"America has entered fascism in a democratic fashion"—was
considered to be the *ne plus ultra* of political sagacity. Curiously
enough, I myself had the impression that I had written a book to the
glory of the U.S. Left (to the extent that the book was devoted to the
United States, which it was only partially, my main aim having been to
study a new type of social mutation). Had I not stressed the originality
of the United States' "cultural revolution" in the literal sense, since it
had emanated from the universities, and of the racial and media revolutions, both of which had started in the United States only to wash over
Europe considerably later, after 1968? Had I not emphasized the novelty
of a public opinion that for the first time had thwarted its own government in the hitherto "reserved" domain of foreign policy, and this for
essentially ethical reasons born of the Vietnam War (whether rightly or
wrongly was another question, which the future alone could answer)?
Looking back on my book today, I find that it was marked by a greatly
exaggerated left-wing optimism. If I was pretty much on target in de-

scribing the internal transformations, I underestimated the disasters that the new state of mind was going to prepare for us in foreign policy—and which the very structure of democracy perhaps renders inevitable. But what I said in 1970 was that the U.S. Left had won, both politically and culturally. In my opinion this was a deeper and more momentous fact of civilization than what could happen at the level of executive power. But the U.S. Left, like the European Left, refused to believe it. It had to have its "fascist" America, a kind of werewolf needed for its ideological comfort. On both sides of the Atlantic, leftists could interpret my disagreement, even though enunciated from a left-wing viewpoint, only as constituting a "shift to the right."

The acrimonious Rabinovitch, whom I met several months later at a friend's house in Washington, analyzed me in the same way in his article and later displayed the same attitude in our conversation. During our brief exchange he kept looking at me with the ambiguous commiseration one reserves for a criminal who is dying of cancer. Expressing compassion for the dying man combined with severity for the assassin, his gaze pierced me with its psychic laser, while his voice assured me that in principle he felt some esteem for the residual traces of *homo sapiens* that survived within me.

To return now to the heart of the matter, some degree of cheating is involved when a highly subjective opinion is wrapped in the authority conferred on it by scientific works that have nothing to do with that opinion. On the other hand—and this is something I am prepared to repeat six times, if necessary, to make the point—the element of imposture is enormously aggravated when science is introduced into the heart of the political bias, by conferring the appearance of demonstrable truth on phony data and fanciful inductions. In this case the scientist is no longer content to exploit his celebrity in order to propagate an ideological platitude that has nothing to do with his specialty. He abuses the confidence of the public by passing off as a product of scientific research a thesis that in reality did not emanate from it, which in fact was dictated by motives having nothing to do with his field of competence but which he clothes with the external trappings of scientific procedure, knowing that most of the persons receiving the message are incapable of verifying or even doubting the seriousness of the arguments advanced.

Many scientists have lent their support to a maneuver of this kind by helping, for example, to elaborate and spread the fable of a "nuclear winter." This expression means that any employment of atomic weapons would envelop the earth in a screen of radioactive dust which, by preventing solar energy from reaching us over a prolonged period, would hasten the death of all life on our planet, or at least assure the extinction of the human race. This terrifying vision of the future first made its appearance in 1982 in the form of a horror novel bereft of all scientific merit which was published in the Swedish ecological journal *Ambio*—a publication which, by the admission of its editor, was inspired by SIPRI—the Stockholm International Peace Research Institute. At the outset, therefore, the vision of a nuclear winter emanated from pacifist circles and organizations, which used it as a scarecrow in order to prod the democracies into adopting a policy of unilateral disarmament, and in particular to keep them from deploying medium-range "Euro-missiles" in NATO countries. Highly partisan groups of scientists advocating unilateral disarmament then came to the rescue— Physicians for Social Responsibility, the Federation of American Scientists, and the famous and particularly active Union of Concerned Scientists. These organizations collected funds from a host of eager foundations and then asked a team of researchers, directed by the astrophysicist and media star Carl Sagan, to prepare a report on the peril. Normally it is the custom, before an article on a particularly controversial subject is published in any top-level scientific journal enjoying an international reputation, to submit the text to what is called an evaluation by at least three of the author's (or authors') peers. But the report drafted by the Sagan team was, oddly enough, not subjected to this particular formality.* It was duly published without hindrance in the magazine *Parade*, whose editor in chief, a certain Carl Sagan, formulated no objection against himself. More serious in terms of negligence was its later appearance, again without the usual evaluations, in the prestigious journal *Science*. After which another article by Carl Sagan on the same theme—"Nuclear War and Climatic Catastrophe"—appeared a few days later in the most venerable of American magazines in the field of political science, *Foreign Affairs* (winter 1983–84).

In late October a conference, specially timed to coincide with the publication of the special issue of *Parade*, was held in Washington on the theme "The World after a Nuclear War." The speeches delivered on this occasion were quickly gathered together and published in a volume entitled *The Cold and the Dark*—as one can see, an innocuous title far removed from the frightening headlines used by the tabloid press to scare the wits out of casual readers, a method which, as we all know, "liberal" intellectuals scorn. Even before the TTAPS Report had ap-

*It is usually referred to now as the TTAPS Report, a name derived from the initials of its five authors—Turco, Toon, Ackerman, Pollack, Sagan.

peared in a scientific journal and before any "nonconcerned" scientists had had a serious chance to study it, the Kendall Foundation had offered the Washington public relations firm Porter-Novelli an $80,000 grant to launch a series of highly simplified and truly scary slogans, peremptory assertions that were bereft of any rational argumentation. Still not subjected to any scientific control and at the same time orchestrated in the name of "science," this media campaign was encouraged and promoted by the issuance of many videotape clips and the preparation of several films, the best known of which, *The Day After,* was distributed all over the world. Everywhere the prospect of a "nuclear winter" imposed itself as something scientifically proven, the press limiting itself for the most part to reproducing information contained in press kits and summary dossiers that had been made available to newspapers and TV networks before the integral publication of the TTAPS Report and before the critical reactions which, in spite of everything, eventually came forth from the scientific community.

These critical reactions, truth to tell, were initially of a notable discretion, doubtless inspired by the authors' fear of being accused of favoring nuclear war. The moral elegance and intellectual honesty a partisan spirit can display in this kind of debate are well known, particularly in university circles. If a strong conviction was soon reached in the plush lounges of the National Academy of Sciences that the climatological model of a nuclear winter was what, in popular parlance, might be called "hocus-pocus," few persons dared speak up and say so; for, to quote the pithy language used in 1984 by renowned physicist Freeman Dyson, the TTAPS report was "an absolutely atrocious piece of science, but I quite despair to set the record straight. I think I am going to chicken out on this one: who wants to be accused of being in favor of nuclear war?"*

Notwithstanding the natural fear of retaliatory blows from which the carnal envelope of the greatest minds is not exempt, within two years Sagan's report and *The Cold and the Dark* (which a book reviewer in *The San Francisco Chronicle* rhapsodically hailed as "the most important book ever published") fell into total disrepute in the eyes of the scientific community. Mouths at last began to open, and magazines began to publish refutations. Gripped by remorse, the editor of *Foreign Affairs* opened the pages of his quarterly (the summer issue of 1986) to an article written by two scientists employed by the National Center for Atmospheric Research, which made mincemeat of the article Carl Sagan had written three years before. Among other things the authors

*Quoted by Russell Seitz, "In from the Cold," *The National Interest,* autumn 1986.

wrote that "on scientific grounds the global apocalyptic conclusions of the initial nuclear winter hypothesis can now be relegated to a vanishingly low level of probability." Other articles that were every bit as severe began to appear in *Nature, Science,* and even *Ambio;* added together, they left no stone standing of the imaginary edifice built around the notion of a nuclear winter. The term, however, retained its force as a slogan, and throughout the world it continues to produce the effect desired by the pacifist groups that launched it. The devastating studies published in scientific journals will never be able to efface the impressions produced by the initial press, TV, and film campaign, particularly since the newspapers, which had given the latter great play, showed little interest in reporting the later critical reevaluations.

This example proves how a piece of intellectual hocus-pocus can receive the stamp of approval of "science" and be taken for Gospel truth by millions of human beings. As Pierre Bayle wrote close to three centuries ago: "If only we could see what goes on inside the minds of men when they choose an opinion! I am sure, were this possible, that we would reduce the suffrage of an infinity of people to the authority of one or two persons who, having propounded a doctrine which it was supposed they had profoundly examined, then pass it on to others who find it more convenient, given their natural indolence, suddenly to believe what they were told rather than to examine it painstakingly. In such a wise the number of credulous and idle sectarians, increasing from day to day, is a new encouragement to other men to rid themselves of the trouble to examine an opinion which they see to be so general and which they fully persuade themselves has become such only through the solidity of the reasons which were first used to establish it; finally one is reduced to having to believe what all believe, for fear of being taken for a troublemaker who wishes to know more by himself than all the others."*

There is no use being naïve about the truth in this matter. Even though refuted, the vision of a "nuclear winter" will survive in people's imaginations. In its January 23, 1986, issue, Great Britain's leading scientific journal, *Nature,* one of the foremost in the world, deplored the growing decline of objectivity in the manipulation of scientific data and the alarming casualness displayed by certain researchers in the affirmation of theories devoid of solid foundation. "Nowhere," *Nature* went on, "has this tendency been more striking than in the recent literature on

*Pierre Boyle, *Dictionnaire historique et critique,* first published in 1697; enlarged in 1702 and again in 1704–06.

Nuclear Winter, research which has become sadly notorious for its lack of scientific integrity." But according to Russell Seitz's disabused commentary in the previously quoted article, these belated rectifications in serious publications did not reach the masses. The harm to world opinion was done, and it is without remedy. A couple of months after the appearance of *Nature*'s refutation, *The New York Times* saw fit to publish an article in which Frederick Warner of SCOPE (Scientific Committee on Problems of the Environment) predicted that the lethal effects of a nuclear winter on the environment would cause four billion deaths. One year before, in September 1985, SCOPE, in an article published by *The Washington Post,* had contented itself with a mere two and a half billion dead.

Was this the case of a "useful lie," which might be excused to the extent that it really served the cause of disarmament and peace? But even if this had been the case, we should still ask ourselves if scientists have a mandate for falsifying data, even with praiseworthy intentions. If we say yes, then we also grant them license to falsify them in a blamable intention. Nobody denies Carl Sagan and his acolytes the right, as citizens, to profess and to propagate pacifist opinions. Their imposture arises because they present these opinions in their capacity as scientists and as though derived from duly verified scientific discoveries. Each man tends to believe that his political, religious, or ideological cause is a moral justification for all manner of deceits. But to yoke science to this hocus-pocus and to abuse the ignorance of the majority of human beings is to annihilate the authority of the only procedure Man has so far invented for subjecting himself to criteria of truth that are independent of his subjective preferences.

Or rather, impostures of this kind, which are more frequent than is commonly supposed, prove that even among scientists passion can win over professional conscience, once the uncertainty and the complexity of the data introduce enough confusion into the debate to allow an ideological lie to be disguised as the truth.

Furthermore, the cause for which the authors of the "nuclear winter" twaddle betrayed science is far from being pure. For in reality they were fighting not for universal disarmament, but solely for the disarmament of the West. Their campaign was designed to combat American military programs, which depended on the voting of congressional appropriations in 1983 and 1984, to stimulate anti-Americanism in the Third World, and to support European pacifists who were hostile to the deployment of intermediate-range missiles on the continent. It would have led not to an overall reduction but to an upsetting of the balance of armaments levels to the detriment of Western countries and the advantage of the Soviet Union. The latter was not taken in for a second, playing up in its concerted propaganda a "nuclear winter" theme that had been composed in the West. Ironically enough, it was the Soviet Academy of Sciences, as well as certain Soviet scientists attending the Fourth International Conference on Nuclear War in Sicily, who courageously expressed reservations about the seriousness of their U.S. colleagues' overly bold hypothesis. Their scruples were immediately swept aside and their voices reduced to silence by their own propaganda services, led by the veteran Central Committee member Boris Ponomarev.

Using a long-tried and -tested technique, Soviet propaganda organs are particularly adept at relying on investigative work accomplished by Western scientists or authors in order to propagate theses hostile to the West. For example, in an article that was published in 1984 by *Moscow News* and later distributed in the form of a booklet by UNESCO's documentation service (need this surprise us?), they invoked the ideas of Paul Ehrlich, one of the "traveling salesmen" of "nuclear winter" and a biologist already known for having palmed off an earlier pseudoscientific prophecy in 1968 with his book *The Population Bomb*—of which more later.

If scientists guilty of abusing the prestige of science and the credulity of their fellow citizens had been seriously concerned about peace, they would not have worked so hard to create a current of opinion favoring an upsetting of the nuclear arms balance to the benefit of the Soviets. For as a result of this current, it is the peoples of the West alone who put pressure on *their* governments to reduce *their* armaments. But the real risk of war resides in unilateral disarmament. If they were willing to study the experience so far acquired with a certain impartiality, if they were truly honest, they would surely have noticed that since 1945 all the zones of the planet that came under the influence of mutual and *balanced* nuclear deterrence have—for the first time over such a long period of human history—remained zones of peace. On the other hand, they would also surely notice the 150 conventional conflicts that could take place only *because they lay outside the area of nuclear deterrence,* and which in round figures have claimed some sixty million victims in forty years—more than perished during World War II.

The ideal solution, of course, is not that peace should be maintained

by the fear of mutually assured destruction. Mankind should make
every effort not to install itself in this kind of situation, which is no more
than a *pis-aller,* a better-than-nothing expedient. But the way out of the
dilemna is not to harass the democratic camp alone and to incite it to
disarm unilaterally—something that can only give free rein to totalitarian imperialism. Such a point of view can be regarded as honestly held
by simple citizens who have every right to profess an opinion other
citizens may find false and dangerous. But those who pretend to base
such an opinion on science or on religion (for that, too, occasionally
happens) are behaving dishonestly. The "responsible" scientists who in
December 1987 applauded the signing in Washington of the Soviet-
American accord on the withdrawal from Europe of intermediate-range
missiles would have done well to reflect that this agreement could never
have been concluded if their advice had been heeded five years earlier—
that is, if NATO had refrained from deploying several hundred Pershing
II missiles on European territory, something that would have left the
United States without any bargaining chips. And above all, that no such
agreement would have been needed if the USSR had agreed in 1982 to
withdraw its SS-20s in exchange for the noninstallation of the Pershing
IIs.

If any further proof is wanted of the extent to which ideology outweighs
science in many scientific decisions, it can be found in the reaction of
the American scientific community to the Strategic Defense Initiative
(SDI), more popularly known as the "Star Wars" project. Given this
community's inveterate hostility to atomic weapons, it might have been
thought that it would respond favorably and that it would welcome the
possibility of moving over to a strategy based on a system of active
defense founded on the creation of a spatial "shield." Simple deterrence
rests on the possession by the two antagonists of offensive weapons that
by themselves, in the context of mutually assured destruction, are capable of paralyzing each other. This is security founded on the reciprocity
of the worst eventuality—what Winston Churchill called the "balance
of terror." This had always been condemned by U.S. scientists and also
U.S. bishops, first, because of its immorality—one cannot eternally
resign oneself to a form of security based on a permanent and mutual
menace of death—and second, because of the risks of an accidentally
triggered nuclear exchange. This kind of accidental catastrophe had
often been imagined in fiction, notably in Stanley Kubrick's classic film
Dr. Strangelove in 1964. But in the case of SDI, what happened? No

sooner had President Reagan announced the initial SDI research program in 1983 than the U.S. scientific community reversed itself with a velocity of transformation worthy of the great Leopoldo Fregoli, of whom it has been said by historians of the theater that he could play up to sixty different roles in the same play! A significant segment of the U.S. scientific community underwent a swift metamorphosis, coming out unreservedly in favor of offensive weapons, as opposed to active defense. The May 1985 *Bulletin of the Atomic Scientists,* as Pierre Gallois noted ironically, "sang the praises of MAD (mutually assured destruction), which it had previously condemned ever since it had first been enunciated. . . . On the other [i.e., American] side of the Atlantic, people have evolved to such an extent that they are now prepared to praise a military policy that was once harshly criticized." Indeed, no sooner had Reagan exposed his active defense plan than the MAD doctrine, which had hitherto been the *bête noire* of the Union of Concerned Scientists, the Physicians for Social Responsibility, and the Federation of American Scientists, became in the eyes of these intellectual eggheads and "concerned" scientists the last refuge of pacifist humanitarianism and philanthropic virtue. From that point on, the Strangeloves were recruited from among Nobel Prize winners, who in unison could chant the film's subtitle: "How I Learned to Stop Worrying and Love the Bomb."

To be sure, the "responsible" scientists continued to show concern, but this time because of SDI. For them, it seems, what suffices to earn a military doctrine's condemnation is not its intrinsic characteristics; rather, it is the fact that it is the doctrine of a U.S. administration. As soon as it ceases to be such, it becomes a good policy; the one that succeeds it automatically becomes bad in its turn.

The scientists who tackled the Strategic Defense Initiative in the *Bulletin of the Atomic Scientists* set out to prove, on the one hand, that it was unrealizable and could not be effective; on the other hand, that it was so fearsome that it would pressure the Soviets into constructing new and even more powerful weapons in order to pierce the spatial shield. These scientists did not seem to notice the contradiction between the two arguments, nor did they appear to foresee their mutually assured destruction on the plane of logic. If the "militarization of space"— to borrow a tendentious phrase coined by the communist press and certain West European governments—risked unleashing an armaments race, it proved that it was far more than an empty dream. Otherwise, why would the Soviets expend so much effort, as they have been doing for years, trying to persuade the Americans to abandon the SDI program? On the contrary, they should be overjoyed to see the Americans setting out on a road that would lead them to a reduction of their offensive weapons, thanks to an excess of confidence in an illusory spatial protection. The Soviet Union should have leapt on this stroke of good luck. This was not what it did; far from it.

Furthermore, U.S. scientists seemed not to know, or did not wish to know, that the Soviets had themselves for years been working—in flagrant violation of the 1972 ABM treaty—on their own program of active defense, something that Mikhail Gorbachev finally admitted officially during a press conference held in December 1987 at the Washington summit meeting, and which none of those who were so harshly flaying the West for its strategy had the right to ignore. It was impossible not to agree with Zbigniew Brzezinski when he wrote: "If the initiative is technically unfeasible, economically ruinous, and militarily easy to counter, it is unclear why the SDI would still be destabilizing and why the Soviets should object to America's embarking on such a self-defeating enterprise; and even less clear why the Soviets would then follow suit in reproducing such an undesirable thing for themselves."*

I do not propose to examine the technical aspects of the Union of Concerned Scientists's (UCS's) work, which sought in 1984 to prove the practical inanity of SDI, for I lack the necessary competence. But one soon had the impression that the technical argumentation was specious simply because it was promptly attacked by scientists who were as renowned as the UCS authors. For example, Professor Lowell Wood of the Lawrence Livermore National Laboratory found gross errors of calculation in the UCS's report. At a conference held in Sicily on August 20, 1984, Wood showed how these errors ruined the entire "demonstration." Robert Jastrow, Professor of Physical Science at Dartmouth University, likewise attacked the figures advanced by the UCS and exposed the enormous weaknesses of the report.† The authors of the report replied to these refutations by modifying and altering the assertions contained in the first version to the point of rendering them unrecognizable. Confronted with such a spectacle, even the most incompetent nonspecialist could perceive that scientific "certitudes" were anything but unchallenged in a debate in which the same physicists, reworking their calculations, had to concede arithmetical rectifications going from the single to the double, and even from one to fifty! Not only that; these revisions were themselves assailed by their scientific colleagues. Fasci-

*Zbigniew Brzezinski, *Game Plan, A Geostrategic Framework for the Conduct of the US-Soviet Contest* (Boston: Atlantic Monthly Press, 1986).
†See "The War Against Stars Wars," *Commentary*, December 1984.

nating though it is to watch such a display of intellectual emulation among scientists, it was less than honest on the part of the UCS scientists to bombard the public with doubtful hypotheses, not to say fallacious speculations, presented to the public as absolute truths.

Notwithstanding these rather pitiable mishaps, the politicostrategic dogmatism of the physicists lost none of its cutting arrogance. In 1987 a task force from the American Physical Society published a 424-page report on "energy-directed weapons"—which is to say, on active defense. Even before qualified commentators had time to analyze the report attentively, the press and other media rushed to proclaim that its conclusions were distinctly negative as regards SDI. PHYSICISTS EXPRESS STAR WARS DOUBT; LONG DELAYS SEEN headlined *The New York Times* on April 25. Can a culture be regarded as "scientific" when hypothetical conclusions based on dubious research are served up to the public in the form of peremptory affirmations, while the press does not bother to communicate the arguments giving rise to them, still less the objections to those arguments?

What the newspapers and television networks, furthermore, did not deign to inform Americans was that among the authors of this report, though they were eminent scientists, there was not a single specialist in energy-directed weapons—not even Charles Townsend, who, though one of the inventors of laser beams, had little experience in the practical handling of the weapons being tested. This relative amateurishness doubtless explains a disconcerting wobbliness in the argumentation. In one passage, for example, we read that the motors of long-range rockets need three to six minutes to burn up their fuel; in another passage it is between two and three minutes.* In matters concerning the possibility of intercepting rockets in space, crucial points such as these cannot be left to vague approximations.

Great as the role that science plays in an age of mass communications is, it must be admitted that the convictions of mankind as a whole owe virtually nothing to a greater access to scientific reasoning, nor to an improved comprehension of the elements of the debate, which would allow for a genuine participation in and democratization of knowledge, even of a summary kind. All the public has access to are grossly simplified conclusions, not the arguments that buttress them, even when the problems involved (those of AIDS, for example) are relatively simple to expose. The present-day public continues to live, much as people did in

---

*See Angelo M. Codevilla, "How Eminent Physicists Have Lent Their Names to a Politicized Report on Strategic Defense," *Commentary,* September 1987.

the Middle Ages, under the sway of an "authoritative" argument: "It is true because So-and-So, a Nobel Prize winner, has said so."

For example, there has been no surer way of arousing anxiety over deterrence, and likewise active defense, than by propagating the myth about an "unlimited" arms race. Why, then, it was said, continue to increase a stock of weapons capable of "destroying the planet several times over"? Nothing was more misleading than this hallucinating image. Because weapons have gained in precision, they have been reduced in their destructive capacity. There is no longer any need to devastate everything for miles around when one can hit a target with a margin of error of only a few yards. Modern nuclear weapons are no longer designed to "overkill" civilian populations. They are targeted not on cities but on other nuclear weapons: silos, submarines, and strategic bomber bases. The latest ballistic technology has the capacity to destroy specific targets without devastating inhabited areas. This is even truer of tactical weapons. The number of civilian and even military victims would be far less than the losses occasioned by a protracted conventional war, such as the Iraq-Iran bloodbath, the war in Afghanistan, or the civil wars of Central America. This is not to say that we should not do everything we can to avoid such conflicts! Deterrence has precisely this objective, as does the balance of forces and also SDI. But contrary to what is constantly being dinned into us, the U.S. nuclear stockpile has steadily declined. The number of nuclear warheads reached its zenith in 1967. In terms of megatons, the yardstick used for evaluating capacities of mass destruction, the stockpile reached its highest level in 1960. It then added up to four times as many megatons as today—simply because, as has been noted, precision has made it possible to reduce the power of each missile.

Scientists are part of the intellectual community. U.S. intellectuals, above all university teachers, are much farther to the left than the country in general, at any rate if being "to the left" consists of wanting to offer strategic superiority to totalitarian regimes. U.S. intellectuals tend to think that the sole danger of war is the one that comes from their own government, no matter what system of security it may adopt. The best solution, in their eyes, would be to have no system at all. Their natural hatred for the government of the United States, furthermore, was multiplied in the case of SDI because the government was headed by Ronald Reagan. For my part, I have no absolute certainty as to the feasibility of SDI, although I am inclined to follow certain specialists in strategic matters whose arguments in favor of SDI strike me as being serious, in particular Albert Wohlstetter.* What, on the other hand, I am sure of is that this program was debated within the U.S. scientific community primarily under the sway of political and ideological passions. This adulteration of the scientific debate becomes possible each time an ideologically charged question is too lacking in scientific certainties to make it possible to close the door on nonscientific influences. When such is the case, the only brake on falsification becomes the personal probity of the scientists. And in the absence of any truly binding methodological constraint, this probity can be found among them as much as among other human beings—which is to say, precious little.

The power of ideology is rooted in a human lack of curiosity about facts. When a new piece of information reaches us, we react first by wondering if it is going to reinforce or weaken our habitual mode of thought. But the predominance of ideological factors would defy all explanation if the need to know, to discover, and to explore the truth operated as powerfully on our psychic makeup as is generally supposed. Considerably stronger seems to be our need for mental calm and security. The ideas that interest us the most are not new ideas, they are ideas we are accustomed to. The prodigious progress of science since the seventeenth century prompts us to invest human nature with a congenital appetite for knowledge and an insatiable curiosity for facts. But what history teaches us is that if Man does indeed display an intense intellectual activity, it is above all to construct vast explanatory systems as verbose as they are ingenious—systems that induce mental calm by providing an illusion of global comprehension, rather than by encouraging us humbly to explore reality and to expose ourselves to unknown information. To grow and develop, science has always had to struggle against this primordial human tendency which surrounds it and combats it from within: indifference to knowledge. The opposite penchant, for reasons that still escape us, is to be found in only a tiny minority of human beings, and even then only in certain, not all, aspects of their behavior.

This is why the rejection of a new piece of information, or even the refusal to examine an old one that has the drawback of being exact, often manifests itself in the absence and outside the influence of any ideologi-

*Wohlstetter has written many studies criticizing the doctrine of simple deterrence. A good résumé of his arguments can be found in "Swords Without Shields," *The National Interest*, summer 1987.

cal motivation. Confronted by an unexpected phenomenon or event, Man, unaffected by any prejudice, is quite capable of displaying a lack of interest due solely to mental inertia.

What, after all, could be more inoffensive than Assyriology? From what academic discipline could someone in our day expect less ability to dominate one's colleagues and use ideology to further one's career? It might therefore be thought that this is the last domain in which the "scientific community" would experience the slightest urge to reject new information. What motivation, what ambitions alien to science could possibly prompt such a rejection? Yet precisely this occurred. A simple refusal to learn was the evil elf that perched on the cradle of this discipline. It is easy to understand why certain areas of history should be jealously watched over by ideologists—for example, the French Revolution, whose territory is littered with ideological debris that are still radioactive and upon which we venture to tread as though entering a castle, haunted by ghosts eager to be enrolled posthumously in our contemporary battles. But Assyriology! Only the thirst for ignorance, the *libido ignorandi,* can explain its laborious beginnings. For when, in 1802, a young Latin scholar, Georg Friedrich Grotefend, informed the Royal Society of Sciences of Göttingen University in Germany that he had found the key to "the so-called cuneiform inscriptions of Persepolis"—something he had indeed achieved—the news left this particular society completely cold. And yet, as a present-day Assyriologist, Jean Bottéro, has written, it was Grotefend who "first advanced along this road at the end of which, after half a century of effort, scholars were finally able to master the formidable triple secret which for two thousand years had defended Assyrian and Babylonian inscriptions."* Discouraged by the indifference of Göttingen's Royal Society, the young Latin scholar abandoned his research. This reaction of apathy toward information is a basic fact that we must take into account if we wish to understand the mishaps of communication and comprehension. It comes before any invasion of ideology. As soon as the latter intervenes, it simply triples or quadruples the powerlessness of pure knowledge to retain our attention; it does not create this impotence from scratch.

Among the minority who are motivated by the anomaly of intellectual curiosity, who possess a taste for facts and an interest in truth, it sometimes happens that the trailblazer is a rank amateur. Such was the case

---

*Jean Bottéro, *Mésopotamie* (Paris: Gallimard, 1987). It was a "triple secret" because, as was gradually discovered, cuneiform served as a script for three languages—ancient Persian, Elamite, and Akkadian.

with this Latin scholar from Germany. It was also the case with Henry C. Rawlinson, an amateur researcher who finally succeeded in deciphering the Mesopotamian script. Rawlinson, who began his professional life in the military service of the East India Company, was, Bottéro tells us, a researcher "whose intelligence, stubbornness and genius made him, after Grotefend, the greatest name in the budding history of the ancient Near East."

In the twentieth century it was also thanks to an amateur, the architect Michael Ventris, that the so-called "linear B" script of Crete was deciphered. Academic Hellenists did not welcome this decisive breakthrough with much enthusiasm. In his preface to the French translation of John Chadwick's book *The Deciphering of Linear B,* the eminent French Hellenist, Pierre Vidal-Naquet, wrote in 1972: "We shall see farther on how Mr. Ventris's sensational discovery was greeted. With nineteen years of hindsight we can say that, *all things considered,* things did not go too badly, and that contemporary Hellenism, albeit an eminently conservative discipline, *on the whole* greeted the novelty *quite rapidly.*" (Italics mine.) "Which," Vidal-Naquet continues, "does not keep the story of these intellectual resistances from being highly instructive." Despite these prudish euphemisms, one can easily imagine how much idiocy and ill will the unfortunate Ventris must have had to endure.

Let no one think that I am advancing the absurd idea that science progresses only thanks to the work of amateurs. Such exceptional cases can be found only in the early stages of a science. Besides, discoverers like Ventris and Rawlinson, even though their main activities did not make them part of the university world, were by no means dilettantes. They simply lacked academic degrees. Well prepared for the tasks they tackled, they had personally undertaken serious and even more exhaustive studies than those of the professionals of their discipline. If their cases merit attention, it is because an amateur, by definition, is not backed by any power, by any network of alliances and friendships in the social milieu of the scientists and the university bureaucracy. The recognition grudgingly accorded to such persons can only be based on an exclusively scientific perception of the discovery's real merits. These rare examples thus provide a good touchstone for measuring the strength of purely intellectual impulses in human beings in general, and in scientists in particular. But let no one doubt it: Hatred and dishonesty are every bit as powerful and all-determining among patented professionals.

All ideology does is to aggravate and envenom this natural fear of facts. The kind of intellectual sorcery practiced by the U.S. sovietologist

Moshe Lewin, which I have already mentioned, offers an amusing example of this animosity. Sorcery—a magical practice aimed at exorcising adverse influences—consists of mentally nullifying a troublesome fact by proclaiming it to be minor and ridiculous. Confronted by the recent anti-Sovietism of the French intelligentsia, Lewin, as I earlier explained, first tried to pass it off as a "Parisian" phenomenon, thus as something worldly, a superficial and somewhat stupid fad: this being, he said, the childish idea that Soviet tanks could reach the English Channel at any moment. Admittedly, in 1985 a television program, devoted to the subject of what this kind of conflict would be like in Europe and presented by Yves Montand, had focused attention on strategic realities which—no matter what Mr. Lewin, comfortably installed six thousand kilometers from our shores, may think about it—is not for Europeans a matter of sheer mythology. Nonetheless, a haunting fear of a frontal assault, which Lewin made so much of, was not the decisive factor in the ideological turnabout that upset him so. The decisive factor was far more the intellectual realization of the specific originality of totalitarian reality, along with the risk of Europe's being "Finlandized" without a war. Thus, when Lewin scoffs at the (for him) baseless "phobias" of the "Parisian intellectual class," which is "interested above all in itself" because it has freed itself from pro-Soviet ideology, he is behaving not like a scientist analyzing a historical phenomenon, but like a politician confronted by hecklers in the back of the hall. The sincerity of others is something that to him seems impossible. Without blaming him for such a human trait, I notice in him an indifference to information and a reluctance to admit a new development—faults that should normally have been eliminated by a historian's sound training. Lewin is unable to absorb a cultural fact such as the ideological evolution of Europe (and not simply that of France or of Paris), because this fact contradicts his initial postulate: to wit, that—according to him—the suppression of freedom is not an intrinsic feature of the Soviet system.

"History would be an excellent thing, if only it were true." This quip of Tolstoy's goes farther than it seems. To be sure, to dream of a totally true history is a piece of epistemological nonsense. The philosophers of history, in particular Max Weber and Raymond Aron, clearly proved it: a historian's point of view is relative. This is because he operates from a certain moment of history. But I am not referring here to these philosophical considerations; or rather, I assume that they are taken for granted and are self-evident. I am referring to brutal deviations from the truth, those the historian has ample means for avoiding. It is not a question of knowing if a historian can attain the absolute truth, it is a question of knowing if he strives to do so; not a question of knowing if a historian can know all the facts, but if he gives due consideration to all the facts he knows, or if he really seeks to find out all those that can be known. But this is seldom the case, or at any rate it is the exception. Within the inherent relativity of the observer's position—this being a simple epistemological truism—there exists or can or should always exist a mixture of methodological objectivity and of personal probity known as impartiality. It seems almost impossible to unite the qualities required of the historian to be able to approach this level of rigor, and indeed they are very seldom united. Certain ancient historians possessed it, even if their documentation is now "outdated," whereas present-day historians lack it, even though they have the finest methods of research available.

The procedure we too often encounter—even among historians of a high scientific level (I am not speaking here of books of sheer mendacious propaganda, where the process of falsification does not even respect the appearance of impartiality)—reposes on the selection of proofs; it treats facts as a collection of examples from which one picks out those that suit the illustration of a theory, while concealing the others as much as possible. If we disregard the kind of history that a minority of conscientious, fact-respecting minds have practiced at one time or another, each with the resources of his day, then we can say that history has almost always been used as an instrument of ideological combat, whether political, religious, nationalist, humanitarian . . . or even scientific, by which I mean, conditioned by the defense of theories and suppositions of a particular historical school.

It is easy to appreciate the weight of this ideology, and it is almost excusable when a historian chooses as his subject some current phenomenon: for example, communism, the Soviet Union, socialism, totalitarianism, the Third World. It is understandable, even though what one might expect from a scientific researcher would be to enable us to escape a bit from the vagaries of daily polemics instead of belaboring us with them even more. However, we must admit that here detachment is less easily attained than when dealing with a distant past. The incessant upheavals of the present, opportune or inconvenient revelations, constantly interrupt the construction of the explanatory model on which the historian is working. It is often the very successors of Soviet or Chinese leaders who shatter the models fashioned by Western sovietologists or Chinese specialists. What a bitter moment it must have been for a Moshe

Lewin or a Stephen Cohen when they read in the *Literaturnaya Gazeta* of September 30, 1987, that the number of victims of hunger and terror during the 1930s and during the war, according to the no longer tongue-tied Soviet demographers, far exceeded the harshest evaluations of anti-communist historiography. In 1940 the Soviet Union had a population of 194.1 million inhabitants. By 1946 the figure had dropped to 167 million. The war having cost the lives of 20 million Soviet citizens, the difference—7 million—must be due to internal repression. But the truth is even starker, for this difference is even greater if one takes as the basis of calculation not a static population—this being a demographic im-plausibility—but the population of 1940 augmented by a foreseeable increase in population over the following six years. If we prolong the average birthrate of the 1930s, which was particularly low given the abnormal number of deaths due to famine and terror, we end up with a figure of 213 million inhabitants, which is what the Soviet Union should have had in 1946. This means that 46 million citizens disap-peared, which is to say, 26 million died of famine or repression.* A figure of this magnitude leads one to suspect that there are many un-imaginable things in the history of communism that we still know little about. But why would our Western historians strain to pierce this secret when they already pay little heed to things that are easy to determine? Just think—prior to the bombshell effect produced by Solzhenitsyn's *Gulag Archipelago* when it was first published in the West and momen-tarily aroused our sovietologists from their dogmatic slumbers, more than sixty books on Soviet concentration camps had been published in France alone, all of them listed in the catalogues of the Bibliothèque Nationale from 1920 to 1974.† Before paying any attention to communist atrocities, many historians wait for the communist leaders themselves to denounce them—and of course lay the blame on their predecessors.

Such official acts of recognition as that of *Literaturnaya Gazeta* give rise, furthermore, to a diverting and agile recovery. They provide proof that the regime is in a healthy state and once again making headway, since its frankness shows it is conscious of its scars and that much more alert in the race toward progress. Never are communist regimes the object of a more fervent cult in the West than when they proclaim that their subjects are in a critical pass or close to starving. When, on October 17, 1987, Gorbachev proclaims that in the USSR "the problem of food-

---

*The *Literaturnaya Gazeta* text, consisting of a debate between a historian and a philoso-pher, was summarized by *Le Monde* on October 2, 1987.

†The inventory was drawn up by Christian Jelen and Thierry Wolton in *L'Occident des Dissidents* (Paris: Stock, 1979).

stuffs has not yet been solved, above all in the countryside," he is given an enthusiastic ovation in the West. In the USSR, as in China, Poland, and Vietnam, recognizing errors and crimes seems to confer an additional right to exercise power. Just think what would have happened if a French newspaper in August 1944 had come out with this headline: REGIME'S POSITIVE EVOLUTION: VICHY GOVERNMENT RECOGNIZES ERRORS OF COLLABORATION. NEW START PROMISED! How many historians, commentators, and governments, when forced to adopt positions they previously combated, thus succeed in never seeming to have to eat their words!

All these intellectual turbulences can in large part be explained by the fact that in the chosen example, the past and the present, the historical and the political debate are mixed up and influence each other. Such and such a historian of communism is at the same time a political editorialist who is periodically asked by leading newspapers to diagnose the meaning of the latest developments and recommend a line of conduct. Direct involvement in the present inevitably increases the difficulty of remaining impartial about the past. On the other hand, when the past is long since passed, serenity should prevail. But nothing of the sort occurs. Specialists have often exploited the distance of an inaccessible Soviet Union in order to depict it not as it was, but as it should have been. They thus—as with Maoist China—create a fictitious ideal, an ideological diversion. But alongside diversions in space there exist diversions in time. Nothing shows this better than the historiography of the French Revolution.

The incurable controversy over the French Revolution interests us less for the divergences of interpretation between historians, these being normal manifestations of living research, than the nonscientific interdictions and taboos that cross it and constantly rekindle the debate. These interdictions first of all relate to facts before affecting interpretations. The faithful disciples of Jacobinism feel greater hatred for a scholar who unearths or confirms facts that are troubling for the Jacobin version of the Revolution than they do for doctrinary counterrevolutionaries such as Edmund Burke, Joseph de Maistre, or Charles Maurras, who constitute their ideological counterparts in a kind of fraternal antagonism. Battles between opposing doctrinaires who slug it out with the help of assertions are fought with a certain relish. Far more feared are new elements of knowledge that slice the shinbones of the war-horses themselves. This is why the historiography of the Revolution, and notably the history writing that was indulged in in schools and universities during the Third Republic, consisted more of selecting from among known proofs than of seeking new ones, of protecting some of these than of establishing others. The ideological, political, and militant imperative dominated scientific exigency, often managing to do so all the more perfidiously by giving itself the appearance of science—this with the aid of the great names of the university world, such as Albert Mathiez or Alphonse Aulard, and of school textbooks by Ernest Lavisse or Malet and Isaac.

It is also worth noting that a lack of curiosity about sources set in early. In the middle of the nineteenth century, Jules Michelet was the first to take the trouble of poring through the archives, followed by Tocqueville, who even explored certain provincial archives. It is no accident that these two great intellects were precisely those who did not think themselves capable of dragging historical truth from the well-depths of their thought. Before them, the conservative Adolphe Thiers and the socialist Louis Blanc, each of them the author of a *History of the Revolution,* or Lamartine, in his *History of the Girondins,* which is of a very conformist revolutionary sentimentality, worked with secondary sources, relying on already published documents and memoirs and oral tradition. It was not until 1986, after two centuries had passed, that the first serious evaluation was made of the number of victims claimed by the brutal repression of the "Chouans," the rebels of Vendée, thanks to research undertaken in village parish archives. Nor before that time had anyone undertaken to inventory the number of needy persons at the time of the Revolution, compared to the number of paupers under the Ancien Régime, nor even sought to draw up an overall economic balance sheet for the new régime. And even these statistically supported studies were greeted by a furious hue and cry from the adherents of the "revolutionary catechism."

The intellectual sway of this catechism is all the more surprising, since at a relatively early date reasonable persons, even François Guizot, whose father had been guillotined at the time of the Terror, considered the political and social accomplishments of the Revolution to be irreversible. Furthermore, the sectarianism of the "catechists" actually increased with the passage of time and became more pronounced, while the danger of a restoration of the Ancien Régime or even of a modern constitutional monarchy gradually faded into nothingness. For republicans, therefore, the mummification of a mythical image of the Revolution responded to a need quite different from that of warding off a political threat that was becoming less and less plausible with each passing day. Even though, prior to 1939, the monarchists, with their Action Française, still played a significant part in French political debates, they themselves never believed in their chances of success. Admittedly, democracy in the twentieth century has had to ward off attacks launched from the right as well as from the left, but the assaults from the right have been mounted by totalitarian regimes, generated by schools of thought entirely different in philosophical complexion from those of the traditionalists. Can it be that the wary vigilance and fear of facts exhibited by the high priests of the revolutionary cult stem from the essentially equivocal nature of the Revolution, that Revolution which was the mother both of democracy and of the adversaries of democracy? Is it not that the catechists' stormy susceptibility to and insatiable appetite for censorship, momentarily calmed by the official adoption of university teaching in accordance with their wishes, spring from the profound ambiguity of their task? They must protect the original Jacobin kernel, from which emerged the major political innovation of our times: the propagation of servitude, masked behind the defense of liberty.

Of the two deadly foes, of the two irreconcilable systems born of the Revolution—liberalism and totalitarianism, or, in present-day terms, democracy and communism—the faithful heirs of Jacobinism have been working to promote the latter, while claiming to be the guardians of the former. Hence their injunction: You should accept Terror in the name of Liberty. For *"la Révolution est un bloc"* ("the Revolution is of one piece"), and "one doesn't make an omelet without breaking some eggs." Consequently, the need to rewrite the history of the French Revolution, to rectify it, expurgate it, idealize it, absolve it, to make it sacred and "renew" it with each passing day, stems from the same ideological need that has given rise to the constant reshaping and dissimulations of recent and contemporary history which have been taking place in the Soviet Union.

What makes the longevity of the revolutionary catechism even more interesting is the fact that it has flourished in the name of science, in a free culture without direct political constraint and without any threats to the security of individuals, except through their careers. The basic issue is the justification or refusal of what in the twentieth century came to be known as totalitarian dictatorship, not simply of the Revolution as a form of democracy that replaced the Ancien Régime. This debate, I insist, has been raging between authors who all essentially approve of the Revolution; some of them, however, consider that the Revolution had the right and even the duty to resort to terror in order to survive, while the others argue that in practicing terror it betrayed and destroyed itself. During the nineteenth century the school "admiring" the Terror included Adolphe Thiers—a right-winger *par excellence* and the man who crushed the Paris Commune of 1871 in a sea of blood—the opportunistic Lamartine, and socialist historians. In the twentieth century this school notably included Alphonse Aulard, Albert Mathiez, and Albert Soboul. As early as 1796 Gracchus Babeuf had given this school its motto: "Robespierrism is Democracy." The liberal school, which on the contrary considered the Terror to be a sign of the failure of democracy and judged it to be as unjustified as it was unacceptable, included the names of Michelet, Tocqueville, Edgar Quinet, and Hippolyte Taine. Despite the enormous superiority of its literary talents and its scientific conscientiousness, this latter school, that of liberal democracy, has always been crushed by the former.

I can personally testify that, shortly before the middle of our century, I was able to study for my *baccalaureat* (high school) degree and then prepare for competitive admission to the École Normale Supériere—in each case with the French Revolution figuring on the program—without my otherwise excellent teachers once mentioning Alexis de Tocqueville's *L'Ancien Régime et la Révolution* in their lectures. On the other hand, the three small volumes of Albert Mathiez's *Révolution française* had to be practically learned by heart. It was only around 1960 that a return to Tocqueville began to be seen in French university teaching. If the French Left has always included Michelet in its patrimony, it has never paid any attention to his severity toward the Terror. The polemical uproar provoked by Edgar Quinet's *La Révolution* in 1865 provided the framework for the ideological melodrama which since then has been dragged out and replayed umpteen times, right up to the commorative bicentennial "spectaculars" staged in 1989. In this ceaselessly repeated scenario, the vital thing in the discussion is not to know whether what the author says is true or false, but what cause or whom it serves or disserves.

Quinet's most violent detractors, first and foremost Louis Blanc, accused him of weakening and betraying the democratic movement. We should not forget that the "traitor" in this case had chosen exile rather than go on living under the reign of Napoleon III (as had his attacker). Thus, already in the 1860s part of the French Left wanted to impose on the rest the duty to lie about the past on the pretext that this was vital to safeguard the cohesion of the present.

But what past? Quinet had begun by pointing out a bitter truth, concealed by the Left with a vigilance made all the more acute by its very obviousness. The Revolution had been a failure. Begun in order to establish political liberty, it had led first to the Terror, then to the military dictatorship of Napoleon. Its social reforms could not be denied; but, as Tocqueville had already explained, in this respect the Revolution had already begun under the Ancien Régime; it could almost be said to have been three quarters completed when the Revolution began. Its real success would have been to have implanted in France a durable and peaceful system of political freedom. But what it succeeded in doing above all was to open the road to aggravated forms of tyranny. Even worse—the "repetition" of 1848 also engendered a Republic incapable of governing and culminated in a new coup d'état and a second confiscation of sovereignty by an authoritarian regime!

What a series of failures! For any political family other than the French Left this would have been enough to question the validity of its ideas. And the first idea that needed to be challenged, said Edgar Quinet, was the legitimacy of the Terror. In a page of striking modernity Quinet laid bare what was to become one of the greatest sophistries of the twentieth century: "Equality without freedom, and outside of freedom, such is the supreme chimera our theorists have been making us pursue throughout the course of our history. This is the bait that has kept us panting. . . . I adjourn the search for political guarantees until such a time as the social level [needed to assure freedom] will have been reached. . . . I assume that the chimera will then have been attained. . . . But who is to judge whether it truly has? . . . So liberty is once again adjourned. It would have been better to have stated from the outset that this would eternally be the case!"

Jules Michelet's reservations about Quinet's thesis had less to do with the Terror, which was condemned with equal severity by both historians, than with his manner of explaining it. Whereas Quinet regarded the Terror of 1793–94 as simply a relapse into an ancient form of absolutism, Michelet grasped the fact that the phenomenon was mentally unprecedented, a kind of historical "first." The historian François Furet has drawn attention to a little-known (or perhaps deliberately neglected) aspect of Michelet's analysis of Jacobinism.* For the author of the *History of the French Revolution,* the 3,000 societies and the 40,000 committees of the Jacobin Club had already subjected France, before the term was invented, to the regime of a single party, one of "democratic centralism," as we would now say.

This technique of club domination is one with whose ingredients we of the twentieth century are all too familiar. Furet, translating Michelet

*François Furet, *La Gauche et la Révolution française au milieu du XIXe siècle* (Paris: Hachette, 1986).

into our vocabulary, lists them as follows: "The drill-like handling of an ideological orthodoxy, the discipline of a centralized militant apparatus, the systematic purging of adversaries and friends, the authoritarian manipulation of elected institutions." Michelet was right. This new technique of power was of another, different species from that of the absolutism of the Ancien Régime.

In 1869 Michelet added a bitter preface to his *History,* entitling it "The Tyrant." "Under its so troubled form," he said of the Terror, "this period was a dictatorship." This dictatorship later led to that of Bonaparte. "The talkative, Jacobin tyrant brings forth the military one. And the military tyrant brings back the Jacobin." Here Michelet teaches us that dictatorship and democracy constitute primary, original realities, which are to be found under any socioeconomic conditions. So let us share his astonishment when he asks: "Through what sort of obstinacy can something so thoroughly elucidated still be doubted?"

It should be noted that Michelet's considerations on the *quadrillage* and systematic surveillance of France by the local sections of the "clubs" (today we would say, by party cells) anticipated the analyses of Augustin Cochin, a historian who was killed at the front during World War I before he had completed his work and who was rediscovered fifty years later by François Furet. Cochin—in this lay his originality—was the first to have identified in Jacobinism the totalitarian phenomenon in its pure state—a kind of dictatorship of the mendacious word, which has nothing to do with ancient authoritarianisms, or class domination, or populist Caesarism. Published for the most part after his death, Cochin's works were massacred by the ineffable Alphonse Aulard, who with a honey-tongued dishonesty demolished a book without breathing a word about what it contained and even attributed to it things it did not contain. Thus Aulard claimed that all Cochin did was to resuscitate the old thesis of Abbé Barruel, according to which the Revolution was the product of the Masonic Lodges. There was nothing of the sort in Cochin, but there were many other things that were omitted by Aulard in his appraisal. This dissuasive method did not fail to bear its fruit: Cochin sank back into oblivion. For having rescued him from this oblivion, Furet also brought down on himself several severe episcopal admonishments from the inquisitors of the Jacobin catechism, who are still very active. Their moral is clear. The question is not one of knowing whether one should or should not make use of Cochin's texts in order to refute them eventually; the best that could happen is simply that they should not exist, that they should remain impossible to find.* To cause to disappear—such is the sovereign technique of this kind of "thinking."

This, as a matter of fact, was what the school of the Terror had already managed to do in the case of Hippolyte Taine, who was unjustly executed by the unsinkable Aulard early in this century. By a strange coincidence Taine, in 1908, had been defended with verve and acuity by Augustin Cochin in his *Crise de l'histoire révolutionnaire.*

No sooner had Taine published those parts of his *Origines de la France contemporaine* that were devoted to the Revolution, to the Jacobins' conquest of power, and to the Terror, than the "republicans" mobilized their forces in order to launch a counteroffensive. Charles Seignobos and Aulard, holder of the Chair of the History of the French Revolution at the Sorbonne (which had been specially created for him), strove to prove that Taine had no competence as a historian. Aulard subjected Taine's work to a meticulous examination in order to expose errors in his footnote references. After Taine's death Augustin Cochin counterattacked; he found that in a sample of 140 pages containing 550 source references, the percentage of Taine's errors amounted to 3 percent, whereas Aulard's errors in criticizing Taine amounted to 38 percent. Nevertheless Taine, the great mind, was the posthumous loser of a battle in which the mediocre Aulard was the winner. After having enjoyed a great success with booksellers at the end of the nineteenth century, *Les Origines de la France contemporaine* gradually ceased to be reprinted.

Why? Because Taine's work had won for itself the infamous status of a counterrevolutionary engine of war. This, it seems to me, was a mistake—for two reasons. First of all, while Taine's indictment of the Jacobins was certainly very violent in tone, and even at times disagreeably ferocious, his judgments on the Terror were no more withering than those of several historians usually regarded as being of the Left, as indeed Taine himself had been regarded prior to the publication of *Les Origines.* Secondly, *Les Origines de la France contemporaine,* as the title indicates, was not concerned solely with the Revolution. Many of its early pages were devoted to the twilight years of the Ancien Régime and many others, later on, to postrevolutionary developments—what Taine called the "modern regime"—from the start of the Napoleonic system down to 1880.

*Unfortunately for the inquisitors, Cochin's writings, as a result of Furet's analysis, were republished. Augustin Cochin, *L'Esprit du jacobinisme* (Paris, Presses Universitaires de France, 1979), with a preface by Jean Baechler.

Furthermore, Taine cannot be accused of being a reactionary in the sense that he was pleading for a restoration or even rehabilitation of the Ancien Régime. His portrayal of the last decades of old France, which comprises some of the most brilliant pages of the book, is much harsher than that of nineteenth-century historians who were more favorable to the Revolution than he was. According to Taine, the Ancien Régime was neither viable nor reformable. Poverty was rampant, the ruling classes incompetent, the political system in a state of putrefaction and incurable paralysis. The case made out by Taine thus had nothing at all in common with the cause that right-wing historians such as Pierre Gaxotte, for example, later sought to uphold.

While pretending to defend democracy, when in fact all of its targets are partisans of democracy, the Terror-admiring school seeks in the Revolution an argument to justify totalitarianism. After the Bolshevik coup d'état of 1917 the "stars" of revolutionary historiography in France became the advocates of Leninist dictatorship in the name of 1793 and the Committee of Public Safety. In *Study on the Situation in Russia,* published in 1919 by the French League of Human Rights (Ligue des Droits de l'Homme), one can read this: "The French Revolution was carried out by a dictatorial minority, Professor Aulard maintains. At Versailles it did not consist of the actions of your *Duma,* but developed in the form of soviets. With us as with you, the municipal committees of 1789 and then the revolutionary committees employed methods that caused people in Europe and throughout the world to say that the French were bandits. It was thus that we succeeded. Every revolution is the work of a minority."*

Aulard, for his part, offered these words: "When I am told that there is a minority that is terrorizing Russia, what I understand is this: Russia is in a state of revolution." What an encouraging definition of revolution!

"I do not know what is going on," Aulard continued, "but I am struck by the fact that in our French Revolution we, like you, had to repel an armed intervention, we had émigrés, like you. I therefore wonder if it was not all that which gave our Revolution the violent character it had. If, at that time, the forces of reaction had not decided on and practiced that well-known intervention, we might perhaps not have shed any blood, or we would have shed but little. It was because people tried to keep the French Revolution from developing that it shattered everything."

*Quoted by Christian Jelen, *L'Aveuglement, les socialistes et la naissance du mythe soviétique* (Paris: Flammarion, 1984), p. 56.

Here one encounters the system of excuses that was to serve as a passport for so many twentieth-century totalitarian regimes claiming to be of socialist inspiration, even the bloodiest and the most famine-inducing of them. After spending a few days in Ethiopia during the worst moments of the repression carried out in 1977 by the communist regime, the high-ranking Italian communist leader Giancarlo Pajetta declared that the present atmosphere of Addis Ababa recalled that of Paris during the French Revolution. As in Paris in 1792 and 1793, remarked Pajetta jokingly, one could learn at midday that the person one had dined with the previous evening had just been executed. Such "surprises," according to Pajetta, are part of the charm of this kind of situation, his evocation of Parisian life under Robespierre being intended to invest it with historical respectability and the poetry of folklore. If "Robespierrism is democracy," then massacres, starvation, concentration camps, and the boat people of Vietnam matter little. The Khmer Rouge, the Sandinistas, Fidel Castro, and the masters of Hanoi have historical reason and socialist morality on their side. Their violations of human rights and their inability to feed their peoples can no longer be held against them. These are dismissed as superficial criticisms, lamentations of a flatly empirical kind, whereas every revolution works itself out according to a long-term dialectic whose term is never reached. The circumstances in which a revolutionary regime lives are always exceptional and unfavorable, which means that it cannot be judged according to its actions, which are always justified. This magic formula, which allows one perpetually to refuse the tests of empirical reality, is the service the Jacobin school rendered the Left. Albert Mathiez, who was far more intelligent than Aulard, thought in almost the same terms, for ideology has a leveling effect on intellectuals: "Jacobinism and Bolshevism are two dictatorships of the same kind, born of civil and foreign war, two class dictatorships operating with the same means—terror, requisition, and taxes—and in the final analysis proposing a similar aim, the transformation of society—not simply of Russian society or of French society, but of universal society."* In making this parallel, Mathiez does not limit himself to describing; he specifically approves.

And yet, while bizarre and contradictory in its behavior, this kind of "historical science," which glorifies the Terror as the only road to the "transformation of universal society," does everything it can to conceal relevant facts. Why? If terror is an instrument for the salvation of

*Le Bolchevisme et le Jacobinisme (Paris: Librairie de 'L'Humanite,' 1920).

mankind, its extension cannot be encouraged too much. Why belittle the scale on which it was practiced by our great ancestors for the common good? Under the sway of what timidity should one dissimulate the scope of the massacres of the Vendée, if they were indispensable for the welfare of the homeland and mankind? And yet, what roars of outrage were heard when, in 1986, a book appeared on the royalist revolt of 1793–95 in the Vendée province and the massacre of its inhabitants. Written by a new "heretic" and earmarked for the ideological guillotine, it was a book full of unpublished documents and data and adorned with a title which, I won't deny, was provocative: *The Franco-French Genocide.* *

Nothing could have been more French than the fact that this doctoral thesis, a masterpiece of research by a thirty-year-old historian, should first of all have stirred up a quarrel over vocabulary. Was the first response to weigh the interest of the archival materials that had been brought to light after being allowed to gather dust for two centuries in various cellars? To measure the scope of the new information provided? To evaluate the progress accomplished by the assimilation of new facts? Not at all! Without further ado the Ph.D.s took to arguing with one another as to whether the author was justified in using the term "genocide" in his title.

Forged in the twentieth century, the term, it was objected, is an anachronism in the context of 1793. But why? It seems to me that one has the right to apply the notion of genocide when one is confronted by certain circumstances that have nothing vague about them—for example:

- when the violence employed against enemies or rebels aims, in a patent and sometimes openly proclaimed way, not only to subdue but to exterminate them.
- when this extermination is extended to the entire population, whether combattant or not, with no distinctions of age or sex, according to a premeditated plan worked out in addition to military operations.
- when, in the same spirit, the means of livelihood and subsistence of civilians, along with their dwellings, fields, workshops, tools, and livestock, are systematically destroyed, all this being undertaken deliberately and not due simply to the lawless looting of a rampaging soldiery.
- when the organized killings, due to fixed design and not to random

*Reynald Secher, *Le Génocide franco-français, la Vendée 'vengé'* (Paris: Presses Universitaires de France, 1986).

anarchy, are continued after order has been reestablished and the adversary rendered powerless.

It cannot be denied that these four aspects were often combined during the Vendée war, under the impulsion of a policy decided on at the highest political level. The Convention, either directly or through the voices of representatives in the field, more than once proclaimed its firm intention of "exterminating the brigands of Vendée," of "entirely purging the soil of Freedom of this accursed race," of "depopulating Vendée." The drive against the rebels was carried out to the letter with the massacre of prisoners, of women (even when pregnant), of children and aged persons. It was accompanied by the destruction of goods. "Vendée has not sufficiently been put to the torch," the Convention wrote to the Committee of Public Safety. "For a whole year no man or animal should be able to find subsistence on that soil." There was even a move to efface the name Vendée from human memory, one member of the Convention proposing that in the list of departments, "Vendée" be replaced by "Vengé" ("Avenged"). It would thus become the "avenged department" (the subtitle of Secher's book).

As for the prolongation of the massacres over and beyond the aims of maintaining law and order—excesses which clearly proved the intention of finishing off this rebellious people—it aroused the indignation of a historian as little royalist in his inclinations as Edgar Quinet, who wrote in 1865: "The mass drownings of Nantes took place in December 1793. How could these drownings have saved Nantes, which had already been saved five months before? [Jean-Baptiste] Carrier continued the exterminations after the Vendéens had been routed at Le Mans. . . . It was thus that the Great Terror showed itself almost everywhere after the victories."

The lexicographic purists of the Bloodbath School nevertheless argued against Secher that "genocide" can properly be applied only to murders against a foreign population. Does this mean that what we saw happening in Cambodia during the "reign" of Pol Pot was not genocide? That the "dekulakization" of the 1930s in the USSR was not genocide? That the 200,000 Ugandans who were massacred from 1982 to 1985 by the soldiers of President Milton Obote did not constitute genocide? Were the Armenians who were exterminated in 1915 not Ottoman citizens? And the *communards* of 1871, who were mowed down en masse by gunfire after their utter defeat, were they not French? To make this kind of distinction is to split linguistic hairs. As for the quantitative criterion, how can it be determined? Certain historians frown at the very mention of the "massacres" of the Vendée, finding the death toll to be on the feeble side. One can always do better, of course; but it would be a good idea to fix a precise limit above which a mass purge deserves the rank of "genocide."

The repression in the Vendée exceeded what was called for to such a highly embarrassing degree that in France's secular schools the scope of what happened and the atrocious details have for the past century been effaced from high school textbooks and university teaching. The Vendée was effectively driven underground, into the catacombs of text-books of royalist or clerical inspiration—with a most paradoxical conse-quence. Relegated by the choice of his subject to the fenced-in dog patch of the "counterrevolutionaries," Reynald Secher, thanks to the serious-ness of his research, actually rectified the factual record to a degree no republican historian had dreamed of. He established with impartiality that the number of human lives lost in the Vendée was in fact very much smaller than had always been thought.

Lazare Hoche, who for a while had commanded the local republican army, estimated the number of dead at 600,000. Later, and right up until recently, even the historians who thought this figure excessive never descended lower than 300,000. Secher, however, after painstakingly checking parish registers and other primary sources, concluded that of the 815,029 inhabitants of the Vendée in 1792, 117,257—or some 15 per-cent of the population—perished in battles or massacres. Although less than what was commonly thought, this is still a lot. Such a percentage, applied to the population of present-day France (around fifty million), would amount to 7.5 million victims. Needless to say, the extermina-tions and destructions varied greatly from one township to another. Certain villages lost almost half of their inhabitants and houses, others less than 5 percent.

Admittedly, the authorities in Paris could not tolerate the Vendéean insurrection, above all at a moment when a foreign war was brewing. But the transformation of the repression into genocide was ideologically, not militarily, motivated. This is proved by the acts of savagery that took place in other areas of French territory where no civil war was threatening. Thus the tiny village of Bédoin, in the department of Vau-cluse (north of Marseille), was punished for having allowed its Freedom Tree to be chopped down one night. Unable to ferret out the culprit, the Convention's emissary decided to impose a collective punishment: sixty-three persons were guillotined or shot, the rest were driven out, and the entire village was put to the torch. "There is not one spark of civic spirit in this commune," the emissary commented with virtuous placidity in his report.

Like all regimes that found their legitimacy on an ideology, the Committee of Public Safety seemed incapable of asking itself why the people resisted it, either actively or passively. In its eyes, the genuine "people" was itself. An abstract, absolute, monolithic entity, it could not imagine that the flesh-and-blood living, changeable, and diverse people could have sincere and real motives for discontent. Curiously enough, before the Revolution the regions of Western France were to the "left," as we would say today. It took Jacobin sectarianism to push them to the "right," where by and large they have remained ever since in the history of French elections.

Clemenceau, who was anything but a fool, uttered the idiocy of a lifetime when he coined the famous slogan *"La Révolution est un bloc!"* ("The Revolution is of one piece"). But no! Nothing that is human is a bloc. Those who reason in terms of blocs are tyrants. One can feel oneself to be an heir of the France of 1789 without making it one's duty to justify the Vendée, Bédoin, and the Terror.

All scientific research takes place within a framework fashioned by one's epoch, a "paradigm," to employ the term used by Thomas Kuhn in his *Structure of Scientific Revolutions.* Works like Ptolemy's *Almageste,* Newton's *Principia,* Lavoisier's *Chimie,* and Keynes's *General Theory* defined—for a decade, a century, or a millennium thereafter—the terms in which problems were posed in a specific field of research. To this extent all human thought is conditioned by a kind of ideological background. But it is fallacious to try from this to argue, as Michel Foucault and Louis Althusser did, that there is no difference between knowledge and ideology, and to affirm that the only intellectual reality is, in fact, ideology. Such a stance leads to skepticism. Knowledge comes to be regarded as no more than a succession of ideological interpretations. Even more, this attitude engenders a dogmatism of ideology, elevated to a superior status as the only true form of knowledge. In both cases the thesis confuses two quite distinct phenomena. The paradigm, in the sense meant by Kuhn, may perhaps possess the characteristics and properties of a general background which unwittingly predetermines the scientist's activity. But what is involved is a scientific representation of reality, an "internal" viewpoint *pertaining to and emanating from that science;* thus it is not an ideology but precisely what is called a theory, the assumption of a coherent working hypothesis based on the latest established data, within which the researcher works according to criteria that remain scientific.

Of a totally different nature is the penetration of a nonscientific ideology into the very heart of science, of which I have already provided several examples; or, stated with even greater precision, the falsification, the perversion, and the mutilation of science to benefit an ideology. There is no doubt that this deceit grows more difficult to carry out as the domains it is meant to penetrate gain in intellectual rigor. But in many scientific disciplines there is still such a margin of uncertainty as to make them vulnerable to tendentious manipulations, particularly since it is not so much the scientific community that they are intended to influence as a public which lacks the means of checking and which is ready to take renowned scientists at their word. The scientist who works within the Kuhnian paradigm does so with total honesty. He is not aware of being conditioned by the epistemological substratum of his times, from which viewpoint he respects objectivity. But this is not the case, for example, when a "revisionist" American sovietologist, Arch Getty, declares during a conference of Slavic scholars held in Boston in 1987 that the total number of victims of collectivization and of Stalin's purges in the 1930s did not exceed . . . 35,000!* This is a patently ridiculous figure, even when measured by the deliberately low estimates of Soviet apologists, and it reflects the naïve clumsiness of the propagandist. But the fact that Mr. Getty, professor of history from the University of California, could advance such a figure at a high-level university conference, without being asked to quit his post on the spot, shows how shallow the respect for facts too often is in so-called "research."

As regards the French Revolution, we are more precisely confronted by a struggle between two paradigms—that is, if we limit ourselves to authors who regard it as generally beneficial. According to the first, the Revolution served as a transition from absolute monarchy to liberal democracy, was accompanied by regrettable "blunders," could probably have been carried out at a smaller economic and human cost, but did in the end realize or seal the ineluctable passage from an old world to a modern political society founded on equality of conditions, identical law for all, choice of leaders by popular vote, freedom of culture and

*This incident was reported by one of the participants in this conference, Jacques Rupnik, in "Glasnost: Gorbachev's Profs; A New Generation of American Academics is Rewriting Soviet History," *The New Republic,* December 7, 1987.

information, and inviolability of human rights. According to the second paradigm, the Revolution prefigured and sanctified in advance the socialist classless society, the dictatorship of the proletariat, the single-party system, the omnipotent State. The "blunders" were therefore not accidental errors. Far from being failures or perverse consequences, they were necessary to thwart counterrevolutionary plots, both internal and external.

The striking thing about the adherents of this second version is that, like the advocates of contemporary totalitarian systems, they proclaim the necessity and the legitimacy of a Terror whose scope and cruelty they simultaneously strive to deny and to hide! Penury, repression, and economic failures are likewise as far as possible dissimulated, soft-pedaled, and in any case dissociated from the responsibility of those in power. Thus, during the twentieth century we have heard Stalin impute the famine to the kulaks, Hanoi blame the "money-grubbing bourgeoisie," and the Kabul regime attribute all popular resistance to its policies to "imperialist interference." To deny and to justify the facts at one and the same time stems here from a vitally important motive: the need to avoid having to abandon the paradigm itself. The partisans of this paradigm do not defend all present-day totalitarian regimes; they pick and choose among them. Some more or less consciously use the Jacobin model in order to praise the Sandinistas but not the Khmer Rouge, who were too heavy-handed in their brutality. They close their eyes to the reality of the Sandinista regime, the old dialectic will go to work, and abstraction will expel those concrete cases that contradict the overall thesis. With respect to other regimes this will not happen. The Jacobin paradigm, like every totalitarian ideology, both proclaims and hides its secret, which is that any revolution carried out according to the Jacobin model in the name of Liberty in fact increases the power of the state and destroys the freedom of civil society. Long before Lenin and Mao, Mirabeau had grasped it well; in an effort to "sell" the incipient revolution to Louis XVI, he wrote in one of his confidential memoranda: "Compare the new state of affairs with the old regime; it is there that consolations and hopes are born. One part of the acts of the national assembly, and it is the more considerable, is clearly favorable to monarchical government. Is it therefore nothing to be without a parliament, without local legislatures, without a constituted body of the clergy, of the privileged, of the nobility? The idea of forming one sole class of citizens would have pleased Richelieu: this even surface facilitates the exercise of power. Several reigns of absolutist government could not have done as much for royal authority as one year of revolution."* This passage constitutes one of the oldest on-the-spot analyses ever made of the famous distinction between authoritarian and totalitarian regimes, a distinction the totalitarians reject because it puts the finger on the most significant of the dividing lines separating political regimes. To the king who was clinging to the old authoritarian type, Mirabeau vaunted the far superior merits, from the point of view of the state, of totalitarian "modernity."

The historiography of the French Revolution thus enables us to verify the aptness of Benedetto Croce's aphorism, or let us rather say truism, according to which "History is always contemporary history"—in the sense that it is part of the history of the moment.† But this unwitting relativism of vision should not be confused with the willfulness of falsification. The first in no way excludes scientific probity, while the second excludes itself from science.

Farther on, in dealing with history and contemporary questions, I shall provide other examples of falsifications and wild extrapolations from given data: for example, concerning the demographic "explosion" of the Third World, the equality of chances in democratic societies, the relationship between development and underdevelopment. But the subordination of knowledge to ideology springs from diverse roots. In daily life casualness with facts and arguments is all too rampant. Rudimentary opportunism commonly colors the thinking of those who are euphemistically called politically "responsible" leaders. Thus, after having sounded the alarm bell against the "fascist" danger in France, the Communist Party suddenly assures us that "it would be a mistake to think that we are faced by a fascist threat in the country."‡ Why this sudden shift? The answer is simple. It is part of left-wing tradition that in a case of fascist danger, the Communist Party should ally itself with socialists and other "republicans" against the supreme peril. In 1934 it suddenly swung from "class against class" tactics and the theme "Our enemy is social democracy" to the Committee of Anti-Fascist Intellectuals and the Popular Front. In 1987 the French Communist Party chose a policy of hostility toward the Socialist Party, "the agent of the Right in the policy of austerity." An entente with the socialists being out of the question, *ergo* there was no "fascist danger." Neither in 1984 nor in 1987 was the political reality of Le Pen's National Front analyzed for

*Quoted by Tocqueville, *L'Ancien Régime et la Révolution,* Book I, Chap. 2.
†In *La Storia come pensiero e come azione* ("History as Thought and Action"), 1938.
‡*L'Humanité,* September 10, 1987.

and in itself. In 1984 the "fascist danger" had been inflated so that the "liberals" could be accused of having engendered it. In 1987 it had to disappear so that the Communist Party could rid itself of the Union of the Left.

During the military regimes in Argentina and Uruguay the communists, on the contrary, sought to constitute a union of all democrats against fascism. Did this mean that once democracy had returned to their countries, they would finally accept political pluralism and defend "socialism with a human face" in communist countries? To believe that such a thing could happen is to remain blissfully ignorant of what ideological opportunism really is or, if one prefers, of how imperturbably fixed and static an ideology can be.

In Uruguay—to cite a single, precise, and revealing episode—at a moment when democracy was in the process of being restored, a huge popular meeting was held in a Montevideo park during the afternoon of Sunday, November 27, 1983. The podium had been set up at the foot of the obelisk erected to honor the memory of the Constitutents of 1830 (the date of Uruguay's first constitution). Sympathizers and militant members of all of the country's political currents turned out in force. The crowd was immense. It was the biggest demonstration Uruguay had seen in a long, long time. Opposite the speakers' platform and a bit to the right, the first rows of the public were composed, as though by accident, of militants belonging to the Communist Party (very much a minority in the country). The meeting began with the solemn reading of countless messages of congratulation, sympathy, and encouragement from all over the world, hailing the rebirth of democracy in Uruguay. Each message was greeted with a ritual burst of applause, cheers, and ovations. But then came the moment when the reader, after delving into the basket in front of him, pulled out and began to read a telegram of friendship sent by Lech Walesa in the name of Solidarity to the Uruguayan people, "just delivered from fascism." Immediately the first rows of the public began to whistle, jeer, and boo, cursing Solidarity and shouting, "Down with Walesa! Down with American imperialism!"

At a higher level we encounter the involuntary prejudice, generally shared by an entire epoch and overlaid with no more than a portion of personal dishonesty. Thus Jules Ferry, the man who had combated the Second Empire of Napoleon III, who had proclaimed the restoration of the Republic on September 4, 1870, who was the father of the republican Left, the minister to whom France owes the great democratic laws on freedom of the press, right of assembly, and free, secular, and compulsory primary education, could on July 28, 1885, declare from the rostrum of the Chamber of Deputies in Paris: "Gentlemen, one must speak more loudly and more truthfully! We must say openly that the superior races have a right vis-à-vis inferior races. I repeat, the superior races have a right because they also have a duty. They have the duty of civilizing inferior races."

Today it is commonly supposed that racism comes from the Right. This is to overlook the fact that in the nineteenth century the inherent inequality of races seemed self-evident to the Left as well as to the Right. In the preface to *L'Avenir de la science* ("The Future of Science"), penned in 1890, two years before his death, Ernest Renan, in looking back at the message of this book, which he had written half a century before, indulged in this piece of self-criticism: "At that time I did not have a sufficiently clear idea of the inequality of races." It is thus interesting to observe how one of the most critical minds of the century could quietly regard as proven a thesis that had not been scientifically demonstrated, and how an open-minded humanist could subscribe to an assumption that was pregnant with redoubtable practical consequences for human rights and tolerance.

The word "race," furthermore, was then often used as much in a cultural sense as in a biological one. The mistake made by the men of the nineteenth century was to attribute to "race" economic, social, or political forms of behavior that they judged severely. The mistake we make today is to absolve such condemnable forms of behavior and even racist attitudes in non-Western countries, for fear of being accused of "racism." When in May 1987 Colonel Sitiveni Rabuka overthrew the regularly elected government of the Fiji Islands because most of its members were of Indian origin, whereas the colonel wanted to reserve power for the Melanesians, there were few in the West who dared to raise their voices to condemn the creation of a new regime founded on an explicitly racist principle. A majority of citizens of Indian origin but born in the Fiji Islands, along with several other ethnic groups, thus find themselves deprived of their political rights for racial reasons. (Ethnic Fijians represent 43 percent of the population.) Rabuka's regime was duly excluded from the Commonwealth, but protests against this new form of apartheid quickly died down and ceased to trouble the planet. After having carried out a second coup d'état on September 25, 1987, and promoting himself to the rank of general, Rabuka was forced to turn power over to civilians on December 5. An interim government, headed by a prime minister who had held office *prior to* the elections of April 1987 (one therefore who refused to accept the result of those elections), was given the task of preparing a new constitution and new elections. Neither, so far as I know, have yet materialized.

In early September 1987 Colonel Jean-Baptiste Bagaza, the ruler of Burundi, who had been invited to attend a summit meeting of "francophonic" (i.e., French-speaking) leaders in Montreal despite the distinctly racist domination of his country, was overthrown by Captain Pierre Buyoya. The Vatican was delighted when the captain announced that he was ending the harsh measures his predecessor had taken against the Church. But Rome did not demand any modification in the ethnic relationships between "superior" Tutsis and "inferior" Hutus, which had led to the massacres of 1972. The new captain-president in fact made it clear that he was not going to alter anything in the status quo—which meant that the existing regime of tribal discrimination, of black apartheid, would be maintained with the blessing of the religious authorities and of the international community.

When, on October 15 of this same year of 1987, in Burkina Faso (formerly Upper Volta), Captain Blaise Compaoré decided to practice "governmental alternance" by assassinating Captain Sankara (whom he wanted to replace) and a dozen of his closest associates, the defenders of human rights and democracy in the West were no more worked up than they had been in 1983, when on the Caribbean island of Grenada the Politburo of the Marxist-Leninist New Jewel movement (a member of the Socialist International!) had decided to murder 150 others, including their chief, Maurice Bishop, who had himself come to power thanks to a coup d'état in 1979. Bishop was "liquidated" by a clan that was even more pro-Soviet than he was, but the "liberals" in the United States preferred to reserve their outcries of indignation for the American landings in Grenada, which took place a little later.

The silence observed by people in the West about such bizarre political practices—if only because of the incredibly high number of military men who govern those countries (a military dictatorship not seeming to be an infraction of democracy unless the dictator is called Pinochet or Stroessner)—can only be explained by the simple inversion of the ideological filter which, one hundred years earlier, would have caused them to attribute these aberrations to the incapacity of "inferior peoples" to govern themselves. In one case it was the racist principle, in the other it is the antiracist *taboo* that keeps people from analyzing these phenomena as they deserve to be—which is to say, as a complex of political, social, economic, religious, and cultural factors, which deserve to be studied like any other facts of the same kind and eventually to be subjected to the same moral standards. When the Italian communist leader Giancarlo Pajetta jokingly compares the Addis Ababa of 1977 to the Paris of 1793, he declares himself to be charmed by the atmosphere reigning in the Ethiopian capital at a moment when it contained more than 100,000 political prisoners and when even children under twelve years of age were being shot. (In Ethiopia persons above this age can, thank Heaven, be shot, but they are no longer children as far as the state is concerned!) For such a reaction to be possible, ideology and the cult of revolution must have encased Pajetta in a kind of bell jar, absolutely impermeable to the fresh air of reality.

Let us look once again at the fourfold function of ideology. It is an instrument of power; a defense mechanism against information; a pretext for eluding moral constraints in doing or approving evil with a clean conscience; and finally, a way of banning the criterion of experience, that is, of completely eliminating or indefinitely postponing the pragmatic criteria of success and failure.

The sentinel who mounts guard before this psychic fortress sifts the incoming information solely according to its capacity to reinforce or weaken ideology. In an edifying book of reminiscences entitled *Reluctant Farewell,* Andrew Nagorski, a former *Newsweek* correspondent in Moscow, described the reactions he encountered during a period of home leave in 1982, when the so-called "Euromissile" debate was at its peak. The issue was whether Pershing II and cruise missiles should be deployed in Western Europe to counterbalance the Soviet SS-20s. "On my short excursion to the West, I found that as a rule minds were already made up on these issues. People who endorsed the NATO decision to deploy new missiles welcomed my observations about Kremlin thinking as ammunition for their team, while opponents dismissed what I had to say about Soviet perceptions of the West as irrelevant. I felt distinctly uneasy with how quickly I was categorized in any discussion of this subject. It was a matter of choosing up sides in a domestic political debate, and what relation all this bore to Soviet intentions hardly seemed to matter."

Can it be that Man is an intelligent being who is not guided by intelligence? Intelligence, considered from one point of view and without prejudging its other properties, can spare us a harmful experience by enabling us, each time it is possible, to analyze the components of a situation in order to foresee or at least to imagine the consequences of a particular course of action. In essence, it is a faculty for anticipating and simulating action, thanks to which we can guide ourselves without necessarily having to put overly dangerous experiments to the test to see what may result. However, not only do we use this faculty all too rarely; placed in an almost identical situation, we often repeat behaviors that have already failed.

CHAPTER 10

The Adulterine Power

Ah! nous n'avons que trop, aux maîtres de la terre,
Emprunté, pour régner, leur puissance adultère;
Voilà de tous nos maux la fatale origine.

Ah, all too often, in order to rule, have we borrowed
Their adulterine power from the masters of the earth;
This is the fatal origin of all our woes.

> — Alphonse de Lamartine, *Aux chrétiens*
> *dans les temps d'épreuves.* Harmonies, I, 6.

Aucune profession n'est plus décriée que celle de
journaliste. Aucune n'est plus flagornée.

No profession has been more disparaged than that of
journalist. None is more fawned upon and flattered.

> — Robert de Jouvenel, *La République des camarades*
> (Paris: 1914). (Robert de Jouvenel was Bertrand
> de Jouvenel's uncle.)

It would doubtless be excessive and unfair to write that information about current events is severely hamstrung in one half of the world and false in the other. For in fact it is severely hamstrung in far more than half the world.

Indeed, if one estimates that there are about fifty countries in which nothing resembling a free press exists and about thirty-five in which it does exist, this gap grows even larger if one takes into account not so much the number of countries but the number of human beings involved; for some of the countries where the news is the most severely controlled are among the most populous of the planet. Between these two groups, whose numbers fluctuate, one can generously concede that there are about thirty other regimes in which the press enjoys limited freedom. Paradoxically, such mixed situations comprise greater personal hazards for journalists than do systems of complete censorship. Every year some of them are victims of reprisals, including murder, due to the very imprecision of the limits tacitly imposed on their curiosity.

Because in most countries of the world current news is either suppressed or severely censored, or else inaccessible, difficult to come by and transmit, it becomes in our eyes so precious and sacrosanct that we come to regard journalistic information in those rare countries where freedom reigns as exempt of every defect and free of all error. In such countries criticizing the press becomes a kind of sacrilege, committed often enough but nonetheless reproved in principle. Yet even in societies that have a long democratic tradition and in which freedom of expression is greatly respected, only a small fraction of newspapers and other media are specifically designed and operated with a view to providing the public with accurate information and serious commentaries— within, of course, the realm of human possibility; for here I refer only to intentions.

Furthermore, in a democracy the law guarantees freedom of expression to its citizens; it guarantees neither infallibility, nor talent, nor competence, nor probity, nor intelligence, nor the verification of facts— all of which are supposed to be provided by or are the responsibility of journalists, not of legislators. But when a journalist is criticized because he is inaccurate or dishonest, the profession as a whole lets out a howl, pretending to believe that the very principle of free expression is under attack and that a new attempt is being made to "muzzle the press." The journalist, it is explained, was merely fulfilling his "task of informing." But what would we think of a restaurant owner who, after serving

232 The Flight from Truth

spoiled food, fended off criticism by exclaiming: "Please, let me fulfill my mission as a nourisher, that sacred duty! Or are you in favor of starvation?"

In reality, most of those who launch newspapers or other means of communication do so to impose a point of view and not to seek the truth. It is simply that when one wants to impose a certain point of view, it is better to seem to be seeking the truth. Just as, among the millions of books that are published, only a tiny proportion are devoted to literature in the highest, artistic sense of the word, or to the communication of knowledge, so only a minority of press and communications enterprises are founded and managed with the primary aim of informing. Newspapers geared to this particular objective occupy a tiny niche in the gigantic mass of the purely commercial or partisan press.

The confusion between freedom of expression, which has to be accorded even to liars and madmen, and the task of informing, which carries its own built-in constraints, goes back to the very origins of liberal civilization. Before the second half of the nineteenth century—which is to say, before the birth of wire services, reporters, the electric telegraph, and so on—all published considerations on freedom of the press—from Milton and Voltaire down to Tocqueville—focused exclusively on freedom of opinion.* As modern democracy developed, it became evident that one of its components consisted of the freedom for each citizen, as Voltaire put it, to "think in writing." We must, he said, defend the right of each individual to make his viewpoint public, even if this point of view appals us, and we should ourselves combat it only through words and arguments, never by force and calumny, this being the basic principle of tolerance.

However, the right to speak rationally or talk nonsense as one wishes has nothing to do with the right to print false information, which is a very different matter. In the early years of democracy the issue of press freedom was not debated in the context of the right to inform or to be informed; it was concerned solely with tolerance and diversity of opinions. This is why the famous First Amendment to the U.S. Constitution, which established the right to a free press, deals in the same sentence with religious freedom, freedom of expression, and the right to assemble publicly and to present petitions.† But the prohibition laid down by this

*John Milton probably wrote the oldest pamphlet in favor of freedom of the press (in its most literal sense): "Discourse on the Freedom to Print without Authorisation and Censorship" (1644).

†"Congress shall make no law respecting an establishment of religion, or prohibiting the

amendment against "abridging the freedom of speech, or of the press"—
placed on the same plane as the prohibition to restrict the right of any
person to choose his religion—does not in any way imply that the
Reagan administration, for example, violated the Constitution, as some
maintained, when it decided that no reporters would be present with
U.S. troops during the early hours of the invasion of Grenada in 1983.
Neither does the First Amendment imply that a newspaper has the right
to publish a confidential state document that has been fraudulently
obtained. The right of the public, or at any rate of the press, to be
informed in advance of all military operations is one that can be established theoretically; but in neither case can such a "right" be derived
from the First Amendment, for the simple reason that this amendment
did not deal with the acquiring of information.

In France, too, after the collapse of the First Napoleonic Empire and
during the period of the Restoration (1815–30) and the July Monarchy
(1830–48), all discussions concerning the press and the laws that might
or might not be desirable for regulating it were concerned solely with
the notion of opinion. All the liberal thinkers—Benjamin Constant in
his *Principes de politique* (1815), Royer-Collard* in his 1817 speech to the
Chamber of Deputies on freedom of the press—begin by assuming (here
I quote Royer-Collard) that "the free publication of individual opinions
by the press is not only the condition of political liberty, but is the
necessary principle of this liberty, since it alone can form within the
bosom of a nation a general opinion on its affairs and interests." Thereafter, the question that engaged the reflections of these political thinkers
the most was deciding how to punish abuses of the freedom of expression: opinions damaging the honor, dignity, or security of others or
threatening civil peace. Can one, they asked, prevent such abuses without infringing this very freedom? Generally speaking, they concluded
that it was better to accept the inconveniences than to try to remedy
them by legislation; for public wisdom, fruit of the experience of freedom and the habit of confronting different theses, would take care of
discrediting defamers and factious elements. Benjamin Constant rejected both the "frenetic souls who in our time sought to demonstrate
the need to chop off a number of heads which they designated, and who

free exercise thereof; or abridging the freedom of speech, or of the press; or the right of the
people peaceably to assemble, and to petition the Government for a redress of grievances."
    *Pierre-Paul Royer-Collard (1763–1845)—philosopher, writer, and politician, was, along
with François Guizot, Prosper de Barante, and Charles de Rémusat, a member of the liberal
group known as "the Doctrinaires."

then justified themselves saying that they were doing no more than expressing their opinion" and "the inquisitors who would like to make an issue of this delirium, in order to subject the manifestation of every opinion to the jurisdiction of authority." As can be seen, what was at issue in all these speeches was the right to express a personal point of view, never what today we usually understand by "the problems of information and the media."*

For Tocqueville newspapers played the role that regional papers and cable television fill in local communities today. They serve both as a social cement and as links between inhabitants. Without the press, citizens could abandon themselves to the individualism toward which they are pushed by egalitarian democracy: "When men are no longer bound to one another in a solid and permanent manner [e.g., in aristocratic societies], it is not easy to prevail upon a great number of them to act in common. This cannot habitually and conveniently be done save

*Chateaubriand, to whom are often mistakenly attributed reactionary ideas, also vigorously defended freedom of the press under the Bourbon Restoration, coming out against any form of censorship and accepting the risk of abuses. But it should be noted that he too, like the other authors I have cited, envisaged the press solely as a conveyor of opinions and not of information; as, for example, when he wrote in *Le Journal des Débats* of June 21, 1824: "No doubt newspapers are nothing in comparison to social power, the throne, the tribune. They are not even comparable things; they are of two different orders. No one has ever thought of considering a newspaper to be a political power; it is a written work expressing an opinion; and if this opinion unites around itself the plurality of enlightened and highly esteemed men, it can become a great power. This is the power of the truth; there is nothing higher in the moral order, there is nothing that does not vanish before this eternal force."

Chateaubriand here committed the *péché mignon* (the "charming sin") of journalists of all periods in confusing freedom of opinion and the expression of an eternal truth, as though having the license to print what one wishes and always being right were but one and the same thing. But he showed himself to be astoundingly modern in sketching the contours of the "fourth power"—as when, in another passage, he posed the question of government by the media: "But, it is said, if ministers should resign before the clamor of five or six newspapers, then is France governed by newspapers?

"Is England governed by newspapers, which are far freer there than in France? And yet English ministers withdraw when public sheets of different political principles agree on their ministerial incapacity. The radical vice of this eternal reasoning made by the foes of freedom of the press is to take the newspapers as the cause of opinion, when they are but its effect. If you have clever ministers, truly monarchist and national, you will see if the newspapers can succeed in rendering them unpopular; far from it being so, such newspapers would themselves become unpopular in attacking men whom the public would have taken under its protection."

If we leave to one side the thorny question—which is without juridical foundation—as to an elected government's responsibility to newspapers, we must admit that Chateaubriand perfectly perceived the democratic circulation of opinion moving from that expressed by the press to public opinion and vice versa, each nourishing the other mutually in putting pressure jointly or separately on political leaders. However, what is involved here, too, in this vibrant portrayal of the budding role of a strong future press, at once mirror and power, is solely opinion, never information.

by a newspaper; only a newspaper can come and deposit the same thought at the same moment in a thousand minds." Viewed from this angle, the exuberance of the press in the United States, according to Tocqueville, stems from the flourishing of associations, that is, of local democracy, wherein he rightly saw the fundamental trait and the genuine source of American democracy. The passage I just cited from *Democracy in America* is in fact drawn from a chapter entitled "On the Relations of Associations and Newspapers." The press, in this conception of society, has a mobilizing function. It helps to draw the citizens together around a common project—which is a good thing, Tocqueville goes on, even if the project is worthless, because it at least tears them away from their individualism. "I will not deny that, in democratic countries, the newspapers often lead the citizens to undertake in common most unconsidered enterprises; but if there were no newspapers, there would hardly be any mobilizing action. The evil they produce is thus far less than the one they cure."

Tocqueville thus persisted in viewing the press solely in terms of its mobilizing function, that is, counteracting the slump into solitary torpor, this being a consequence of democratic atomization. It is disconcerting to realize that one of the greatest modern theorists of democracy and one of its most intuitive observers should not have perceived the importance of the other function that makes the press indispensable in a democratic system: the function of providing information. Now, if democracy is a regime in which the citizens determine the general orientations of domestic and foreign policy by voting for the diverse programs of the candidates they designate to represent and govern them, this regime can operate sensibly and follow a course in the interests of its members only if the electors are correctly informed about the state of affairs of the world and their nation. This is why falsehood is so serious for democracy, a regime that is viable only when the truth prevails and which can lead to catastrophe if the citizens make their decisions on the basis of false information. In totalitarian regimes the leaders and the state-controlled press deceive society, but the governments do not conduct their policies according to their own lies. They have files and sources of information available only to the elite. In a democracy, when the executive power deceives public opinion, it is obliged to have its acts conform to the errors it has inculcated, since it is public opinion that designates the leaders or else votes them out of office. Is it not to avert this deadly risk that the press intervenes, or should intervene; is it not this function that renders it indissociable from democracy itself?

But in this respect, alas, the original confusion between the function of opinion and the function of information or, more exactly, the precedence of the first over the second, as well as its preponderance, have given rise to a misunderstanding which has lasted till this day. On the one hand—and here everyone is in agreement—democracy is a system in which all opinions should be able to express themselves, provided they do so peacefully. On the other hand, it is a system that can function properly only if its citizens can have access to a basic minimum of exact information. Yet no matter what people say, this latter function has never been completely distinguished from the former, nor properly understood. And above all, it has always been underestimated.

Nothing illustrates this more clearly than the usual tiresome platitudes one has to listen to at round-table discussions or academic debates about the press. The press, it is endlessly repeated, should be pluralist. But only opinion can be pluralist, not information itself. By its very nature, information can be true or false, but not pluralist. I am well aware that not every item of information attains that ideal degree of certainty that dispels all hesitations and puts an end to controversy and dispute. "Pluralism" thus affects it only to the extent that the information is doubtful. One might say that the more a piece of information is pluralist, the less it is information. In essence, it must always tend toward certainty; and, it may be added, far more information can actually attain this degree of certainty than is generally supposed, this supposition being a convenient way of not having to heed it. The cliché of an unattainable objectivity is too often a refuge for mental laziness—or mere trickery.

In any case, in settling a question of fact, objectivity does not consist of opposing contrary opinions in the course of a debate, as is so often erroneously assumed. If the two opinions are both based on false information, of what use is the debate? Such differences may reflect the differing moods and viewpoints of a country's ideological families. But the mission of the press does not stop there. The confrontation of arbitrary opinions has never replaced factual knowledge. The duty of the press is to acquire this kind of knowledge and then to transmit it. Pluralism regains its rights and reveals its necessity when the moment comes to draw conclusions from established facts, to propose remedies, to suggest specific measures. Unfortunately, in practice "pluralism" intervenes prior to this stage; it sifts the information, eliminating certain facts, passing them over in silence, denying them, amputating or amplifying them, and even inventing them, in such a way as to adulterate the process of opinion formation in its embryonic stage.

Those who invoke "pluralism" shamelessly refer to the right claimed by every newspaper to present information in its own way. This is so much the case that every time the French socialist daily *Le Matin* (which finally went under) entered a new crisis, the new rescuer would guarantee that the newspaper would remain "anchored to the Left." But someone who really believes in his own political tenets has no need to "anchor" himself. He is—or should be—persuaded that the validity of his tenets will be sustained by the accuracy of the information provided. If he feels the need to announce that he will present information in a light favorable to his theories, this means that he is no longer as convinced of their validity and admits that impartiality would be fatal to his "camp."

Another ritual piece of nonsense consists of defining the press as a "counterpower." It is true that the role of the press is to tell the truth, and that the government in power does not much like the truth when it is unfavorable. But it is also true that the truth is not always unfavorable. Thus the press has no business claiming to be a counterpower by virtue of a selective automatism and in every circumstance. Besides, the very notion is absurd, for if things really happened in this way, and if the government in power invariably deserved to be opposed, it would be sufficient reason to despair of democracy, for it would mean that a democratically elected government is always mistaken, and therefore that the people electing it are afflicted with a congenital, incurable idiocy.

This idea that a good newspaper is one that always combats a government is not without its consequences in the overall presentation of the news, simply because local constraints make it virtually impossible for the media of free countries to do a really serious job of reporting in totalitarian communist countries such as China, Vietnam, Cambodia, Albania, Ethiopia, and Cuba. As a result, nine tenths of the information provided in the democratic press consists of critical appraisals of the democracies themselves. The latter are taken to task above all for associating with less democratic allies, which are particularly vulnerable to such accusations since they are at once permeable to information and exposed to moral condemnation. By virtue of this "logic" the democratic system of information can all too easily find itself coasting down the easy slope of permanent indictment of democracy itself; and thus, though invented to defend democracy, it helps to undermine it.

This was particularly true during the long period of the Cold War, when the Western democracies were confronted by a militarototalitarian system whose undisguised aim was to undermine and destroy capitalist societies. A great deal of the "reporting" then done by Western journalists was primarily aimed at justifying the existence of such systems and soft-pedaling the threat they posed to democracy in various parts of the world. This was a classic example of how democracy can unwittingly transmute its lifeblood into a poison, by fabricating arguments to prove that, unless absolutely perfect, it does not deserve to exist. In effect, this amounted to stipulating that democracy's only choice is between saintliness and death.

Far be it from me to prescribe some kind of scared conformism or absolute perfection in order to save democracy. All I ask on democracy's behalf is the truth, the whole truth. Once again, what matters is clearly to delimit the informative function of the press, radio, and TV media, given the disastrous consequences for democracy a poorly informed public opinion can entail.

The role of watchdog, judge, and even inquisitor that the press arrogates to itself, while healthy and necessary, amounts, it would have us believe, to a kind of magistracy. Like all magistracies, it should be surrounded by guarantees of competence and impartiality. However, the "fourth power" or the "counterpower" is only a *de facto* power. It has no constitutional substance save for that derived from each citizen's right to write and say what he wishes. Whereas the other counterpowers—the judicial and the legislative—are powers in themselves, recruiting their members according to criteria of representativity or competence or morality as defined by the Constitution and by laws or regulations, nothing of the sort conditions the hiring of journalists. The professional diplomas handed out by schools of journalism have only an indicative value. They guarantee little and they are not obligatory, unlike the degrees the law demands for doctors, lawyers, and professors. As a result, the journalistic community is the supreme judge of the capacities and honesty of its own members and the quality of their work—along with the public, to be sure; but the public almost never has the means of disputing the information offered to it, since most of the information available to members of the public is derived from the newspapers they usually read, the TV programs they watch, and the radio broadcasts they listen to. When, by chance, an ordinary citizen possesses a firsthand source of information—when, for example, his newspaper or TV network deals with a familiar problem concerning his work, his neighborhood, a foreign country he happens to have lived in, or events in which he was personally involved—he most often passes a severe, sometimes scandalized judgment on the way in which the subject is treated. This is a disquieting symptom, though frequent enough, as each of us has been able to discover. The more a reader or TV viewer knows about a certain subject, the more harshly the media are judged. When a journalist invokes the "right to inform" and the "right to information," he or she refers to the right to present the facts as he or she pleases, almost never to the public's right to be accurately and honestly informed. When the media commit errors—often gross mistakes that can have harmful consequences—these errors can be effectively denounced only by the press itself—something that rarely happens and which is ill regarded by the journalistic community, especially in France. Blunt attacks on other newspapers are normally launched only by extremist rags, and the public then attributes them to political passion. Such attacks concern the political bias rather than the professional quality of the reporting. But it is solely on the terrain of professionalism and by rigorously supervising the quality of the informational service it renders society that a "fourth power" could claim some degree of legitimacy and the right to assume the mission of being a "counterpower." With some newspapers and networks, furthermore, this "mission" is transformed, as though by magical metamorphosis, into one of "propower" when power falls into the hands of or reverts to the party that enjoys their preference.

To counter this reproach, journalists often entrench themselves behind the so-called distinction between opinion and information—another standard cliché from the high-sounding but hollow platitudes one so often hears. Yet the distinction is seldom observed. The controversy over the present-day press comes precisely from the fact that the right (the first to be recognized) to express all opinions—even the most extravagant, the most hateful—the right to be wrong, to lie, to say stupid things has spilled over and influenced the mission of information gathering and transmitting, which appeared only later. If today one accuses a journalist of being a falsifier of facts or an ignoramus on a precise point of information, one is immediately accused of indulging in a "witch-hunt," of assailing the freedom of the press, of rejecting "pluralism."

According to a famous maxim, "Commentary is free, information is sacred." I must confess that I have often had the impression that the very opposite holds true. Information is free and fanciful, commentary is sacred. But the most pernicious ill is opinion disguised as information. U.S. journalists often speak slightingly of their European counterparts, especially of French and Italian journalists who, they say, mix facts and commentaries in the same article, imposing value judgments on the news items they pour out and on the declarations and actions of politicians, which they should be reporting in a neutral fashion. It is true that many journalists are in such a rush to make it clear that they have a poor or good opinion of this or that politician, to avoid being regarded as accomplices or adversaries, that they run out of breath in the first lines of their article and provide a wretched presentation of the facts. It is also true that the U.S. journalist displays a rigorous discipline in his way of drafting articles of pure information, adhering to a deliberately impersonal style, but without the necessary dryness of wire service dispatches. He avoids resorting to allusions and each time recalls the basic facts needed to understand the case, as though the reader had never read anything on the subject before. News items, news "stories," news "analysis," and syndicated columns are clearly separated categories in their conception and presentation, just as unsigned editorials reflect the opinions of the paper's management. But the most serious peril for the objectivity of information does not stem from the confusion of genres—which of course would be a good thing to banish, though this precaution in itself would not suffice. The bad journalist, who sprinkles subjective remarks through his article which are not derived from the facts and thus give it a partisan coloring, is not the most dangerous. For the reader is not long in perceiving the clumsy hocus-pocus that is being attempted before his eyes. The real danger comes from the feasibility of presenting false or altered items of information in an utterly neutral tone—a practice indulged in by the best newspapers in the world. It is easy to present a highly partial judgment as an established fact without this being immediately apparent, just as anyone can pass off an interpretation as an integral feature of information. And U.S. journalists of the printed press and electronic media indulge in such tricks just as much as their European colleagues, although, I admit, in a less gross and visible manner.

Here is an example of the European method, which I have culled at random—in this case from the February 10, 1988, issue of the Spanish daily *El País* concerning a relatively anodine event: the result of primary elections carried out by party caucuses in Iowa at the start of the U.S. presidential election campaign. The article was entitled "The Victory of Fanaticism." What fanaticism? That of Pat Robertson, an evangelist preacher and television star, virtuoso of "electronic religion," who in Iowa had come out ahead of Vice President George Bush. "A victory obtained thanks to the unprecedented mobilization of fanatical Christians by the evangelical churches, which wish to do away with the right to abortion, to rid the world of Soviet 'tyranny,' and to reestablish prayers in public schools." The reader thus reaches the middle of the article without having learned much of what primarily interests him—to wit, the percentages obtained by the different candidates of the Democratic and Republican parties. On the other hand, he is amply informed of the personal emotions of the newspaper's correspondent in Des Moines, emotions for which I feel as much respectful consideration as profound indifference. I did not spend sixty pesetas to be informed of the vibrations unleashed in this Spanish correspondent's soul by Pat Robertson. Instead of undertaking an inquiry, he began naïvely by asserting that never before in history had a comparable mobilization of "Christian fanatics" been seen—something that indicates an alarming degree of crass ignorance in this reporter; above all, he did not ask any questions as to the causes of the evangelical church's capacity to mobilize its faithful and the social roots of its popular success—the only truly pertinent subject, about which we would have liked to have obtained information and elucidation. Above all the Spanish newspaperman wanted us to know that he despised Robertson, and that for that reason he himself merited our esteem. Without harboring any greater sympathy for the United States' "moral majority" and Pat Robertson than for this newspaperman, I must recall that in a democracy one has no right to term a citizen a "fanatic," even if one detests his ideas, so long as the citizen does no more than give free expression to his or her opinions (that sacred right!) in the context of an electoral campaign. Since abortion had been authorized by the voting of a law, did no one have the right to appeal to electors to have a contrary law voted through? Or to wish to make the reading of prayers compulsory in public schools? Those who disagree need only campaign in their turn, using persuasion and arguments. Fanaticism is measured not by the content of the opinions one professes but by the manner in which one seeks to impose them. So long as it is not through violence, nor through intolerance, persecution, and terror, one has not transgressed any fundamental principle of democracy. However, *El País*'s correspondent seemed totally unaware of such fine distinctions, the very foundation of pluralism, since he chose to put Soviet "tyranny" in quotation marks, thus flaunting his reprobation of such black malevolence—just think, calling communist totalitarianism "tyranny"!—and his own warped conception of true tolerance.

I have cited *El País*. But at the time the same crazy amplifications of the ridiculously short-lived Robertson intermezzo could be found in many other European newspapers of the same political orientation, particularly in left-wing newspapers in France and Italy.

This tiny sample is just one of thousands that occur every day in the free press; instead of undertaking an honest inquiry, the journalist delivers a sermon. Of a higher degree of refinement is the opinion that is no longer substituted for information but presented as an element of information in both form and style. Let us take, for example, the speech Mikhail Gorbachev delivered to the Central Committee of the Communist Party of the Soviet Union toward the end of October 1987. On November 3, *The New York Times* and *The Wall Street Journal* both devoted a banner headline to this harangue—the former proclaiming GORBACHEV ASSAILS CRIMES OF STALIN, LAUDS KHRUSHCHEV, the second GORBACHEV BENDS TO HARD-LINERS BY HEDGING HIS ATTACK ON STALIN. His speech could be interpreted from both these angles. But what was involved in each case was interpretation, not information. In reality, Gorbachev had severely criticized Stalin, but international opinion was disappointed, for it had expected him to go even further. He was not as severe as Khrushchev had been in 1956, indeed far less so. He praised Stalin's "resolution" and his wartime "talents as an organizer," whereas Khrushchev had revealed his incapacity and paralytic inertness during the first weeks of the German invasion of 1941. Gorbachev, furthermore, did not rehabilitate Bukharin, who had been shot after a prewar Moscow show trial (though his rehabilitation came a short time afterward in February 1988). He bore down heavily on Trotsky, whom many had hoped he would absolve. We can therefore say that of the two, *The Wall Street Journal*'s headline was, for that date, closer to the reality of the speech than that of *The New York Times,* but that is not the point; the two headlines constituted value judgments rather than reports and reflected the secret desires of the editors, implicit conjectures as to the factional struggles dividing the Politburo, Gorbachev's determination, his future intentions and sincerity. As Karl Marx himself once wrote, with common sense: "Discussions on the reality or irreality of thought, isolated from practice, are sheer scholasticism."

It will be noted that I have referred only to excellent newspapers, and also to independent ones. In this connection I would add to my list of superficial commonplaces about the press and the media the cliché that attributes the virtue of objectivity to independence, as though this went without saying. When one speaks of "a big independent morning [or evening] newspaper," one has the impression of having said everything needed to justify the confidence of the public, and newspapers like to describe themselves in this way. But just as freedom does not guarantee infallibility, so independence is no guarantee of impartiality. It favors, but does not replace it. One can perfectly well be both independent and dishonest. I can, if I find the money needed, and furthermore if I am known to a sizable segment of the public whose prejudices and passions I satisfy, create a newspaper with the deliberate intent of quite independently presenting a deceptive version of contemporary reality and a vile portrayal of persons who don't share my point of view. For this it is not essential that I be bound to a political party, to specific financial interests, or to a government. Man does not have to be forced to be intellectually dishonest to become that way. He can achieve this very well all by himself. Nor does he need some external power to force him to be incompetent, so great is his capacity to achieve this spontaneously. For independence guarantees competence or discernment no more than it does impartiality. There are as many incompetent journalists working for private U.S. and European television networks as for public networks. Like pluralism, independence constitutes *one of the conditions* that make it *possible* to provide honest and exact information, but which do not render it certain.

Favorable conditions are not enough. There must also be capable individuals wishing to take advantage of the opportunity to produce solid information. This end product cannot be taken for granted in advance, by virtue of some kind of natural determinism, any more than freedom of creation suffices to bring forth a constant stream of talented writers, painters, and composers. This explains why certain newspapers, among the most universally well reputed and highly esteemed, the pride of the most developed democratic civilizations, and certain of the most venerable radio broadcasting and TV companies have at times been able to deceive their contemporaries on fundamental issues, and this to a truly surprising degree, considering their enormous means of information gathering and verification. During the decade preceding the outbreak of the World War II, the London *Times* adopted a position which, though not openly favorable to the Nazi regime, favored conciliation and disarmament as the best ways of calming Hitler and preserving peace. Similarly, as an attractive gamble and a hypothetical basis for diplomatic action in dealing with totalitarian systems, the notion of détente periodically came, and will doubtless continue to come, back into favor in the democracies.* Anyone has the latitude to ask that it be tried out, and *The Times* had every right to recommend such a policy, if this choice was dictated by its conscience. But the imposture, viewed from the angle of the "job of informing," began when *The Times* took to concealing information tending to show that the spirit of conciliation of the democratic governments in no way was moderating

*The fluctuations of public opinion in the Western democracies with regard to Saddam Hussein's totalitarian regime in Iraq are a bitter reminder of how deep-seated in the democratic psyche is the desire for détente no matter what—that is, for avoiding tough decisions.

Hitler's bellicose ambitions. In particular, *The Times* concealed the scope of the German rearmament effort, which, though at first clandestine and a violation of existing treaties and accords, later became more and more visible.

Here again, information was tailored to suit the newspaper's opinion, not the other way around. All indications pointed toward a final dénouement, which logically could only be a Hitlerian aggression, but *The Times* deliberately ignored them or denied their significance. The reminiscences of a French diplomat serving in London at the time offer us a detailed account of the mechanisms whereby governments reject elements of information that are incompatible with their particular interpretational filter, and those whereby the press, resorting to the same process of selection, instills in public opinion a distorted vision of looming threats.* The deceit is not easily perceptible, and it is hard to counter because it takes place at the stage of information gathering and transmitting, which it intercepts and colors, not that of commentary. Given the enormous influence wielded by *The Times* on prewar British public opinion in general and on the Foreign Office in particular, and given the leading role played by the British cabinet in the conduct of foreign policy by the democratic countries—Paris at the time having neither the authority nor the means to contradict London—one can regard the great "independent" newspaper as being partly responsible for persuading the country's political leaders and public opinion to accept Neville Chamberlain's docile policy, which encouraged Hitler to launch the war.

Today *The New York Times* is no less read, feared, and admired than was its London cousin in 1938; it may even be more read, given the worldwide diffusion of the U.S. press, and in particular of the *Times*'s overseas extension, the *International Herald Tribune.* Although one of the most complete and best-informed newspapers of the planet, no matter what its variable and varied political preferences may have been or may be, *The New York Times* has not been deprived by nature of one of *homo sapiens*'s most distinctive gifts—that of not seeing what exists, and of seeing what does not exist.

This gift was imparted with prodigality to *The New York Times*'s regular correspondent in Moscow during the late 1920s and 1930s—the famous Walter Duranty. The picture this journalist offered of the Soviet Union during the years of the giant famine (1931–34) and then the Great

---

*Girard de Charbonnières, *La plus évitable de toutes les guerres* ("The Most Avoidable of All Wars") (Paris: Albatros, 1985).

Terror (1936–39), and this in the most influential newspaper in the world's most powerful democracy, the homeland, furthermore, of rigorous "investigative" journalism, differed not at all from the most slavishly Stalinist articles then being published in communist newspapers in the USSR and in the West. During a tour of the Ukraine in 1933 Duranty could joyfully inform his transatlantic readers that he had seen enough to be able to assert categorically that all rumors about a famine in that region were ridiculous. Four years later, during the Moscow trials, the famous correspondent informed his readers no less categorically that it was unthinkable that Stalin, Voroshilov, Budenny, and the Military Tribunal had been able to condemn their friends to death without crushing proof of their guilt.

Duranty, we should remember, did not claim to be indulging in analysis or interpretation; here he was transcribing "facts." Let us imagine that a European journalist, finding himself in the United States around 1860, had been able to write in his newspaper that after having made an on-the-spot inspection, he could categorically assert that "rumors of civil war are ridiculous," and that it was "unthinkable" that gunfire could break out in any part of the territory of the Union. What would a U.S. historian think of the level of nineteenth-century journalism if he came across such a piece of "reporting"?

Gentlemen of the press, so little inclined to self-criticism, do not sufficiently study the mistakes of their predecessors. They thus commit similar errors in their turn. Who took to heart the outrageous and dishonoring imposture of Duranty? It was also in *The New York Times* that Harrison Salisbury, another "star" of contemporary reporting, wrote that during the Vietnam War U.S. Air Force planes had bombed nonmilitary targets in the north and gave for the civilian casualty counts figures supplied by the communists.

Time unwittingly did even better, since one of its correspondents in Saigon during the war, an English-speaking Vietnamese named Pham Xuan An, was not an occasional "stringer" but one of the magazine's staff reporters. After South Vietnam had been overrun by communist armies in 1975 he revealed that he had been a communist agent all along. Shortly thereafter Pham Xuan An could be seen seated in the grandstand next to Pham Van Dong, along with the entire Hanoi Politburo, during a military march-past.

As for Sydney Schanberg of *The New York Times,* after the fall of Saigon and Phnom Penh in 1975, he saw with his own eyes a sudden, substantial rise in the general standard of living of the population—this in the Cambodia of the Khmer Rouge, as well as in the Vietnam of the concentration camps and mass executions. The article he wrote in April 1975—"Indochina without Americans: For Most, a Better Life"—deserves to be analyzed in all contemporary schools of journalism. I doubt, however, that analysis is their favorite occupation. Nor, I imagine, would they bother to analyze an article like the one James Brooke, *The New York Times*'s correspondent in Angola, wrote in the January 3, 1985, issue of that paper—"Angolan Writers Bloom in Independent Climate." I must confess I searched in vain for documentary evidence of this flourishing renaissance of letters, which took place, according to Brooke, under the aegis of a new, unexpected form of Platonic academy—the Politburo of Luanda. However, since we must never despair of the human mind's capacity for adaptation, we can but rejoice at the tidings that the "climate of independence" of which Brooke spoke—a climate characterized at the time by the presence in the Angolan sector controlled by Luanda of 50,000 Cuban soldiers, 2,000 Soviet "advisers" (one of them a general), and 1,000 North Koreans—could have stimulated artistic creativity to the point of transforming the communized segment of Angola into a new, Medician Florence!

Believe me, I am not especially attacking *The New York Times.* It is a newspaper I enjoy reading. I try to read good newspapers only. But it is in good newspapers, there where one does not expect to find them, that aberrations surprise and scandalize. The transient decline in the reputation of *Le Monde* during the 1970s was due to distortions of the truth and to the rearrangement of information according to ideological prejudices, which were more shocking in this newspaper than in others known for the mediocrity of their professional ethics. One is not surprised, for example, when one reads in *The New York Times* Richard Bernstein's excellent reporting on Mozambique (September 3, 1987). But when Mr. Brooke goes into ecstacies over Angolan esthetes of the MPLA, one is dumbfounded.

Is it, then, legitimate to plead once more for the right to make mistakes? One can and must grant this right to articles of reflection, opinion, analysis, forecasting. But the right to make mistakes is admissible only if one can first establish that the journalist has done his best to discover the truth and to gather all the available evidence, and that he has not glossed over anything he knew or invented anything he didn't know. There is no point here in invoking the impossibility of ever attaining definitive information on this or that subject. But it is easy enough in an article to indicate clearly the extent to which one has been able to obtain solid information, beyond which limits uncertainty and conjecture begin. An attentive study of the media teaches us, alas, that errors and omissions—leaving aside the many that are due to sheer incompetence—are very often willful. When, in 1933, Walter Duranty denied the existence of famine in the Ukraine, it was not at all because he had been unable to obtain any factual information. In fact, he did not say this. On the contrary, he said he had been able to inform himself thoroughly and could assert that there was not the slightest starvation in the Ukraine. Why? He could see that it was a famine that had been deliberately provoked, that it was not just famine but genocide. Since he was understandably reluctant to write this, he preferred to deny its very existence. But why? Though not a communist, Duranty probably felt it would be better for the Soviet Union to have a good reputation in the West. From that moment on he treated information not as an end governed by a criterion of accuracy, but simply as a means of obtaining a desired effect.

Unfortunately, in that part of the contemporary world in which press and media are free (and what a small part this is!) information is often handled in this spirit. To be sure, not all the time and everywhere, nor in all papers, in all media, every day; but still consistently enough to impair the healthy functioning of democracy. Instead of informing their fellow citizens, too often journalists want to govern them. What, in effect, is a democracy? It is a system in which the citizens govern themselves. What purpose do the press and other media serve in this system? To place at the disposal of citizens information without which they cannot govern themselves wisely or at least pick out and judge those who are to govern them. It is this organic link between self-government and information, without which the citizen's choices would be made blindly, which justifies freedom of the press and makes it so necessary to a democracy. When the information the press feeds to the public is false, the process of democratic decision making is itself falsified. All the more so since the media likewise influence political leaders, first of all directly and then through currents they stir up in public opinion and which in turn affect the people in power.

It is difficult not to attribute a role to the U.S. press, and above all to certain of its most respected newspapers, in the formulation of concepts that American leaders, beginning with President Franklin Roosevelt, took with them to the wartime conferences at Teheran and Yalta. These concepts generated a spirit of conciliation and concessions in the U.S. delegation that was the source of most of the later difficulties encountered by the West during the years of the Cold War. If, during the 1930s, the U.S. press had done more to familiarize its readers with Lenin's statements on the irreversibility of communist conquests, the leaders of the West would perhaps not have been so ready to deliver Central Europe and North Korea into Stalin's hands in exchange for a simple promise that the Soviet Union would evacuate those territories after free elections had been held or a peace treaty had been signed. The same newspapers, which had refused to pay serious attention to the program Hitler had expounded with great clarity in *Mein Kampf,* based their hopes of building a "better" postwar world on an idyllic vision of the Soviet Union. They either did not know or chose to ignore and to regard as "accidents" of the system the famines due to forced collectivization, the mass terror, the bloody methods of repression. Most of the Moscow correspondents of apparently serious and impartial newspapers had concealed these facts—which were revealed primarily by extreme right-wing newspapers, automatically suspected of partisan passion. It is thus not surprising that the negotiators at Yalta thought they could rebuild the postwar world, using the cement of Stalin's "good will" and his respect for his pledged word! Roosevelt kept insisting on the importance of this factor in his private conversations with his aides, notably with Admiral Leahy, who was then the White House chief of staff.

Another of the favorite fantasies of the press during the 1930s consisted of forecasting the Soviet Union's imminent conversion to democracy and capitalism, indeed of claiming that this sensational development was already under way. This absurd notion first appeared in the West in 1922 and periodically resurfaced thereafter. This, for example, is what one could read in May 1936 in the *New York Herald Tribune* under the title "Russia Progresses." (Dateline Paris, May 12, 1936):

Rufus Woods, American newspaper publisher, passed through Paris after two months of scouting in Germany and Russia. "Russia is finding itself," he said, "by a process of evolution away from Communism toward Socialism, with the adoption of the production methods of capitalism. The fetish of equal wages has been given up in favor of a graduated scale such as exists in capitalistic countries. Secondly, payment to laborers is made on a piece basis for goods actually produced; this has boomed production. Thirdly, the Soviet Union has given up its attempt to control all distribution and now sanctions public markets in competition with government markets. All this is putting Russia on its feet with a solidity never dreamed of."*

If we could forget the date, we might have the impression that what is here being described is the *perestroika* of Mikhail Gorbachev.

*Text reproduced in the May 12, 1986, edition of the *International Herald Tribune,* in the section entitled "75 and 50 Years Ago."

It is noteworthy that, alongside of exact albeit wrongly interpreted observations (the piecework wage system, which the legendary "shock worker" Stakhanov had done so much to promote, being presented here as a liberal measure, when in fact it was a new device for exploiting labor by increasing work norms), Rufus Woods listed as sure information and as "facts" he had duly observed an imagined freedom of commerce, not to mention an increase in production, which he could not possibly have witnessed. Like generations of other newspapermen both before and after him, he seems to have harbored not the slightest doubts as to the limits of what one can correctly perceive in a totalitarian country. He was as happily convinced of having been able to take everything in, according to his wishes, as if he had just completed a journalistic trip to the Swiss Confederation. How many Western journalists were to make idiots of themselves thirty or fifty years later, without it affecting their prestige, fooling their readers and TV viewers by providing similar impressions of Red China, Cuba, or Nicaragua?

Let us not exaggerate the power of the press, but let us not underestimate its influence in the genesis of misconceptions acquired by political leaders. For example, in 1943 Tom Connally, one of the most influential U.S. senators, asserted that Stalin was preparing to dismantle the Soviet economy, throw socialism overboard and steer his country toward democratic capitalism.* This was an excellent reason—was it not?—to have confidence in Stalin during the forthcoming negotiations, since, all things considered, he was beginning to resemble Roosevelt, while the USSR was becoming a country like the United States. This was an anticipation of a later product of wishful thinking during another golden age of Western misconceptions—the so-called "convergence" theory, which created such intellectual havoc in the 1960s. (Still later, in 1988, Valéry Giscard d'Estaing could write in a French weekly magazine— *Paris-Match,* July 15—that, thanks to Gorbachev, the Soviet Constitution was becoming "analogous" to the U.S. Constitution.) Senator Tom Connally, it should be remembered, was neither stupid nor a nonentity. A key congressional figure in the field of foreign affairs, he later became one of the U.S. architects of the Atlantic Alliance. But in the meantime, during the decisive wartime years that culminated in the conferences of Teheran and Yalta, he, like so many others, helped to contribute the false and fatal postulate that underlay Western diplomacy, to the effect that the USSR was gradually transforming itself into a democracy and

---

*These remarks, made by Senator Tom Connally—not to be confused with Governor John Connally of Texas—were published in *The New York Times* on May 25, 1943.

had abandoned all idea of conquest. Had it not proved that it was abandoning its imperialist ambitions by dissolving the Comintern? This turned out to be another propaganda trap, one that led countless Western leaders hopelessly astray. From 1945 on the Soviet Union quickly demonstrated that it did not need a Comintern to pursue an expansionist policy and that a Communist International could remain redoubtably active everywhere in the world without the help of an official, visible structure.

One cannot, I repeat, hold the press responsible for errors of analysis made by political leaders. But the press cannot be regarded as entirely innocent. In a democracy public opinion is largely swayed by information and commentary supplied by the press, and political leaders cannot buck such currents with impunity. Anyone daring, in the late autumn of 1987 prior to the "summit" meeting between Gorbachev and Reagan, to arouse a sentiment of elementary prudence with regard to the accord on intermediate missiles was immediately thrust from the mainstream of general opinion and popularity and relegated to the ghetto of ultra-conservative diehards—an unenviable confinement for a politician. Furthermore, active participation in democratic politics leaves one with precious little leisure time for properly informing oneself and even less desire to do so. One is often surprised by the ignorance, the "holes," that certain leading politicians reveal in private conversations or even in public debates, simply because what can be called "professional deformation"—the strains of overwork and the ever-increasing amount of time that has to be devoted to mediatic questions—leads them to interest themselves less and less in the documentary paperwork involved in tackling specific issues and more and more in what public opinion, which is to say the press, thinks of them. The polemics and the student demonstrations which put an end to the Chirac government's attempt in December 1986 to reform the universities in France had absolutely nothing to do with the actual contents of the legislative bill (prepared for the National Assembly), which most of the demonstrators knew next to nothing about. It was a classic example of triangular interaction—in this case between the apprehensions of *lycéens* (high school students), the amplification of these fears by the media, and their exploitation by certain political parties. Basically, there was nothing new in this phenomenon. After all, from 1933 to 1936 Roosevelt had a very perspicacious ambassador in Moscow in the person of William Bullitt, who foresaw everything, including the Hitler-Stalin pact. But Roosevelt, preferring to believe what Walter Duranty was writing, had Bullitt replaced by the incredibly naïve Joseph Davies, whose view of the Soviet Union was, if anything, even more rosy than Duranty's.

As soon as journalists, while pretending to provide information, consider that they have the right to present current happenings in such a way as to orient public opinion in a manner they regard as salutary, democracy is amputated of one of its main supports. It is affected just as perniciously as it is by a corrupt judiciary or electoral fraud. Let us never forget this elementary principle. Totalitarianism can only live thanks to falsehood, and democracy survive thanks to the truth. Too often journalists regard this principle as of secondary importance. Freedom of expression seems to them to include that of "highlighting" information according to their individual preferences. There are even newspapers where the journalists insist on a "coloring" or "balancing" of political affiliations, not among editorialists but in the news-gathering services—as though a newspaper staff could become a kind of parliament destined to reflect the spectrum of political parties in the country, and as though information, in its final state, could result from a compromise between partisan falsifications! This perversion of the notion of objectivity, derived from an exemplary pluralism of opinions, supposes that true information can emerge from a potpourri of prejudices. In Italy, for example, this practice has given birth since the 1970s to a monster baptized *lottizzazione* (parceling out of lots). This operation, in the recruiting of a newspaper staff, consists of distributing "lots" of prereserved posts: so many posts for Communist journalists, so many for Christian Democrats, so many for Socialists, and so on. One of the chief editors of the *Corriere della Sera,* who was appointed in 1986, told me it was impossible to get rid of certain incompetent journalists because their departure would cause the "quota" for this or that party to fall below the agreed-upon level!

How could journalists more ingenuously admit just how shallow their confidence in their own integrity as simple information gatherers is? We return to the same basic, sempiternal fallacies and confusions that crop up in all controversies over the press. Is it a valid counterpower? Has it become too powerful? Is it not powerful enough? Is freedom of the press not more threatened with every passing day? Has it become too arrogant, or does it properly fulfill its investigative mission for the welfare of the citizens? Among all these standard interrogations there is one that is almost invariably missing. In the information provided about a certain matter by the press and electronic media, what is true and what false? Notwithstanding the interest of the preceding questions, it seems to me that this is the fundamental point for the health of a democracy. However, it is the one that is the least discussed.

In January 1987 the director-general of the BBC, Alasdair Milne, had to resign after five years of running battles with the Conservative government and the corporation's board of governors—sometimes caused by mistakes of management, at other times by protests from journalists. A few days before, the journalists had asked for Milne's resignation, arguing that he had lost the confidence of his team.* However, in both the British and the foreign press the affair was usually presented under the sole angle of an attack on the legendary independence of the BBC. On January 31, 1987, *Le Monde* headlined a front-page editorial: BBC: END OF A MYTH. The "myth," of course, was that of its supposed independence of the government in power. At no time did it occur to the editorialist that the "myth" might also be that of the BBC's objectivity. Now, independence in a public service or with respect to a private owner is defendable only in the name of objectivity, which supposes both competence and probity. It would seem abusive to claim independence in the name of the right to lie or make mistakes. In the struggles that regularly pit editorial staffs against public or private owners, this is a question that is almost never raised, as though it had been proven once and for all that the members of the journalistic profession always execute their work in a perfect manner, without committing mistakes or villainies. An editorial staff must defend its independence with respect to the government in power and to the stockholders, but it is not entitled to use this independence as it pleases.

Can the journalistic community claim to be the only vocational group that enjoys a privileged independence that is not bound by any technical, professional, or ethical rules, save for those that may be dictated to the journalist by his own conscience and of which he is the sole judge? To denounce as an infringement of human rights and public liberties any critical assessment of this supernatural immunity is to adopt an untenable position. What would journalists say if they were asked to grant the same privilege to politicians, industrialists, businessmen and financiers, trade union leaders, intellectuals, policemen, civil servants, parliamentarians—in a word, to all those they spend their time hauling over the coals? The democratic journalist exists only as a the product of a civilization in which freedom to criticize exists. He cannot, therefore, without flagrant hypocrisy, raise an uproar and protest this "profanation" when the freedom to criticize—which is what he lives off—is applied to himself.

The Times (London), January 30, 1987.

After the forced resignation of the director-general of the BBC, I carefully read the British press and a number of continental newspapers. I came upon many editorials regarding questions of principle, assaults on the independence of the BBC, and relations between a state-controlled television service and the government in power. Opinions naturally differed, but all remained in the realm of generalities. Nowhere did I come across an article beginning with these simple words: "I have had the controversial TV sequences played back to me, each time in the company of a specialist on the subject dealt with. Here are the facts and the arguments that can permit one to maintain that the BBC has failed (or not failed) in its mission."

The first piece of reporting that had unleashed a serious conflict between the BBC and the Conservatives was devoted, in the spring of 1982, to the war in the Falklands. It was a documentary that was favorable to the Argentinians. Without going so far as to claim that England has always conducted herself well in this matter, I find it easy to understand the indignation felt by the Conservative electorate, and even by certain Labour members, over a biased recapitulation that blamed the British side for everything. The authors of the documentary counterattacked, invoking the freedom to inform and their sense of professional ethics. They were supported by their colleagues of the printed press until the day when one of the presenters of the documentary revealed that he himself had been dismayed by the contents of the broadcast version. His complaint was that it contained too many "minority"—or anti-British—views. The editor's defense was that the program clearly stated at the outset that it contained other material that demonstrated that it was not anti-British overall.

In January 1984 a *Panorama* show on TV featured the results of an "inquiry" according to which the Conservative Party had been infiltrated by extreme right-wing activists. In this program two members of Parliament, Neil Hamilton and Gerald Howarth, were accused of racism, anti-Semitism, and fascism. The two MPs protested and demanded a retraction. Nevertheless, the BBC stubbornly maintained that what the program alleged was true. The two victims of this defamation then started a lawsuit, which was eventually settled in their favor. The BBC agreed to pay each one £20,000 in damages to which were added £250,000 to cover court proceedings and lawyers' fees.* The BBC also apologized to the two members of Parliament. As can be seen, a grave professional fault had been committed, one that had cost the BBC a lot

The Sunday Times (London), February 1, 1987.

of money and which had stained its honor and reputation. To present the reaction provoked by this error as a political "encroachment on the independence of the BBC" was, under the circumstances, to apply another twist to the sacrosanct "duty to inform."

Another controversial broadcast aroused a storm in July 1985, because it presented an Irish Republican Army apologist, Gerry Adams, in a curiously sympathetic light. It was quite evident that the producer who had interviewed the IRA spokesman was with him heart and soul, welcoming his justification of terrorism as being a valid form of "resistance to oppression"—that hackneyed cliché and shallow sophistry, so utterly absurd when brandished in a democratic state, but which subversive movements of totalitarian inspiration resort to, exploiting the very freedom they are granted by the state in order to destroy it.

This apologia of violence and bloodshed happened to coincide with a marked recrudescence of terrorism. In particular, it followed closely on the wild shooting spree that had taken place in Saint James's Square in London when a number of "diplomats" had opened fire with machine pistols from the windows of the Libyan embassy and killed a young woman police constable, who had been posted there to protect the embassy premises from a threatening crowd of anti-Gaddhafi Libyan demonstrators. Since public indignation over this outrage was already running high, the home secretary, Leon Brittan, asked the BBC's board of governors to have this most inopportune documentary, which amounted to a quasi-provocation, removed from the program for which it had been announced but not yet shown. After the board of governors had acceded to this request and had the showing of the interview postponed, BBC journalists staged a one-day protest strike, supported by many of their colleagues from the private ITV television network.

Unlike the preceding case, this controversial feature did not, literally speaking, involve a falsification of information. A TV network that invites many persons of varying tendencies to take part can perfectly well organize a debate with a terrorist—even if it is in doubtful taste. The problem of professional ethics was posed by the manifest complaisance shown by the interviewer toward the terrorist. What is a "debate" when there is no reply or objection? Even if the program had consisted of two equally "respectable" opinions—on the one hand, that of a terrorist making an apologia for murder as a normal form of political expression in a law-abiding state, and on the other, of a citizen requesting that the rule of law be respected in a democracy—it could have been shown that the symmetry between the assassin and his potential victim was an essentially fallacious form of "equity," but the debate at least would have taken place and brought out the basic asymmetry involved. But to grant the terrorist the right to speak unopposed, with the blessing of a benevolent interviewer who was virtually an accomplice, was really to commit a crime against the "duty to inform." For this duty should have made it mandatory that the public also be offered arguments and facts against terrorism, not simply those that glorify it. The question of whether this feature was one of information or opinion can be debated endlessly, but it was certainly not scandalous to think that in this particular case the BBC did not respect the impartiality which is the necessary counterpart of its independence.

Nor was there anything scandalous involved when the BBC again came under fire for the way in which its news features and magazines had covered the U.S. bombing raid on Libya in April 1986. In October of that year the Conservative Party chairman, Norman Tebbit, published a twenty-one-page report that anyone could consult—and contest, for this report was anything but empty. Tebbit made clear, on the basis of detailed evidence, that the "coverage" of the U.S. bombing raid had been presented in a tendentious fashion, the information being deliberately distorted by an anti-American and anti-Conservative bias (Margaret Thatcher's government had authorized the U.S. fighter-bombers to take off from airfields in Great Britain). A polemical debate as to the necessity and timeliness of the U.S. operation was quite legitimate; indeed, the more the question was debated, the better it would have been. But this was not what the BBC had done. The available information had been selected in an insidious and surreptitious fashion, with the result that the captive audience had been taken for a ride. The news and commentaries had been offered in a seemingly objective fashion, but a vital portion of the information required to be able to form a reasonably sound opinion had simply been done away with.

The uproar with which the Tebbit report was greeted seems to me an ominous portent for the future. There was talk of "censorship." But since when has it been forbidden to publish critical assessments of news features that have *already been shown,* and to challenge their conformity or nonconformity with the facts? Since when have dictionaries taken to defining as "censorship" the retrospective examination of published documents? Did not the act of censorship emanate rather from those persons who would have liked to prohibit all control over the veracity of televised news features and who would have preferred to see the Tebbit report remain unpublished? By virtue of what exorbitant dispensation should journalists escape from the monitoring of reliability to which the greatest historians, the greatest memoir writers, the greatest scientists are subjected? And this in the name of the freedom of the press? Does a scientist have the right to falsify an experiment in the name of the freedom of scientific research?

BBC director-general Milne finally left following a feature that had been prepared in January 1987 about a top secret military spy satellite designed to overfly the Soviet Union. Here it was no longer a matter of opinion; the very security of the country and its defenses was imperiled. To be sure, documents concerning the secret satellite had already been published in the left-wing weekly *The New Statesman.* Should one publish everything one knows? The problem is as old as the press itself. But there is a difference in kind between a private newspaper, which can be managed by its editors as they wish and at their own risk, and which the reader is free to buy or not to buy, and a national institution that is entirely financed by viewers (the BBC does not broadcast advertising) and whose journalists have a special responsibility as representatives of their country.

For a long, long time the BBC was regarded as just about the sole example of a truly successful official radio-television corporation in terms of quality as well as impartiality. It was able to resist the pressures of successive governments, whether Conservative or Labour. During the 1960s, for example, Harold Wilson, although a socialist, was probably the prime minister who had the worst relations with the BBC of any premier since the war.

But this miraculous success of total independence for an official radio-television corporation depended on a no less total probity in the presentation of information and debates of ideas. Alas, this probity began to weaken after 1968, when Great Britain was invaded by an all-too-facile ideology, one that claimed that there is no such thing as neutral information, only an "information of combat." From 1970 on, this tinselly Marxism became the fashionable doctrine among elite Cambridge and Oxford scholars, which is to say, with the young recruits of the BBC. For years I have listened every morning to the BBC's admirable World Service, which certainly provides the most complete radio news coverage of international events in the world. Yet I could not help noticing subtle but flagrant departures from neutrality of information in connection with such delicate topics as Nicaragua, the Strategic Defense Initiative, and Gorbachev's reforms.*

*Certain formulas of a seemingly descriptive nature conceal a bias beneath their apparent neutrality. Thus I have seldom heard the World Service of the BBC refer to the Nicaraguan Contras other than as "CIA-backed Contra rebels." But the BBC never referred to the Sandinista government as "the Moscow-supported dictators of Managua"—a formulation that

Anybody with the financial means to do so can launch a newspaper designed to explain that the earth is flat and the sun turns around it. If he obtains clients, so much the better for him. If not, he will go bankrupt. But an official radio-television network is a public service that is viable and acceptable only if it rests on competence and honesty—for the public has no way of sanctioning it, as it can sanction a private newspaper by ceasing to buy it. Journalistic probity does not consist solely of resisting governmental pressure, it consists of resisting *all* pressures—ideological, political, cultural—from wherever they may come. The miracle of the BBC will not take place again until its future managers remember this principle and return to it.

Even in the relatively small portion of the world press that is free, most journalistic professionals speak or write not to inform but to prove something. What distinguishes the serious press from the mass or "gutter" press is the proportion of greater or lesser exactitude to be found in "oriented" information. Good newspapers give priority to accuracy, striving to render their political orientation credible or, failing that, more or less invisible; and often they resign themselves to publishing information capable of undermining their cherished interpretations. They know this is the price they must pay to retain their authority, thanks to which they continue to be read or listened to by a multitude of readers and TV viewers, not all of whom subscribe to their political or ethical postulates. Bad newspapers or broadcasters, for their part, select, arrange, or alter information in such a patent and clumsy fashion that only partisan minds, whose sole interest is in finding the confirmation of their *idées fixes,* can go on reading or listening to them.

would have been the pure and simple reflection of the reality. All of the BBC World Service's news reports on Nicaragua have tended to suggest that the Contra movement was a totally artificial phenomenon sustained exclusively by the CIA, and that it enjoyed no popular support inside Nicaragua—something that was manifestly untrue. Any honest correspondent could easily perceive the unpopularity of the Sandinista regime through many signs: the flood tide of Nicaraguans seeking political asylum in neighboring countries, even without joining the Contras; the fact that even Sandinista soldiers captured by the Contras and later freed thanks to cease-fire agreements refused to return to Nicaragua; the demonstration by more than ten thousand people in Managua in early 1988 to demand democratization of the country; the continuing presence in Sandinista jails, at the end of 1987, of about nine thousand political prisoners, of whom less than one thousand were former Somozistas, and so on. Notwithstanding these eloquent facts, a BBC correspondent in Managua, during a *News Desk* broadcast on April 3, 1988, could still claim that the Contras represented nothing and were simply afraid of losing "their handsome CIA salaries." I couldn't help wondering if this correspondent's own "handsome salary" was really justified.

It nonetheless remains true that even organs of information that enjoy the highest professional repute and great international prestige allow themselves to deform the simple chronicling of facts. In 1984 the New York–based Institute for Applied Economics published a study on the way in which the three major TV networks—ABC, NBC, and CBS—had, day by day, reported the economic recovery the United States began to experience in 1982 and which became extremely vigorous in 1984. The institute examined all the economic reporting the three networks had done over a period of six months. In 1983 the United States achieved one of its highest growth rates since World War II and the highest for that year of all the industrialized nations—7.7 percent in constant dollar estimates; the lowest rate of inflation—0.3 percent; and a notable decline in unemployment, which had dropped to 8 percent from 11 percent in 1981. An examination of all the economic statistics, whether official or private, that had been published (from four to fifteen per month) over the half-year period from July 1 to December 31, 1983, revealed that 95 percent of them indicated positive results and provided evidence of an economic recovery. But during the same period, which saw the three networks produce 104 evening programs devoted to information, analysis, interviews, or commentaries concerning the U.S. economy and employment, 86 percent portrayed the overall situation as bad or catastrophic. In other words, the immense majority of U.S. citizens, for whom, as in any modern country, televised prime-time news is the chief source of information, could not possibly guess that their country was experiencing an economic surge, in fact the biggest since the start of the crisis in 1973 and even since the end of World War II.*

From time to time television viewers got wind of the economic recovery, only to be warned that the so-called "progress" indicated by the statistics had no practical value and would lead to no improvement in conditions of daily life. The media could not, of course, simply ignore the stream of statistical data indicating a recovery. But, when they mentioned them, the effect was immediately nullified by a commentary or piece of reporting tending to rob the statistic of any overall significance. Thus, between December 1982 and December 1983, the level of unemployment among the country's working population fell from 10.7 percent to 8.7 percent. In one year the recovery had created four million new jobs. But on December 2, 1983, the day on which the Department

*A summary of the report published by the Institute for Applied Economics appeared in *The Wall Street Journal* of March 7, 1984 in Holmes M. Brown, "How Television Reported the U.S. Recovery."

of Labor announced these figures, ABC focused its attention on the situation in the Midwest, "where unemployment is most severe." Unemployment had receded in forty-five out of fifty states, but ABC chose one of the five states that had lagged behind in order to do some on-the-spot reporting. The network's correspondent managed to unearth two "upper-middle-class employees" who had been without employment for a year and a half. Their case was not in the least representative of the usual length of unemployment; for in the United States since World War II, as all well-informed journalists should know, even the darkest periods of unemployment have rarely lasted more than three to four months—unlike unemployment in Europe, where the periods tend to be longer. The selection of these two cases, added to the geographical choice of one of the five least favored states, was bound to engender a negative impression. For four minutes—an enormous proportion of the twenty-minute evening news (commercial breaks excluded)—the network transmitted the pessimistic comments of the two blue-collar workers, who were so understandably gloomy and depressed that one of them suggested he was thinking of committing suicide. And on this macabre, lugubrious, and desperate note the evening news program ended—a program whose salient item had been the announcement that the unemployment rate in the country taken as a whole had dropped by 2 percent!

It goes without saying that a journalist, when an item of good news of this kind reaches him, has a duty to point out that there are nevertheless persons and places it unfortunately does not affect. By all means let him say so, but not to the point of making this the highlight of the evening news! For what moral right have journalists to reproach politicians for lack of honesty when they gloss over the dark shadows in their speeches, boasting only of the bright spots in the picture, if the journalists themselves practice amputations in the opposite direction? They do so, indeed, in a more pernicious fashion; for the public does not expect a politician to provide objective information. It grants him a latitude to embellish his achievements, whereas it usually assumes that the journalist is impartial.

When Dan Rather, the famous editor and anchorman of *CBS Evening News* wrote in to *The New York Times* in 1987 to protest personnel cuts in the network (which was losing TV viewers), saying that "Television news is a tool of democracy. . . . News is a light on the horizon . . . a beacon that helps citizens of a democracy," he was once again confusing principle and practice. Just as a political boss loses the right to call himself a democrat in a country where elections are rigged, so a journalist forfeits this right when he knowingly distorts information. The one thing that clearly emerges from the study of the TV evening news programs of 1983, and also—from what I saw of them myself—those of 1984, is that the U.S. media made frantic efforts to hide the economic recovery, so as not to give the Reagan administration credit for its economic policies. During the first quarter of 1984 the gross national product bounded forward at the unheard-of tempo of 9.7 percent, calculated on an annual basis. During the first six months, two million new jobs were created, 1,950,000 of them during the two months of May and June, as the Department of Labor announced on July 7. This meant that six and a half million Americans had once again found work since the start of the recovery, late in 1982. Yet in June 1984 I saw Dan Rather devote a good third of *CBS Evening News* to the "crisis of agriculture in the Midwest," as portrayed in apocalyptic terms. It is common knowledge that farmers in rich countries, supported as they are by government subsidies, which enable them to obtain fancy prices for their harvests that are way above world levels, spend their time bewailing their "poverty" in order to retain those privileges. We were accordingly treated to a whole series of terrible tales trotted out by Midwest wheat and corn growers, all of whom seemed on the verge of suicide. Dan Rather could thus wind up that evening program with the suggestion that the worsening of the economic situation was serious enough to compromise Reagan's chances of being reelected the following November.

In fact, as we now know, Reagan in November 1984 carried forty-nine out of fifty states. Gradually the TV media had to yield to the bitter facts. During the summer of 1987 the unemployment rate actually fell to close to 5 percent (generally regarded as a rock-bottom level), while inflation was eliminated. In a news roundup during the first days of September I saw a totally resigned Dan Rather admit what all the world now knew: that the United States had just traversed, and was continuing to enjoy, the longest sustained period of uninterrupted growth in peacetime since the end of the Civil War.

Many well-founded objections to Reagan's economic policies have been made; above all, there was the chronic balance-of-payments gap and the budget deficit. The stock market crash of October 1987 also illustrated the fragility of the Wall Street financial system. But one has the right to formulate such objections only if one also has the honesty to give those against whom they are leveled credit for good results; and in any case, when one is a journalist, one should give up trying to conceal them.

Surveys undertaken by *Public Opinion* have shown that as a group U.S. journalists are considerably more "liberal," not to say "radical," than the country as a whole. This is their right. To be concerned by this state of affairs would amount to "witch-hunting" if their personal opinions and professional behavior were kept rigorously separated. But all too often this is anything but the case. For a number of U.S. media managers Reagan's economic policies *had to be* shown to be a failure. They clung to this thesis for as long as it was tenable in the face of contradicting facts and figures. More seriously, they also travestied the truth by presenting their opinions in the guise of "information."

In Europe, too, the pathological anti-Reaganism of the media (including many influential newspapers, such as *La Repubblica* in Italy, *The Guardian* in Great Britain, and *El País* in Spain) made it utterly impossible for their listeners or readers to understand how in 1988 the United States should suddenly have been able to eliminate most unemployment—after in fact, five successive years of economic growth without inflation, an achievement they had hardly heard anything about. Or, more exactly, when they were finally obliged to recognize these facts, the same media and newspapers had a ready-made explanation—the U.S. budget and trade deficits! But if such deficits were enough to ensure a prosperous economy, Brazil, Mexico, Peru, Nigeria, Poland, and Yugoslavia would boast the strongest economies in the world!

Journalists justify themselves by arguing that the press is a "counterpower" and a "watchdog" whose role is to supervise, criticize, even harass the government. Here again we encounter the ambiguity of this notion of "counterpower." If it is a question of opinions, then they can be freely expressed, no matter how false, unfair, hate-ridden, sycophantic, well remunerated, sincere, or hypocritical they may be. But when it comes to information, the press, in proclaiming itself to be a "fourth power," is conferring on itself a kind of magistracy, although it has no reason for being *a priori* for or against the government. If information happens to be unfavorable to the government, it dispenses it. But it must also transmit the information when it is favorable. This is the only way it can exercise its "magistracy," assuming it can play this role. A magistrate does not open a trial session by assuming *a priori* that he must condemn the defendant and that it would be a dereliction of duty were he to acquit him or allow him attenuating circumstances. Furthermore, the government of the country in which newspapers and media are operating is not the only power against which the "counterpower" of the press must be arrayed. There are also the opposition parties, which, even though not actually in office, still exert some power; and there are also financial and cultural, trade union and religious powers—and of course the press itself. Foreign governments, too, whatever their political coloration, ought to be covered on a totally equal footing, with no biased filtering of information; just as *in all countries* opposition parties and movements, guerrilla fighters, economic realities, corruption, violations of human rights, military forces, repressions, successes, and failures should all be reported. Criticism directed against all—not simply against one's own government—should, for a press that considers itself to be a "magistrate," *result* from correctly established information; but it is not the task of critical journalists to *direct* the choice of this information under the sway of a selective bias, which metamorphoses a pitiless ferocity toward some into a boundless indulgence toward others.

Unfortunately, the weight of the "fourth power" is not always thrown behind the cause of the truth, far from it; and yet, only steadfastness in the service of the truth would lend it the principled legitimacy it so far lacks. For if the "fourth power" has been cosubstantial with the basic institutions of democracy from the very beginning, the formula itself is meaningful only as an analogy. I return to this point, for I have often noticed that this is one of the least well understood of distinctions. The three other powers are defined by constitutional texts. The men and women who exercise those powers (whether executive, legislative, or judicial) must, to be legitimate, be recruited according to precise rules—through election, academic tests and examinations, or nomination by qualified authorities. They are exposed to specific sanctions in cases of abuse, maladministration, or serious error. But these criteria become vague in the extreme as soon as it is a question of the power to inform and to communicate. To offer the public information and opinions, pictures, photos, articles, or exhortations to choose one party rather than another is a right included in the general rights of the ordinary citizen. The law goes no further. It does not in this case confer on any particular category of citizens a specific power over others as it does for the three constituted powers, whose mission and limits it both describes and prescribes. Freedom of expression belongs to all, but, like freedom of movement, it does not indicate the itinerary to be followed. The power enjoyed by the press ultimately stems from its success; it is a pragmatic power, just as is the legitimacy accorded to it by the public, by the unseen audience, due to its good professional reputation; or, for that matter, to its bad reputation, in the case of libelous scandal sheets and the tabloid "gutter press," which also have their clients. One can succeed, in the press and other media, either because one is scrupulous or because one is scandalous. In both cases you will have power, even a kind of legitimacy, since part of the public follows you, buys you, listens to you, watches you. For this reason certain excellent observers of our times have been willing to grant only a kind of metaphorical resonance to the notion of "fourth power."

The resulting situation is quite disconcerting. In most countries the press is the slave of the regime or enjoys a strictly limited freedom, subject to reprisals and persecutions. In the democracies it is honest and exact in its informational function only to a limited degree. The powers that be fear the press less for what is true in its affirmations than for its ability to stir up public opinion, regardless of whether what it reports is true or false. It was a French socialist, Michel Rocard, a member of a party that had shaken off Leninism, a man little inclined to seek a monopoly over forms of speech, who one day said: "The mediatic power today is much stronger than the political power." And it was a "liberal" (in the European sense) or a "conservative" (in the American sense) politician, certainly a democrat, Raymond Barre, who could muse aloud: "Has the fourth power become so powerful as to keep the three others from functioning?"* It is a power that was clearly not foreseen when the first democratic constitutions were drafted. And a power (if it exists) which cannot be accepted unconditionally, inasmuch as it reposes on neither a guarantee of authenticity of news nor on integrity in daily practice. The immediate effect produced on public opinion by a given piece of "information" is no less if the news is false than if it is true. This can be observed as much in international relations as in domestic politics. The inaccuracy or poverty of daily information makes it hazardous to claim that even the most democratic of peoples are motivated in their votes primarily by the real achievements of their governments and thanks to an understanding of the international situation in which their country finds itself.

Most curiously of all, the upholding of the truth rarely constitutes the criterion the press itself uses when it rebels against the encroachments of the regime or deplores the commercial collapse of a newspaper. There is then much talk of threatened "independence," of necessary "plural-

*These statements were made by Messrs. Rocard and Barre in speeches delivered at a symposium, "The Media, Powers, and Democracy," which was organized in Paris in May 1987 by the Institut International de Géopolitique and presided over by Marie-France Garaud.

ism," but very little of credibility and almost nothing of competence or of a working knowledge of the topics dealt with—which to some people would seem accessory conditions for working in any field of communication. When the socialist newspaper *Le Matin* had to close its doors in January 1988, the French press corps, almost to a man, shed tears over the resultant shrinking of "the space of freedom"—a shallow cliché if ever there was one, and a most undefined notion—but nobody dared to say that *Le Matin* had died because of its partisan viewpoint and professional incapacity. Kept alive artificially for several years with funds supplied by the French presidency, which in 1985 had even gone as far as to place the newspaper under the management of the former socialist minister of information, Max Gallo, *Le Matin* was doomed to see the void inexorably widening around it, as happens with a newspaper of such strident militancy that all know in advance exactly what it is going to print.

Lacking in impartiality, *Le Matin* furthermore exhibited a professional incompetence which sometimes exceeded acceptable limits. To cite but one example: On November 14, 1986, it hailed the legislative elections in Brazil with this front-page headline: ON SATURDAY, FOR THE FIRST TIME IN FORTY YEARS, FREE ELECTIONS IN BRAZIL. The error of the "forty years" was repeated in the body of the article—proof that it was not due to the clumsy intervention of a headline writer and that the managing editor and editor in chief had willfully endorsed it. Let us be charitable and suppose that the journalist had forgotten the democratic election of the president of the republic on January 15, 1985, admittedly voted in by a restricted electoral college; and that he had also forgotten the municipal elections of the following November 15, which had been the first truly free election based on universal suffrage since the end of the military dictatorship. And let us further suppose that *Le Matin*'s Latin American affairs specialist had wished to refer to the start of the aforementioned military dictatorship and to the coup d'état that had marked the interruption of the democratic process in Brazil; nevertheless this putsch had taken place in 1964, which is to say twenty-two rather than forty years earlier. Any reasonably complete contemporary almanac could have provided him with this information. When a politician loses an election, it is commonly said that he was "disowned by the electorate" because he had not properly fulfilled his mandate. Why, then, when a newspaper goes bankrupt, do people never say that it has been "disowned by its readers" for the same reason?

On the other hand, if the talk show interviewer Michel Polac was dismissed from TF1 (France's first television channel) several months after its privatization in 1987, this was not due to any lack of TV viewers, since his *Droit de Réponse* ("Right of Reply") program attracted millions of Saturday-evening TV watchers, notwithstanding its late hour. I should add, for readers unfamiliar with French television, that *Droit de Réponse* was an informal roundtable debate produced and conducted by Polac, usually about political, social, and international issues and less frequently about scientific, historical, or philosophical subjects. In addition, Polac regularly invited half a dozen newspaper or magazine editorialists to debate contemporary issues. Appointed by the socialists to TF1 when this channel was state-controlled, Polac ardently defended the socialist ideology for six years, displaying a slick ferocity against liberalism. When the "liberals" (which is to say the conservatives) returned to power with Jacques Chirac in March 1986—TF1 still being a state-controlled channel—they did not put an end to this talk show, which continued to serve as a weekly tribune for the airing of left-wing gripes and grudges. During the student demonstrations of November 1986, when a young man was all too brutally killed in a police roundup—an accidental murder the authorities had certainly not planned and which was in no way due to the essence of the French political system—Michel Polac devoted an almost hysterical *Droit de Réponse* program to these turbulent events, violently attacking the Chirac government and likening it to the most infamous Fascist dictatorships of past and present. Still, he did not lose his post. He lost it, however, once and for all for allowing the channel's new owner, Francis Bouygues, to be insulted after TF1 had been privatized and his channel publicly mocked during one of Polac's shows as a *chaîne de merde* ("a shitty channel").

Fired by his "shitty" boss as a result of this exploit, Michel Polac was able to mount a vast publicity campaign, which went on for weeks after his dismissal, in which he portrayed himself as a victim of political persecution, a martyr for freedom, and so forth. That such a thing could happen is proof enough that journalists do not apply to themselves the criteria they use for judging others. I see no reason why the "art" of television should not include programs of a pamphleteering kind, in which free play is given to dishonesty, tendentiousness, and polemical fireworks, since literature offers us a multitude of talented works in the genre of which it would be a pity to be deprived. But the authors of such works have always written them in full awareness of the risks they were running, without claiming to have a permanent right to a lavish monthly salary paid out by those they were attacking: the state or a private businessman. Polac could not be defended in the name of the duty to inform, for fulfilling this duty had not exactly been his dominant concern; nor could he be defended in the name of freedom of public debate, for the manner in which he had run his own had been anything but fair. His show was a tribunal in which the results were known in advance. Opponents of the thesis Polac wanted to put across were made to look like defendants in the box, were usually represented in small numbers, reduced to silence, mocked by others present, ridiculed and reviled as narrow-minded cretins and enemies of "progress." The TV camera skillfully abandoned the face of any contradicter who seemed about to articulate an argument that might damage the producer's cherished doctrine.

A show of this kind could provide amusement, but how could anyone maintain that objectivity, tolerance, and a respect for others had been its essential ingredients? In principle, we should all have access to the pleasures of sectarianism, but no one can demand to be guaranteed a lifelong salary in order to indulge in it. In this particular case, no other televised show of the same kind, but representing an opposite ideological viewpoint, existed—either on TF1 or on any other channel. The usual justification, based on a "pluralism of contrary excesses," could not even be provided. The other televised political debates, although more serene, were largely produced by socialist journalists, whom the Socialist Party had durably enthroned while in power. The "freedom" incarnated by Polac was thus that of a monopoly. It had nothing to do with genuine information, nor with a well-balanced debate of contemporary issues. To attribute Polac's dismissal to purely political vengeance, to a freedom-strangling tyranny, to a desire to asphyxiate the press, information, opinion, and thought did not stand up to serious analysis. Once again it was wretched journalism, and journalism is rarely worse than when it deals with journalism itself.

In this respect I can add a personal testimonial—from my experience as editor in chief of *L'Express* (1978–81). Whenever a crisis arose among the editors or between the owner and myself, I would often read articles about this crisis written for other publications by journalistic colleagues who had not bothered to get in touch with me to confront my version of events with the one they had been given. This latter version usually emanated from a particular clan within the staff, which in the heat of political controversy and internal intrigues used a network of friendships to publish elsewhere an account arranged in such a way as to serve its cause. No one at the other end bothered to verify this account by resorting to the elementary precaution taken by any journalist or historian worthy of his calling: comparison of sources. I have often seen this professional fault (most particularly a French one, it is true) committed with respect to false or semifalse "information" concerning myself or some activity I was in a position to know a great deal about, without the person responsible having taken the trouble to obtain the information that was ready to hand. Clearly, the journalist was less interested in offering the public solid information than a thesis.

The primacy of thesis over fact sometimes rises to almost comic heights. Early in 1988 Daniel Ortega, president of Nicaragua's communist government, undertook a propaganda and public relations tour of Europe and the West. Sweden, in particular, gave him a warm welcome. While there, he explained that Nicaragua was suffering from a food shortage due to a prolonged drought. This news was enough to galvanize the Swedes into upping their previous offer of annual aid from $35 to $45 million. No one could deny Sweden the right to ease the burden Moscow was carrying; but why do it by swallowing such a flagrant untruth? Anyone who has spent any time in Central America cannot help being startled by this "long drought." Let me simply quote what the *Grand Dictionnaire encyclopédique Larousse* (1982 edition) has to say about the climate of this region: "Hot and humid tropical climate. The Caribbean littoral, lashed by prevailing winds, has an *almost constantly rainy* climate, whereas the leeward regions and the Pacific coast are *less watered* and enjoy a carefully delimited *dry season.*" (Italics mine.) Four fifths of Nicaragua's territory are situated along the Caribbean side. The rest of the country is subject to a regime of tropical rainfalls at fixed dates and hours. In this region unexpected droughts are an unknown phenomenon.

With this text before me, I phoned an old Swedish friend, editor of one of Stockholm's leading dailies, to ask if the press in his country had done its homework in rectifying Daniel Ortega's climatological leg-pull and if he himself, to open the eyes of his countrymen, had written one of those eminently commonsense editorials which had made him so famous. "You're crazy!" he replied. "I don't want to be attacked as a reactionary." This is how, in the country that awards annual Nobel Prizes for science, the Sandinistas were able to invest Central America with the aridity of the sub-Saharan Sahel.

On the other hand, it was raining in Paris on the December day in 1985 when President François Mitterrand officially greeted General Jaruzelski. Many persons were amazed, and even the prime minister, Laurent Fabius, could not understand why this honor was being accorded to the sinister figure who had tried to throttle Solidarity and Polish hopes of liberty. What political calculation could justify this strange complaisance? People scratched their heads in vain for the answer. At which point a curious rumor began to spread: The secret reason behind this incomprehensible hospitality was Mitterrand's belief that, thanks to this concession, he would soon obtain Moscow's authorization to have Soviet Jews emigrate via Warsaw, from which they would be flown on to Israel in Air France planes. This implausibly fictitious plan, however, was "unveiled," notably by two famous journalists known to be "close to the Elysée" (Palace)—as the saying goes—and to be the customary confidants and privileged dispensers of presidential thinking: Serge July and Jean Daniel, the editors, respectively, of the daily *Libération* and the weekly *Le Nouvel Observateur.* Both their editorials ended on the same general note—"He laughs best who laughs last" and "Those who shout today will look grotesque tomorrow."

Questioned about the likelihood of the airborne operation Mitterrand was trying to put over, the historian and sovietologist Michel Heller prudently replied that this hypothesis struck him as fanciful. There was no indication at the time that Soviet Jews wishing to emigrate were about to receive massive quantities of visas. Even if such a thing had been the case, there was no compelling reason to believe they would come out via Poland. Nor was it clear just what Jaruzelski had to do with this scheme. Nor, finally, would a fleet of Air France jets have sufficed to transport this human swarm, unless the airline chose to suspend its flights to all other destinations.

Questioned in his turn by a radio network regarding Michel Heller's skepticism, Théo Klein, president of the CRIF (Conseil Représentatif des Institutions Juives de France—Representative Council of France's Jewish Institutions) replied in an obviously confident and optimistic tone: "God preserve us from the sovietologists!" I hope God will continue to keep Théo Klein and a few others under his sacred protection, for over the next few years nothing ever came of the fabulous plan, concocted by François Mitterrand with General Jaruzelski, for evacuating Soviet Jews via Warsaw. But the most striking thing of all is that none of those who had spread this phony information later felt the need to retract it, to explain its origin, or to apologize for the error made.

Confessing one's errors is not the predominant passion of the press. When the media agree to consider self-criticism, it is usually only a lordly self-examination dealing with lofty questions such as these: the limits of intrusion into the private lives of citizens; the risk of letting oneself be manipulated by terrorists by giving too prominent a play to bomb blasts and the seizing of hostages; a growing numbness to horror, which might overtake the public if shown too many pictures of war; the possible contagious encouragement of violence by the showing of violent scenes to the young; indifference to contemporary happenings due to the very accumulation of news items; the anesthesia of the critical faculty and the weakening of the memory induced by the uninterrupted flow of news dispatches. These are highly estimable, highly interesting questions. They are all, it is worth noting, ethical questions which certainly honor those who raise them, albeit not without a certain narcissism. But unfortunately, they have nothing to do with the most important of all questions—for they are not self-criticism having to do with the truth or falsity of information or with the raison d'être of journalism relative to error, falsehood, and competence. Do the media help us to have a better knowledge of our world, or not? How much truth is there in what they transmit? This, let us admit, is the crucial problem; but it is one that is seldom broached.

When such a question is raised, the negative reactions manifested by the journalistic community are exceedingly sharp, not to say ferocious. It refuses to be challenged on the terrain of the true and the false, though this is the only one that counts. When in 1976 Michel Legris, a former newspaperman with *Le Monde,* published a book entitled *Le Monde tel qu'il est* ("The World As It Is"), a book in which he exposed what he regarded as that newspaper's partiality, citing precise examples of falsification or amputation of information, Jacques Fauvet, who was then the editor in chief of the famous daily, did not bother to reply to the objections nor eventually did he seek to rectify the errors, either his own or those of Legris. He spent all his time denigrating the author of this sacrilegious book by every possible nonintellectual means, intent on destroying him professionally. Other newspaper editors, while secretly delighted by this challenge to the infallibility of a paper that loved to distribute lessons of morality to the French press, were careful, however, not to offer employment to the poor Legris, so fearful were they of *Le Monde*'s vindictive wrath and power. Legris was thus plunged for a long time into the most soul-shattering unemployment.

"Investigative journalism" suddenly ceases to be sacred when journalism itself is involved. A newspaper executive then adopts the same attitude of rancorous extermination that he condemns with such haughtiness when he discerns it in a politician or business executive. In the same way *Time* magazine and CBS did almost everything they could in 1986 to stop the publication of *Reckless Disregard,* a book written by the journalist and legal expert Renata Adler. In 1983 the retired army general William Westmoreland had started a lawsuit against CBS for having broadcast a feature called "Vietnam Deception," in which he was taken to task for his role as commander in chief of U.S. forces during the Vietnam War. During that same year General Ariel Sharon had instituted legal proceedings against *Time* because of an article in which he was accused of having ordered the massacre of Palestinians in the refugee camps of Sabra and Shatila during the Israeli's army's invasion of Lebanon in 1982. This particular butchery had been perpetrated by Lebanese Christian troops financed by Israel, it is true, but it had not been proved that they had acted with the agreement of the Israeli High Command, and indeed from the trial proceedings it seemed more likely that the Israelis were not responsible. Both trials ended with out-of-court compromises between the respective parties. The plaintiffs obtained only partial damages. *Time* and CBS thus escaped formal condemnation for defamation.

Renata Adler then went through the stenographic recording of all the trial proceedings, the detailed cross-examination of witnesses, and so on. After painstakingly analyzing them, she came to the conclusion that *Time* and CBS, though they had managed not to be sentenced for libel, had nevertheless gravely distorted the facts and had then lied, after the first protests were made, in order to cover up the mistakes their journalists had made. During the summer of 1986 *The New Yorker* published long extracts from *Reckless Disregard* in two successive issues. Thereupon, instead of replying to arguments with arguments of their own, *Time* and in particular CBS launched a massive steamroller operation in an effort to intimidate the publishers, Alfred A. Knopf, by threatening a lawsuit in order to have them postpone publication of the complete book indefinitely. What terrified Knopf was not so much the possibility of a lawsuit as the prospect of falling out with *Time* (with the result that it would never again review Knopf books) and of seeing its authors henceforth blackballed and debarred from taking part in CBS debates. Paradoxically, far-left newspapers and small groups took up the cudgels for the two giant media conglomerates! They denounced the publication of the book, doing everything they could to discredit Renata Adler with all sorts of calumnious accusations simply because they were convinced that the United States was totally to blame in Vietnam, just as Israel was totally to blame in Lebanon. A charming exhibition of intellectual and moral probity.

Rare are those, even when news is their stock in trade, who do not suppress information when it is unfavorable to them. The press sees itself, and wants to see itself, as a counterpower. But it acts like an executive power, and even more brutally than that, to stifle everything that embarrasses it, for it is less disciplined—I am speaking here not of political or ideological control, but of professional discipline such as exists for doctors, lawyers, or engineers, which in its case is nonexistent. Journalism is even the only profession—or more exactly *métier* (trade)—in which such inherent discipline does not exist. In this context, far from being the antithesis of the powers that be, it is rather a copy thereof, enjoying a degree of arbitrary latitude no political power in a democracy is allowed to enjoy. It is thus the adulterine child of anarchy and absolutism—the "adulterine power" of which Lamartine speaks, the wild imitation of the "masters of the earth." Sometimes in the democracies the worst offenses against freedom of the press come from the press itself. "This," wrote columnist William Safire, thanks to whom *Reckless Disregard* was at last able to appear after having been delayed several times, "is a case of prior book restraint triggered by powerful news organizations that are quick to denounce prior restraint by government."*

The difference between censorship exercised by governments and that exercised by the press in democratic countries is that the former is usually denounced and impeded, whereas the latter is not, since the press would have to undertake the task of criticizing itself. No doubt those who are not part of this particular fraternity frequently contest its statements, often in violent terms, but they seldom do so in public for fear of sounding a "fascist" note. When politicians or economic experts undertake to criticize the media, they usually make themselves unpopular, even when they are right, and gain a reputation of being adversaries of freedom of expression. Newspapers sometimes engage in polemics with one another according to ideological prejudices, but never or rarely over the professional quality of their work. I am not taking sides regarding the fundamental issues of the Westmoreland and Sharon trials; I am simply saying that CBS and *Time* should have replied on the merits of the evidence, as they insist that others do, rather than have sought to smother the evidence by bringing pressure to bear on the publisher of an embarrassing book.

Are journalists the last citizens in a democracy who still enjoy the privilege of being able to stifle news that annoys them? In 1977, when Indro Montanelli, editor in chief of *Il Giornale,* was seriously wounded by bullets fired at him in the street by Red Brigade terrorists, the *Corriere della Sera,* for which he had previously worked but with which he had had a falling out, reported that an apparently unidentified "journalist" had been the victim of an assassination attempt. A personal

*In a column entitled "The Book Criticizes Giants, so Publication Is in Doubt," *The New York Times,* reprinted by the *International Herald Tribune,* October 28, 1986.

quarrel thus culminated—O sacred duty of informing!—in this supreme idiocy: the most famous editorialist of the Italian press did not even have the right to have himself gunned down in his own name! And this in the *Corriere della Sera,* of which he had been the "star" for thirty years!

The press is forever on the lookout for mistakes committed by political leaders, but it does not enjoy having its own errors exposed, and it usually is as reluctant to admit to them as to rectify them. On April 21, 1982, for example, CBS broadcast a prime-time TV documentary prepared by Bill Moyers, featuring three poor families that had been hard hit by reductions in social security payments—in other words, for the message was unmistakable—who had been deliberately plunged into poverty thanks to Ronald Reagan. The White House protested. It pointed out, to begin with, that, contrary to repeated allegations in the press, Reagan had not reduced social security expenditures, but had simply reduced the annual *growth* rate of such expenditures (which meant that, taking inflation into account, more money had been spent in this field in 1982 than in 1981). The White House spokesman further argued that the three hardship cases had been deliberately chosen to denigrate the president, for they were not at all representative. Two of the three families had had their social security benefits suspended thanks to decisions taken by local (i.e., state or municipal) authorities, and not by the federal authorities, while the suspension in the third case had been ordered before Reagan had become president! The White House communiqué made it clear that it did not contest CBS's right to broadcast what it wished, the First Amendment to the Constitution being sacred; nor was it invoking the "fairness doctrine" of the Federal Communications Commission. All it asked was a right of reply, so that its spokesman could inform the public of the facts I have just enumerated. CBS, however, refused this right of reply, and Bill Moyers justified this refusal by declaring that "Mr. Reagan has chosen not to offend the rich, the powerful and the organized in his budget cuts, but to take on the weak, with a budget which falls most heavily on the poor."* In other words, he replied by vague and general imputations, without deigning to consider the specific objections that had been made.

This example illustrates the absurd situation in which mankind today finds itself with respect to information. In many countries of the planet the political regime muzzles the press. In countries where the press is

*The New York Times, April 23, 1982.

free, it can fulminate against the government in power, or against any other institution, even against individuals, leveling unjust accusations without observing standards of accuracy or being obliged to correct its errors. Thus it is that CBS can simply refuse a right of reply to the president of the United States on *questions of fact* without furnishing an explanation. Furthermore, U.S. journalists have never really accepted or admitted the validity of the Communications Act of 1934, in which the "fairness doctrine" of impartiality was enunciated and according to which in exchange for a licence to broadcast on a certain frequency every station pledges itself not to abuse its power by making one-sided presentations of the news or by maintaining silence on essential subjects. The profession's point of view is that nobody, other than itself, is fit to judge the way in which it does its job—again, a truly unique privilege in the world we live in. And it is true that honest newspapers are worthy of the trust placed in their reporting thanks to the abilities and scruples of the journalists who work for them. The others, regurgitating the mangled fragments of an old philosophical half-truth, go on sententiously declaiming that "there is no such thing as objectivity"—a dictum which, as Kant would have said, belongs to the "asylum of ignorance" or, let us say, of arrogance. For the thing that does not exist is, of course, infallibility. Impartiality is something that does exist—that is, not an unattainable, absolute objectivity, but the effort to attain it. In few cases of serious errors detected in the press is any effort at objectivity at all apparent. And in a great many cases it is even the contrary impulse that is most manifest.

Earlier I cited the case of the hubbub that was stirred up in left-wing and left-of-center newspapers in Europe over the semivictory of the "televangelist" Pat Robertson during the primary elections in Iowa in February 1988. The Inquisition was on its way back, we were given to understand, a typhoon of fanaticism was sweeping over America, a bigoted totalitarianism was about to engulf the White House. But three weeks later the Reverend Pat Robertson was swept into oblivion. In the New Hampshire primary, then in South Carolina's, and finally on "Super Tuesday" (March 8, 1988) the states of the South plunged his electoral pretensions into the depths of political nothingness from which, for any serious observer, they had never really emerged. In Illinois, on March 15, the number of delegates he won was nil—which eliminated him from the race altogether. But did the same newspapers that had played up his original emergence feel the need to rectify their analyses and explain the reasons for their hyperbolic overestimation of the reverend's importance? Not at all.

The press of free peoples will not serve democracy, will not fulfill its mission to public opinion, and will not serve as a model for the future press of peoples that are currently enslaved so long as it dresses up militant publications to look like organs of information. An organ of information is not a newspaper in which no opinion is expressed, far from it; it is a newspaper in which the opinion *results* from analyses of the printed information. A militant publication is one in which the opinion precedes and orients information, imposes its choices, and regulates the focus. Thus the German weekly *Der Spiegel* ("The Mirror") as was once noted by Ralf Dahrendorf, who is both a German citizen and the director of the London School of Economics, "stands for an anti-European and anti-Western position on German unity."* Let us put it even more plainly by saying that *Der Spiegel* was for years markedly pro-Soviet, having in 1981, for example, assumed a position hostile to Solidarity and favorable to Jaruzelski. Elisabeth Noelle-Neumann, director of West Germany's most important public opinion institute, could even say that "the basically leftist orientation of younger Germans was probably fashioned by *Der Spiegel*"—which supported the pacifist movement and aroused hatred against the Atlantic Alliance. This is its unquestionable right. But the famous weekly does not have the right to pretend that it is a magazine of information, indeed the most powerful, not to say the only, one in the Federal Republic. If it publishes a great many articles, some of them very good, it picks and chooses them according to ideological criteria. But the supreme failing in matters of the press is not to defend an opinion, but to do it while seeming not to do so.

Obviously, the press does not systematically oppose what any government does. When there is a change in the political majority, such-and-such a newspaper, which had been in the habit of soft-pedaling the previous government's successes, suddenly begins soft-pedaling the failures of the present government. Furthermore, information does not concern only domestic politics. The magic formula of "counterpower" must also be placed in its international context. In a democracy, to attack one's government without respite when it is defending itself against the encroachments of a totalitarian and imperialist power is not to play the role of counterpower; it is, on the contrary, to go over and join the camp of the strongest power. It is not true that *Der Spiegel* was pitiless toward just any government; it was above all pitiless toward

Newsweek, April 19, 1982.

democratic governments, rarely toward communist governments, and almost never toward the Soviet government, whose goodwill, sincerity, and peaceful intentions seem to have been spared its universal suspicion.

Similarly, how was it that since the coming to power of Mikhail Gorbachev in 1985, the "watchdog" function that the liberal press and media in the United States attribute to themselves should have played so small a role with respect to the Soviet leader, while concentrating exclusively on Ronald Reagan? To be sure, information should not be censored if it is unfavorable to a democratic regime and favorable to a totalitarian regime—provided it is true. However, rest assured. This is not the most frequent type of censorship. The U.S. press conceives of its watchdog role almost solely with respect to the U.S. administration, especially if it is Republican, and with respect to its allies and supporters in the world. But is that really fulfilling a watchdog role? A good watchdog should have an instinct for what is most dangerous, not for what is closest. A strong man is not one who beats his wife, while allowing the murderer of his son to go scot free and even lending him his car to get away.

The simplistic "counterpower" and "watchdog" theory leads to the aberration of thinking that the work of journalism should be determined by the sole "duty" to be "for" or "against" this or that. This oversimplified conception causes people to forget that a journalist's work should first of all be geared to collecting the data involved, to gathering substantive information, and that only thereafter should one decide to condemn or to approve, and to what extent. Never, perhaps, was this disregard for the importance of solid information, this indifference to what was at stake—in contrast to an exclusive overconcentration on the conflict between press and administration—so glaringly revealed as in the case of the U.S. invasion of Grenada in 1983. It may be recalled that no newsmen were allowed to accompany the expeditionary force during the first two days of an operation that was aimed at dislodging a fairly bloody Soviet-Cuban dictatorship. But to make clear what was involved, let me briefly recapitulate the basic elements of the case. This particular dictatorship had not a shred of legitimacy—something that never troubles "liberals" so long as the dictatorship is Marxist—as it had in fact toppled a democratic government in 1981. For two years Grenada's New Jewel movement (a communist party that had been admitted to the Socialist International!) had exercised a tyrannical rule, effectively controlled by Soviet and Cuban overlords and amiably assisted by North Koreans, East Germans, and other notable philanthropists, under the ostensible leadership of a local communist, Maurice Bishop. However, in early October 1983, Bishop, during a heated discussion in the Marxist junta presided over by the Cuban ambassador, was assassinated, along with his friends, their families, and his own family, women and children included—a massacre in which some 200 persons (or 140, according to the lowest estimates) lost their lives. The Bishop "government" was then "replaced" by a junta composed of officers, which called itself the Ruling Military Council. This RMC stepped up the repressive measures taken against a long-since-terrorized population whose sufferings were well known to Washington but which were of no concern to U.S. liberals. The Sovieto-Cubans, furthermore, had built a vast military airport and a submarine base on the island. All of which indicated clearly enough that a new Soviet bridgehead was being established in the Caribbean at the very moment another (Nicaragua) was being installed in Central America.

After Bishop's liquidation a wave of panic swept over the neighboring islands, which suddenly saw themselves within easy range of the devouring wolf. They sent discreet messages of distress to Washington after having vainly appealed for help to London, which turned a deaf ear to their plaints. (This did not keep Mrs. Thatcher from later protesting the U.S. operation. The fact that Grenada was a member of the Commonwealth did not, it seems, entitle it to be aided, but it did include the right to grumble against those who liberated it after maintaining a long silence about the misdeeds of those who had enslaved the island.)

About this devastating record the U.S. press hardly breathed a word. The only scandal about which it got worked up was the outrage it felt it had undergone thanks to its exclusion from the theater of operations on October 25 and 26. U.S. newspapers had previously been almost totally disinterested in the situation in the Caribbean and did not bother to explain to the public the political and geostrategic reasons that had prompted Reagan to order the operation—while of course reserving the right eventually to contest these reasons on the basis of their own analysis. In any case, this question of national and international interest was sidetracked. The restoration of democracy to Grenada, which was perfectly achieved, to the great relief of the local population, was quickly lost sight of in the face of the enormity of the greatest crime against humanity committed in modern times—excluding the media for forty-eight hours! Edward M. Joyce, at that time president of CBS News, denounced this crime as heralding "the dawn of a new era of censorship, of manipulation of the press, of considering the media the handmaiden of government."* The journalists invoked the eternal First Amendment, once again overlooking the fact that while it guarantees freedom of expression and opinion, it nowhere stipulates that the army of the United States has an obligation to carry reporters in its baggage trains to cover every military operation. The American Association of Newspaper Publishers raised an outcry over the "secret war"; yet this war was not secret (another case of false information indulged in by the press); it had been announced and played up by the administration in Washington from the very outset of the landings. It is true that during the first two days it was covered solely by communiqués and filmed documents issued by the High Command. This is a bit different, even if insufficient. *Editor and Publisher,* the press's professional weekly, deplored the "fact" that Americans had ceased to be the *best informed people in the world* (no less!) "particularly about what their government is doing supposedly on their behalf." This "supposedly" is admirable. For, as far as we know, this government, having been democratically elected and having not transgressed the constitutional limits imposed by the Constitution on the executive branch's freedom of initiative, could justifiably claim that it had legitimately acted in the name of the people. *Editor and Publisher,* on the other hand, could not.

It can happen, of course, that democratic governments keep journalists from doing their proper job as informants. During the war in Algeria the French governments of both the Fourth and Fifth republics sinned greatly in this respect. There is every reason to reproach them for betraying their own principles in so doing. But this is not the case with totalitarian powers. The USSR never said that foreign journalists had a right to move about freely in Afghanistan. What violates human rights in a totalitarian regime is not a denial of press freedom; it is the regime itself. The regime must be entirely democratized if information is to be democratized. Free journalists, who maintain a strict and unflagging vigilance over the democracies themselves, face lesser difficulties. This is notably the case in the United States, of all the democracies perhaps the most willfully transparent. But the professional conscience of journalists should be on a par with this transparence.

Let us put this Grenada affair into its proper perspective. Some U.S. newsmen realized that their recriminations against Reagan often reflected the narcissism of the journalistic tribe rather than solidly

*Quoted by Leonard Sussman, "Press versus Government," *Freedom at Issue,* May–June 1984.

founded objections; besides which, the journalists were unconvincing. Already, prior to the invasion, barely 13.7 percent of Americans questioned in a public opinion poll considered the media to be trustworthy. After the Grenada operation, according to a poll taken in early December, and after six weeks of media broadsides against the administration's "censorship," only 19 percent of U.S. citizens thought correspondents should have accompanied the landing troops from the first minute on. *The Washington Post*'s accusation—according to which those forty-eight hours of press absence affected "the whole character of the relationship between governor and governed"—had the hollow sound of melodrama. *Time,* with greater lucidity, wondered why the media had been able to arouse such a wide-ranging resentment in the general public, and why their temporary exclusion from the scene of action had caused such delight and even aroused a "gleeful and even vengeful public attitude." Why indeed? Instead of inflating soap bubbles to sustain a fatuous quarrel, the journalists would have been better inspired to search for answers to those questions.

The answer was that the administration, in accord with the immense majority of Americans, had no confidence in the impartiality the media might exhibit in reporting the first phases of the expedition. It felt they would do everything imaginable to transmit as one-sided and as black a picture as possible of U.S. "atrocities," accompanied by a telling interview with a Castrista, who would indignantly denounce this "imperialist and Yankee crime," in ways calculated to arouse a wave of pacifist revulsion in the general public. Three quarters of the newspapers in the United States were hostile to the strategic and political motives that had dictated Reagan's decision. They tended in advance to dismiss them, to deny their urgency and pertinence *a priori.* Since Vietnam and Watergate the U.S. press had above all concentrated on its mission of being an unconditional adversary of the government in power. There are ways of working up public antipathy for the government that are far removed from reasoned political criticism. The Reagan administration knew perfectly well by what gimmicks the TV cameramen could, during the first hours of the landings, focus on painful scenes of violence in order to damn the operation by diverting public attention from its overall objectives. For example, during the first hours of fighting against the Cuban occupants of the island, U.S. shells fell on a psychiatric hospital. This clearly was a dreadful happening, and one that deserved to be talked about—but only along with other aspects of the operation. But this is probably all that a hundred million American TV viewers would have seen if TV camera crews had landed with the troops. "What would have happened," Leonard Sussman wondered, "if color television on the first night of the Grenada intervention had shown the blasted hospital, dead bodies, and perhaps a wounded mental patient wandering through the rubble? Would that single picture have proved that the political basis for the American intervention—eliminating a Cuban-Soviet beachhead—had been erroneously conceived? That the murder, days earlier, of the prime minister and civilians had been justified? That Americans should pull out before the murderers were apprehended? That Grenadians would have been better off if no American soldier had landed?"*

This was not in any case the opinion of most Americans. For a public opinion poll undertaken shortly afterward by CBS revealed that the administration's analysis of the situation on the island coincided with that of the local inhabitants of Grenada, who welcomed the invasion as a liberation. A massive 91 percent majority of the Grenadans who were interviewed declared themselves happy that the U.S. had intervened; 85 percent declared they had been living in a state of fear and trembling for themselves and for their families; 76 percent felt Cuba definitely wanted to control Grenada; and 65 percent were certain that the huge airport had been built to serve Soviet and Cuban objectives, not for tourist purposes.

It should be added that several weeks later the U.S. troops left the island, where free elections were held and democracy was restored. Yet despite the blinding clarity of the facts, three and a half years later (in May 1987), at a conference held in Paris on the subject of "The Media, Power, and Democracy," which I have already mentioned, I could still hear dozens of U.S. newspapermen and professors from schools of journalism furiously stigmatize their two-day exclusion from Grenada as the most abominable crime ever committed against human rights. When a tribe whose task it should be to heed public opinion and to know how to talk to the public isolates itself so much from both public opinion and that of the liberated country that is at the center of the controversy, it can only be said that it has taken refuge in a kind of tribal "autism" hardly compatible with its mission. Autism, for the person who is afflicted by it, is a "focusing of one's entire mental life on one's internal world and a loss of contact with the outer world."† This is a sorry state of affairs for professionals whose job it is to observe the outer world.

*From the previously cited article. From 1967 to 1988 Leonard Sussman was executive director of Freedom House, an institution specializing in the study of totalitarian constraints and upholding the cause of liberty in threatened or oppressed countries.

†Antoine Porot, *Manuel alphabétique de psychiatrie* (Paris: Presses Universitaires de France, 1969).

Whence comes the trouble? Simply from the fact, once again, that too many journalists are preoccupied not by what is, or what happened, but by what must be proved to be.

In this chapter I am concerned with countries in which the press is free. It is superfluous to speak of the others. But—and this is the vital point—it is interesting to examine what Man does with freedom when he has it, and also—the subject of this book—what use he makes of the faculty of knowing and of saying what he knows. In countries subjected to censorship, I have often noted the paradoxical fact that ordinary citizens, and above all intellectuals, are on many points better informed about the affairs of the world than are those of free countries, simply because their minds are more sharply conditioned by the very existence of censorship and are that much more apt to be able to distinguish the true from the false and to recognize the genuine information of which they are so often deprived.

I am not trying to maintain that governments, even when democratic, are always right and do only good things. The press often attacks them, and quite rightly so. I am, however, taking issue with the caricatural and childish attitude of a press that scorns everything that does not consti- tute an attack against the government in power and all established authorities. Governments obviously strive to hamper the diffusion of unfavorable news and to amplify news that is flattering for them. No less obviously, the raison d'être of the press is to reestablish a proper balance and to make known things that governments (and opposition parties also, in matters concerning them) would rather see concealed. But this role of the press is valid only if it is based on a scrupulous respect for accurate information. However, in any given democracy there are as few newspapers or networks that respect this as there are countries in the world that respect democracy. In the latter the press is not a counter- weight or antidote to political dishonesty; it is part and parcel of it, and constitutes one of its chief instruments. When we look over the newspa- pers and media of the country in which we happen to live, we spontane- ously classify them as favorable or unfavorable to this or that political current, to certain financial, cultural, religious, racial, or sexual circles. In our judgment of them it is almost never the quality of their informa- tion that is the foremost criterion. To publish such-and-such a piece of information is to show that one holds such-and-such an opinion. Whether it is true or not is secondary.

Even the way in which a commonplace crime is presented, above all when it is pompously termed a "phenomenon of society," can "classify" a newspaper as surely as its political prejudices. On December 1, 1987, for example, the Paris police arrested a mysterious "assassin of elderly women," a man who over a period of several years had killed at least thirty aged ladies, all living alone, in order to steal the money they had saved up. Now, it so happened that the murderer was black, homosexual, and a drug addict. For a full week the left-wing newspapers—*Le Matin, Libération, Le Monde, La Croix, L'Humanité*—more or less kicked the story under the rug, banishing it to their inside pages and concealing details about the murderer. The story, half hidden away in the body of each paper, was presented with grudging headlines and sometimes simply omitted. When the story was mentioned, it was usually done in such a way as to deflect attention from its criminal aspect and to give the sordid tale a political slant. Thus, on page 13 of the December 3 issue of *Libération,* beneath the headline AN ASSASSIN KNUCKLES UNDER, one could read: "In July 1986, after three and a half months in the government, Charles Pasqua could already deplore nine assassinations of grandmothers. Exactly the same number as under the Left since 1984." Now was this really the issue? Exploiting a successful police operation mounted after a difficult investigation, *Libération* could find nothing better to do than pin the blame on the conservative minister of the interior!

This passage inaugurated a journalistic technique worth enshrining. If someone you don't like achieves a success, instead of publishing the news—which irks you—publish a news item from three years back, choosing a circumstance in which your *bête noire* failed lamentably. The motives underlying such discretion are patent: fear of antiblack racism and antihomosexual "racism." However, in this case there was no risk of rekindling hatred for foreigners, for the murderer, Thierry Paulin, was a French citizen. There was also another factor: a desire not to reinforce reflexes of "exclusion" toward drug addicts. But how could the authors of this occultation, professionally so unacceptable, not realize that it was bound to boomerang against the cause they thought they were serving? In the hierarchy of twentieth-century crime in France, Paulin was very high up for the number of his personally killed victims—behind Dr. Petiot, who murdered dozens of Jews during World War II in order to rob them, but ahead of the equally notorious Landru. Not to speak of such a thing in a handful of newspapers, when it was the number one topic of conversation for French men and women everywhere, was quite simply clumsy, for this silence could not keep the entire population from hearing about it.

In 1979 Jimmy Goldsmith, owner of *L'Express,* had asked me to say nothing in his weekly about the "affair of the diamonds"—the ones

Giscard d'Estaing had received as a gift from the "emperor" of the Central African Republic, Jean-Bédel Bokassa—an affair that had greatly affected the prestige of the president of the Republic, for whom Goldsmith felt considerable sympathy. I naturally refused, first as a matter of principle and then by arguing that our silence would not help Giscard in the least and would be damaging for *L'Express*. In the same way, racism can only be aggravated when the public begins to realize that influential newspapers are minimizing the responsibility for a series of atrocious crimes simply because the criminal happens to be a black and a homosexual. They thereby arouse the irritation of many people, who can only wonder how such a series of crimes would have been played up if the murderer had been a white man and a killer of Arabs. These wretched journalistic tricks do not calm racism; on the contrary, they tend to revive it, they form part of the vicious circle of complementary paranoias from which we can emerge only by ceasing to regard race and homosexuality as factors modifying anything, whether for good or for evil.

Let us congratulate an antiracist newspaper that explains in a clear and open way why racism constitutes an almost self-contradictory stance, scientifically stupid and morally indefensible, but not a newspaper that suppresses information when it thinks it might excite racism. It then reasons exactly like the politician it criticizes for so doing when the latter imagines a problem can be solved by keeping silent about it. Furthermore, it implicitly admits in doing so that it has little confidence in its case, since to plead it the paper feels the need to lie, if only by omission.

The fact that in nine cases out of ten the journalist's opinion determines information and not vice versa, is admitted in the private conversations editors and correspondents have among themselves and with those they deal with. "Come off it! It's not in X——— newspaper that you're going to find this kind of information" is a standard comment enunciated as a commonsense axiom. At international conferences devoted to journalism, the religious cult of Information as something sacrosanct is celebrated, while censorship is stigmatized as an evil imposed by the diabolical powers of money and political expediency. But among themselves journalists know very well that newspaper A won't deal with this topic and newspaper B won't cover that topic—"this" and "that" both being, from a neutral point of view, newsworthy items of information.

In 1980, when Juan Luís Cebrián, editor in chief of *El País,* called me from Madrid to ask for a letter of support to be read at a trial where he was being accused of libel, I naturally agreed to write one. Then I asked how it happened that his newspaper had been just about the only one in Europe that had not mentioned the "Marchais affair"—that is, the publication by *L'Express* of a document that had been found in the German archives and which proved beyond the shadow of a doubt that the secretary-general of the French Communist Party had in 1942 and 1943 gone to work in Nazi Germany as a *volunteer* laborer and not as someone who had been deported, as he had always claimed. Cebrián replied with laudable ingenuousness and no trace of embarrassment: "Yes, I know, it really is regrettable—but the foreign editor was off on a trip and his assistant, who had taken his place, is a communist. So naturally he kept quiet on the subject." This was a candid admission of the fact that even the editor in chief of a newspaper has trouble keeping information from being influenced by the political preferences of the person transmitting, or refusing to transmit, the news. My friend Cebrián and his newspaper have—in case you doubted it—received many "journalistic awards" in all sorts of countries.

With rare exceptions, it is generally admitted in newspaper circles—despite protests to the contrary destined for the outer world—that the political preferences of journalists serve as a criterion in their presentation of the news. In Italy this capitulation to partiality has even been institutionalized—the term for it, as I have already explained, being *lottizzazione* (dividing up into lots). Let us go back to it for a moment. At a UNESCO conference Paolo Romani, Paris correspondent of *Il Giornale* during the 1980s, went into some detail describing this curious practice, explaining how the political parties intervene directly in the hiring and internal promotion of journalists. The parties maintain a close watch over the "respect for equilibrium," as the innocuous saying has it. Thus, contrary to what happens in other countries, where such ties are usually denied or dissimulated, Italian journalists often openly proclaim their membership in a particular party, which then basically takes charge of their "career plan." Many, Romani said, were officially registered party members, while others openly situated themselves in a Socialist, Christian Democratic, Republican, or Communist "area." With respect to this "area," they maintain themselves in what, in a charming locution, is called a state of "constructive disposability." The art of distributing journalistic "lots" proportionately, according to the varying strengths of the different parties, attains the summit of perfection at RAI—Italy's state-controlled radio and television setup (private channels are not authorized to deal with news). Each TV channel quite officially possesses a political coloration: The first channel is Christian

Democratic in orientation, the second is Socialist, the third is Communist. It could not be admitted with greater frankness that no one, even in the journalistic world, has the slightest confidence in the much touted "professional conscience" of journalists, nor in the "professional ethics" of newsmen. Thus, on March 17, 1988, when a ministerial crisis was opened by the collapse of the Goria government, RAI's second channel devoted the first ten minutes of its 7:45 P.M. news roundup to the Socialist leader, Bettino Craxi, even though the president of the republic had just entrusted the Christian Democratic leader, Ciriaco de Mita, with the task of forming a new government. Let's hear no more of that old saw about "pluralism"! The communist journalists who in 1981 were appointed *directly* by the Party to posts at French TV channels were not chosen by any kind of "pluralism."

During the years I have spent observing and working in journalism, what has most struck me has been the small number of journalists who really behave like professionals—that is, whose curiosity focuses on facts above all else. This limited contingent of professionals also has opinions and formulates judgments of its own, often very emphatic ones. That is not the point. Impartiality is not indifference. On the contrary, the more value one attaches to ideas, the less prepared one is to see them based on a lack of information. *In journalism, opinion is interesting only when it is a form of information.* By this I mean that an editorial is of no interest unless it is based on solid documentation, solidly analyzed. The *bête noire* of censors and ideologists is not pure opinion, nor is it the arbitrary "mood" of some random newsman; it is opinion backed by information, in other words, a form of factual demonstration. What the ideologist fears is not that you should say: "I don't like Vietnamese communism," but that you should say, with the accompanying proof: "The communist regime in Vietnam has killed a million innocent persons in ten years." It is not that you should say: "I am against what French socialist governments did between 1981 and 1985," but that you should say, with supporting evidence: "The socialists managed around 1984 to re-create mass poverty, which had disappeared from France several decades before."

The root cause of poor reasoning is often poor information. From then on, it encrusts itself in public opinion, and nothing can dislodge it. Let's take the widely held notion that François Mitterrand is the person who, thanks to the "Union of the Left" and its 101-point Common Program masterminded the collapse of the French Communist Party. Anyone familiar with elementary logic knows that the concomitance of two facts does not suffice to establish a cause-and-effect relationship

between them. Communist parties have collapsed or considerably declined all over Europe—in some cases without an alliance with the
socialists or participation in the government, as in Spain and Portugal,
or with a participation in the government, as in Finland. They declined
when they were Stalinist, like the French and Portuguese Communist
parties, and when they were Eurocommunist, like the Spanish Communist Party, which has virtually disappeared. Even the powerful Italian
Communist Party dropped over a period of twelve years from 34 percent
to 21 percent of voters, at a time when Craxi's Socialist Party was
violently hostile to it and yet continued to gain ground.* Finally, the
truly significant collapse of the French Communist Party took place
between the legislative elections of 1978 and the presidential election of
1981—which is to say, precisely during the three years when the communists and socialists were at daggers drawn, when the Common Program
had been declared "foreclosed" by Mitterrand, and when the Union of
the Left lay shattered at the bottom of the ravine after the rupture in
the autumn of 1977. On the other hand, when this union was fully active
it allowed the French Communist Party to pull off one of the greatest
triumphs in its history, in the municipal elections of the spring of 1977.
Yet all these arguments will not keep commentators from continuing to
flaunt this unpuncturable platitude.†

*Results obtained in the so-called "administrative" elections of May 29 and 30, 1988.

†From 1968 to 1988 the communist vote in France evolved as follows: in the legislative
elections of 1968 the Communist Party obtained 4,435,337 votes; in those of 1973 (that is, one
year after the setting up of the Union of the Left and the signing of the socialist-communist
Common Program), 5,085,108. In the legislative elections of 1978, it won 5,791,525 votes (part
of this rise being due to an increase in the number of voters, notably of the youngest, since
President Valéry Giscard d'Estaing had lowered the minimum voting age from twenty-one to
eighteen years). The years of the Union of the Left thus unquestionably helped the French
Communist Party, and not the Socialist Party alone. Shattered in the autumn of 1977 because
of the ill will of the French Communist Party, the Union experienced a brief resurrection
between the first and second runoffs of the elections of 1978, then collapsed completely. Even
when Mitterrand took Communist Party members into his socialist government in 1981 and
1984, there was no more Common Program. The French Communist Party's hostility to the
Socialist Party was at times violent and openly declared, at times underhand and relatively
muted (during the period from 1981 to 1984, when there were four Communist Party members
in the successive governments of Pierre Mauroy). During the presidential election of 1981, the
Communist Party vote, after three years of rupture and polemics, fell to 4,003,025, and in the
legislative elections of 1986, to 2,663,734. Finally, in the presidential election of 1988, it fell
to 2,055,995 votes—rising slightly during the subsequent legislative elections of June 5, to
2,663,734. The collapse of the French Communist Party thus began *after* the burying of the
Union of the Left and the Common Program. It continued throughout the years when the
Communist Party had entered as a privileged partner into the socialist government, where it
had the misfortune of sharing the blame for the policies pursued by this government, notably
in 1984, when the Socialist Party, like Mitterrand himself, hit a rock bottom of unpopularity.

Often, during the last, rasping stages of international conferences, the possibility is envisaged of creating "professional commissions" for journalism—along the lines of the councils that supervise the legal and medical professions. But who is to judge whom? To a certain extent, such commissions already exist in some countries in the form of newspapers and reviews devoted to press and media. But these specialized publications, which hand out good and bad marks, are almost never concerned with the accuracy of information. Such is the case with what is probably the most prestigious of such reviews, *The Columbia Journalism Review,* published by the school of journalism that is reputed to be the finest in the United States. The review prides itself on distributing praise and blame with no regard to ideological bias, on not espousing any partisan cause, and on being to neither right nor left. Yet in 1984 *Public Opinion* published a study examining all of the articles criticizing the media that *The Columbia Journalism Review* had published over a period of ten years. The findings showed that 78 percent of the articles had been written from a frankly left-wing or "liberal" viewpoint, 12 percent from a "conservative" viewpoint, and 10 percent without its being possible to discern any partisan orientation. The conception of "good" journalism, as propounded by *The Columbia Journalism Review,* is that of an aggressive journalism which should, as a matter of principle, attack established authorities and be wide open to the complaints of oppressed minorities. The *Review* tirelessly lashes the lukewarmness of the press in the pursuit of these objectives. In 1983, for example, it took both press and television to task for their partiality in favor of Reagan. The media, it declared, were "the *Pravda* of the Potomac, a conduit for White House utterances and official image-mongering." This is how a professional publication, which is supposed to keep watch over others, can reveal itself to be unable, or at least reluctant, to verify its own information. Indeed, according to a study undertaken by a group of sociologists of the news programs of the three main TV networks during the period under consideration, it emerged that the news flashes presenting Reagan in a favorable light totaled 400 words, and that those that were hostile to him, 8,000 words—a ratio of twenty-two to one in favor of "negative" stories.*

Escaping from this trap in July 1984 and resuming its attacks against the socialists, the French Communist Party was nevertheless unable to recoup its losses and became a marginal political formation. Thus, in France as elsewhere, the great decline of European communism during the 1980s took place independently of the local context, a context that was itself in a perpetual state of flux.

The Wall Street Journal (European edition), June 19, 1984.

In foreign policy, too, *The Columbia Journalism Review* (*CJR* to the initiated) applies criteria that are more ideological than professional in its appreciation of the work of newsmen. Thus, reviewing the American reporting of events in Iran, it deplored the fact that the media were lacking in fairness toward Khomeini and depicted his regime as authoritarian and reactionary. Pushing Third Worldism to a pitch of hysteria, the *CJR* insinuated that the U.S. press had made a caricature of the "battle for freedom" which, it would have us believe, the ayatollahs were waging. As one can see, we are far removed from the technical yardsticks this publication is supposed to employ in judging the merits and demerits of the media.

Schools of journalism, I might add, do not appear to be places where people are primarily taught to seek out and verify information. Rather, students develop a sense of their social mission in the service of a noble cause, which they themselves define and are expected to promote. For CFJ (Centre de Formation des Journalistes) in Paris during the 1970s, this noble cause was the Common Program of the united Left. One day during this period a delegation of CFJ's "best pupils" asked to meet me and came to *L'Express.* The question they had come to put to me was this: "Why did you devote a cover story to the Marchais affair and not to Giscard's affair of the diamonds? Isn't there in this case a proof of your political partiality, of your complaisance toward the government in power and of your hostility toward the Left?" I began by replying that my personal opinions were clearly expressed in my editorials, where I had never sought to hide my aversion for Georges Marchais's ideas and my (relative) preference for Valéry Giscard d'Estaing's. However, my decision in the matter that preoccupied them did not stem in any way from my personal opinions; it was motivated by purely professional criteria.

The "affair of the diamonds" had been simultaneously aired by the daily newspaper *Le Monde* and the satirical weekly *Le Canard Enchaîné* and then taken up by the entire press, including ourselves. But we had no new, unpublished elements of information which might have justified our giving this story major play. I had in fact tried to obtain additional information for *L'Express,* and for this purpose (and though the owner did everything he possibly could to dissuade me) I had sent a team of journalists to interview ex-"emperor" Bokassa (the presumed distributor of the diamonds), who had taken refuge in the Ivory Coast. However, the Ivory Coast police had prevented any contact with him. On the other hand, the document from the administrative files proving what had long been suspected but not definitely established—to wit, that

Georges Marchais had collaborated with the Germans during the war by willingly going to work for Hitler in an armaments factory—was a *L'Express* scoop. It had cost us a lot of time and cross-checking before one of our reporters could gain access to the list of French volunteer workers in Germany, which was preserved at Augsburg, and simply locating this particular file had required a lot of work. Since this was a scoop, it was logical that we should have made a cover story out of it. Furthermore, this was not simply a private matter; it was a highly political affair, since it made a significant difference if the secretary-general of the French Communist Party had indeed collaborated with the Nazis—which probably meant that the Soviets had a dossier with which to blackmail and control him.

I cited several articles in which we had severely and even violently criticized Giscard d'Estaing's policies when they seemed to us to merit criticism. But I realized, from the stony look on the faces of my visitors, that I was speaking to them in Etruscan. My language was totally hermetic. For them professional ethics had nothing to do with the search for genuine, unpublished information, with the gathering of new, original documentary material, with a debate of ideas founded on factual arguments alone. The First Commandment of their credo was to uphold the Left and, failing that, to treat Left and Right on the same level of equality, no matter what the available information might be, and never to say that the Left was in the wrong. That was their conception of "objectivity." Needless to say, the observance of this scrupulous egalitarianism was binding only on the liberal (i.e., conservative) press. Our colleagues of the Left had the moral right to reserve all their attacks for the Right and to support the Left exclusively. Therein lay complete and exemplary objectivity. Though unable to attain such a degree of perfection, we, the lesser mortals of the liberal press, at least had the right to respect this inferior form of objectivity—*a priori* egalitarianism—no matter what the latest news might be. Why, they asked me, do you devote so much space to communism, totalitarianism, Soviet expansion, socialism, Maoism, Third Worldism? I replied that it was not my fault if, since 1945, these were the visions of the world and the political forces that had dominated the international scene. In short, the brightest pupils of this school of journalism were behaving as politicians often do, accusing me of deforming reality because I was reflecting it.

This is the kind of deformation politicians have in mind when they blame their woes on journalists. It is a childish accusation, which we routinely dismiss with an ironic shrug: "Naturally, it's the fault of the journalists once again!" What politicians tend to regard as a good press is one that serves to enhance their personal prestige. This, of course, exists—certain newspapers being systematically hostile to this or that party (whether in power or not) or to such-and-such an ideology in their treatment of information, others being systematically favorable. Such being the case, with insincerity reigning on both sides—that of the journalists as well as that of the politicians—the quarrel is without possible issue.

The journalist assumes a double role in public life. He is at once actor and informant. If he sincerely believes in the cause he is advocating, he should encounter no conflict between his role as an actor, the influence he seeks to exert, and his role as an informant. On the basis of information he tries to describe and to analyze conscientiously, he elaborates arguments, makes choices, and recommends solutions. If, on the contrary, he is moved to truncate and falsify information, it is probably because his cause is not a very good one. The disjunction between a "press of information" and a "press of opinion" is fallacious. If the opinion is good, the information can be so, too, without any difficulty; if the information has to be made bad, then the opinion is not worth much. The presumed antagonism between the two components of journalism is a phony problem. Criticism of the press from within its ranks is usually frowned upon, simply because freedom of expression, in the world we live in, is such a rare and fragile blessing that solidarity is spontaneously displayed with any journalist who is raked over the coals, even when his cause is anything but excellent.

This rule of solidarity, however, suffers exceptions—these being, as might be guessed, of an ideological order. In 1984, during the International Television Festival in Seville, Christine Ockrent, who was then the director of information for France's second TV channel, Antenne 2, proposed to the jury, of which she was a member, that they sign a text calling for the freeing of Jacques Abouchar, a journalist working for her network who had just been arrested in Afghanistan and accused by the Soviets of spying. Presided over by Robert Escarpit, a former columnist for *Le Monde* and a professor in the "sciences of communication" at Bordeaux, the jury was composed of Sean McBride, winner of a Lenin Prize and also the founder of Amnesty International, which won a Nobel Peace Prize; a Spanish journalist named Antonio Gala; Enrique Vásquez, director of information for Spanish television (TVE); and a representative from Soviet television, a Mrs. Formina or Formida (my sources are not sure of the spelling). In any case, Formida, Formina, or Formica launched into a diatribe against Christine Ockrent's "provocation," and everyone groveled before her. Everyone, that is, except Christine Ockrent herself, who, realizing the vainness of her efforts despite several attenuations of the proposed text, resigned from the jury and flew back to Paris. Particularly instructive was the attitude of Enrique Vásquez (we can forget about Escarpit, who has always been pro-Soviet); though selected by a moderate Social Democratic government, he upheld Moscow against a journalistic colleague who had been thrown into prison in Afghanistan for simply "doing his job"—according to the standard expression, which had never been truer. After such an exploit, the shrill protests made by these same jury members against violations of press freedom in Chile and South Africa can only make one laugh.

Newspapers sometimes go overboard in demanding privileges that cannot be accorded in a democratic country. They then conduct a dubious juridical campaign when, in the name of press freedom, they demand that they be allowed to violate existing laws. In March 1987, for example, two Italian journalists were arrested for having in their respective newspapers, *L'Unità* and *La Repubblica,* published a document that was part of an examining magistrate's file in a criminal affair. They had managed to obtain the document only with the help of a "mole" who was one of the employees in the Ministry of Justice. The ministry called on the journalists to name their source. They refused—thus conforming to the profession's code of honor, one that normally arouses general esteem. But a code of honor is not necessarily consistent with democratic rules of justice, for otherwise a murder committed as part of a family vendetta should not be the occasion of an indictment. The two Italian journalists were accordingly imprisoned.

Such cases occur in the United States when journalists refuse to obey a subpoena issued by a federal judge (or the attorney general's department) calling on them to name their sources or face a prison sentence for contempt of court. Immediately the newspapers raise a hue and cry, denouncing "fascist" methods and an "end" to freedom and human rights. "The Handcuffed Press" was the headline in *La Repubblica* on March 18. Now, in all democratic countries, particularly in Great Britain, which has been far more democratic than Italy for a far longer time, even to comment on a judicial inquiry while it is in process is something that is punished with extreme severity. In this case, furthermore, a public functionary was guilty of an offense foreseen by the penal code, and the publication of the confidential document was bound to affect the course of the inquiry. How, then, can one claim for oneself the privilege of illegality when one makes a practice of denouncing it in other sectors of society? One can decide to run a risk in publishing a document of great importance in defiance of the law, but one cannot accuse those who then take legal action of being fascists. Journalists should understand this. They cannot, on the one hand, continue to behave with the opportunism they denounce in politicians, without even having the same excuses, since they have no responsibility for political decisions and, on the other hand, claim an immunity due to the servitors of pure truth—which in effect they sometimes are, but by no means always.

Partiality is not the only vice that dogs the journalistic profession. To this we should add a scourge which has also had ravaging effects: incompetence. As strange as this may sound, journalism is doubtless the only profession one can enter without any formal preparation. I have already expressed my skepticism about schools of journalism, although they sometimes turn out first-class graduates, but ones who probably would have been excellent news gatherers without having to attend such schools. The teachers who are supposed to form future journalists do not themselves always practice the art they teach with any particular brilliance. Fortunately, having a diploma from a school of journalism is not yet a requirement. The hiring of journalists for both nationalized and private news staffs is carried out above all through "connections," chance, or political choice. It is fondly hoped that the talent will then develop. But if it doesn't develop, the inadequate journalist must often be retained, for firing him, at any rate in Europe, is either impossible or very difficult and costly. Many journalistic staffs abound in uncooperative "contributors" who, though practically useless, are, alas, employed. But even intelligent journalists can be victims of preconceived ideas about the subjects they deal with, and they do not always acquire the culture necessary to understand what they see or read. This is true above all in countries where information, or rather disinformation, is cleverly manipulated by the regime—all the more so since, as I have repeatedly stressed, journalists, who are so wide awake and distrustful in their own democratic lands, have a tendency to fall dangerously asleep in totalitarian countries of "the Left." All one need do is to go back and read what *The Guardian* was regularly publishing about Poland from 1980 to 1984 to want to howl with laughter.*

In *Reluctant Farewell* Andrew Nagorski, a former *Newsweek* correspondent in Moscow, well described the lack of preparation, the credulous naïveté, and even the absence of zeal in the search for information displayed by so many Western journalists posted to the Soviet capital. Most of them, at the time he was there, did not speak Russian and were

*Lovers of comic literature should leaf through the anthology provided by the English quarterly review *Survey* in its special issue on Poland, Vol. XXVI, No. 3, summer 1983.

thus dependent on the TASS agency's foreign-language handouts. For the rest they had to rely on their Soviet translators, all of them employees of the famous "organs" (of the KGB, etc.), or on what they could glean from Western diplomats, who were as cut off from reality as they themselves. Almost none of them, in questions of sovietology and the history of communism, possessed the knowledge that can be acquired without knowing Russian. Even among the rare ones who did speak the language, Nagorski found few who wanted to roam around the country and talk to Soviet citizens who were not officials. Most of them distrusted the dissidents, who bored them with their recriminations and whose points of view, they said, did not interest people in the West. So for the most part the dispatches filed by the Western press corps in Moscow consisted of rehashes of what the Soviet authorities offered them—in other words, the message these authorities wanted them to convey to the West. Typical in this respect was the attitude of Michael Binyon, the London *Times* correspondent in Moscow from 1980 to 1984. In his book *Life in Russia* he candidly admitted that he had based most of his "reporting" on what he could obtain from the Soviet press, adding: "It is far wiser and more tactful to let the Russians make their own criticisms of their society than to judge them and pontificate as an outsider with different assumptions and outlook."* It would be hard to flaunt with greater fatuity the triumphant cult of voluntary ignorance. This gentleman, furthermore, was the correspondent of a "conservative" newspaper. This can only be regarded as a highly "original" *modus operandi* in a country like the USSR, where the state controlled all forms of communication. As one can see, the much touted valor of the press in acting as a "counterpower" wilts most oddly when the regime is not democratic—which is to say, precisely when that regime most needs to be countered, or at any rate contradicted. One trembles at the thought of how many Western journalists applied exactly the same methods, sometimes for decades on end, while covering events in Peking and Hanoi, Havana and Managua, Warsaw and Ethiopia.

The professional indolence of such journalists makes them, all too obviously, docile instruments of disinformation—doubtless without their realizing it, but this is precisely the essential aim of disinformation. In *Para Bellum* Alexander Zinoviev defined it by putting these words

*Cited by Andrew Nagorski in *Reluctant Farewell,* p. 48. Many correspondents, Nagorski noted, found Binyon's views perfectly acceptable in Moscow, whereas elsewhere they would have rejected this justification of their work as slavishly echoing the statements of a state-controlled press.

in the mouth of one of his characters, nicknamed "the Westerner" because he had made a specialty, while working for the "organs," of deceiving the West: "The enemy should act according to what we want, while remaining convinced that he is acting according to his own will and against our interests." In this book I have deliberately not dealt with disinformation, because my aim is not to show how a free press lets itself be spoon-fed by totalitarian disinformation agencies—a subject about which there already exists an abundant literature—but to show how a free press deceives itself, wittingly or unwittingly, through ideological bias or journalistic incompetence.* I mention disinformation here merely to point out that it is too easily confused with similar but technically different notions.

Disinformation should be understood in the real meaning of the term. Nowadays, we tend to employ it erroneously as a synonym for counter-truth, deception, a tendentious version of events. Disinformation is doubtless all of these things, but it is also something far more subtle. It consists of managing things so that it is the adversary himself, or failing that a neutral third party, who first publishes the false news or upholds the thesis that is to be spread. In this way falsehood takes in many more persons, since no one suspects its true source.

In October 1985 a New Delhi newspaper, *The Patriot,* was reported to have published an article "revealing" that the AIDS virus was the product of experiments in genetic engineering undertaken by the U.S. Army with a view to improving weapons of biological warfare. The virus had later spread to New York, and from there it had been transmitted by U.S. servicemen to Third World countries. On October 30, 1985 the Soviet weekly *Literaturnaya* Gazeta "picked up" the story published in *The Patriot* and stigmatized these American "crimes." This is the truly subtle aspect of disinformation technique. It allows one to clamor loudly: "Look, it's not we who say so, all we're doing is citing a foreign newspaper." A pro-Soviet newspaper, *The Patriot* has a reputation in India for indulging in this kind of operation. But who knows this outside of India? The most extraordinary thing of all was that the original article had not in fact appeared. The Soviet secret services had obviously sent it to the editorial staff, not doubting for a moment that it would be published on the agreed-upon date, and had accordingly given the green light to *Literaturnaya Gazeta.* Negligence or sabotage? A woeful lack of coordination? In any case, nobody took the trouble to verify the

*I touched on this question in *How Democracies Perish,* Chap. 16.

source—save for a journalist working for *The Times of India,* who one year later undertook an investigation and discovered the awful truth: The article had never been published by *The Patriot!**

This mix-up, however, did not in any way keep this rumor from prospering and circulating through the Third World, picked up from *Literaturnaya Gazeta* by news agencies, even though they did not accept responsibility for the report. In Brazil the *Estado da São Paolo,* a serious and respectable newspaper, fell into the trap and lent its credibility to the theory. In September 1986, at a summit meeting of nonaligned countries held in the Zimbabwean capital of Harare, a thick report which had all the looks of a serious scientific study, with charts, tables, annexes, and a bibliography, was distributed to all the delegates. The report concluded that the AIDS virus had originated in experiments conducted in a laboratory at Fort Detrick, Maryland. The report was signed by two "researchers of the Pasteur Institute in Paris," Drs. Jakob and Lilli Segal. Queried on the subject, the Pasteur Institute replied that it had never heard of the two "scientists," who were finally run down— in East Berlin. But, needless to say, the representatives of the nonaligned states were not informed of this rectification when they returned home from Harare.

However, the disinformers' greatest triumph was unquestionably scored on October 26, 1986, when *The Sunday Express* of London picked up the story. In the art of disinforming, the farther to the right the newspaper that peddles the rumor is, the more authentic it looks; for the reader assumes that such a paper would pick up such a report and publish it only with extreme reluctance and after having made sure it was based on solid evidence. Five days later, on October 31, 1986, *Pravda,* the official daily newspaper of the Central Committee of the Communist Party of the Soviet Union, published a cartoon in which a white-clad doctor was shown handing a U.S. officer an enormous test tube inside which blackish things were swimming, while the officer slipped a wad of dollar bills into the doctor's other hand. The cartoon's caption read: "AIDS, a terrible and incurable illness, is, in the opinion of certain *Western* scientists, a creation of the Pentagon's laboratories." (Italics mine.) The Soviets reaped an additional dividend, for *The Sunday Express*'s article unleashed a new flurry of wire-service dispatches, which flashed around the globe. It was now too late to efface the mystification, even though the *Estado de São Paulo* tried very honestly to

---

*Bharat Bhushan, "AIDS, a Soviet Propaganda Tool," *The Times of India,* November 19, 1986.

do so—by apologizing to its readers in late November 1986 for having deceived them "on the basis of false information coming from the Soviet Union." In the Soviet press the Brazilian daily was severely taken to task for this act of self-criticism. The Soviet papers recalled that they had humbly limited themselves to reproducing information "furnished by the Western press itself" and confirmed by "the greatest Western experts."* In any case, the authors of this hoax had won a sensational victory; for in the Third World it is now hard to find anyone who is not convinced that it was the Pentagon and the CIA that unleashed the AIDS epidemic.

In 1987 Soviet disinformation agencies even managed to persuade a leading French publisher to include on his list a book in which the KGB's tall story was lengthily repeated and further adorned with a new burlesque flourish: the Pentagon had succeeded in fabricating the HIV virus *in such a way that it would selectively hit blacks while sparing whites!* This piece of scientific rubbish presupposes a thick dose of racism among those who spread such a story: that is, the conviction that blacks are *biologically* different from whites—for otherwise the virus could not be selectively effective. These incredible lucubrations have been refuted by countless scientists in the West. I won't cite them here, since, according to the disinformers, these scientists conceal their true thoughts—some because they themselves are working for the CIA, others because they are scared. I will merely cite Soviet scientists. One of them is Viktor Zhdanov, director of Moscow's Institute of Virology, who is considered to be the Soviet Union's leading AIDS specialist. In the December 5, 1985, issue of *Sovietskaya Kultura,* Dr. Zhdanov, replying to those who claimed that the CIA was responsible, wrote that the AIDS virus had doubtless existed in Africa for thousands of years. In June 1986, during the Second International AIDS Conference, held in Paris, Dr. Zhdanov, replying to a journalist who had asked him if the Americans had concocted the AIDS virus, declared: "This is a ridiculous question. And why not the Martians?"† The other Soviet scientist is Valentin Pokrovsky, president of the Soviet Academy of Medicine. In a statement made to *Le Monde* on November 6, 1987, he declared: "No Soviet researcher has ever spoken of the artificial fabrication of the virus. Like all the scientists of my country, I think the virus has a natural origin."

The honesty of these declarations saves the honor of the Soviet scien-

Literaturnaya Gazeta, December 3, 1986.
†Reuters, AP, UPI, June 25, 1986.

tific community. The disinformation campaign found fewer suckers and accomplices in its midst than in certain Western media! Not only is the HIV virus far too complex to have been fabricated in a laboratory, but cases of AIDS were detected before 1981, the year in which the disease really began to spread and long before the period when the diabolical witch doctors of the Pentagon were supposed, according to the KGB, to have worked on their deadly brew. In 1960, for example, the British medical review *The Lancet* published the results of a clinical observation undertaken on a patient who had died of an unidentified malady in 1959, and which retrospectively was discovered to have been AIDS.*

Despite countless refutations of the story spread by the KGB, one could still read in the 894th number of the Spanish weekly *Cambio 16* (January 16, 1989) an article that calmly repeated the phantasmagorical and scientifically untenable theory according to which AIDS is a disease created by the Pentagon. Once again the inevitable Jakob Segal appeared as the guarantor of the grim police joke invented by the Soviet secret services. Thus, three years after first launching this incredible canard, a leading Western European weekly could pick up the "story," having with sublime incompetence not bothered to do any research on the case.

I will close this parenthesis on disinformation by stressing the point that though it has no direct bearing on my subject, it is nevertheless linked to it in the sense that only bias and incompetence make it possible for the newspapers of free countries to be made such utter dupes. We have a right to expect greater perspicacity from our media people, which would make journalists less gullible when confronted by the often gross ruses of disinformation. It being my purpose to ask why it is that Man—whether journalist or not—embraces what is false with such avid impetuosity when he can so easily find out what is true, it behooved me at least to cite a spectacular triumph of the disinformers, one due to an all-too-careless predisposition on the part of the victims or, if one prefers (for it is not innate) to an acquired immunodeficiency in critical appraisal. Furthermore, by an interesting convergence in disinformation similar to one that is frequently encountered in the field of terrorism, the extreme Right here finds itself aligned with the extreme Left. In 1988 the magazine *Éléments,* organ of the so-called "New Right" in France, picked up the KGB tale in its turn, in its sixty-third issue, with an article entitled, "AIDS—the Pentagon Accused."

To put it as succinctly as possible: The world today is split into

The Lancet made this observation in its issue of November 12, 1983.

countries in which the government wants to replace the press, and countries in which the press wants to replace the government. The illness of the former will be cured only by introducing the virtues of democracy or the beginnings of freedom. The curing of the latter—in countries that are already democratic—lies in the hands of the press itself. It is high time all journalists, not simply a handful of them, should at last decide to exercise their real professionalism in the full sense of the word: that is, by providing exact and complete information, after which they can add all the opinions, analyses, exhortations, and recommendations they like.

Anyone who wishs to can opt out of a civilization in which the global flow of information is the determinant factor in collective decision making rather than astrology, palmistry, or dice throwing. But the fact is that we have entered this kind of civilization and that we ourselves have made it what it is. We must, therefore, at the risk of destroying it, respect its rules and principles. By its very nature it can function properly only if nourished by knowledge. Accordingly, in this specific type of civilization, the falsity of perceptions, the forgetting of experience, and dissimulation as a prime ingredient of political talent have particularly devastating consequences. Let us not poison the fountain from which flows our drinking water.

CHAPTER 11

The Betrayal of the Profs

*Comme tous les faiseurs de bouc émissaire, ils
tiennent leur victime pour coupable. Il n'y a donc
pas, pour eux, de bouc émissaire.*

Like all scapegoat makers, they consider their
victim to be guilty. For them, therefore,
there is no scapegoat.

—René Girard

Western civilization revolves around knowledge, and all other civilizations revolve around Western civilization. To enunciate the latter proposition is not to wallow in ethnocentrism, and in any case it is true only to the extent that knowledge is concerned, and perhaps also human rights and democracy. Everywhere there is a desire for development, and thus there exists everywhere an implicit or explicit acceptance of the principal condition for development—which is to apply knowledge to activity.

Claims of "cultural identity" are often no more than ways of denying this necessity without renouncing the benefits of development. They amount to saying: Give us development in the form of subsidies, in such a way as to spare us the effort of establishing an effective relationship with the real and the concrete. For this is basically what is involved in Third Worldism, if not in the Third World itself—I mean the fiction, as opposed to the reality. For Third Worldism is a philosophy not of development, but of a transfer of resources destined to perpetuate under-development while attenuating poverty and, above all, alleviating the dire financial needs of the administrators of that poverty. By "defense of one's cultural identity" Third Worlders do not mean so much the defense of culture proper as the preservation of the right to inefficiency in production and corruption in management. For it is hard to see why esthetic values, the creations of art and literature—which in the final analysis are the only distinctive features of the cultural originality of civilizations—could not preserve their individuality simply because a society chooses to do what is rationally and universally necessary in the economic, technical, and political fields in order to emerge from a condition of poverty. I note that no society today rejects the objective of development *a priori,* which must mean that all more or less grudgingly accept as axiomatic the central role of knowledge.

But is this theoretically central role really such in practice? And above all, is it so in the daily functioning of Western civilization, in the very heart of which it is lodged and which it indeed defines as a cultural prototype? I would say that knowledge occupies this central position more or less *in spite of this civilization* or, more exactly, because of its nature but in spite of ourselves. If there is one thing guaranteed to reassure the jealous guardians of the spiritual and esthetic identity of individual cultures (and I am one of them), it is the force of resistance to the rational that is deployed within the very civilization that has been constructed on the basis of rationality. However, the most radical internal antagonism toward reason is not even located on the purely cultural level. Is it not true that the sickest civilizations—for example, the pre-Columbian civilizations, entirely built up and organized around an astrological delirium, which was as bloody as it was totalitarian and from whose cruel ravages nobody could escape—also brought forth one of the grandest and most original art forms in the history of mankind? The real antagonism, therefore, is that which introduces division, contradiction, and incompatibility not between "cultural identity" and rationality, but in the very heart of rationality itself; that is, the antagonism which, in a cultural system built upon, by, and for knowledge, thwarts the progress of knowledge in its own particular domain. This domain, admittedly, is not the only one that makes life worth living, but as a framework for action it cannot without harm be both posited and denied.

In a pertinent essay, "The Defeat of Thought," Alain Finkielkraut has very well described a fundamental aspect of this alienation. But in my opinion, the internal contradiction which a civilization based on knowledge is now encountering and which threatens to paralyze it goes far deeper than the superficial zones affected by the fatuities of mass media and by the leveling of values due to a refusal to accept any notion of hierarchy between cultures. The sources of knowledge are poisoned at a far deeper level than the point at which they gush forth in the form of press and media.

Now what, in a civilization founded on knowledge, is the situation of those who are responsible for it—that is, the intellectuals? This term is generally regarded as covering thinkers, writers, artists, and also scientists, to the extent that they express themselves on political or moral issues—just how I have already shown in several passages. The term "intellectuals" is far less often taken to include schoolteachers. Yet it is they who transmit knowledge, or what passes for knowledge, who mold culture at its roots, and who possess the key that grants to each successive generation access to a representation of the universe—from the humblest elementary school teachers right up to the most distinguished and famous university professors, and in between those who are perhaps the most influential in molding a society's vision of the world, the secondary school teachers, who direct the thinking of children from ten to eighteen years of age. Their influence has become even more decisive during the final years of our twentieth century, since the progress of economic equality in modern societies has caused an ever-greater number of young persons to receive instruction from them.

Not all teachers, of course, are "intellectuals." Only some of them participate or are regarded as participating in the elaboration of culture. Very few of them, indeed, have with this culture the personal relationship of judgment and taste which, for better or for worse, typifies the intellectual—or, in less pedantic terms, the cultivated individual. It by no means denigrates schoolteachers to define them as the rehearsers of culture, and even more as those who reconstruct and recompose its image, simplifying it for the benefit of the young. From time immemorial, but above all since compulsory education penetrated down to all levels of society, the pedagogue has fulfilled this function as an interpreter who provides each generation with a condensed translation of the state of knowledge and of certain values at a given moment. But every translator, as is well known, can prove unfaithful to the original text, and pedagogues have never deprived themselves of the opportunity of rewriting the text according to their prejudices and the educational mission they have conferred on themselves.

To be sure, such transmitters of knowledge do not operate alone and independently. They follow ministerial circulars, directives handed down by their superiors, by bureaus and commissions of all kinds, preset programs which impose general orientations and sometimes the precise content of the education that is to be dispensed. However, in free countries the "teaching body," as we say in France, exercises an irresistible ascendancy over the authorities that are supposed to direct it, notably because of powerful trade unions and associations. The administrative and pedagogic managers, who are naturally recruited from among professors and teachers, thus think twice before tackling the "Teaching Fortress"—to borrow the title of a book written about the Fédération de l'Éducation Nationale.* The basic issue, therefore, concerns the mentality of a social group and a particular category of intellectuals—the

*The FEN, as it is popularly known in France, is a very powerful association of teachers' trade unions, so powerful indeed that its decisions, and its pressure tactics in general, often have the force of law. This is because the French educational system is "administered" by the Ministry of National Education, which directly controls and finances more than a million teachers—which in fact means that it does not control them at all; for no enterprise or bureaucracy can be administered by a single management when it exceeds three to four hundred thousand employees. As a result, it is the teachers' unions that really lay down the law and which impose their will on the minister and on the central administration in Paris. These trade unions are grouped into the Fédération de l'Éducation Nationale (FEN), which is divided into the Syndicat National des Instituteurs (SNI—the teachers' union for elementary school teachers); a Syndicat National des Enseignants de Secondaire (SNES—the teachers' union for secondary school teachers); and the Syndicat National des Enseignants de Secondaire—Supérieur (SNES—Sup., the union of university professors and instructors). While the SNI is socialist, the SNES and the SNES—Sup. are communist. This means that the communists have managed to colonize the educational apparatus, since in fact less than 10 percent of the members actually vote communist. This said, French schoolteachers and professors are much farther to the left than the overall national average. In France the left-wing vote oscillates between 45 percent and 52–53 percent of the total, whereas teachers and professors traditionally vote for the Left in a proportion ranging from 70 to 75 percent.

The FEN was one of the prime movers of the "Red May" upheavals of May 1968 and was also heavily involved in the November 1986 demonstrations in Paris, which led to the shelving of a parliamentary law (presented by Jacques Chirac's conservative government) designed to reform the university system in France. *La Forteresse enseignante* ("The Teaching Fortress"), prepared under the auspices of the Fondation Saint-Simon, was published by Fayard in 1985.

302 The Flight from Truth

teachers—and of their attitude toward knowledge, their sense of pedagogical responsibility, and their professional ethics.

Let us first of all note that the teaching profession, which is supposedly motivated by an ideology upholding the impartial transmission of knowledge, has at the same time, with a charming ingenuousness in the art of contradiction, wanted to be an instrument of combat. Even before the nineteenth century, when a number of societies began to feel it was a duty to promote general instruction and the eradication of illiteracy, we can discern a tendency in the behavior of pedagogues that was more didactic than descriptive.* Later, like freedom of the press, popular education developed hand in hand with modern democracy and now constitutes one of its organic components. Just as we should never forget that democracy cannot do without education, so we should not forget that, along with the press, teaching is basically another facet of information dispensing. And yet, for this reason, it suffers from a persistent ambiguity—between informative education and formative education. Personally, I think that, to designate the former, we should revert to the fine old word "instruction," which is the transmission of simple information, and reserve the term "education" for the second kind of work, which aims at endowing the individual personality with a specific conception of reality and style of behavior.

The teacher can either teach or indoctrinate. When the teaching is more important than the indoctrination, education fulfills its principal function in the best interests of those who receive it and in the interest of democracy. On the other hand, when indoctrination takes precedence, it becomes harmful, an abuse of childish innocence, and substitutes imposture for culture.

A sure sign that formative education—to the extent that knowledge is involved (for the rest, it is free to follow the whims of custom and fashion)—indeed, an infallible sign that indoctrination is the evil genius of instruction is the fact that totalitarian societies subordinate an essential part of their educative system to it. Everything that directly or indirectly affects the ideological sphere falls under the sway of censorship and falsehood. Fortunately, certain elementary forms of knowledge, certain fundamental sciences, certain basic techniques can be honestly taught without disturbing the ideology or being disturbed by it. This allows these societies to maintain themselves more or less in

*In Walter Lippmann's *The Public Philosophy*, published in 1955, there is a fascinating chapter on the ways in which the pedagogical theories of Jean-Jacques Rousseau, Johann Pestalozzi, and Friedrich Froebel influenced the development of primary and secondary school education in the United States.

purely practical terms, even though many primary intellectual activities vegetate in a state of semiasphyxiation because they are prevented from being developed according to their own specific logic, the evolution of which would constitute a living refutation of the ideology. During certain periods, however, ideology devours all disciplines and practices; it overflows its natural riverbed and inundates areas usually conceded to pure knowledge and apprenticeship, provided that they remain politically inoffensive. Such a cataclysm occurred in the USSR when, as we have seen, Stalin and then Khrushchev forcibly imposed Lysenko's "biology." Or again, disaster overtook China at the time of the "Cultural Revolution," when one could not plant a lettuce or hammer a nail without following the "method" expounded in *The Little Red Book*— which, being no more than a tissue of hollow fatuities, plunged the country back into prehistoric night. Cuban schoolchildren, in matters relating to general ideas, find themselves restricted to the vaticinations of *el líder máximo,* just as Albanian schoolchildren were long force-fed the plethoric works of Enver Hoxha, and just as young Germans in 1935 had to swallow the rudiments of Nazi ideology. All dictators—it is almost a platitude to say it—have been ravishers of education, as of the press, and for the same reason. "May the school, in all of its stages and in all of its teachings, educate the youth of Italy so as to make it understand the historical climate of the revolution!" proclaimed Benito Mussolini in 1925.* This referred, of course, to the Fascist revolution. In the name of another revolution, an Italian Communist Party pedagogue was still saying exactly the same thing in 1972: "There is in the world and in our country a cluster of ideas which represent the most advanced that the progressive and revolutionary movement has produced over the past half century; we are interested in seeing them asserted at school."†

And asserted they were! Indeed, the mere fact that since the beginning of democratic institutions there has existed, in Italy as in France, a religious as well as secular form of schooling suffices to prove that education has never been neutral and has never consisted simply of providing the young with information and leaving them free to interpret it. The pupils of religious schools have used textbooks different from those in secular schools, including anthologies of literary texts, con-

---

* *"La scuola in tutti i suoi gradi e in tutti i suoi insegnamenti educhi la gioventù italiana a comprendere il clima storico della rivoluzione,"* Benito Mussolini, December 5, 1925.

† *"Vi sono nel mondo e nel nostro paese un complesso di idee che rappresentano quanto di più avanzato il movimento progressista e rivoluzionario ha prodotto da mezzo secolo; abbiamo interesse che esse si affermino nella scuola,"* Giorgio Bini.

stituting two parallel and independent series, edited by different authors in a different spirit, highlighting different events and concepts, and printed by different publishers—even in the case of Latin grammars! They have been two distinct worlds, and it is clear that neither of the two could be objective. Parents who in the early years of this century sent their children to a religious school wanted them above all to have a "Christian education," even in matters that religion had or should have had nothing to do with. The public or lay school, on the other hand, tended to inculcate "republican" values, as they used to be called in France, in its young pupils. It rewrote history and established a literary hierarchy in keeping with this objective. By studying Ernest Lavisse's history textbooks, which set the tone of teaching in French public schools at the end of the last century and during the early years of our own right up until 1914, Pierre Nora has clearly brought out the objective of republican edification which runs like a thread through all these textbooks.*

The evolution of history in these textbooks rests entirely on the principle of explanation through final causes (which the "scientist" spirit of the times vigorously condemned). Thus the history of France is split into two periods: before and after 1789. The first period, which begins with the birth of France in the year 987, is no more than the slow gestation of a French Revolution, groping its way forward, and of a Third Republic, whose advent was slightly delayed by medieval plots and clerical absolutism. In religious schools, on the other hand, the pupils were taught that the decline started in 1789. This way of using the school as a battleground for the ideological struggles of adults in order to harden the intellectual muscles of the young troops who will one day take over from their elders is a fairly widespread pedagogical abuse—as is proven by the fortunately vain efforts that religious associations in certain U.S. states have made to ban the teaching of Darwinian evolution. But though formative and informative education continue to coexist and to compete in free societies, and even though the touchstone of the truth

---

*Les Lieux de mémoire, four volumes, edited by Pierre Nora (Paris: Gallimard), particularly Vol. I (1984), Lavisse, instituteur national; le petit Lavisse, évangile de la Révolution. "With Lavisse," Nora writes, "patriotic duty is the corollary of republican liberty. The history of France is in many respects no more than a repertory of examples for the manual of civic training." In other words, it is the opposite of an initiation into historical knowledge. No matter how praiseworthy it may be to inculcate the cult of the fatherland and of freedom to children, one sets out on a slippery slope in doing so by teaching history or literature, for this legitimizes the principle that the teacher has the right to use knowledge to indoctrinate—a principle that can later be put to far more harmful purposes. Either one teaches or one preaches; one cannot do both at the same time.

by no means guides pedagogy, everything is a question of wise blending. If the indoctrination becomes too invasive, society reacts, provided it remains democratic and can therefore do so. It rejects the attempt made by a single ideology to annex schoolteaching.

This is what happened in France against nineteenth-century clericalism; and again in the spring of 1984 against socialism, when the most gigantic demonstrations the country had seen in almost forty years forced François Mitterrand to withdraw his parliamentary bill for a "unified public service" in the field of national education, which would have passed a death sentence on private schools. Let no one believe that the millions of citizens who paraded through the streets of Paris and several other large French cities were all fervent Catholics, inspired only by their faith—an implausible supposition at a time when active religious worship had been steadily declining. Most of the demonstrators were not even parents with children attending private schools, which, in any case, had ceased to be marked by religious militancy and had long since begun using the same textbooks as the public schools. Even if we subtract the number of demonstrators who, for political reasons, seized on this opportunity to protest against the government, we find that the primary motive, the uneasy presentiment that brought these huge crowds together, was the looming threat of an ideological monopoly. The new religious sectarianism, the real clericalism, was no longer Christian, as it had been in the nineteenth century; it was Marxist. Marx was great, and the Fédération de l'Éducation Nationale was its prophet. As the historian Emmanuel Le Roy Ladurie pointed out quite rightly at the time, it was idiotic to invoke a secular ideal in order to demand an ideological clampdown on the entire youth of France. During the last century the concept of secularism had been forged precisely to combat ideology in teaching and to affirm the principle of *neutrality* of knowledge. Now it was being brandished to demand the exact opposite of what it signified! Society can tolerate a certain degree of tendentious "slanting" in schools, provided that the main core of teaching remains serious and professional. Having myself completed my primary and secondary studies with the Jesuits from 1929 to 1941, I can say that this was already the case in private teaching prior to World War II—otherwise this form of teaching would have disappeared for lack of students. Curiously and paradoxically enough, it was when I entered a state-run *lycée* after my baccalaureate, in order to prepare for the competitive exams for entry into the École Normale Supérieure, that I heard far more talk about religion in the classrooms, indulged in by certain public school teachers who were convinced Catholics, whether of the Left or of the Right, and who mixed far more of their faith into their courses than had the Jesuit Fathers under whom I had previously studied.* But all in all, there existed a zone that was common to both forms of teaching. Within this zone pupils studied what had to be studied according to criteria defined by the standard rules for the transmission of knowledge.

It was this pact of moderation which the extremism of schoolteachers shattered in France during the final decades of the twentieth century.

By a piquant illogicality, it was in 1953, the year of Stalin's death, that French textbooks of history and geography became Stalinist. This was a classic case of the fatal penchant Western Marxists have for espousing the official theses of communist countries at the very moment when the latter are revising or abandoning them. Speaking at a 1987 symposium devoted to "The Perception of the USSR in French School Textbooks," the historian and demographer Jacques Dupâquier noted that, in geography textbooks especially, the achievements of the Soviet economy were described in purely ideological terms and backed up by official Soviet statistics. The illustrations all came from Soviet sources, with captions such as this: "They exude success, good health, and confidence in the future!" The authors of these manuals depict the kolkhozes in glowing colors and praise their productivity! They extol "the Davydov plan for the diversion of Siberian rivers" and the "superb results" obtained by the disciples of Michurin and the students of Lysenko! This approval of the scientific idiocies of Lysenko represented an even more grotesque deceit than the surfeit of credulity shown in welcoming the official statistics. Let us not forget that this approval of Lysenkoist obscurantism was to be found not in partisan newspapers, which no one is obliged to read and which contradict each other anyway, but in *school textbooks imposed on children* as the sole source of information on the subject, and this *under the authority of the Ministry of National Education and the General Inspectorate of Public Instruction.*

The abuse of trust and the betrayal of the teacher's moral duty shine forth here in an ignominious fashion. Nor was this all—the Khrushchev speech of February 1956 did not in the least affect this zeal for imposture and informational inaccuracy. Right up until 1967 all French school

---

*Founded in 1794, the École Normale Supérieure is probably the most prestigious institution of higher learning in France. Admission to it is highly selective, students needing two to four years of special preparation. The year I was admitted, only 24 out of 2,000 candidates were accepted. Today the average number of admissions in any year is around 80, all of whom have scholarships. Famous graduates of the ENS, which comprises a scientific as well as a literary section, include Louis Pasteur, Henri Bergson, Jean-Paul Sartre, and Georges Pompidou.

textbooks provided an idyllic vision of the USSR, in accordance with the most optimistic propaganda clichés. The rosy pictures continued to be supplied by the TASS and Novosti news agencies. The demographic shortfall was explained by the authors as part of the legacy of Tsarism and also caused by the Nazi invasion, never by Stalinist purges. Needless to say, only a minority of teachers and textbook authors actually belonged to the French Communist Party or voted communist. But this sobering fact merely illustrates a phenomenon whose scope must be properly assessed if one wishes to understand the historical and political culture of our epoch: the inundation by communist ideology and a Marxist vision of the world of vast areas of the so-called noncommunist Left. It is difficult to imagine the climate of intolerance that reigned in French schools throughout those years. The expression "witch-hunt" usually designates acts of intolerance committed by rightists against leftists, rarely the other way around. Besides, this witch-hunt in the teaching body was directed not so much against the Right as against scientific and pedagogic probity. Dupâquier learned this to his cost. In 1969 he had succeeded in persuading the Bordas publishing company to put out a textbook based on documentation that was a good bit more serious in covering the USSR than the statistics, the eulogistic propaganda, and the official photos so piously swallowed by other authors. He tells the story: "As might be expected, there was a mighty uproar. We were denounced by *L'École et la Nation,* and at the Bordas publishing company we received some forty letters of protest expressing a whole range of feelings from sadness to anger. The indignation of one of our colleagues was such that she could only express herself in capital letters: 'IT IS APPALLING FOR ITS FOOLISHNESS AND DIS-HONESTY.' Another had the delicacy to write to Mr. Pierre Bordas to say that he had always had confidence in him, that his textbooks on all subjects had been adopted in all the classes of his *lycée,* but that after this 'blow' his colleagues and he himself were going to reconsider everything. In fact, there was a marked drop in sales. The annual sales of the suspect textbook never rose above 20,000, whereas a companion textbook destined for the third *lycée* year easily attained 50,000."

In France the commercial success of a textbook, it is important to realize, depends on the sovereign decision of each teacher, who chooses or does not choose it as a classroom manual for his pupils. It is thus understandable why publishers hesitate to propose works that collide head on with the prejudices of the teaching profession.

Between 1980 and 1985 a thaw finally set in, and one can speak of a belated and partial de-Stalinization of textbooks of history and geography. This must doubtless be attributed to the overall de-Marxization of the French intelligentsia. Even so, in 1983 one could still find books faithful to the Stalinist gospel—such as the Gauthier collection (put out by the ABC publishing house), in which, among other things, one could read that "several elements lead one to think that Yuri Andropov, who succeeded Leonid Brezhnev as the head of the Communist Party of the Soviet Union on November 12, 1982, will continue the policy of openness of his predecessor."

An intrepid newspaper or magazine editorialist is free to indulge in pontifications of this kind and to deem that Brezhnev was "open" and the former head of the KGB more open still. His readers have seen rubbish of this kind before, and the journalist can always change his tune a little later. But the infliction of such inept but by no means innocent textbook prophecies on innocent children, and in the name of a "public service," can only make one sigh: poor public school, poor student, poor parent!

At the same symposium Maurice Decrop surveyed the history of the USSR as related in French textbooks since 1931. He found that of the 24 textbooks he labeled "pro-Bolshevik" (as opposed to 21 that were anti-Bolshevik and 10 that were moderately so), 23 had appeared between 1946 and 1982—which confirms the process of Stalinization that French teaching underwent after World War II. I stress the point—for this is the vital criterion—that the falsifications concern not opinions but facts. For example, the textbooks simply ignore the Kronstadt sailors' uprising of 1921* or attribute the building of the Berlin Wall . . . to the

---

*A graphic account of the Kronstadt insurrection can be found in Michel Heller's *Soixante-dix ans qui ébranlèrent le monde* ("Seventy Years that Shook the World") (Paris: Calmann-Lévy, 1988):

"The workers' demonstrations in Petrograd made a deep impression on the sailors of the Baltic Fleet, 'pride and ornament of the Revolution.' The movement of discontent soon spread to the battleships *Petropavlovsk* and *Sevastopol,* which in 1917 had been among the foremost breeding grounds of Bolshevism in the navy. On February 28 the crew of the *Petropavlovsk* drafted a resolution outlining the new demands of the seamen of the Baltic Fleet. On March 1 it was adopted at a meeting attended by the entire Kronstadt garrison.

"The sailors of the Baltic demanded first of all the reelection of the soviets, freedom of speech and the press for workers and peasants, freedom of assembly, the right to form trade unions and peasant associations. For peasants they demanded the "absolute right to work the land as they wish, and to keep livestock . . . without being obliged to hire it." In their combined Resolution Program, entitled *Why We Are Fighting,* the Kronstadt seamen wrote: 'In carrying out the October Revolution, the working class thought it was obtaining its freedom from bondage. But the result has been an even greater enslavement of the human person. . . . More and more it has become apparent—and today this is all too obvious—that the Russian Communist Party is not the defender of the workers it claims to be, that their interests are alien to it, and that, having come to power, it thinks only of keeping it.'

Federal Republic of West Germany! Quite rightly Decrop regards such gross examples of censorship and historical deformation as due "more to a refusal of information than to a lack of information." And he concludes: "One may well wonder just how much neutrality there is in public teaching. In this connection it is interesting to pick up Jacqueline Freyssinet-Dominjon's book *Les Manuels d'histoire de l'École libre, 1882–1949* (Armand Colin, 1969). The author presents the public school as a model of objectivity, from which the free school* is far removed. The profound differences in the textbook presentation of the history of the USSR lead one to wonder if this opinion is not an illustration of the parable of the mote and the beam."

One has the distinct impression that at a given moment, sometime in the 1960s, the teachers in France, not content to be unwittingly under the influence of their ideology, deliberately decided to use their position of strength in the education of the young to combat liberal civilization and, with this end in mind, to rewrite history instead of teaching it— much as, at the same moment, left-wing magistrates in France were arrogating to themselves the license to refuse the law instead of applying it. Teaching gave way to militant preaching. Thus, in a teachers' guide, the author (Vincent, Bordas, 1980) gave his colleagues the following instructions:

"It will be shown that two camps exist in the world:

- one imperialist and antidemocratic (USA)
- one anti-imperialist and democratic (USSR)

"The sailors' watchword, 'Soviets without communists,' dispelled all possible doubt. They were revolting not against the Soviet regime, but against its takeover by the Communist Party. This was what made the Kronstadt rebellion so dangerous for the Bolsheviks. The Kronstadt revolt, Lenin declared to the Tenth Party Congress on March 21, 'is more dangerous for us than Denikin, Yudenich, and Kolchak combined.'

"On March 2, Lenin and Trotsky signed an order denouncing the Kronstadt movement as a 'White conspiracy.' Fifty thousand men were given the task of crushing the revolt, under the command of Tukhachevsky. During the night of March 17–18, Red Army units burst into the fortress, which was defended by 5,000 seamen. On March 18 all of the Soviet newspapers devoted their front pages to the fiftieth anniversary of the Paris Commune, excoriating the 'bloody butchers, Thiers and Galliffet.' In the stormed fortress the insurgent seamen were shot to death. The survivors were transported to the continent and sent to concentration camps at Arkhangelsk and Kholmogory."

*In France *l'école libre*—literally the "free school"—designates a school that is almost invariably Catholic-run. In 1905 church and state were formally separated in matters of education, and from then on "free schools" were deprived of state subsidies—with the exception of schools in the three departments of Alsace, which had once belonged to ultra-Catholic Austria. In 1959, however, Prime Minister Michel Debré, who was well known for his Catholic fervor, had a law passed that authorized the partial financing of "free schools" with state funds.

and then, specifying the objectives:

- world domination through the crushing of the anti-imperialist camp (USA)
- struggle against imperialism and Fascism, reinforcement of democracy (USSR)."

So now we know. Teachers no longer have the duty to teach; their task is to overthrow capitalism and to bar the road to imperialism. They accomplish this task in every domain, even in books of foreign languages and literatures. Thus the Spanish textbook *Sol y Sombra* (Bordas, 1985), by Pierre and Jean-Paul Duviols, both university instructors, which is used for the final *lycée* classes to prepare for the baccalaureate, contains an entire chapter celebrating the merits of Fidel Castro and another enshrining the mythical version of the reasons for Salvador Allende's overthrow in 1973. The modern Spanish or Latin American authors quoted in *Sol y Sombra* are almost all communists or fellow travelers. While claiming to offer a representative panorama of Hispanic culture in the twentieth century, the authors managed to put together an anthology in which for Spain neither Ortega y Gasset, nor Azorín, nor Menéndez Pelayo, nor Pérez Galdós, nor Gómez de la Serna, nor Pérez de Ayala, nor Maeztu, nor Salvador de Madariaga figured, any more than among the pre-1936 poets did Gerardo Diego, Pedro Salinas, or Jorge Guillén. The only poets who survived were the "martyr" García Lorca (assassinated, notwithstanding the legend, for personal rather than political motives) and the communists Rafael Alberti and Pedro Hernández. Of one of the greatest Spanish-language poets of our time and of all time, the Nicaraguan Rubén Darío, we find one poem cited—the *only* political poem (and one of the few truly mediocre ones) he ever composed, a poem addressed in 1905 to President Theodore Roosevelt. What makes this poem so priceless, in the eyes of the Duviols brothers, is clearly the fact that it is a diatribe against the *Yanquis.* What the brothers forget to mention, assuming they even know it, is that here Rubén Darío attacked the United States in order to defend Spanish colonialism after Theodore Roosevelt had intervened in Cuba in order to expel Spain.* The poet was clinging to an old-fashioned, antidemocratic, reactionary world for sentimental reasons, out of nostalgia for an effete colonial society. Such is the poem that is here presented as an anticipatory manifesto for the revolutionary Left of the 1960s.

*The poem was originally entitled "Teodoro," but the Duviols brothers changed the title to "To Roosevelt," to make their animus more obvious.

As for capitalist society, to judge by the lucubrations of the French teaching profession, it does not deserve to live any more than the imperialism it secretes. The textbook entitled *Initiation économique et sociale,* destined for the second grade (the year preceding the baccalaureate), chooses to illustrate its "dossier" on "Capital in the Enterprise" with a poster from the film *La Banquière* ("The Woman Banker"), which was inspired by the life of Marthe Hanau, one of the stars in the annals of embezzlement between the two world wars.* Why not have chosen Stavisky? The opening page of the "dossier" entitled "What is an Enterprise?" is illustrated in the same spirit by the reproduction of a poster advertising a film based on René-Victor Pilhes's novel *L'Imprécateur* ("The Curser"), a simpleminded indictment drawn up by an extreme left-wing author who blackened his portrayal of an imaginary multinational corporation. Farther on we come upon another illustration: the four Willot brothers, crooked businessmen who, just when the book was published, had been projected into the limelight by several sensational trials. This is what is known as "objectivity." And why not have included Al Capone, while they were at it? Thus, in a work destined to initiate the young in the workings of an economy, the only persons held up and engraved on their memories as models of banking and business— the two institutions which, from the fourteenth to the twentieth century, have created the prosperity of the West—are half a dozen crooks!

Small children too benefit from the anticapitalistic vigilance of the French teaching profession. In *L'Éveil à l'Histoire* ("Awakening to History"), which is used in elementary school classes and which by 1985 had sold 957,000 copies (Heavens, just imagine the intellectual damage!)—a small book which in a hundred pages takes us from prehistoric times right down to the present—one can read in the fifty-ninth and final lesson, entitled "Since 1945, Grave Dangers," this paragraph: "In cities, above all, life is ceaselessly becoming more painful and more unhealthy. How many *apartments* there are that are too small, noisy, and lacking in comfort! How many people spend two or three hours of crowded *commuting* every day to go to their work and to return! The *air we breathe* is full of dust, smoke, gasoline vapors, exhaust fumes; it is becoming more and more toxic. Silence is more and more difficult to find, even at night. Many illnesses result.

"*Food* is not as healthy as it used to be. We consume fewer and fewer natural foodstuffs. White bread, long considered a luxury foodstuff, is

---

Initiation économique et sociale, by J.-P. Cendron, C.-D. Echaudemaison, and M.-C. Lagrange (Paris: Nathan, 1982).

less healthy and nourishing than the second-rate bread of the past. And what should one say of forcibly grown fruits and vegetables treated many times over with insecticides? Or of the meat of vaccinated animals, fattened with abnormal rapidity? The consumption of *alcohol* and the use of *tobacco* cause many illnesses."

One is left wondering how in such dreadful conditions and thanks to what incomprehensible miracle life expectancy in our century has been able to increase, and in a particularly rapid and spectacular fashion since 1950. Mr. and Mrs. Chaulanges do not explain to the little ones in the elementary schools why and how people who have been poisoned by increasingly unhealthy food, asphyxiated by increasingly toxic air, worn out by slower and slower urban transportation, compressed into ever smaller apartments, undermined by chronic insomnia due to nocturnal din, ravaged by alcoholism and tobacco use, infected by insecticides, and stricken by ever more numerous and more varied illnesses nevertheless succeed in living on average twice as long as their ancestors in the previous century.*

The conquest of the schools by the Left—the Marxist, not the liberal Left—has been going on all over Europe. In Italy the "diversion" of the school from its teaching function in order to place it at the service of political indoctrination developed in two stages. In 1968 a leftist campaign was launched to do away with *all* textbooks! "No to the textbook!" one could read in a publication put out by the teachers' union. The textbook, so the argument ran, "is paid for by the workers, even if the state acquires it. It's a business that brings in billions to the publishing industry. It is imposed by the school of entrepreneurs. It promotes a form of instruction that does not help the workers. It favors a discredited class culture."

This reasoning recalls the thesis developed during the 1960s by the French sociologist Pierre Bourdieu in *La Reproduction,* according to which the schoolteacher has never done more than "reproduce" the ruling class. This is why, the above-mentioned manifesto goes on to declare, "the didactic-political collective of the Teachers' Union decided at a general assembly meeting to refuse the adoption of textbooks." This

---

*The USSR, interestingly enough, is one country where the ravages of alcohol have been steadily increasing. In the January 1989 issue of the monthly *Nash Sovremennik* ("Our Contemporary"), Fyodor Uglov, chairman of the Campaign for the Sobriety of the People and a Lenin Prize–winning member of the Academy of Medicinal Sciences, declared that "the number of alcoholics in our country rises by half a million a year, and that includes only those who are registered. Every third death is a victim of alcohol. Alcoholism claims close to one million lives a year!" Further on he added that, as a result of this addiction, 1,600,000 mentally handicapped children would be entering Soviet schools in 1990.

plea for a return to oral teaching unleashed an understandable panic among Italian textbook publishers, who from one day to the next were threatened with bankruptcy. It was then that the Italian Communist Party came to the rescue—this being the second phase of the operation. Textbooks could survive, the publishers were informed, provided they placed themselves at the service of the Good and not of the Bad. It was thus that one could read in a study published by one of the Italian Communist Party's publishing companies that "we need a school in which efforts are made to break down the obstacles to the formation of revolutionary personalities."* The publishers caved in immediately, and from 1976 on they produced textbooks that were aligned with the ideology that had been so heavy-handedly proposed to them. In Italy, as in France, they yielded to commercial blackmail. Since four fifths of the teaching profession were either card-carrying communists or adepts of the "Marxist Vulgate" (to use Raymond Aron's phrase), the publishers had no choice between obedience and financial ruin.

The result was most edifying. A leading Italian journalist, Lucio Lami, devoted a book to describing what happened. In this book, entitled *La Scuola del plagio* ("The School of Falsification," published by Armando Armando, Rome), he surveyed fifty textbooks destined for elementary schools, that is for children under ten years of age, which were adopted by the teaching community as a result of the "intellectual and moral reform" of 1976. The errors of omission and comission so strikingly resemble those of French textbooks that I won't try the reader's patience with repetitions and a new avalanche of quotations. I shall merely limit myself to one, in which the textbook's author, a "professor" of history, manages to tell the story of World War II without mentioning the German-Soviet pact of August 1939 and consequently the invasion and annexation of one half of Poland by Stalin while Hitler was invading and annexing the other half. It seems that, while remaining virtuously and peacefully aloof from the conflict, the USSR was then the victim of a dastardly and undeserved attack, just as Belgium had been. "Hitler" (Italian children were thus obliged to learn) "successively invades Austria, Czechoslovakia, and Poland. The democratic nations, which had sought to avoid the conflict, are forced to enter the war. Mussolini, Germany's ally, foreseeing a lightning victory by the Germans, declares war on France and England (1940). The German

*"Occorre una scuola nella quale si cerchi di abbattere gli ostacoli alla formazione di personalità rivoluzionarie." From "Il libro di testo: pedagogia e politica," *Calendario del Popolo,* January 1972. Many articles in communist newspapers and magazines followed the same general line.

armies invade Belgium in order to outflank the French fortifications and to strike France in the back. After occupying Holland and part of France, Germany turns against Russia, which is forced to enter the war." (An extract from *Quale Realtà,* a textbook for the elementary fifth grade.)

The saddest thing is that this kind of pedagogical charlatanism flourishes in so many school textbooks that in the end we simply laugh it off as ridiculous. This kind of scholastic skulduggery has doubtless always existed to a certain degree, but there have been periods when it remained contained within tolerable limits by a minimum of intellectual honesty and others when these limits were transgressed. Furthermore, the democratization of teaching and our entry into the era of mass education has prodigiously extended the field of influence and increased the number of victims of scholastic brainwashing. Some time ago, while browsing through the bookstalls on the quais of the Seine, I came upon an old history textbook, obviously destined for some Catholic or royalist college* at the start of the last century, in which the restoration of the Bourbon monarchy (which actually took place in 1815) was pushed back to coincide with the end of the Revolution in 1799, and in which Napoleon Bonaparte was transformed into a lieutenant general in the armies of Louis XVIII! I doubt that this daring version of the facts imposed itself widely at the time, and in any case it could not have deceived many young minds, for only a tiny part of the population then went to school. Now that virtually everyone goes to school, we cannot offer ourselves the luxury of a smiling indifference. But few writers bring cases of this kind to the attention of the public and rightfully denounce "scholastic disinformation"—to borrow the title of Bernard Bonilauri's brilliant and demoralizing book on this subject.†

French teachers—at least the dominant faction among them—have thus set themselves the objective of forging a socialist "basic personality" in their students. Just as Christian education was once based on the assumption that certain elements of information and ideas were to be concealed from the pupils—was this not the raison d'être of the Index?—so the kind of education designed to foster a "break with capitalism" justified the expurgation and "correction" of human knowl-

*In French a *collège* designates a private (usually Catholic) boarding school, rather than an institution on the university level, as is the case with certain British "public schools"—like Winchester College.

†*La Désinformation scolaire* (Paris: Presses Universitaires de France, 1983). Bonilauri shows that the dominant objectives in French textbooks are to (1) "embellish sovietism," (2) "condemn liberalism," (3) "corrupt pluralism."

edge according to what it was necessary to get the pupils to believe. From 1968 on, when revolts inspired by America's "counterculture" began to sweep France, a second ideological component was added to the crude practices of cynical censorship—the puerile idea that the very transmission of knowledge was reactionary. It followed logically that learning was equally so. We then witnessed the rise of a so-called "nondirective" pedagogy, which managed in fifteen years to pull off an antieducational tour de force, with the result that after five or six years of elementary "instruction" a good third of the children ready to enter secondary school were practically illiterate, and that almost half of the students entering universities could read but hardly understand what they were deciphering. This devastating decadence was due only in part to the increase in the numbers of students and to a scarcity of qualified teachers. It has been primarily the result of an official doctrine, of a deliberate option, according to which the school *should not* have the function of transmitting knowledge. Let no one think I am joking. Ignorance today is—or at any rate was until very recently—the object of a deliberate cult whose theoretical, pedagogical, political, and sociological justifications have been explicitly expounded in many texts and directives.* According to these directives, the school should cease to transmit knowledge in order to become a kind of "convivial" phalanstery or "place of life" in which boys and girls practice an "opening to others and to the world." The aim is to abolish the "reactionary" criterion of competence. The student is not expected to learn anything, and the teacher does not need to know what he or she is teaching.

Is this not the swiftest method of suppressing classroom failure? The zealous promoters of the new pedagogy deny, of course, that this kind of failure is due to scholastic inaptitude; they attribute it to a sole and single cause: social inequality. According to them, inequalities of capacities, talents, and energy do not exist between human beings, nor are there qualitative differences in their dispositions. The considerable differences that can be observed in their scholastic results are due to the fact that they are either socially and culturally favored or handicapped. It is thus essential above all else to keep such differences from manifest-

*In the case of France, they can be found in a number of books which, from 1982 to 1985, began to denounce the ravages of this crazy fad, and which—a sure sign that many people were worried—were often best-sellers. Suffice it to name, among the most striking, two books by Maurice Maschino, *Vos enfants ne m'intéressent plus* ("Your Children No Longer Interest Me") and *Voulez-vous des enfants idiots?* ("Do You Want Idiotic Children?"); the sparkling *Poisson rouge dans le Périer* ("Red Fish in the Perrier"), by J.-P. Despin and M.-C. Bartholy; from J.-C. Milner, a crushing indictment called *De l'École;* and finally, Jacqueline de Romilly's *L'Enseignement en détresse,* 1984.

ing themselves, for this might engender the illusion and spread the erroneous conviction that certain students succeed better than others because they are brighter or more hard-working or have a better teacher than others. All this, they claim, is nonsense. Social class, economic privileges, and the cultural advantages conferred on the student by his or her immediate background alone explain such differences. What happens at school is due to factors external to the school.* The school thus has but one mission: to neutralize the influence of such factors by reestablishing within itself a rigorous equality of results, which unfortunately is not encountered outside it. To allow glaring gaps to appear between "good" and "bad" students, to allow "good" students to acquire more knowledge more quickly than others, would be to encourage a belief in natural inequalities or qualitative differences and offer an advantage to those who benefit from social injustice. The good student must be pulled down to the level of the bad student, who is regarded as the equitable social mean. Scholastic success is redistributed in much the same way as the socialist state seeks to redistribute incomes. Every attempt to conceive of instruction as being a machine for detecting talents and for providing them with the wherewithal to be developed is stigmatized as "elitist" and for this reason condemned as "reactionary."

It will be noted that this pedagogic philosophy rests on two postulates both of which are devoid of any scientific validity. The first is the postulate of the identity of the genetic heritage of all human beings. The second is the dogmatic assumption that scholastic results are the direct consequence of economic advantages and the student's social surroundings—that is, that no child coming from a neighborhood poorer than another's could ever possibly perform better than the latter. Random observation suffices to negate this gratuitous assumption. Sociological absurdity is thus added to biological absurdity. Instruction, the vehicle for spreading knowledge, is based on ignorance! The holders of this obscurantist pedagogy confuse equality *before* the school with equality *in* the school, as Professor Laurent Schwartz has aptly put it.† What

*The recognized propounder of this theory is Pierre Bourdieu, notably in *Les Héritiers* ("The Heirs"), published in 1964, and in *La Reproduction* (1970). Anyone wishing to measure the sociological fragility of this thesis and the arbitrary nature of its ideological abstractions need but read, with stupefaction, Philippe Bénéton's *Le Fléau du Bien* ("The Scourge of the Good"). In the third and fourth chapters of this book, published in 1983, he lays bare the scientific poverty and the fatuous empirical support of an inquiry Bourdieu claimed to have conducted in a Parisian *lycée*. The sociologist Raymond Boudon had already demonstrated the inability of this dogmatism to deal with real facts in *L'Inégalité des chances, la mobilité sociale dans les sociétés industrielles* (1973).

†Laurent Schwartz, *Pour sauver l'université*, 1984.

the democratization of teaching really means is that a child's economic situation will never keep him or her from undertaking studies corresponding to his or her aptitudes. This does not mean that all children have the same aptitudes. Nothing in the present state of scientific research allows one to assert that all human beings are equally gifted for everything, and there are many reasons for believing the contrary. To decree that all schoolchildren will be first in their class the day society becomes more just—and what kind of "justice" would that be?—can only be the fruit of ideological delirium founded on incompetence.

It is all the more to be regretted that this willful incompetence should nowadays flourish in the very socioprofessional body that has the mission of transmitting the treasures of human knowledge from generation to generation. As François Jacob has written in *Le Jeu des Possibles* ("The Game of Possibilities"), it is precisely because human beings are not naturally identical that the notion of the equality of rights was invented and should be fought for. The equality of rights *remedies* the inequality of gifts—to be sure, between individuals, a phenomenon that can be observed, and not between races, which is neither an observable phenomenon nor a scientific concept. If natural equality reigned, juridical equality would be needless. Besides, it is now clear that in democratic capitalism one can increasingly reduce economic inequality and the influence that economic inequality can have on cultural inequality and on one's scholastic chances in schools and universities.

What is anything but obvious, on the other hand, unless one is prepared to renounce the very essence of the act of teaching and the act of learning, is *why* one should see to it—as though this were something desirable—that all children placed in the same conditions should obtain the same results and accordingly prepare themselves for the same activities, later exercised in the same way and with the same felicity. Added to the falsification of textbooks, this unrealistic principle simply completes the destruction of teaching carried out by the teachers themselves.

Equality in the world of instruction can only consist of creating conditions of access to school studies in which each can succeed according to his or her real intellectual abilities, and not according to one's social surroundings. A child born into more favorable surroundings should not be favored if he or she is mediocre—and for this reason we need a strict, selective system of instruction. The child born into a poor, uncultured family should not be deprived of the benefits of higher education if he or she is intelligent—and for this too we need a strict and selective system of instruction, one that is capable of detecting natural talents, instead of repressing them by keeping them from emerging and by maintaining them on the same level as those of the worst students. This latter conception of equality results in the greatest wrong that can be done to students who have been handicapped by their social surroundings: by *inflicting upon them at school a second unfavorable milieu!* Since they happen to be living in domestic surroundings that asphyxiate intellectual activity, they must be saddled in the classroom with an added load of mind-numbing "snuffers"! A fine piece of reasoning. This system of instruction destroys the great historic function of the school, its veritable democratic vocation, which is to correct social inequalities by promoting intellectual inequalities. The ideology inspiring this "system" postulates the identity and equality of all human beings. Since actual experience does not confirm this postulate, special measures have to be taken to force it to do so—by organizing a generalized failure, one that serves as a kind of purgatory while waiting for the Nirvana of total intellectual equality. This unscientific postulate in fact engenders the most reactionary kind of school, for only the children of well-to-do families have the material means and the necessary contacts to be able to find outside an increasingly sterile teaching system the genuine education that this kind of instruction no longer provides. The intended matrix of "justice" thus gives birth to a monstrous injustice.

The school has been and can once again become an instrument for the perfecting of society and the correction of inequalities, but precisely—since that is its role—by dispensing knowledge, not by denying and interdicting it. What the process of democratization has permitted has been to transform knowledge more and more into a lever for correcting initial economic inequalities. One of the profoundest meanings of the concept of democracy is perhaps this: that democracy serves to undo sociological determinism in making culture accessible to all. But it is thanks to the benefits of culture that it undermines this determinism, not by promoting anticulture and manufacturing "idiot children" all perfectly equal in their idiocy. The dream of the new pedagogues is to transform the school into a tool for the destruction of existing society by distorting the truth and encouraging ignorance.* These tactics will

---

*I trust my American readers will not think that I am here analyzing an exclusively European philosophy of teaching. The havoc this has wrought on U.S. schools, colleges, and universities has been just as devastating. In a review article aptly entitled "La Trahison des Clercs," J. O. Tate quotes this revealing passage from Roger Kimball's *Tenured Radicals: How Politics Has Corrupted Our Higher Education* (Harper & Row, 1990): "The truth is that when the children of the sixties received their professorships and deanships they did not abandon the dream of radical cultural transformation: they set out to implement it. Now, instead of disrupting classes, they are teaching them; instead of attempting to destroy our educational institutions physically, they are subverting them from within. Thus it is that what were once

not destroy society—first of all because the new pedagogues know next to nothing about this society, don't bother to study it, and judge it according to lazy prejudices which are of a flabbergasting and inflexible fatuity; second, because society will not long tolerate a school whose aim is to undermine it from within; and finally, because in seeking to annihilate itself the better to annihilate society, the school ceases to be the accuser it fancied itself to be and becomes the accused. Its very inefficiency discredits it and covers it with ridicule. It thought it was embarking on a revolution; all it did was run itself onto the rocks.

Fortunately, in France and elsewhere, civil society has been defending itself vigorously against the efforts of teaching bodies to plunge it back into illiteracy. The demand for education remains high, indeed it keeps steadily growing, and the pressure it exerts partly thwarts the new pedagogy. Among French postadolescents under thirty years of age, the percentage of holders of degrees equal to or higher than the baccalaureate (end of secondary schooling) has quadrupled in the last quarter century. It is true that the degrees are no longer quite the same. It is also true that a significant increase in the number of diplomas awarded can be noted in a society without that increased number being sufficient, simply because the need for degree holders in higher education has outstripped the available supply thanks to cultural and technological transformations. A progression in absolute figures can be offset by a regression in relative terms. Forms of society are developing in which many kinds of unskilled work have diminished and most are fated to disappear. "Each year in France, 80,000 almost illiterate young people become handicapped adults," as Paul Camous has written.* Forty or fifty years ago they would have been manual laborers, farmhands, factory workers, or artisans, purposefully integrated in agriculture and industry, as they then were. It is not enough to congratulate oneself because the number of degree holders is higher than it used to be in a particular country; one must also know if the number has grown as rapidly as the demand. A society can perfectly well lack both unskilled jobs for its unemployed and young degree holders for its qualified jobs. This explains why, despite the increase in the number of diplomas awarded, the public can still have the impression that the teaching

the political and educational ambitions of educational renegades appear as ideals on the agenda of the powers that be. Efforts to dismantle the traditional curriculum and institutionalize radical feminism . . . now typically issue from the dean's office or Faculty Senate, not from students marching in the streets." Tate's review article appeared in the September 1990 issue of *Chronicles*.

*In *La Vie Publique*, September 1987.

system has failed in its task; it then demands a more effective system of education, as recent public opinion polls in many countries have demonstrated. In France such polls show that in the middle and late 1980s young men and women in the 18- to 24-year age bracket regarded the USSR as an economic fiasco, a graveyard for human rights, and a menace for democracy—something that fortunately proves the flagrant failure of thirty years of brainwashing via school textbooks.*

In recent textbooks the pedagogues have gradually abandoned the increasingly desperate effort to get their students to admire the Soviet model.† Nevertheless, they have since found a new launch pad from which to fire off their attacks on democratic capitalism. This is Third Worldism, according to which the prosperity of developed countries has but a single cause—the exploitation and impoverishment of underdeveloped countries. This thesis has not the slightest foundation in economic and historical reality; it is simply a substitute for and spatial extension of the untenable Marxist ideology of added value. Third Worldism has been so often and completely refuted that I will not return to the subject—except to stress the point that this is a new example of the persistence, notably on the school level, of a false conception, and this notwithstanding the abundance of data that disprove it.

According to one fashionable fancy, the modern child is supposed to compensate for the insufficiencies and partialities of school instruction with the help of information he or she is offered by the media. This is even alleged to be one of the sources of the "demoralization" of the teaching profession, which has been divested of its previous "captive audience" (its young charges) and the authority that was once conferred on teachers thanks to their virtual monopoly in the dispensation of knowledge. I wonder if people who reason in this way have watched their children looking at television or have looked at themselves while they were watching. Aside from the fact that the political prejudices of media journalists are often not far removed from those of schoolteachers—sometimes by choice, sometimes by conformism and indolence—and aside from the fact that education is not simply nourished by the latest events, even when they are "cultural," it is impossible not to notice

*From 1987 on, the "Gorbachev effect" attenuated the perception of Soviet agressiveness among the young, as among other age groups. The change of style in Soviet diplomacy succeeded where scholastic falsification had partially failed.

†The interested reader can find a revealing discussion of this "cultural revolution," as written up by Branko Lazitch and Christian Jelen, in the June 25, 1982, issue of L'Express—five years before the previously mentioned symposium devoted to the "perception of the USSR through French school textbooks."

the fleeting nature of TV information and the semioneiric state in which we watch it. The dominant characteristic of a TV news item is that it is separated from the larger context and its antecedents; it is neither situated nor explained, except by comments so meager that they could often be dispensed with entirely. It is the violence of the image, not the importance of the event, that gives the impression its impact. Now, education, the initiation into culture and apprenticeship in independent thinking, presupposes conditions that are poles apart from passive perception. I am referring above all to televised news. TV "magazines" and documentary features enable journalists to employ the illustrative force of television without renouncing rational explanation, the interpretation of data, in a word everything that is addressed to a wide-awake consciousness and which leaves a trace in the memory. But most items of TV information come from news roundups. The nature of the televisual medium, quite independently of the journalists' volition, promotes in the TV viewer a momentary intensity of impression along with swift forgetfulness. The prevailing rule for this particular genre is a rapid succession of images and extreme brevity for each subject. There is little or no hierarchy of significance. An international or economic news item of extreme importance is followed by a common crime or some local uproar. The necessarily simplified commentary is superficially grasped, even when it is actually heard. The statement "I saw it on TV" does not mean that one has the slightest notion of what the broadcaster said. Isolated from its causes and context, the picture strikes a level of our perception where intellectual analysis and thus the switching on of memory intervene but feebly. We recall the "great moments of television" because they impressed us by their pathos, by their baroque, horrible, or comic nature, not by their explanatory value or their objective influence on the course of history.

We can perfectly well apply to the awareness of the television viewer, who is also a TV voter, the four terms that Freud employed to describe the mechanism of the dream: "displacement" (which means that one person can play another's role), "dramatization" (which means that gesture replaces thought), "condensation," and "symbolization." I would even add a fifth term: evaporation.

This is not a critique of television—a critique which would be as senseless as criticizing trips by air. Let me simply note that televised information—even if we overlook distortions due to bias, censorship, or incompetence—is merely a way of registering facts, not of analyzing them. And even then, it merely registers the external facet of events, enacting before our eyes a play of which we do not understand the text.

A sumptuous play, no doubt, and one that prodigiously and overabundantly enriches our physical vision of the planet and our fellow human beings. But this vision does not enable us to derive a lesson from the facts, to combine them with one another, or to introduce a causal order between prior happenings and consequences. How, then, can we articulate events within a general comprehensible framework and integrate them with sense and value in our memory? One impression quickly follows another—something the cleverest politicians know how to exploit.

There is another drawback that aggravates the weakness of TV as a medium of education: the impossibility, indeed the pointlessness, of rectifying. Any televised news item, no matter how monstrously false or lacking in perspective it may be, sails on, once it has been broadcast, like a stricken, unmasted ship which nothing and nobody can bring back to port to be patched up. Now, the apprenticeship of thought is, to a large extent, a permanent process of rectification by the constant addition of new data to the initial representation, which is thus ceaselessly modified. "Children" wrote La Bruyère, "have neither a past nor a future." Education has the task of providing both one and the other. I doubt that TV sequences can replace or aid it in this role, for they too have neither a past nor a future.

Teachers usually reply to objections such as these first by saying that the fate of teaching has always been linked to political factors, and next that they themselves have the right, like all citizens in a democracy, to emit opinions and to take part in political struggles. Both of these statements are sophistries. The fact that every society and every state had or should have a policy *of* education does not mean that teachers have a right to carry on politics *inside* education. It is better, of course, that they should be consulted on policy concerning education, but each time they have been consulted over the past forty years in France, the advice they have proferred has been so childish, sectarian, and irresponsible that it throws a cloud of doubt over their underlying motives. As for the right of teachers to dabble in politics—and Lord knows, this is one thing they don't deny themselves; many even make something of a career out of it!—in what way would this right be violated by professional scruples and intellectual honesty in the transmission of knowledge? Professors, to be sure, have no reason to remain vestal virgins. In *La Trahison des clercs* ("The Treason of the Intellectuals"), Julien Benda did not condemn commitment in intellectuals. What he requested was that they, above and before all others, subordinate commitment to truth, and not truth to one's *engagé* cause. This duty is even more binding on the teacher, whose audience has no choice between listening and not listening. The teacher who is unfaithful to his or her calling adds to the sin against intelligence that of a dominant position.

Why do so many teachers and professors in democratic countries so hate liberal society, and why, to put it concretely, do they vote more to the left than the average of the society of which they are members and whose children they instruct? During the nineteenth century and the first half of the twentieth, it was often the army that wandered perilously astray from the mainstream of public opinion, toward the right and the extreme right. Today it is the professoriate who have gravitated toward the left and the extreme left. It is not only in the European democracies but also in the United States that this discrepancy has attracted attention. In 1982, for example, Professor Bertell Ollman of New York University was pleased to announce that a "Marxist revolution is taking place today in American universities."* Professor Ollman's textbook *Alienation: The Marxist Conception of Man in the Capitalist Society,* the title of which sounds like a bad Italian joke from the early 1960s, was being used in 1982 in a hundred American universities as prescribed reading, and had by then gone through seven printings. The European observer could not but look on with amusement at this extraordinary spectacle of a Marxism, which in the Old World was and is in full intellectual retreat, enjoying new victories overseas. "Radical ideas," wrote Guenther Lewy in *Policy Review* (winter 1982), "have spread and deepened. Nowhere is this more true than in the colleges and the universities. There are hundreds, perhaps thousands, of openly socialist professors."

A dramatic illustration of this trend is Stanford University, which, yielding to purely ideological though not truly formidable pressures, watered down the only prescribed course in general culture for incoming freshmen, replacing Dante and Dostoevsky with Frantz Fanon and other works far worse than those of that author. Why should this reputedly conservative university adopt positions that are woefully out of date? Perhaps because Stanford is a very rich private institution and is thus more prone to the snobbery of "radical chic" than Berkeley, a university supported by the State of California.

The result, in any case, is that the organizers of European conferences, who were having ever greater trouble finding local participants ready to play the role of forthright Marxist gospel peddlers, were re-

*Quoted by Arnold Beichman, "Karl Marx Goes to College," *The Wall Street Journal,* May 14, 1982.

duced to having to import them from the United States. They paid us back with interest for what we had lent them! But the spectacle of this amiable ideological Ping-Pong match over the Atlantic merely thickens the mystery. Whence comes this fierce hatred of intellectuals for the least barbaric societies of human history, and this rage to destroy the only civilizations to date that have emphatically conferred a dominant role on intelligence?

CHAPTER 12

The Failure of Culture

When one asks oneself how and why it is that a civilization born of knowledge and dependent on it seems bent on combating or deliberately not employing it, one is logically led to reflect most seriously on the role of intellectuals in such a civilization.

According to a cut-and-dried vision of our world, on the one side there are intellectuals, artists, writers, journalists, professors, religious authorities, and scientists, who have always defended justice and truth against all comers, and on the other there are the forces of Evil—governments and establishments, money, warmongers, famine makers and exploiters, the police, racists, fascists and dictators, oppression and inequality, the Right in general, and to a small extent the Left in a tiny number of eminently transient and atypical deviations. This vision prevails all the more easily since the means of communication in democracies are by definition in the hands of those it flatters.

The others, who are onlookers, entertain an entirely opposite conception, but one just as outrageous, of the role of intellectuals. Pitilessly they stress their errors, their dishonesty, their servility to fads and fashion, their irresponsibility when they adopt a position on serious matters. Thus there is not one but two conceptions of the modern intellectual.

The first blames intellectuals for their lack of a sense of responsibility in the exercise of their influence, the nonchalance with which they neglect and even falsify information, their indifference to the damage caused by their mistakes. In France this kind of accusation goes all the way back to Tocqueville and the famous chapter in his *L'Ancien Régime et la Révolution* entitled "How, towards the middle of the eighteenth century, men of letters became the principal political persons of the land, and of the effects which resulted therefrom." Therein Tocqueville explained that "the very condition of these writers prepared them to savor general and abstract theories in matters of government and to entrust themselves to them blindly." From then on, "by taking over the direction of opinion, notwithstanding the almost infinite distance separating them from practice," they created the prototype of the intellectual who behaves like a party chieftain, but without assuming the risks.

The second conception of the role of the intellectual consists, on the contrary, of exalting—as though it were an advantage—his distance from the constraints of practical matters. He is the moral conscience of society, the servant of the truth, the enemy of tyrannies, dogmas, forms of censorship, iniquities. This glorious tradition boasts great moments and accomplishments—from Voltaire's defense of Calas to the Dreyfus affair and the struggle against racism.

This benighted separation of wheat from chaff is based on the crass ignorance of the intellectual history of the past three centuries in the Old World as well as in the New. There have been as many thinkers of the Right as there have been thinkers of the Left who have propagated unrealizable Utopias, pseudoscientific dogmas, and catastrophe-inducing exhortations, notably between the two world wars. Especially since 1945, there have been as many left-wing thinkers as right-wing ones who have employed their talents to justify falsehood, tyranny, assassination, even foolishness. In 1937, for example, Bertrand Russell, a future Nobel Prize winner, could declare: "Britain should disarm, and if Hitler marched his troops into this country when we were undefended, they should be welcomed like tourists and greeted in a friendly way." Lest anyone think I am making this up, let me continue with a few more extracts from this incredible speech, made at Petersfield, Hampshire, England, in early April of that year. "Concerning the hospitable welcome," wrote *The New York Herald Tribune*'s correspondent, "Earl Russell explained, 'It would take the starch out of them and they might find some interest in our way of living.' If the British government stopped arming and turned pacifist, this country would not be invaded and would be as safe as Denmark, according to Russell, who contended that no country attacked another country unless it was afraid of the other's armaments. As a step toward world peace, he proposed dismemberment of the British Empire."*

Bertrand Russell may have been an eminent philosopher in his specialty—symbolic logic—but he was nonetheless an imbecile on the subject dealt with in those sentences. Similarly, Julian Benda, author of one of the fussiest pleas on behalf of the necessary independence of intellectuals, *La Trahison des clercs,* could, twenty years after the appearance of this cleansing work, go off the deep end to the point of acclaiming the sentencing to death of Laszlo Rajk during a trumped-up show trial in Budapest. "Voltaire," he wrote in the November 17, 1949, issue of the communist literary weekly *Les Lettres Françaises,* "was acting fully in his role of learned man in intervening in the Calas affair, just as was Zola in the Dreyfus affair; I claim that I am like them in defending the Hungarian verdict, the justice of which seems to me to be denied only by partisans."†

The seraphic and sacerdotal vision of the intellectual all too naïvely confers on him infallibility, courage, probity, and discernment. On the other hand, the critical view betrays an excessive pessimism, in supposing that the intellectual is afflicted by a congenital flightiness and a fundamental inadaptibility to reality, even if in other respects he might be a profound theorist or a brilliant artist. Both conceptions suffer from a common vice. They attribute to the intellectual qualities or defects that are in a sense innate.

Now, the intervention of the intellectual in public affairs takes place under the sway of considerations, pressures, interests, passions, cowardly concessions, prejudices, hypocrisies, motives of snobbery and *arrivisme* that in every respect are like those that move other human beings. The three virtues needed to resist them—clear-headedness, courage, and honesty—are to be found neither more nor less among intellectuals than in other socioprofessional categories. This is why the contingents which intellectuals have contributed to the formulation and

---

*Quoted in the column "50 Years Ago" *International Herald Tribune,* April 2, 1987.

†In the Middle Ages the French word *clerc* was used to designate a scribe (whence the English word "clerk") who, as one who could read and write Latin, enjoyed certain scholarly privileges. The closest approximation to Benda's twentieth-century use of the word would probably be "intellectual," which he preferred to avoid as too straightforward. (Translator's note.)

promotion of major human aberrations are proportionately equivalent to those furnished by the rest of their contemporaries.

If, for example, for the period between the two world wars we subtract the intellectuals who yielded either to the Fascist temptation or to the Stalinist temptation, there are not many important ones left. Most of the "shining lights" of Italian literature and art encouraged the advent and consolidation of the Fascist state in the name of a "revolutionary" ideal: D'Annunzio, Pirandello, Papini, Marinetti and the Futurists, the poet Ungaretti (who became a Stalinist after 1945), and, to a lesser degree, Benedetto Croce, a somewhat ambiguous sympathizer up until 1925. Like Antonio Gramsci, the communist theorist of the conquest and imposition of total intellectual control, the Fascist theorists detested democratic and parliamentary institutions. They preached a "pedagogy of violence"—the same that resurfaced on the extreme left around 1970 among the "philosophers" who inspired and encouraged the terrorism of Italy's Red Brigades. Throughout Europe the hatred of liberal society became the common denominator of many right-wing as well as left-wing writers. In Germany the intellectuals of the Left detested the Weimar Republic as much as the Nazis detested it, and their blows helped to precipitate its downfall. In Great Britain the most prestigious intellectuals—from George Bernard Shaw to the notorious "Red Dean" of Canterbury—condemned Fascism the better to praise the Moscow show trials and (with lovely logic!) the German-Soviet pact of 1939. Before, as after, the war, these freedom-killing stances were the work not of a few antiquated pamphleteers but of highly celebrated talents.

In France the famous Committee of Anti-Fascist Intellectuals of 1934, which was stuffed with Comintern agents, contained as many adversaries of liberal democracy as the opposite camp did. In his *Révisions déchirantes* ("Heart-rending Revisions," published in 1987), a follow-up on his 1972 masterpiece, *Révolutionnaires sans révolution,* André Thirion describes with an all-too-cruel vivacity the strange vagaries of both right-wing and left-wing totalitarianisms. For example, in 1935 Emmanuel Mounier, an intellectual leader of left-wing Christians and the founder of the monthly review *Esprit,* could write: "We too are critical in our attitude toward liberal and parliamentary democracy. A democracy of slaves set free." After which he added, "We in no way deny that the Fascists, compared to the regimes they replace, provide an element of health." After the liberation of France in 1944 Mounier experienced a momentary weakness for Stalinism.

Fortunately it is possible to offset this wholesale condemnation by citing the names of intellectuals whose anti-Fascism, before or after

World War II, was authentic and did not consist simply of exchanging one totalitarianism for another: André Gide, George Orwell, Arthur Koestler, André Breton, François Mauriac, Albert Camus, Raymond Aron, José Ortega y Gasset, Salvador de Madariaga, Octavio Paz, Mario Vargas Llosa, Carlos Rangel. But there are not many of them, and it cannot be said that their colleagues always behaved toward them with perfect elegance.

When Albert Camus died in an automobile accident on January 4, 1960, at the age of forty-six, he was one of the most famous French writers in the world as well as one of the most spiritually tormented. Also one of the most attacked. A Frenchman born in Algeria, a man of the Left who went on claiming to be one, he was increasingly called upon to adopt a clear position on the subject of the Algerian war. But instead of serving as a moral guide, he shut himself up, from 1956 on, in a sorrowful, stricken silence, which was interpreted by many as a form of escapism. He said nothing, despite the increasingly dreadful tragedies of a conflict that had already entered its sixth year.

How are we to explain this apparent flight before the "responsibilities of the intellectual"? It was, of course, above all the progressives and the anticolonialists, members of the political family he had originally belonged to, who demanded an accounting from the writer. Their explanation was anything but favorable. Camus, they insinuated, was disguising beneath a "noble" humanism his refusal to make a revolutionary choice. Or, more simply, the Algerian settler in him (what the French call the pied-noir—the "blackfoot") had muzzled the progressive. A short phrase uttered by him in December 1957 created a scandal. In Stockholm, whither he had gone to receive the Nobel Prize for Literature, Camus, questioned about Algeria, declared, "I believe in justice, but I will defend my mother before justice."

This phrase immediately touched off a furor in the outraged ranks of the Left. Was this not a French translation of the jingoistic gospel "My country right or wrong"? Camus was thus placing his carnal attachment to his homeland, to the French community of Algeria, above the justice of Antigone, of the "unwritten laws" of the political Good!

How many times, since this phrase was uttered, has this Camus shorthand formula about the "mother" being preferred to "justice" been bandied about in this sense—which is nonsense, or at least somewhat equivocal!

When Camus spoke of his mother, he was, in fact, thinking of Madame Camus, his mother, and not using the word to symbolize his homeland. If symbol there was, it was that of the civilian populations, of innocent victims. Already in March 1956 he had used the same image in a remark made to Emmanuel Roblès: "If a terrorist throws a hand grenade into the market of Belcourt [Algiers], which my mother frequents, and kills her, I would be responsible had I, to defend justice, likewise defended terrorism. I love justice, but I also love my mother."

Camus had from the very start been on the side of the Moslems in combating oppression and injustice. In 1937 he had even been excluded from the French Communist Party for having remained faithful to the Algerian nationalists, with whom the Party had broken as a result of an abrupt shift in Moscow's line. Born in conditions of extreme poverty, son of a farm laborer who had been killed at the start of World War I and a humble woman who never learned to read or write, Camus had in 1938 devoted his first newspaper articles in the newspaper *Alger Républicain* to "Poverty in Kabylia." Later in Paris, after the Liberation, it was the 1945 famine in Algeria, the repression following on the uprisings in Constantine and Sétif, which inspired his editorials in *Combat.* He never ceased to demand bread and justice for the Arabs. He supported the popular movement of the Friends of Ferhat Abbas's Manifesto, partisans of an "Algerian republic" federated with France (at that time a very bold program), and he protested against the arrest of its leaders, a major political blunder on the part of the French authorities, one that alienated young Moslems and, in rejecting them, pushed them toward the most extreme currents.

Why then, ten years later, did Camus separate himself from the French progressives who had unreservedly supported the Algerian revolution? Because he refused them the right to approve *all* of the Algerian rebels' acts indiscriminately, just as he refused to grant the French *pieds-noirs* settlers in Algeria the right to condone all of the French army's and police forces' repressive measures indiscriminately. In fact, what Camus foresaw and dreaded, as being bound to ravage the contemporary world, was mass terrorism—the kind that strikes not leaders, who are too well protected, but defenseless and often innocent civilians. Thus, from July 1955 to January 1956 he wrote a series of articles in *L'Express* in which he sought to obtain a guarantee from both the Algerian revolutionaries and the French military authorities that the civilian populations would be at least spared assassinations and reprisals. In January 1956, during a trip to Algiers, he launched an "Appeal for a Civil Truce in Algeria," which earned him threats from French diehards, the benevolent neutrality of the FLN (the insurgents' National Liberation Front), and the scorn of the progressives. This setback was his last attempt to influence the course of events directly. Subsequently he continually intervened with the French authorities on behalf of arrested persons, whether French or Algerian, and in particular he appealed to the president of the Republic, Vincent Auriol (and later René Coty), on behalf of Algerians who had been condemned to death; but he made no more public statements on questions of general policy.

The truth was that he abhorred the metropolitan French, whose parliament for a century had voted down *all* reforms in Algeria, and who now felt it quite natural that the *pieds-noirs* settlers should be sacrificed on the altar of the revolution. He sensed all too clearly that sincerity could no longer obtain a hearing. Why should an intellectual continue to speak out if he is not asked to say what he thinks but simply to encourage one or the other of two fanaticisms? Was he really needed for such a task? In a climate in which each camp, in the eyes of the other, was crawling with unmitigated "bastards" (*salauds,* in the refined vocabulary of Jean-Paul Sartre), Camus refused to risk the blood of others with "those articles one writes so easily in the comfort of an office." He added, "I denounced collective repression even before it had assumed the hideous forms it has just taken. . . . I will continue, but not with those who have always remained silent about the dreadful crimes and the maniacal mutilations of a terrorism which kills civilians, Arabs, and women."

An easy way of saying "A plague on both your houses!"? Not at all. To understand Camus, one must situate his qualms of conscience in the context of the larger debate born of the polemics aroused by *L'Homme révolté,* of 1951. Having written that there is no absolute Good on the Left, any more than there is on the Right, Camus had unleashed against himself a campaign of personal denigration, the nastiness and dishonesty of which were equaled only by their efficacy. Any declaration he made was forthwith distorted, travestied, ridiculed. So what was the use of speaking out? The silence observed by Camus was also the silence to which he had been condemned by the intolerance of the Left.

In Italy there is the similar case of Ignazio Silone. From the moment he repudiated communism right up until his death in 1978, this writer was the subject of a discreet, tenacious, but terribly effective ostracism on the part of Italian literary society, even though it was by no means composed solely of left-wingers. But the power of intimidation exercised by the Left extends, or extended, far beyond official political frontiers. If Gorbachev ever realizes his project of erecting a monument to the victims of Stalinism, he should engrave upon it the list of Western intellectuals who were treated like plague bearers and cruelly persecuted in the most cowardly manner because they had condemned Stalinism. Whereas a painter like Renato Guttuso could, without losing a shred of honor, glory, or financial benefit, spring with a single leap from Fascism to Stalinism out of sheer opportunism, to the Italian (and also the French) intelligentsia Silone's honest renunciation of communism was absolutely inexcusable. This was a classic case of the equivocal situation so often mentioned in this book, of the snare within which, in Latin America for example, the Mexican Octavio Paz or the Peruvian Vargas Llosa has become embroiled. On the one hand, the local intelligentsia belatedly recognizes the abomination of Stalinism; on the other hand, those who condemn it are nonetheless "reactionaries." There is no use trying to understand why. Before attempting any complex explanation, one must admittedly take into account a very simple factor that operates on the lowest level of spiritual degeneration—left-wing snobbery.

One cannot, of course—and this is important—compare Camus's brief flirtation with communism as a young journalist in Algiers with the national and international role played by Silone in the clandestine Italian Communist Party and in the Comintern between the two world wars. Silone had the profile of a typical "renegade"; Camus, when he achieved fame, did not have the image of an ex-communist. He simply belonged to the "progressive" family. This makes the almost identical ostracism to which both were subjected all the more interesting. For this similarity shows that the dividing line of liberty does not pass between the Stalinist Left and the non-Stalinist Left. It lies, in fact, outside the periphery of the Left. This was made clear by the violent excommunication pronounced by Sartre against Camus in 1953. The so-called "progressive" Left can sometimes briefly condemn communism (over Hungary in 1956, for example); but for a long time thereafter it continues to regard the adversaries of communism as being adversaries of itself.

It would be an act of arrogance to draw up an honors list. Suffice it to say simply that the intellectual does not, by virtue of his calling, possess any preordained preeminence in lucidity. What distinguishes the intellectual is not sureness of choice but the scope of the conceptual, logical, and verbal resources he develops to justify his choices. What distinguishes him furthermore is his influence. Thanks to his perspicacity or blindness, impartiality or dishonesty, slyness or sincerity, he drags others in his wake. Being an intellectual does not therefore confer an immunity rendering everything forgivable; but it confers more responsibilities than rights, a responsibility at least as great as the freedom of expression he enjoys. In the final analysis, the problem above all is moral. When Gabriel García Márquez writes that the "boat people" of Vietnam are vulgar traffickers and that in reality they have been engaged in the fraudulent exportation of capital, he must know this is false. His antitruthfulness is an error not of judgment but of another sort. As was that of Jean Genet when he extolled the assassins of the Baader-Meinhof gang on the front page of *Le Monde* in 1977. Should one claim that such villainies are trivial because they emanate from writers of international repute? One might as well argue that the more one is listened to, the less one should be held to account for what one says.

To the age-old debate on this subject a new one has been grafted—that of the relationship between intellectuals and the media. Every degree of cultural quality can be found on radio and television, from the excellent to the nonexistent. But that is not the real issue, which lies in the modification of behavior that the very existence of the media provokes in intellectuals. The possibility of reaching a vast audience, more through theatrical effect than by scrupulous analysis, prompts intellectuals to adopt strategies of communication worthy of small-time politicos.

It is only right and proper that the intellectual should have access to the media. But only too often he uses them solely to get his ideas across; and he modifies his ideas so that they can be transmitted by the media. It is a case of Harlequin wanting to play Antigone. And woe to the person who would really like to be Antigone! Thus in 1961 Lucien Bodard published a book, *La Chine au cauchemar* ("The Nightmare of China"). He was the first to describe the horrors of the Great Leap Forward, which caused sixty million Chinese to die of hunger. What a scandal! He was shunned, decried, and hissed—*sifflé en quatuor,* as Stendhal would have said. I recall a televised program in the 1960s that showed a "Dossier de l'Écran" on China, in which this same Lucien Bodard, sitting alone against all the others, could not get a word in edgewise.* Later Jean Pasqualini, author of an authoritative eyewitness account entitled *Prisonnier de Mao,* was subjected to the same violent barrage. It was not until after Mao's death in 1976 and the revelations made by his successors, that it became possible to say the truth about China. Simon Leys, whose *Les Habits neufs du président Mao* ("President Mao's New Clothes") appeared in 1971 and whose *Ombres chinoises* ("Chinese Shadows") was published in 1974, was for the first time able to get everything on the subject of Maoism off his chest on French television—in 1983, during a memorable session of Bernard Pivot's Friday-evening talk show, *Apostrophes.* For twenty-five years the media helped to suppress, rather than to make known, books about the real situation in China. It was not the moderators who took the initiative for these public executions . . . well,

*The "Dossier de l'Écran" (literally the "Screen File") is a regular French television feature in which a film on a particular subject is shown and the subject is then discussed by seven or eight "experts."

not always. It was the *other intellectuals* who had been invited to be part of the panel and who ganged up against the blasphemer. What, one wonders, happened to the "wholesome" pedagogy of the media during this quarter century of occultation of the truth about China? If this cowardly dissimulation of the truth cannot be blamed on the radio and TV programmers—not exclusively, at any rate—then it was the intellectuals themselves who decided they must not stray too far from the beaten path of "conventional wisdom" or who instinctively adhered to it. And it is they who, to conquer the vast TV public, feel they have a right to use methods that are at once oversimplifying and distorting. Those means were already described by Julien Gracq in 1950, in his devastating essay "La Littérature à l'estomac" ("Literature with a Paunch"), in which, speaking of radio, he wrote that this was where "the tempestuous howl of literature peters out on the shores of the infinite."

In many cases, intellectuals, whose mission (according to themselves) is to guide nonintellectuals along the road to truth, have been the ones who have most contributed to leading them astray. We have already encountered several specimens of this kind of reverse education. Either the intellectual—Bertrand Russell is a classic case—emerges from his sphere of competence but uses the prestige it confers on him to cloak with his authority theses of which he knows no more than the man in the street; or else he dissimulates or alters the elements of knowledge he possesses inside his speciality so as to make them coincide with a thesis that is outside the scientific realm but to which he is attached for nonscientific reasons; or again, he may have no specialty—none, that is, in the general order of knowledge, none being required outside his particular art, be he novelist, painter, architect, poet, or composer—but this does not keep him from uttering "definitive" pronouncements on questions of which he knows next to nothing.

The intellectual evolution of the German novelist Günter Grass from the realistic social democracy he was supporting in the 1970s to the turgid extravagances of pro-Soviet pacifism he finally espoused in the 1980s, illustrates how difficult it is for a writer to maintain an intermediate and reasonable position, one that will not win him a spotlight with the media. Excessive imprecations—even and especially when they are without serious basis—afford more gratification to their authors than a sincere effort to understand. When Grass decided he had become sufficiently famous as a novelist to have the right to lose his head completely in political matters, he began exhorting his compatriots to "undertake acts of resistance, to resist American leadership in view of the genocide that threatens." Germany, he argued, now had the means for making up for the "lost opportunity of resisting in 1933, when the genocide to come was announced."* In reality, Grass's opposition to the Atlantic Alliance is more reminiscent of the resistance to democracy in the 1930s of pro-Nazis and pro-Fascists, notably in France. They too "resisted" the rearmament of the democratic countries.

I won't bother to comment on the theory according to which the best way to wash away the shame of Hitlerian genocide was to let the Soviet regime become politically and strategically dominant in Western Europe. The hatred of democracy implied in declarations like this made by great intellectuals of the free world is intriguing. Thus Bertrand Russell, who, as we have seen, felt in 1937 that Nazi Germany was not a danger for the democracies provided they consented to disarm unilaterally, could later write in *The Manchester Guardian* (October 30, 1951) that the United States had become a "police state" similar to Hitler's Germany and Stalin's Russia. It is true that this was when McCarthyism was running rampant. But this showed little understanding of the nature and limits of McCarthyism, which not long afterward was eliminated from U.S. political life by the very play of democracy—that same democracy which Russell understood so poorly that he went as far as to bet five pounds with Malcolm Muggeridge that Joseph McCarthy would soon be elected president of the United States! When, sometime later, the senator from Wisconsin, who had been impeached by his senatorial colleagues and forcibly retired from all activity, died in disgrace, Russell had to pay up his lost bet, but he did not for one moment revise his opinions about "totalitarian" America.

In his memoirs, *Out of Step*—an indispensable work for understanding the history and state of mind of the intelligentsia of the United States (and indirectly of Europe) before, during, and after World War II— Sidney Hook lengthily describes his arguments with Albert Einstein.† He cites many conversations and exchanges of letters with the illustrious physicist, which confirm the fact that one can be a genius in one's own domain and totally lacking in judgment in others. And indeed, to such a degree that one begins to doubt that it could be the same mind that applies itself to two different subjects, so intelligent is it in dealing with one and so feeble in dealing with the other. These crevasses of thought, into which the most brilliant intellects tumble, would cause no broken bones save their own were it not that their publicly stated positions

---

*Quotations drawn from Renata Fritsch-Bournazel's *L'Allemagne, un enjeu pour l'Europe* ("Germany—A High Stake for Europe"), preface by Alfred Grosser (Brussels: Editions Complexe, 1987.

†Sidney Hook, *Out of Step,* (New York: Harper & Row, 1987).

influence millions of human beings thanks to the illegitimate transfer of authority from one domain to another.

Even before the war, in a letter written toward the end of 1938 to Max Born (and published in Born's correspondence), Einstein had given the measure of his political discernment by confiding to his friend and colleague that, after due reflection, he had changed his mind about the Moscow show trials. This was one case where he would have done better not to have reflected; for the process of meditation led him from the correct impression that those trials had been rigged to the erroneous conviction that they had been genuine and fair—the result being that those condemned, in his opinion, deserved the death sentence.

After the war Einstein, having become a U.S. citizen, took an active part in the presidential elections of 1948 by joining the committee for the support of Henry Wallace, Roosevelt's vice president from 1940 to 1944, who had set himself up as an independent third-party candidate (against Harry Truman and Thomas Dewey) and whose attitude toward the Soviet Union was that of the standard harebrained "useful idiot."

It is indeed astonishing to note how many political refugees from Europe, intellectuals who had been driven from the Old World by totalitarian regimes and who owed their survival to the fact that the United States existed and had been able to welcome them, adopted pro-Soviet and anti-American positions during the start of the Cold War and Moscow's first "peace offensive" of 1949. During those years Thomas Mann was another celebrant of that edifying and oh-so-novel homage, which certain persons paid to the democracy that saved them.* The great misfortune of the twentieth century is to have been the one in which the ideal of liberty was harnessed to the service of tyranny, the ideal of equality to the service of privilege, and all the aspirations and social forces included under the label of the "Left" enrolled in the service of impoverishment and enslavement. This immense imposture has falsified most of this century, partly through the faults of some of its greatest intellectuals. It has corrupted the language and action of politics down to tiny details of vocabulary, it has inverted the sense of morality and enthroned falsehood in the very center of human thought.

Let us beware of drawing up any systematic indictment against the "intellectual." Rather, I incline to think that the usual antithesis pitting, on one side, the notion that "intellectuals are always mistaken" against the other—the notion that "intellectuals are always right"—rests on nothing

*On Thomas Mann's equivocal attitude toward Soviet concentration camps in East Germany, see George Watson's fascinating article "Buchenwald's Second Life" in *Chronicles*, July 1989.

more than the subjectivity of the observer and his initial assumption. This assumption is chosen solely for emotional, polemical, or opportunistic reasons. But should it turn out that professional intellectuals are, in the final analysis, neither more nor less prone to error than other human beings—the latter being to some degree "intellectuals" too—it is high time to revise our naïve ideas about "intellectuals" as a community invested with a particular capacity for leading mankind toward the Good and the True. And should it turn out that they are in fact more prone to error than other mortals, we would have to determine why and how there has come to pass what deserves to be called the failure of culture.

Einstein's childish political vagaries could easily enough be forgiven, at any rate on the moral plane, but for the fact that at times they extended to domains in which his scientific competence should have served as a barrier and where, consequently, his flight from the truth can no longer be explained by naiveté alone and must unfortunately be attributed to a lack of sincerity. How else can one interpret Einstein's refusal to associate himself with a collective protest against the French physicist Frédéric Joliot-Curie, who in 1952 asserted that after "thoroughgoing personal investigations" he had reached the conclusion that the United States was practicing bacteriological warfare in Korea? This, as we now know, was one of the first and most memorable campaigns of Soviet disinformation in the postwar period. In his book of reminiscences, *J'ai cru au matin* ("I Believed in the Dawn"), Pierre Daix, who at the time was the editor in chief of the French communist daily *Ce Soir,* has given us a detailed account of how this campaign was directed and orchestrated by the international communist movement. With a rare nobility of character in avowing past mistakes, Daix was severe in passing judgment on himself, even though, at the time he committed these mistakes, he had been blinded by ideological loyalty (which was not the case with Einstein, who was simply "sympathetic" to this campaign). "Today," he wrote in 1976, "I consider that my participation as editor in chief of an evening newspaper in the spreading of this lie—the so-called bacteriological war the Americans were waging in Korea— was as serious a mistake as my reply to Rousset [David Rousset had pointed out the existence of concentration camps in the USSR as early as the late 1940s]. False news, arousing hatred—the full gamut of dishonor for a journalist was involved."* The dishonor was doubtless even greater for Joliot-Curie, who prostituted his Nobel Prize in Physics in aiding the propagation of this infamy. It is true, of course, that he had

---

*Pierre Daix, *J'ai cru au matin* (Paris: Laffont, 1976).

already abdicated all intellectual autonomy by declaring in 1951: "Placed in the very center of [human] struggles, disposing of complete information thanks to its militants, and armed with the theory of Marxism, the Party is bound to know better than each and every one of us."* No doubt Joliot-Curie was mentally conditioned, but is this an excuse? "That I was conditioned," Pierre Daix pointed out courageously, "does not exonerate me of responsibility for the kind of brainwashing I helped to foster. Otherwise, the Nazis would not be responsible either." The remark applies even more to Joliot-Curie, since his falsehood was located in the scientific field, where the capacity to fool oneself diminishes with the importance of the imperatives of verification, which were familiar to him. And Einstein? What is one to say about his refusal to be associated with the protest condemning Joliot's imposture? What is the lesson to be drawn? The only clear conclusion, when one sees one of the greatest scientific geniuses of all human history tacitly but knowingly corroborate a politically motivated scientific mystification, is that to date and in their immense majority intellectuals, while flaunting their role as guides, have considered themselves relieved whenever they so choose of any obligation to the truth and of all moral responsibility.

Often, indeed, in their outrageous fanaticism, they surpass the worst monsters of the political arena. Their loss of all moral sense is merely laughable—take the case, for example, of Marguerite Duras, who in 1985 warned the French people in these terms of what lay in store for them if they did not vote socialist in 1986: "I am here to tell you: if you continue, you are going to find yourselves in the company of scarecrows like Gaudin, Pasqua, and Lecanuet†, and all alone, and then it will be too late; you will be part of a society we don't ever wish to know again, and thus you'll be members of a society deprived of us: without truly and profoundly intelligent people, without intellectuals—yes, that's the proper word—without poets, without novelists, without philosophers, without true believers, true Christians, without Jews, a society without Jews, do you realize?"‡

Thus, according to this intellectual lady, the return of the liberals (who favor free enterprise) to power in France would mean the disappearance of all "truly and profoundly intelligent" citizens, among whom of course she places herself ("you'll be members of a society *deprived of us*"), the disappearance of all philosophers, novelists, poets . . . and

*Quoted by Jeannine Verdès-Leroux, *Le Réveil des somnambules* (Paris: Fayard, 1987).
†Jean-Claude Gaudin, Charles Pasqua, Jean Lecanuet—three leaders of the antisocialist opposition.
‡Quoted by Jean-Marie Domenach, *La Propagande du parti socialiste*, 1987.

of all Jews (i.e., what Hitler wanted). Not all excessive utterances are insignificant, for some of them reveal the fantasm* present in the mind of this novelist, as well as of many others who, surprising as this might seem, have not understood what democratic alternacy is and still conceive of it as involving the proscription of the adversary. Furthermore, they do not admit that there can be intellectuals in a camp other than their own. Marguerite Duras's seemingly crazy declaration above all betrays the desire, in the case of a socialist victory, to eliminate all those who do not think as she does. Contrary to what is often believed, today it is the intellectuals who lag behind the politicians, for, at least in the democracies, no politician, not even the most disheveled demagogue, dares use a language as radical as "exclusion"—to employ this fashionable lexicographic incongruity.

But what is simply comic bombast in a country where the citizens are protected by bourgeois law from the scourge of alternation *à la Duras* becomes tragic in other contexts, where the irresponsibility of intellectuals suddenly takes on the ruddy hue of blood. In *Out of Step* Sidney Hook relates a conversation he once had with Bertolt Brecht on the subject of the Old Bolsheviks who were shot during the Moscow show trials of the late 1930s. "It was at this point that he said in words I have never forgotten, 'As for them, the more innocent they are, the more they deserve to be shot.' I was so taken aback that I thought I had misheard him. 'What are you saying?' I asked. He calmly repeated: 'The more innocent they are, the more they deserve to be shot.' (*'Je mehr unschuldig, desto mehr verdienen sie erschossen zu werden.'*) I was stunned by his words. 'Why? Why?' I exclaimed. All he did was smile at me in a nervous sort of way. I waited, but he said nothing even after I repeated my question. I got up, went into the next room, and fetched his hat and coat. When I returned, he was still sitting in his chair, holding a drink in his hand. When he saw me with my hat and coat, he looked surprised. He put his glass down, rose, and with a sickly smile took his hat and coat and left. Neither of us said a word. I never saw him again."

It will be noted that the intellectual here goes farther than any politician ever did in the very exercise of the worst form of tyranny, for he justifies state crimes from a moral point of view by upholding the political

---

*"Fantasm: an imaginary scenario in which the subject is present and which, in a way more or less deformed by defensive mechanisms, transcribes the accomplishment of a desire and, in the final analysis, of an unconscious desire"; J. Laplanche and J.-B. Pontalis, *Vocabulaire de la psychanalyse* (Paris: Presses Universitaires de France, 1967). It was Talleyrand who remarked that "all that is exaggerated is without importance." But though one understands his scorn for verbal excesses, these in themselves are often of great importance.

legitimacy of the utilitarian assassination of innocent persons. "I say," wrote Benda accusingly in his *Trahison des clercs,* "that modern intellectuals have *preached* that the state should not care a hoot about being just; they have given to this affirmation a character of predication, of moral teaching." In 1927, the year in which Benda wrote these lines, the unjust state could be either socialist or Fascist. After the collapse of "rightist" totalitarianisms in 1945 this right to injustice was reserved for dictatorships of the "Left." But after, as before, the war, intellectuals surpassed even politicians in the justification of pure violence. Even Stalin, even Hitler, even Mao, even the executioners of the *communards* of 1871 always felt the need to assassinate the "guilty" only, that is, to claim that they were such and consequently to invent reasons for their guilt. This was the raison d'être of the revolutionary tribunals set up under the French Terror (1793–94), of the rigged Moscow trials, of Vichy's "special sections." Even the Khmer Rouge, whose leaders were eminent intellectuals—they too being philosophers who had been educated at the Sorbonne—did not behave quite like the worthy scions of that refined lineage, since they never dared to assert that innocent persons deserved to be executed all the more so since they were innocent. It was simply that, having become politicians, the Khmer Rouge did not completely exclude the possibility that they might one day have to provide an accounting for what they did.

This prospect, on the other hand, never troubles the intellectual, who claims to be both *engagé* (committed) and irresponsible. Sartre would have been very surprised if he had been asked to account for the millions of corpses piled up by the various totalitarian regimes of which for so many years he was the zealous propagandist. He, the theorist of commitment, he who demonstrated with his implacable logic that we are *all* guilty of the crimes that are committed in the world, *even when we know nothing about them,* doubtless felt that this responsibility ceases when we become aware of them—which was his case.

Intellectual irresponsibility, far from being confined to philosophical abstraction, extends very concretely to the juridical domain. This is an interesting aspect of the contemporary evolution of law. In 1979 the DST* arrested an East German physicist named Dobbertin, who since 1963 had been working under contract with the Centre National de la Recherche Scientifique (CNRS for short—a huge, state-financed research organiza-

*Direction de la Surveillance du Territoire—France's internal counterespionage service, comparable to the United States' FBI or to Britain's MI5.

tion which supports thousands of researchers, not only in the scientific field but also in the sociological, economic, historical, and even literary fields). A specialist in thermonuclear questions, Dobbertin, according to West Germany's counterespionage department, which transmitted the file and all the information it had on him to the French DST, was found to have been working for the East German secret service.

Immediately, without bothering to examine the facts, the French scientific community raised an uproar, demanding that Dobbertin be released and denouncing the "spy mania" that had led to his arrest. Two Nobel Prize winners, several members of the Institut de France, and the director of the Pasteur Institute outdid themselves in evoking the "universality of science." What a superb cliché. Dobbertin himself went them one better in the exercise of macabre humor. He claimed protection under the article of the Helsinki accords that guarantees the free circulation of ideas—how true it is that communist countries faithfully applied this article in questions of espionage! He invoked the spirit of "scientific and technical cooperation" and the "supranational character of research," both of which, he insisted, accorded him immunity from prosecution by a national judicial system. His lawyer shouted that his client had been the victim of a "grave violation of human rights." In November 1981, five hundred French scientists addressed a memorandum to the president of the Republic and the minister of justice in which they argued that the maintenance in prison of the suspected East German spy constituted a threat to their freedoms and to science. Once again, fascism was on the march! In May 1983 Dobbertin was provisionally released, his researcher friends having chipped in to provide the bail demanded by the prosecuting court in Paris.*

In 1986 a worldly psychoanalyst named Armando Verdiglione, who had made himself notorious for his frivolity, was condemned by an Italian law court. From his patients, usually rich society ladies who had fallen under his spell, he had been extorting huge sums of money a thousand times higher than the most outrageous fees any disciple of Dr. Lacan could dream of charging. The money went to finance a fabulous Verdiglione Foundation, which organized lavish conferences attended, in particular, by leading lights of the French intelligentsia. These intellectuals were not ungrateful. They reacted to the courtroom sentence by organizing a huge campaign and portraying Verdiglione as a victim of obscurantism and a scientific martyr. They even went as far as to dress up

*Finally brought to trial seven years later, Dobbertin was condemned by a Paris law court on June 15, 1990, to twelve years of imprisonment for espionage.

the Verdiglione case as a "new Dreyfus affair"—an insulting comparison for the memory of Captain Dreyfus, which could only depreciate the value of future references to the *fin-de-siècle* affair. On August 1, 1986, the weekly *Nouvel Observateur* raised the question "Can a law court pass judgment on the criminal character of the influence a psychiatrist may have on his patient, a professor on his student, a nurse on the sick old man she takes care of?" Even if it is a case of psychoanalytical "transfer," I would reply: Yes, of course, when the professionals in question use their influence to extort money from their charges. Freud's writings on the subject—which condemn the possible exploitation by the psychoanalyst of such a "transfer" of affection for personal or selfish ends—are absolutely clear. It is really exceeding all tolerable limits of hypocrisy to assert so brazenly that there is no criterion of professional ethics that allows one to make an elementary distinction between disinterested influence exercised for purely pedagogic or therapeutic purposes and the influence of a swindler on his dupe. The intellectuals who orchestrated this campaign revealed the dark depths of their thinking. What they really want is to be placed above the common law. "The laws of the civil code and the laws of [psycho]analysis are not made to be reconciled," wrote two psychoanalysts, who added, "It is up to psychoanalytical societies, the only ones competent, to try to remedy certain abuses."*

I do not know if the authors of those lines realize the enormity of their demands. This is quite simply a return to the judicial system of the Ancien Régime. Prior to 1789, in effect, there were a code of law and corresponding courts for the nobility, others for the clergy, and still others for commoners. Furthermore, in none of those systems did crimes and misdemeanors go entirely unpunished, whereas today it is impunity pure and simple which the above-cited intellectuals claim for themselves and their peers, notwithstanding the fact that it was for the most part the same intellectuals who clamored for the suppression of the special tribunals and the Court of State Security, which were established under De Gaulle for dealing with terrorist attacks and other acts of sedition perpetrated by the advocates of a French Algeria.

Such intellectuals have even been willing to sign petitions in favor of terrorist murderers, as happened during the trial of a number of Action Directe members in 1987. In their eyes terrorism becomes positively beneficial when it is an intellectual who initiates it, elaborates its theory, and incites others to follow his example. In 1987, moved by the same sentiments that had inspired them in the Dobbertin affair, members of

*Maud and Octave Mannoni, *Le Monde,* September 2, 1986.

the French scientific community protested the arrest of an Italian biologist, Dr. Gianfranco Pancino, who was suspected of once having headed the terrorist movement Workers' Autonomy, which in the 1970s was responsible for almost as many murders as were the Red Brigades. The target of no less than forty-two arrest orders on different criminal counts issued by the Italian judicial authorities from 1980 to 1983, Pancino, who in 1982 had fled to France, was in 1987 the object of an extradition request. At which point 317 scientists and doctors signed a petition (published in *Le Monde* on January 13, 1988) asking that he be "returned to his family and his scientific activities." "He had begun a new life in France," explained one of his colleagues, Dr. Fabiano Calvio. "This unjustified incarceration has ruined both his personal life and his life as a researcher. We are not taking a position on the fundamentals of the affair, but we wish that he be enabled to return to work here and to make up for lost time. He must be released."

It is worth noting that, as had happened in the Dobbertin case, Pancino's defenders declared that they were not judging the fundamentals of the affair. This amounts to stating as a principle that, even should he be guilty—a hypothesis they prudently did not exclude—Pancino *should not* be tried by the law courts of his own country. When an intellectual is involved, the question of guilt or innocence should not be raised. No matter what he may have done, an intellectual should not be arraigned before a law court, even to be acquitted. Even if he is condemned on the basis of overwhelming evidence, this does not prove his guilt, since he belongs to a higher order than that of ordinary mortals (as long as he is a leftist, of course), since his kingdom is not of this world. Thus, in the United States Alger Hiss, one of President Roosevelt's chief advisers, was condemned in the late 1940s for perjury in seeking to deny the links he had established with Soviet agents (in particular, he had been Stalin's "mole" inside the U.S. delegation during the negotiations at Yalta, with all-too-evident results). Nevertheless, Alger Hiss, in the eyes of "liberal" American intellectuals, was regarded and is still regarded as a political martyr and a "victim of McCarthyism." So much so that when, thirty years later, a young university student, Allen Weinstein, decided to devote a thesis to this affair, he was initially convinced of Hiss's innocence but—to the intense fury of the latter—he was led by his own historical research to change his mind and to conclude that Hiss was in fact guilty of the charges brought against him.*

*Allen Weinstein, *Perjury: The Hiss-Chambers Case* (New York: Knopf, 1978). See also Nadezhda Ulanovskaya's *Istoria odnoi serni* (New York: Chalidze Publications, 1982), in

I wonder if intellectuals realize the damage they do to themselves by making such claims. What moral credit can they still possess for struggling on behalf of human rights and for crying "Fascism!" on every street corner when elsewhere they calmly demand that a foreigner in France, maintained at the French taxpayer's expense, has a right to indulge in espionage, that an American in the United States has the right to betray his country, that a psychoanalyst has a right to abuse the trust placed in him, and that a biologist has the right to kill or to incite others to murder? Rights which, fortunately, are not enjoyed by popularly elected deputies and senators, whose parliamentary immunity can, if necessary, be rescinded.

I too deplore the fact that a valuable researcher should find himself in prison.* But I deplore even more, in this case, the reasons that led him there in the first place. For after all, he was arrested not because he was a researcher—contrary to what an unscrupulous propaganda campaign alleged—nor because some obtuse police apparatus was pursuing the annihilation of culture. He was suspected of having participated in a violent plot against democracy, and, being a man of thought and reflection, he did not make this choice in ignorance or naïveté. On the contrary—for this was the accusation that was brought against him and to which he must absolutely answer—he was one of those who *influenced* the ignorant and naïve. Unless the Penal Code is to be reformed to authorize intellectuals in general and doctors in particular to carry out or recommend murder, it seems iniquitous to reserve for manual laborers alone the sentences prescribed for the punishment of terrorist bombings and murderous assaults on individuals.

The fundamental question posed by the Pancino affair, as well as by the case of the philosopher Toni Negri, who also enjoyed the benevolent complicity of France's left-wing intelligentsia, is this. Why from 1970 on did so many Italian intellectuals approve, recommend, or practice terrorism? The standard reply to this question is that they were revolting against the injustices of Italian society and the corruption of the political system. But how can such a theory be sustained, since the wave of terrorism was unleashed at a moment when Italy was enjoying a degree of freedom it had never previously enjoyed in all of its history, and at a moment of triumphant success for its capitalist system, when the

which it was revealed that "Ulrich," who provided Whittaker Chambers with damning information, was in reality Alexei Ulanovsky, like his wife an agent of Soviet military intelligence (the GRU).

*After three weeks of imprisonment, Gianfranco Pancino was provisionally released from jail on January 13, 1988.

standard of living was rising steadily and social inequalities were steadily being reduced? In twenty-five years this evolution had transformed an underdeveloped dictatorship into a democracy with a modern, dynamic economy. Tocqueville's thesis—that it is when improvements begin to occur that residual inconveniences are the least readily endured—can perhaps explain the unrealistic cult of violence of ill-informed masses but not that of intellectuals possessing all the elements of appreciation needed for a correct analysis. Now, it was precisely intellectuals, whether professors or students, who furnished the ideology and most of the practitioners of active terrorism. We must therefore seek the origins of their conversion to terrorism elsewhere rather than in a rational interpretation of the ills and injustices of Italian society, which, though real enough, had ceased to be incurable, and which, far less than at any other period, could be traced back to the despair and destructive rage of the "wretched of the earth."

In the same manner, it was among the ranks of the intelligentsia (both the word and the phenomenon are in fact creations of Russian nineteenth-century culture) that the "populists" of the 1860s to 1880s developed a kind of domestic Third Worldism. Russia, they preached, would leap right over the capitalistic and democratic phase and immediately achieve a state of direct government exercised by the socialist peasantry. These ideas, too, served as an alibi for terrorism, which does not always choose well (or perhaps chooses all too well?) its targets—the most spectacular victim being Tsar Alexander II, who was assassinated in 1881 even though it was he who had done away with serfdom.

Gradually the current of Russian thinking that regarded freedom and individual happiness, in actual, concrete terms, as the only valid criteria of progress was overwhelmed and defeated. Aleksandr Herzen—in opposition to Tolstoy—had predicted this historic orientation: "Socialism will develop in all its phases until it reaches its own extremes and absurdities. There will then burst forth from the titanic breast of the revolting minority a cry of denial. Once more a moral battle will be joined, in which socialism will occupy the place of today's conservatism and will be defeated by the coming revolution, as yet invisible to us."*

The intellectuals of Italy were not influenced by a direct knowledge of Italian society. Prompted instead by their lust for revolutionary messianism, they constructed a vision of society which served as an imaginary justification of this lust. Unfortunately, in particular cases they were not content to go into paroxysms in their tiny corners; they killed.

*Isaiah Berlin, *Russian Thinkers* (London: Hogarth Press, 1978), p. 98.

In a study devoted to "Intellectuals and Terrorism," Sergio Romano employed the phrase "revealed revolution" to designate the psychic makeup of intellectual terrorists. It is a curious mixture of Christianity and communism.* On the one hand, they await some future event that at one devastating stroke will metamorphose our world and ourselves; on the other hand, thanks to Marxism, they can present their desires as scientific truths. For example, when a major breakdown in electrical power in 1977 plunged New York into a massive blackout, Toni Negri saw in it the collapse of the "factory state," as he calls industrial society. Sergio Romano quite rightly stresses the mystical and ridiculously primitive character of this interpretation, which transforms a technical incident into a structural crisis, or else sees in it a historic break with the past, comparable to the storming of the Bastille or the Winter Palace. The philosophy of the intellectuals of terrorist revolution combines the visionary foolishness of the astrologer, the pedantry of the Marxist doctor of philosophy, and the automatic weapon of the Mafia killer.

We are here in the presence of an ideological alienation of a classic type: intellectuals rewriting facts according to their own ideas, not the reverse. Thus they betray the original mission of the intellectual, which is to understand reality; and then they yield to a parody of action, after going through a parody of comprehension. For in a democracy a terrorist bomb blast lacks the power to transform society. It is a symbolic act whose only practical mark is the blood spilled on the sidewalk—as though terrorists needed to reassure themselves, to be able to say that in killing a passerby on a street corner or by leaving a corpse in the trunk of a car, which will be the talk of the evening TV programs, they prove to themselves that their vision of the world is not entirely a dream. But in a democracy this corpse is but the absurd symbol of their impotence and revolutionary delirium; it does not and cannot have any influence on the course of history.

A less bloody aspect of the behavior of terrorist intellectuals is what I will call "pedagogic usurpation." I have already cited cases of intellectual abuse in the exploitation of one's scientific, literary, or academic prestige, the intimidation of the general public by one's reputation, titles, and awards. This amalgam is common to terrorists and to many intellectuals, who fortunately do not employ terror, at least not physical terror. In Italy this takes the form of revolutionary "collectives" orga-

*Published in *Commentaire,* spring 1980, No. 9.

nized by university professors who transform their lecture courses into what Sabino Acquaviva has termed "word factories"—"those words that are ceaselessly redefined and which progressively purge the social world of the individuals concerned," as Augustin Cochin wrote in *L'Esprit du jacobinisme*. Then, "banishing the dissidents, they impose a distinction between a truth held by society at large, which reposes on facts, and a truth pertaining to the social group that must guide the revolutionary struggle."*

The decisive factor here in the diffusion of ideas comes from the aura superimposed on the intellectual message thanks to the prestigious charisma emanating from the "master" who expresses it. This type of superposition is to be found almost everywhere under other forms and with other materials, wherever we encounter forms of communication that rely on emotional rather than intellectual means.

I don't know if one should regard the clergy as being composed of intellectuals. Certainly, many of its members are. But their intellectual value, strictly judged, is greatly enhanced by their spiritual ascendancy and position inside an established religion. Their prestige and authority are thus invested with a double degree of superiority: that enjoyed by the terrestrial intellectual over other human beings, and that of the supraterrestrial intellectual over terrestrial intellectuals. But is the priest-intellectual—be he bishop, cardinal, or pope—really supraterrestrial even for believers? When he makes statements about economic, political, social, or strategic problems, is his "enlightenment" divinely inspired? Even the most fervent Christian knows, or should know, that this is false. Neither the Old nor the New Testament, nor the Fathers of the Church, nor the various councils have ever taught that the assumption of sacerdotal functions imbues all those who have been ordained as priests with omniscience. Even the doctrine of papal infallibility (which, as the name shows, is limited to the pope) concerns only questions of dogma, those that affect the very foundations of faith. When "liberation theologians" or U.S. bishops in a pastoral letter, or the pope himself in an encyclical, make declarations on economic or strategic issues, the value of their opinions depends on exactly the same factors that confer value on the opinions of anyone else: on their knowledge of the subject, their competence, their sureness of judgment, their capacity for reasoning intelligently, their intellectual honesty. Their texts and declarations ought to be evaluated according to the same criteria that are applied to the writings and remarks of other human

*Sabino Acquaviva, *Guerriglia e guerra rivoluzionaria in Italia* (Milan: Rizzoli, 1978).

beings. Consequently, to invoke the authority of the Christian religion and to imprint a kind of divine stamp on considerations that possess neither more nor less value than that of the information, intelligence, and probity of their authors is a regrettable imposture. "Liberation theologians" in fact propose nothing more than the most elementary kind of Marxist gospel. As far as they are concerned, the suppression of capitalism is sufficient to bring about the end of underdevelopment. If it is objected that all Third World countries in which capitalism has been suppressed have sunk even lower, into a still deeper abyss of poverty, whereas the only Third World countries that have been able to take off economically have been capitalist, they make no reply. They don't wish to know it.

I can vouch for this on the basis of personal experience, for I have spoken with a number of them. As Swift once wrote: "You cannot reason a person out of something he has not been reasoned into." As individuals and citizens, liberation theologians can adhere as much as they please to the economic opinions of their choice, even if they are founded on an abysmal ignorance of the most elementary facts and on a stubborn refusal to inform themselves about present-day realities. In this, alas, they are merely following patterns of behavior that are habitual with the rest of us poor mortals. But intellectual poverty becomes a moral swindle when they claim that their political opinions are *deduced* from Christian theology. I would like to be shown how. None of them has ever demonstrated the unbroken link between the principles of Christianity and the wretched Marxist clichés that provide them with a second gospel. The Church, they say, must side with the poor. Fine. This is not very original, and I don't know of anybody, whether Christian or not, who pleads for an aggravation of poverty. If liberation theology had something new and definite to offer, it should be able to show us an original remedy. But theirs is merely a borrowed remedy, copied from the shopworn clichés of the past and still mouthed by ideological "healers" who have gone bankrupt in all the countries they have preyed on. I am not, I repeat, contesting their right to adhere to this ideology if it suits them; I am reproaching them for deceiving millions of poor folk and sincere believers by raising the Christian flag over spoiled goods.

Why? Doubtless because the influence of Catholicism, considered strictly as a religion, has been regressing. Liberation theologians prefer a Marxist orthodoxy to no orthodoxy at all. The principal target of their hatred is liberal society, which is uncontrollable because of its billions of individual variations. That kind of society, they know, they will never be able to take over and unify. On the other hand, collectivist society, having already been streamlined and unified by Marxism, can, they think, one day fall into their hands, simply by changing the mold. Theirs is consequently not a struggle against poverty. They do not protest the existence of poverty in Ethiopia, Cuba, Mozambique, or Nicaragua, for those are "good" poverties. They have already covered themselves with as much ridicule for having, in the 1980s, chosen the Sandinistas as their preferred political model as did the intellectuals who flattered Fidel Castro with such abject obsequiousness during the 1960s.

The theologian Joseph Comblin, author of *La Teología de la revolución* (1974) and of *Teología de la práctica revolucionaria* (1974), wrote in the latter: "If liberation is thought of as a process of emancipation with respect to the imperial domination of developed nations, it can be conceived only within the framework of a worldwide revolution. The change must necessarily be universal. In this sense the liberation of Latin America is one of the aspects of the worldwide revolution of contemporary society, a unitary society embracing all nations." It would be difficult to plagiarize in a more servile fashion the letter and the spirit of Leninist texts. It is also worth noting that Comblin indulges in geopolitical, economic, and historicofuturological considerations which ought to be tested on their own grounds for each Latin American country and not be presented, as they are here, without the slightest technical proof, according to a tutelary magic, which is as miraculous and abusive as his "theology."

Liberation theologians like to argue that the confrontation between East and West leaves them indifferent, that they are concerned with down-to-earth problems, that they are not at all out to promote communism, any more than they are to praise communist states, even indirectly. Nothing could be more false. Whereas nobody can ever get them to utter a good word about the slightest social successes of liberal societies, their tongues are miraculously unloosed when it is a question of repeating the standard falsehoods that abound about and within communist countries. In August 1987 Father Leonardo Boff, one of the "stars" of liberation theology, paid a visit to the Soviet Union. When he returned to Brazil, his homeland, after a two-week trip, he held a press conference at which he declared, among other things: "Socialism guarantees better conditions for a true Christian existence than the social order of the West" and added that "prejudices and calumnies" concerning the conditions of Christians in the Soviet Union abound in the West. If, he went on, "socialism grants better conditions to authentic Christians," it is because Soviet society, according to Boff, "is founded not on exploitation, individualism, and consumerism, but on work and the fair dividing-up of profits."*

According to an often-heard platitude, the Catholic Church is supposed suddenly to have realized, after sixteen hundred and a few-odd years, that it has always been in the camp of the strong and that it was high time that it conform to its evangelical mission and pass over into the camp of the weak. It therefore crossed over into the anticapitalist camp. But it would be an error to believe that the Church did so out of a sudden love for weakness. If it has embraced the socialist interpretation of the world, it is because it fancies—I hope wrongly—that the communist camp is that of the future victors, particularly in the Third World. It thus remains faithful to its ancient tradition: to be on the side of the strong.

I do not blame it. I wish simply to draw attention to the fact that, in this piece of intellectual sleight of hand, the confusion between knowledge and faith constitutes one of the finest examples of the triumph of ignorance that is so typical of our times.

Even more than a case of confusion between knowledge and faith, this is a case of faith placed at the service of ignorance, which it serves to guarantee. For example, in 1984 the Catholic bishops of the United States published a "project for a pastoral letter" on the U.S. economy and the relations between the Third World and developed countries. Here they asserted, among other things, that poverty had not ceased to grow in the United States over the past twenty years—something that is quite simply belied by a mass of easily accessible statistics. Next they asserted that the Third World had grown steadily poorer, while the industrialized world was growing richer. This proposition is, to begin with, false, but in addition it contradicts the first. For if the rich world has steadily grown richer, poverty in the United States could not at the same time have increased. There really is a limit to incoherence. The practical solutions then proposed by the bishops were borrowed from the old arsenal of social democracy and the all-providing welfare state. Their amateurishness shone forth in every line. As Robert Samuelson commented ironically in a *Newsweek* (December 3, 1984) article devoted

*Quotations from an article published in the *Neue Zürcher Zeitung,* August 14, 1987. The Swiss daily reported that the Brazilian media had given a big play to Boff's declarations. This elicited the following comment from the French monthly *Est et Ouest:* (September 1987): "It is high time we asked ourselves why the other Western media, in particular the European, said nothing (so far as we know) about these statements. When Boff appears as a victim of Vatican 'oppression,' he deserves a blaze of publicity. But when the same Boff comes out in praise of the Soviet Union and thus gives the game away by revealing this capital aspect of liberation theology, he is ignored."

to the flashes of genius emitted by the above-mentioned prelates: "The bishops who drafted the recent pastoral letter on the American economy could usefully spend a few weeks touring Europe. They might learn there what they obviously did not learn here: social conscience is not enough; it won't produce economic justice. The principles the bishops admire most are enshrined in Europe and, partially as a result, Europe's economy is mired in massive unemployment."

If the bishops want to deal with economic problems, they should acquire a competence in *economics,* obtain serious *economic* information, and observe the criteria that are used in providing *economic* proofs, instead of flaunting their dignity as bishops as a guarantee of scientific competence.

I will say as much about the pope in person, particularly regarding his encyclical of February 1988, *Sollicitudo rei socialis.* Needless to say, everyone knows that the encyclical was not personally written by the pope. It was the work of the pontifical Commission for Justice and Peace, presided over by Cardinal Etchegaray, a former archbishop of Marseille and author of a 1976 book, *Dieu à Marseille* (God in Marseille), which certainly helped make Marseille better known, if not God. The same author further deepened his meditations and in 1984 he gave us *J'avance comme un âne* ("I Advance Like a Donkey)—a title one might almost risk numbering among the revealed truths, since Cardinal Etchegaray, as is well known in the Vatican, was the principal inspirer of *Sollicitudo rei socialis.* What can one say about this wretched mumbo-jumbo devoted to economic and social problems and the relations between the Third World and wealthy countries—save that it could just as easily have been composed in 1948, that it is forty years out of date, that it betrays a flagrant ignorance of everything revealed by systematic research and economic experience between 1948 and 1988, and that it winds up its archaic and ignorant condemnation of capitalism by dismissing it along with socialism, as it was then the fashion to do ("a plague on both your houses")? The two systems are held to be incapable of transforming themselves and to be equally perverse. Both are "imperialistic." There is no hierarchical differentiation of values between the two. Nowhere is there the slightest mention of the fact that the liberal system in 1988 is not at all what it was in 1948, nor that it has by and large succeeded where the totalitarian system has no less globally failed. On the subject of underdevelopment, the encyclical is not even able to rise above the hackneyed cliché, so many times refuted, that "we are rich because they are poor." The two "ideological blocs" are paired as equivalent (how familiar we are with this misleading parallelism, as though the unfortunate liberal world were no more than a monolithic "bloc"!), and the two of them end up being equally maleficent "structures of sinfulness." What a scholarly formulation!

As A. M. Rosenthal wrote in *The New York Times* (March 15, 1988), Mikhail Gorbachev must surely have "grinned" at the rigorous parallelism established by the pope, or at last by his surrogate "thinker." What dismays us in all this is that here too the available knowledge was not heeded. The Vatican's Commission on Justice and Peace did not deem it necessary to undertake the elementary work of research and documentation needed for a serious study, it made no effort to keep abreast of current developments in this field, and it tarnished the prestige of the papacy in order to concoct a witches' brew of Third World and antidemocratic sorcery.

My complaint is not that Roger Etchegaray, speaking as an individual, should profess the belief that democratic capitalism is worse than, or with the indulgence of the commission perhaps merely equal to, totalitarian communism. Each human being has the right to take sides as he chooses. Nor am I complaining because he knows nothing about economics. No one is obliged to learn its rudiments, provided he leaves the subject alone. What is inadmissible is that he should use his spiritual prestige—in this case that of the Catholic religion and the Vatican—to dispense gross errors to millions of defenseless souls. When members of the clergy resort to such abuses of prestige—much as one speaks of abuses of confidence—they behave like intellectuals, this being a favorite *modus operandi* with intellectuals. Only too often they seem to be saying to the public: Don't adhere to an idea because you've understood it and find it correct; approve it because I am intelligent, because I have adopted it, and you should follow me because I am famous! Celebrity should not be a safe-conduct pass for banality or error.

Let me cite another example of this penchant. On December 27, 1987, the Sunday newspaper *Journal du Dimanche* published an interview that had been granted to it by Cardinal Decourtray, archbishop of Lyon, chairman of the French Episcopal Conference and Primate of the Gauls. In this interview the cardinal smothered his readers beneath an avalanche of platitudes about the French election campaign, which no one would have been masochistic enough to read if their author had not been an archbishop. "The level of debate is sordid, there is too much talk of scandals . . ." he opined, unburdening himself of similarly profound thoughts of the kind we endure with weary patience coming from a garrulous traveler when the journey has been long and the train is late, thoughts which, it seems to me, could have prospered on their own without having to receive the transfiguring seal of the cardinal's purple. Since it is nowhere written in the Bible that God dispenses powers of revelation to bishops in order to judge current politics, the opinions of Albert Decourtray are the opinions of Albert Decourtray, nothing more. To confer on them a bogus authority simply because the person expressing them holds a high office in the Church in effect degrades the public, instead of elevating it by appealing to its freedom of choice.

Promoting "prestigious" opinions in this way is a practice resorted to frequently. Thus, at the invitation of the president of the French Republic, seventy-five Nobel Prize winners assembled in Paris from January 18 to 22, 1988, in order to reflect on the "threats and promises [confronting us] at the dawn of the twenty-first century." On January 22 the fruits of their deliberations were solemnly divulged in the form of sixteen conclusions. The most indulgent comment one can make about this conference is that, if it had assembled seventy-five *concierges* (janitors) or barbers or café waiters, the results would probably have been more original.

I have the highest esteem for the three aforementioned professions; this is why I say that with them the results would have been *more* original, for no member of those amiable trades would have agreed to endorse the web of platitudes and errors the Nobel Prize winners inflicted upon us. This cultural fiasco reminds us of a truth of which history has offered many demonstrations: that intellectual powers, even genius, are not automatically transferable outside their bearers' sphere of competence.

Clearly, the Paris conference was above all meant to be a propaganda operation for President Mitterrand. As a French taxpayer I am happy to have contributed modestly to the travel and hotel expenses of those eminent persons, who so badly needed distraction. I should add that among Mitterrand's guests—which is to say, guests of French taxpayers, become hosts *malgré eux*—were many Nobel Prize winners for Literature or Peace. These were gentlemen of admirable talents and merits, no doubt, but ones whose futurological vaticinations have rarely been regarded by the public as mathematical truths—something that helps limit the damage. However, also present at the Elysée Palace was a strong contingent of scientific Nobel Prize winners.

Now, what were we offered in the "Sixteen Conclusions" of this august assembly? First of all, that "all forms of life should be considered as an essential patrimony of mankind" and that we should therefore protect the environment. Magnificent! Farther on, that "the human species is one, and each individual composing it has the same rights." We seem to have read this somewhere before, enunciated two centuries ago. Farther on still: "The richness of mankind is also in its diversity." The sheer boldness and novelty of these aphorisms is positively breathtaking. But this is nothing compared to what follows. We tremble with gratitude in measuring the cerebral force, the imaginative creativity needed to discover that "the most important problems confronting mankind today are at once universal and interdependent." With instructions like that in hand, we can confidently await the "dawn of the twenty-first century."

All the more so since, farther on in the document, the Nobel Prize winners were so fearless and ingenious as to dare assert that "education should become an absolute priority . . . particularly in underdeveloped countries"; or again, that "nutrition and birth control are essential instruments for a demographic policy." And imagine the stunned awe with which we learn that "molecular biology permits one to hope for progress in medicine." The minds of our scientific pioneers teem with novel notions, as for example this one: "Television and media constitute essential means of education." However, being shrewd and circumspect, they hastened to add that "education should help to develop the critical spirit, over and against what the media diffuse." To think that this had never occurred to anyone before! Our great men then offered the charmed public proposals as unexpected as one to reduce armaments expenditures in order to use the money thus budgeted for other purposes, or one to convene an international conference to examine the problem of Third World indebtedness. But since they didn't unveil any practical suggestions as to how to resolve this latter problem, to which innumerable conferences have already been devoted, there is every reason to fear that this pious wish will remain a mere project. Disarmament, too, is a hackneyed cliché that has haunted newspaper offices and chancelleries since 1919; but until we are told just how the political, strategic, nationalistic, economic, and ideological obstacles opposing it can be removed, nothing new or useful will have been said on the subject.

Today no conference worthy of the name can be held without emitting an opinion on the subject of AIDS. This one, too, proved no exception. And what was enunciated on this subject illustrates all too well, alas, the deplorable drift that can be exemplified by a genuine scientist when, in the name and under the cover of science, he is led to emit nonscientific opinions dictated by political or other prejudices.

Proving that ideology is stronger than science, even in a scientist, the British biologist John Vane, who won the Nobel Prize for medicine in 1982, launched a diatribe against pharmaceutical laboratories, which, he said, were guilty of not yet having found a vaccine against AIDS because they were solely motivated by their "search for profits." At the moment he was making this remark, it was well known that the very nature of the HIV virus had been holding up the discovery of a preventive anti-AIDS vaccine. The main obstacles were certainly not of an economic order. As for profits, if Professor Vane had taken the trouble to study history a bit—that is, *if he could preserve a scientific attitude when leaving his specialized field*—he would have had little trouble realizing that all the pharmaceutical discoveries that have transformed medicine in our century have been made in five or six capitalist countries. They were achieved in private laboratories which, taken together, spend far more money on basic research than do states or even independent organisms such as the Pasteur Institute, which is financed in large part by profits accruing from the sale of vaccines. On the other hand, not a single specialized pharmaceutical product has been discovered in the Soviet Union over the last seventy years, even though it was a purposively profitless society. All Soviet medicines are copies of Western pharmaceutical products, and it is common knowledge that the doctors who take care of Soviet leaders import their medicines and instruments from the West. Thus the Nobel Prize winners gathered in Paris could escape from banalities only by lapsing into falsification.

From their august cogitations not a single concrete application can be drawn. Once they unburdened themselves of their vapid generalizations, they had nothing further to suggest. No, I am being unfair. They did formulate one thing that was perfectly concrete—the only one, and for them of an inestimable value. This was their sixteenth and ultimate Conclusion: "The Conference of Nobel Prize winners will meet again in two years to study these problems."

Similarly, one may wonder what purpose is served by the science of sociology when one considers the stupefaction with which the French, on the evening of the preliminary presidential campaign vote on April 24, 1988, discovered that close to 15 percent of the citizens had voted for Jean-Marie Le Pen, the extreme right-wing candidate of the National Front. Their surprise was due to the fact that since the onset, in the early 1980s, of an economic crisis rendering the position of immigrants precarious in view of the rise of unemployment, false methods of interpretation had been applied to the understanding of the growth of Le-Penism. The mistake made by virtually all French politicians was not to have realized the specific nature of the Le Pen phenomenon, an error all the harder to forgive since it was in part deliberate. The Left was interested only in using the rise of Le Pen's National Front as a weapon for leveling accusations against the classic Right, without realizing this could be a two-edged blade.

To compare the National Front to the prewar fascisms of the 1930s is, as I have pointed out, a piece of historical foolishness. The National Front's electorate has no general ideological motivation. It was formed in poor urban quarters as a result of the usual frictions with large concentrations of immigrants. The proof that the National Front has no solid consistency can be found in the fact that in the elections of June 5, 1988, its percentage of the vote fell by 10 percent. A party that loses two million votes in six weeks is not a serious party. Its concertinalike electorate switches camps with each new election. In fact, one and a half million NF voters switched to Mitterrand during the second and final runoff of the presidential election on May 8.

Instead of coldly and efficiently analyzing the problem in its sociological, economic, educational, and security contexts, the Left did everything it could to turn it into a political football—until the moment came when it perceived, to its dismay, that entire urban quarters that normally voted communist or socialist were switching over to Le Pen. More than 18 percent of those who voted for Le Pen in the European elections of 1984 were workers; in the legislative elections of 1986 they made up 26 percent; and they made up 37 to 40 percent in the first round of the presidential election of 1988. More than a quarter of Le Pen's electorate changed sides to the socialist candidate during the second round, assuring Mitterrand's election and not that of the liberal candidate, Jacques Chirac.

The Right, for its part, had let itself be trapped in the snare created by the intellectual terrorism of the Left. It was afraid to grapple with the fundamental problems—above all, material, practical, and psychological—caused by immigration for fear of being accused of racism. Simply declaring that such a problem existed was enough to have the infamous accusation flung in one's face. As a result, the problems were not dealt with, and an abstract ideological campaign was waged against Le Pen, who was thus able to strengthen his position, since the ideological debate was way over the heads of the suburban dwellers most immediately concerned. Interested only in exploiting tensions and mis-

understandings in order to indulge in demagogy, the Left in fact opened
the gates to demagogy—but one practiced by someone else.

Not a single courageous voice spoke up—I mean without immediately
being silenced by insults—to wrest the problem away from its false
ideological context. The left-wingers were interested solely in destabliz-
ing the Right, rather than in destabilizing Le Pen. The classic Right,
torn between its desire to retrieve lost votes and its fear of contracting
an unholy alliance, simply reacted passively.

Of what utility, then, in one of the most cultivated countries of the
world, had been the accumulated work of hundreds of sociologists on
problems posed by the concentration of various ethnic groups in certain
urban areas, by overcrowded apartment blocks, by poorly adapted
schooling, a higher-than-average unemployment rate, conditions of life
favoring delinquency, and violent gangs of idle and often drug-consum-
ing youths? Had our intellectual and political leaders derived the slightest benefit from the thousands of studies that were published in the
United States during the 1960s on such subjects and which in many cases
dealt with identical problems? Had they even seen *West Side Story*? But
how could French sociologists who were watching the upheavals caused
by a high level of immigration report their findings and analyses impartially and recommend measures to be taken, without being called racists
and accomplices of Le Pen? For purposes of political propaganda the
Left absolutely had to describe the Le Pen phenomenon as a repetition
of the "rise of Fascism" of the 1930s, in order to create the illusion that
France was like Germany on the eve of Hitler's assumption of power.
Given the intellectual climate of French university life, any scientist
daring to denounce the inaccuracy of this comparison would have been
morally lynched, ostracized, and ignominiously booted out of the sacred
progressive family into the fascist cesspool. I have heard so many research scholars say things in private about such poisoned topics, private
opinions which differed radically from their published writings, that the
only conclusion I can draw is that the instinct of self-preservation is
more developed in scientists than the love of science is.

This example graphically illustrates one of the most frequent forms
of the "defeat of thought"—which is to say, the taboo that keeps one
from linking a social phenomenon to its true cause. Just as in earlier
times, during periods of plague or drought, the disaster was attributed
to some sin rather than to natural causes, so today the social scourge
is isolated from its historical antecedents and a phony origin is fabricated that is compatible with the ideology one is interested in impos-

ing. The difference is that the "intellectuals" of yore did not know and did not have the means to determine the real causes of an epidemic, whereas we can far more easily trace the authentic genesis of a social reality. In our case, therefore, the obstacle to knowledge is erected by a mental block or interdict; it is lodged in ourselves far more than in the objective difficulties posed by the problem to be solved.

I have more than once had occasion to point out the inversion of causal sequences which, in the case of civil wars, move people to mistake the effect for the cause—as, for example, in Mozambique, where the rebellion of the RENAMO movement, rather than a governmental policy that engendered both famine and revolt, was made responsible for famine. The reign of terror unleashed by RENAMO (the National Mozambican Resistance movement), its massacres, rapes, plunderings, and destructions, can only inspire horror. But this feeling should not keep us from asking why, despite the military aid furnished to the communist government of Maputo by the USSR, the German Democratic Republic, and several democracies (Great Britain, France, the United States), RENAMO was able to become so powerful. Content with the explanation that it is all due to South African aid, observers rarely raise the question, particularly in the terms so clearly and soberly used by James Brooke of *The New York Times*. Here, after fully and objectively describing RENAMO's atrocities, is his assessment, with my comments in brackets:

At independence, about 90% of the colony's 250,000 Portuguese settlers left, many to neighboring South Africa. The new leaders made virtually no effort to win back this bitter exile group. [I should remind the reader that most of these whites had been born in Mozambique of parents and grandparents who had lived there for several generations.]

When independence came, 93 percent of Mozambique's African population was illiterate. The departure of the Portuguese led to economic collapse. Into the vacuum stepped FRELIMO, a guerrilla group with a vision of a Marxist Mozambique that one day would become the first African member of Comecon, the Soviet-dominated, East-bloc economic union.

Portuguese-speaking FRELIMO operatives, who generally had a better command of Marxism than of local tribal languages [in other words, local intellectuals], brought revolution to a conservative countryside.

Churches were closed and traditional leaders dismissed. Abandoned plantations were turned into East European–style state farms [an idea that could have occurred only to intellectuals]. Hundreds of thousands of peasants were herded from ancestral lands into 1,400 communal villages. [The same methods had been used in Ethiopia and Tanzania, the Western press displaying the same lack of curiosity at the time this was happening; this represents a second intervention on the part of intellectuals, who are responsible for such noninformation, not to mention an absence of compassion manifested when the tormentors are good "leftists."]

Dissenters were sent to detention camps euphemistically termed 'reeducation centers,' [exactly the same methods as those applied in the USSR, Vietnam, Cuba, and other communist countries, where the intellectuals in power naturally accord a great importance to education] where beatings and starvation were frequent. Renamo rebels, preying upon disenchantment with the government, raided them for recruits. [*International Herald Tribune,* May 12, 1988.]

I have interjected these parenthetical comments into Brooke's soberly factual explanation of events to stress the point that when people set out to change a society overnight by force, and in deliberate ignorance of what that society really is, they are displaying a mind-set in which intelligence is completely subordinated to an omnipotent ideology. No matter what the doctrine may be, it is therefore by definition an intellectual *modus operandi.* One and a half years after independence, *Le Monde* published a series of articles about FRELIMO, the first of which was entitled "Creating a New Man" (August 10, 1976). Once again, this murderous *idée fixe* of all socialist utopias. The third article was entitled "An Economy in Difficulty" (August 12). The initiatives of the Marxists had thus already failed before RENAMO appeared on the scene.

Now, when their program fails, do they draw the logical conclusions from the setback? Not at all. The leaders of communist Poland during the first ten years of its existence, almost all of them intellectuals, gave us one of the most appalling examples of this pigheadedness—in a book entitled *Oni* ("They"), which I earlier had occasion to mention when comparing the stubborn impenitence of Polish communists in the committing of horrors with that of Darquier.*

In this case "they" are the leaders who communized Poland from 1945 to 1956, the year of the first popular revolt against the regime. "They" created this communist Poland—or rather they made themselves the instruments of a creation whose real author was Stalin. Docile instruments, most of them leaders of the Polish Communist Party (or what was left of it, for in 1938 Stalin had ordered most of the senior Polish communists who had taken refuge in the Soviet Union to be shot) arrived from Moscow, where they had spent their decisive years. Some of them had even taken Soviet citizenship. During the eighteen tumultu-

Them, by Teresa Toranska (New York: Harper & Row, 1987).

ous months that separated the fall of Edward Gierek, in the summer of 1980, from the imposition of martial law by General Jaruzelski in December 1981, a talented young Polish journalist named Teresa Toranska had the ingenious idea of going to interrogate them in their various places of retirement and managed to get them to talk with astounding frankness. Was this due to the corrosive effect of the general feeling of euphoria engendered by a new atmosphere of freedom? Whatever the cause, these old Stalinist diehards proceeded to unravel the secrets of their past careers without restraint—though probably not without some lying—thus providing a mine of information which future historians will be able to exploit for decades to come. But the great lesson of this book far exceeds the circumstances that inspired it. It has to do with human nature and its relationship to truth, evil, and itself. Can it be that our intelligence is nothing more than a machine for justifying our errors and our crimes, without regard for our fellow human beings? Is it perchance a prison into which no light penetrates because we ourselves stop up all the apertures? From these astonishing discourses, during which stubborn octogenarians proudly quibbled over their bloody work of enslavement and impoverishment, there radiates the mystery of primordial falsehood, perhaps Man's very center.

Those who spoke had, in fact, carried out the sovietization of Poland. They had inflicted terror and the classic gamut of proscriptions, extortions, executions, and deportations on their people, only to end up with a pitiful record of economic and human failure, having made themselves so monstrously unpopular that it had provoked the revolt of 1956, which swept them from power.

Yet, try as she might, the interviewer could not get them to say that they had been mistaken! Communism seems to be something that failure never refutes, which the hatred of the people never demoralizes. Marxism-Leninism, we should remember, for communists themselves never cease to repeat it, is founded on the primacy of praxis—that is, the exactitude of the theory is judged by the test of facts, not of ratiocinations. But "they" spend their time eluding the facts by resorting to devious arguments and abstract justifications. With extraordinary cowardice they denied all responsibility for the acts they had committed. All Toranska was able to extract from them was a vague "Yes, errors were made." After which they immediately added that the errors were "recognized" and even "corrected"—usually by the sacrifice of one or several scapegoats who were condemned to death or to a hard-labor camp on trumped-up charges of sabotage or spying.

Is our responsibility abolished when our harmful behavior stems from a sincere conviction? To be sure, an individual becomes a fanatic almost unwittingly, but that is no excuse. Each of us should realize that one possesses within oneself the formidable capacity to construct an explanatory system of the world and along with it a machine for rejecting all facts contrary to this system.

In the autobiography of his younger days, Pierre Daix, the former editor of the communist daily *Ce Soir,* tells how one day in 1953, when he was visiting Moscow, he came upon a column of prisoners whom guards were leading to a worksite. So indoctrinated was he at the time that he could not and did not want to see that this was the distinctive feature of a totalitarian system. "I was persuaded that they were common criminals or Nazi prisoners-of-war. I would have needed someone to put me on the right track, in order to understand that these prisoners were being marched through the streets of Moscow, like our own concentration camp prisoners, who were paraded through the center of the town of Mauthausen for purposes of common dissuasion."* To which he added this judicious observation: "Terror, when it is truly generalized and daily, is not easy to detect." Whence no doubt the blindness of Jean-Paul Sartre, who around the same time could write during a journalistic foray into the Soviet Union: "Freedom of criticism in the USSR is total."

How are certainties formed and how are they undone? Why is the intelligent and courageous individual not more immunized against sectarianism and "happiness in submission" than the cowardly and narrowminded one? How does one free oneself from fanaticism?

Rare are those persons who, in curing themselves of their ideological obsessions, have really deeply probed the intellectual motivations that gave rise to them, first in order to free themselves truly and completely, then in order to explain them without trying to excuse them, and finally in order to recover complete freedom of thought. Pierre Daix is one of them—like Arthur Koestler, who, in his autobiography, describes with exceptional thoroughness the gradual acceptance of a totalitarian interpretation of the world and the logic that enables it to sink into the mind and to induce massive blindness.† Thus Koestler, while traveling through the Ukraine in 1933, was simply unable to realize that its people were suffering from massive starvation. He *saw* people who were visibly famished, but he was unable to *construct the concept* of a famine based

*Mauthausen, located near Passau in Austria, was a concentration camp to which the Nazis sent many French men and women, particularly those who had been active in the Resistance.

†Arthur Koestler, *Arrow in the Blue* and *The Invisible Writing.*

on these particular perceptions. Emmanuel Le Roy Ladurie, in *Paris-Montpellier,* and Alain Besançon, in *Une génération,* have also managed to describe with detachment the edification and dislocation of such psychic conditioning.* Usually, however, those who have "been through the mill" emerge only half cured, and they harbor a greater feeling of resentment against those who refrained from sharing their errors than against those who led them astray.

"If you were not mistaken, like them, then you have no right to be heard!" Indro Montanelli one day reminded me during a demonstration staged in Paris in December 1981 against General Jaruzelski's proclamation of martial law in Poland. "You have no right to be here! Go away!" shouted the socialists at liberals who were taking part in the demonstration. In their warped view of the world only those who had previously supported the authors of Poland's enslavement now had the right to protest against it, whereas those who had never been their accomplices were automatically disqualified. Those who have had a monopoly of error thus reserve to themselves a monopoly in the rectification of error. Furthermore, they present this not so much as a rectification as an "evolution," as a taking into account of new elements in order to "save what is essential." In other words, they have "refined" and modified their theory thanks to ceaseless creative reflections. However, at the time they made their false analysis, it was nevertheless the best possible one for the moment. Such being the case, the mere existence of persons who during the now incriminated period combated their positions is a disagreeable reminder that their own aberrations were by no means inevitable and were due more to their own intellectual makeup than to external circumstances. They must therefore crush these people with even greater firmness than their former companions. Former Maoists and the former champions of the "liberating progressiveness" of the Iranian revolution want to reason as though all mankind had previously endorsed their blunders. Pioneers they were in the process of hallucination, pioneers they are determined to remain in the bitter process of awakening. The paragon of singleminded pluralism, that is, of pluralism without the others, always reverts to his natural bent. "To recognize my errors, yes!" he cries. "But for me, recognizing my errors means guillotining both those who agreed with me yesterday, since they were mistaken, and those who yesterday were saying what I am saying today, since they were expressing their opinions from a reactionary point of

*Emmanuel Le Roy Ladurie, *Paris-Montpellier* (Paris: Gallimard, 1982); Alain Besançon, *Une génération* (Paris: Julliard, 1987).

view, which I must not allow to be confused with the leftist logic that inspired my conversion."

The need to believe things that are implausible—and what, more than the implausible, satisfies the need to believe?—engenders in fellow travelers an intolerance toward nonbelievers that is more ferocious and a rancor which is more tenacious than those displayed by militants—as though Man finds it more difficult to shed a half belief than a whole belief. U.S. "liberals" and European "progressives" are less magnanimous in forgiving others for their own errors than dedicated communists are. In the process of self-criticism their semiblindness gives way only to a kind of semilucidity and semisincerity. In his *Voyageur dans le siècle* Bertrand de Jouvenel did not succeed in looking himself in the face and explaining his hesitant and passing adherence to extreme right-wing ideologies during the late 1930s.* He sounds astonished, writhes and wrings his hands, but finally gives up trying to diagnose this intellectual waywardness, which, in a person of such intelligence, must have had a genesis it would have been instructive to reconstitute. Particularly since Jouvenel, from 1945 on, had driven such recollections from his conversation, if not from his mind. Admittedly, from that date on nobody could expect absolution for having "strayed to the Right" either before or after the moment of conversion. On the other hand, to have flirted with the totalitarian Left afforded and still affords one the right to the most flattering compensations, as much for the period of wandering as for having put an end to it.

———————————— ✕ ————————————

Everything thus boils down to the erroneous way in which the elusive problem of the "function of the intellectual in civil society" is usually posed. How can the intellectual be the rudder of society if he proves himself incapable of playing this role in his own thinking? The function of the intellectual in public life cannot be properly filled if the intellectual doesn't begin by assuming the role of the intellectual in intellectual life. How can he be a teacher of honesty, rigor, and courage for the whole of society when he is dishonest, inexact, and cowardly in the very exercise of intelligence?

Max Weber once established a famous distinction (one that is not as limpid as it sounds) between the ethics of conviction, that of the pure intellectual (*Gesinnungsethik*), and the ethics of responsibility (*Verantwortungsethik*), that of the man of action. The first obeys only his own

*Voyageur dans le siècle (Paris: Laffont, 1979).

principles and truth; the second, under the pressure of a real environment and a desired result, must compromise with both reality and his own convictions. In practice this distinction applies to few concrete cases, for most intellectuals (and this from time immemorial) participate in action, either directly or through the influence they wield, and are thus compelled to effect a compromise between their convictions and the imperatives of a particular situation—just like men of action, who, fortunately, are not all of them total opportunists. But the root question, above all, is to know if an ethics of pure conviction exists, that is, if a human being can conform to total honesty even when engaged only in debating ideas, with no relevance to immediate practice. I think he can, but only to such a statistically negligible and marginal degree that it will exercise no influence on human events, at least in the short run. On the other hand, in a larger sense we have frequently seen how the intellectual generally declines all responsibility for the practical consequences of his affirmations, just as he likes as much as possible to dispense with the obligation of providing proofs in the elaboration of his convictions. Thus among intellectuals the ethics of conviction and the ethics of responsibility can often be reconciled in the ethics of irresponsible conviction.

This irresponsibility is first affirmed in the strictly intellectual phase of the elaboration of a conviction, then by a refusal to face the consequences, as much scientific as moral, of the errors committed. When in 1968 Paul Ehrlich, who then headed the Biology Department at Stanford University, published *The Population Bomb,* which was crammed with apocalyptic exaggerations based on unsubstantiated demographic forecasts, he was not displaying any more intellectual responsibility than the moral responsibility he displayed, twenty years later, in not bothering to provide any explanation for his past errors and their ideological motivations. He simply shifted to another subject—to, as we have seen, strategy and space defense, in which he displayed the same talents.*

After having manhandled linguistics for twenty-five years by using it simply as an ornament for its fantasies, French philosophy today has quietly written everything off in order to "square up the books." Its representatives feel no obligation to regret this mystification, to analyze its origins, its causes, its development, and the intellectual damage it

*A French translation of Ehrlich's book, entitled *La Bombe P,* was published by Fayard in 1972. The book was raked over the coals for lack of serious corroborating evidence by Jean-Claude Chesnais in *La Revanche du tiers monde* (Paris: Laffont, 1987). Equally worth consulting is Chesnais's *La Transition démographique* (Paris: Presses Universitaires de France, 1986).

inflicted. When in 1988 Thomas Pavel brought out *Le Mirage linguis-tique,* a book of destructive serenity, the literary and philosophical fortnightly *La Quinzaine Littéraire,* which for a quarter century had been one of the fortresses defending the many errors denounced in Pavel's book, published an entirely laudatory review with disconcerting complacency, feeling no need to look back over its own past.* I wonder how the faithful subscribers to *La Quinzaine* can have reacted. Let us imagine for a moment a reader of the *Osservatore Romano* (the Vatican's official organ) opening his daily newspaper and finding inside an article written by a cardinal who, without making an issue of it, quietly declares that all the Gospels are apocryphal and were in fact concocted by Nero and Petronius during a night of wild drinking. The reader would natu-rally think that, all things considered, the Vatican owed him an explana-tion. There was nothing of the kind in *La Quinzaine.* Instead we were offered this, written by Vincent Descombes: "As for the balance sheet offered by *Le Mirage linguistique,* it is all the more crushing for being so measured and precise. It is not our intention here to take issue with anybody, or to demand a return to sure values. Rather, what is involved here is, in keeping with the duty of philosophers and scientists, to keep the *account book* of intellectual enterprises." It will be noted that, without making the slightest attempt to exonerate the imposters on the terrain of linguistics and philosophy, *La Quinzaine* maintains its claim to irresponsibility. "It is not our intention here to take issue with any-body . . ." (Why not? What justifies this immunity granted to those who, precisely because of their culture, deserve it the least?) Mr. Descombes continues: ". . . or to demand a return to sure values." (Which values? What exactly is involved? What is the meaning of this irony? Does there, yes or no, exist a science of linguistics which was led astray by the fashionable jugglery of the structuralists?) The right to make errors can be accepted only if it is accompanied by a respect for well-founded objections and sincerity in discussion.

This is a state of mind one all too rarely meets, in a cultural universe in which what predominates is more like an exterminating fury against contrary arguments—even on a terrain as distant from the great geo-strategic issues of our times as, for example, the history of art. In 1985, an important English art historian, T. J. Clark, who now teaches in the United States and who is all-powerful at Harvard, published a book entitled *The Painting of Modern Life: Paris in the Art of Manet and His*

*Pavel's *Le Mirage linguistique* was published by Éditions de Minuit. The laudatory review appeared in the May 1, 1988, issue of *La Quinzaine. Littéraire.*

Followers. In this book Clark maintained that the scandal caused by Manet's *Olympia* at the Salon of 1865 was not because the painter had accomplished an esthetic revolution that shocked the habitual perceptions of public and critics, but because he had painted a "proletarian nude" and because the hand of the young woman hiding her cunt in reality designated "penis envy" and "regret for the missing phallus," which Freud had described as being a stage in the evolution of the sexual psychology of little girls. I need hardly add that there is not a trace in the mass of written and illustrated material concerning Manet and his contemporaries of something that even remotely begins to sustain this ham-handed and woefully unsubtle interpretation, a hangover from the psychoanalytical clichés of the 1950s. I greatly admire Protagoras, but I don't approve when he says: "One does not think that which is not." Heavens! Does he want to reduce us to unemployment? To think of what does not exist is almost all we ever do. I am thus not opposed to false ideas, provided they are entertaining. But to blunder in the most oafish fashion, as Clark does, by striving to revive the nauseous doctrines of "socialist realism" which Stalin and his henchman, Andrei Zhdanov, were proclaiming in 1946 is quite different from being elegantly and wittily mistaken. We here encounter the strange predilection displayed by so many late-twentieth-century intellectuals in the United States for the reheated scraps of a ramshackle provincial Marxism, which today is an object of scornful laughter even in Ulan Bator.

As for the "loss of the phallus," I can vaguely remember hearing somebody arouse a spark of interest back in 1967 by alluding to this theory in a Saint-Tropez discothèque around three in the morning, although I can't swear that his audience was really following attentively, and in any case that was the last time I heard it. Professor Clark, of course, has every right to cling to this shopworn idea and even to feed off it, but he has no right to claim he has been doing the work of a historian, still less to heap gross insults on those of his colleagues who, being more serious than he, showed his thesis to be both primitive and mistaken. This is what Françoise Cachin proceeded to demonstrate in the May 30, 1985, issue of *The New York Review of Books.* Two years before, Françoise Cachin had helped to stage a major Manet exhibition, the most complete and meticulously organized since the painter's death a hundred years before and the likes of which we shall probably not see for another century. For this occasion she had overseen the preparation of a 550-page quarto catalogue, one of the handsomest monuments of erudition an exhibition of painting has ever brought forth.

What, then, was Clark's reply to the long, detailed article in which

Françoise Cachin refuted the thesis that Manet's painting constituted an indictment of capitalism and prostitution? First of all, Clark insulted Madame Cachin. This happens far more frequently than is generally supposed in the upper spheres of "thinking." He accused her of trying to "settle old scores" (another old saw used when one doesn't know what else to say) for reasons that had nothing to do with the subject at hand. "Cultural apparatchiks like Mrs. Cachin have a state machine set up for the purpose, which never stops vomiting retrospectives. The animus informing Mrs. Cachin's review was provoked in great measure, I believe, by my lack of enthusiasm for most of its products."*

The elegance of the formulation here is on a par with the loftiness of the sentiments expressed. None of this rubbish, of course, had anything to do with the basic issue. When finally Clark deigned to get around to the subject, in the second part of his rebuttal, he accused Madame Cachin of having falsified quotations from his book. The old trick of speaking of "truncated quotations" or quotations "taken out of context" can lead a desperate author to paradoxical inconsistencies. Thus quite shamelessly Clark sought to obscure the fact that he had ever written something about a hand signifying a phallus. In her reply to his rebuttal Madame Cachin was obliged to provide the complete quotations from Clark's own book! Intellectuals often deform quotations from their adversaries' writings, but generally those who are actually accused of such misdeeds are the rare souls whose quotations are exact! The social history of art requires a minimum of scruples in the supplying of proofs. And Clark's inanities were not born in the lower depths of militant imbecility; they echoed through the glorious temples of university thought.

Here too one cannot but admire the clear conscience with which intellectuals indulge massively in knavish tricks, one tenth of the volume of which they are not prepared to forgive in political or economic leaders. The exploits of which they are capable when caught in the act, in order to deny all responsibility, are on a par with the finest acrobatic stunts of veteran politicos. When I speak of behavior worthy of "politicos," I am resorting to a technical description; for the main problem for intellectuals, as for politicians (but even more frequently and with fewer excuses) when confronted by a problem, a difficulty, or an objection, is never to ascertain what is true or false, but to determine how it will affect

*The New York Review of Books, August 15, 1985.

the interests of the cause. In 1987, for example, there appeared *Heidegger et le Nazisme,* written by Victor Farias, a Chilean author whose book was nonetheless first published in French translation.* Whether by astute design or fortunate accident we were not told, but one thing is certain. For the past fifty years the groveling idolatry of French philosophers toward Heidegger and the author's shameless dissimulation of his Nazi sympathies constituted an ethical-conceptual mix of intellectual nitroglycerine ready to explode with a deafening roar at the first bump. Which is exactly what happened. The moment the book was published, we were treated to a display of fireworks—essays by the dozen, articles by the hundred, editorials, "open letters," special magazine issues, roundtable colloquies, and televised debates. The famine in Ethiopia was soft-pedaled, Gorbachev was momentarily deprived of advice and left to his own devices, the crushing of General Pinochet was adjourned, for the honor of the tribe that had been besmirched by the infamous Farias required the mobilized energy of all its sons. Pure logic, as usual, was extolled and fêted, as could be seen from the series of defensive arguments rolled out for the occasion: (1) What Farias asserts is false; (2) we already said so; (3) we had no knowledge of those horrors, but in Heidegger's case they constitute an individual misapprehension, which offers no proof against his philosophy; (4) in any case, it's not up to Farias to say so, it's up to us; (5) this is why we were keeping silent about this and effacing all traces of the evolution of Heidegger's thinking in the realm of politics.

Why did the French intellectual community consider itself so directly targeted, stung, and challenged by "revelations" which, it claimed, were anything but new, which were true and yet false, and which, in addition were of no importance? Why was a veto suddenly imposed on this Farias fellow, who overnight was transformed from someone totally unknown into an accredited whipping boy, an infamous henchman of ontological obscurantism, and denied the right to investigate Heidegger's Nazism?† As regards the last point, we are already familiar with the principle. Only those who have lied or have been mistaken enjoy the privilege of rectifying the error (without, however, admitting they were wrong). The others, those who didn't spout nonsense, are disqualified in advance and invited to hold their tongues in the name of good taste and propriety. But French philosophy had little cause to congratulate itself with regard

*Paris: Verdier, 1987.

†In his philosophical system Heidegger distinguishes ontology, the science of Being, from the "ontic"—which concerns "existants" on a level of "inauthentic existence."

to the Heideggerian trap and the sinister family secret—whence the fright induced by the publication of *Heidegger et le Nazisme,* the panic fear of bigoted old women discovering that the priest has been titillating little boys.

The German philosopher's Nazism has long been known. Each time it resurfaces, the philosophical tribe raises the same yelps. Why these repeated cycles? Because Heidegger's Nazism, which is not accidental but profoundly inherent in his doctrine, poses a direct challenge to philosophy itself. When, between 1935 and 1945, French philosophy, which was low in alcoholic content, needed to be laced, a strong dose of Heidegger was poured into it to give it more punch. No heed was paid to the label or the political soil of the brewer. Ever since then, French philosophy, though by and large leftist, has been living with this reactionary virus in its bloodstream—something that periodically produces unspeakable tremors.

For indeed, behind Heidegger's personal and militant commitment to Nazism there arises the problem of the links between his philosophy and this political commitment. Does the Nazism of Martin Heidegger the individual stem logically from his philosophy? Is this philosophy itself a sample of totalitarian thinking? Personally, I have always thought so, and this was what I wrote in 1957, in the third chapter of *Pourquoi les philosophes?** There I emphasized the archaic nature of Heidegger's thinking, his hatred of "technical folly," liberal civilization, of industrial and commercial society, the old-fashioned, mystical cult of the primitive rural community—all of them familiar themes of Nazism. I particularly stressed the totalitarianism inherent in Heidegger's discursive approach to problems and his method of exposition, with the accumulation of affirmations all repeating the same idea in five or six different ways, as well as his predilection for placing a "Therefore" at the start of the last sentence of a paragraph, when in fact there is no deductive chain of thought between earlier propositions and their supposed conclusion. This characteristic procedure, which I shall call "terrorist tautology," marks Hitler's speeches, just as it does those of Stalin's "theoretical" writings.

Now, it is precisely this procedure that assured Heidegger's success among philosophers. Inasmuch as philosophy, in our day, could no longer prove anything, the sanctification of the pure, intransigent, unexplained affirmation offered an ideal life raft. Since Heidegger appeared on the scene, philosophy has become increasingly assertive and peremp-

*"Wherefore Philosophers?"—as yet unpublished in English.

tory. It is no longer founded on the proof, but on the scorn felt for any recalcitrant skeptic who is unwilling to let himself be bewitched. That as verbal and verbose a body of work as Heidegger's, that such a tissue of hollow platitudes could have been taken for a monument of thought simply shows that, for lack of substance, modern philosophy is in desperate straits, so much so that it is condemned to become totalitarian. Heidegger's political behavior is not an accident of character, not a subjective cowardice; it is an integral feature of his philosophy. In an article on totalitarian culture written years ago I already cited a sentence taken from his November 3, 1933, *Appeal to Students,* a sentence that was exhumed and often quoted after the appearance of Farias's book: "Do not seek the rules of your being in dogmas and ideas," wrote Martin Heidegger. "It is the Führer himself, and he alone, who is the German reality of today and tomorrow."*

As one can see, the acceptance of the transcendant model quickly turns into a metaphysics of incarnation, the consequence of which is the cult of personality. Hitler, I might add, had already been juridically recognized as the "titulary holder of the idea of the State" (law of March 1, 1933). Note that he was proclaimed the titular holder of the *idea* of the State, not simply of the State. For a regime to be able to legitimize this despotic property of an idea, totalitarian philosophers are needed. Heidegger was one of them. If certain persons have had doubts about the intrinsic connection between Heidegger's philosophy and Nazism, he himself at least had none, since it was in his theoretical vocabulary, aided by technical terminology, that he justified his commitment. "The national socialist revolution," he declared on November 12, 1933, "brings with it the complete overthrow of our German *Dasein.*" (Let me add, for the benefit of civilized nonphilosophers, that in the Heideggerian vocabulary, *Dasein*— "There-being"—means "human reality.") In a book of reminiscences published posthumously, Karl Löwith relates how one day on the outskirts of Rome, where he had taken refuge from Nazism, he went for a walk with Heidegger, who had come there on vacation. The philosopher of the *Dasein* was sporting a swastika emblem in his buttonhole. "On our way back," wrote Löwith, "I steered the conversation toward the controversy that had been stirred up in the *Neue Zürcher Zeitung,* and explained that I was in disagreement with both Barth's political attack against him, and also Staiger's defense, because in my opinion his commitment in favor of National Socialism was the essence of his philosophy. Heidegger approved wholeheartedly,

*L'Express, June 7, 1971; reprinted in *Idées de notre temps* (Paris: Laffont, 1972).

adding that his notion of 'historicity' was the basis of his political 'commitment.' "*

This controversy, furthermore, had already taken place at least once before, after *Les Temps Modernes* in 1946 had published a text by Löwith entitled "The Political Implications of the Philosophy of Existence in Heidegger's Work"—a text that prompted the philosopher's apologist and commentator, Alphonse de Waehlens, to propound the lamentable thesis, one deeply insulting for philosophy, that there is no link between Heidegger's doctrine and his personal politicomoral commitment. A new proof was thus afforded of the casualness of intellectuals with respect to the consequences of their official attitudes! After the collapse of Nazism, complete morons were shot for having committed crimes against humanity on the grounds that obedience is no excuse, yet here it was claimed that the greatest philosopher of the twentieth century (according to his defenders) could invoke an absolutely watertight separation between his thought and his acts! A strange system of defense, indeed. For there are only two alternatives. Either Heidegger's political commitment is derived from his philosophy, and if so, that challenges the meaning of this philosophy; or it is not derived from it, and if a philosopher can make such a grave choice without any relation to his thinking, this can only prove the futility of philosophy itself. However, the recollection of the polemical debate of 1946 was repressed by the philosophical community, just as was that of the intervention Lucien Goldmann (author of *Le Dieu caché,* "The Hidden God") had made ten years later during a symposium held at the Abbey of Royaumont, when he had read some of Heidegger's Nazi texts and was treated to lively reprobation and indignant criticism. The philosophers knowingly rejected the historical information, thus avoiding an examination of the philosophical implications. In a discreet footnote to *Critique of Dialectical Reason* (1960), Sartre wrote: "The case of Heidegger is too complex for me to be able to expose it here" (p. 21, note 1). Coming from an author who considered a thousand pages to be a modest preface for meager prolegomena and who, as far as I can recall, never judged a question to be too complex for his all-devouring voracity for ratiocinations about everything imaginable, this sudden, passing modesty comes as something of a surprise. Let's say it sounds hollow. As for Heidegger's intellectual offspring, who after the appearance of Farias's book distinguished themselves by the moral and intellectual baseness of their

*Karl Löwith, *Mein Leben in Deutschland vor und nach 1933, ein Bericht* (Stuttgart: J. B. Metzler, 1986).

reactions, they merit attention only as symptoms of the shipwreck of modern philosophy.

The history of philosophy can be divided into two different periods. During the first, philosophers sought the truth; during the second, they fought against it. This second period, of which Descartes was the precursor of genius and of which Heidegger has been the most putrid manifestation, entered its heyday with Hegel. Between Descartes and Hegel there were several heirs of the truth-seeking epoque, the most pathetically sincere of whom was Kant and the most subtle Hume, who vainly sought a middle way in order to stave off the ineluctable triumph of imposture.

The sole interest of the Heidegger affair was to have revealed the poverty, masked by the supposed profundity, of modern philosophy, and also the scope of what might be called "the culture of evasion." Of it one might say that commitment was asked at the entrance, never at the exit.* Those of Heidegger's contemporaries who were not Nazis but who, like many left-wing intellectuals under the Weimar Republic, judged the *Zentrum* (Center) party and the Social Democrats to be more reactionary than the Nazis, paid dearly for their mistake, since the final exit for many of them was the concentration camp. But how many of those who escaped and took refuge in the United States—preferring, in Walter Laqueur's phrase, "California to Siberia"†—really assimilated the lessons of their blindness in the 1920s after World War II was over? Too many of those intellectuals, who survived only thanks to the United States, promptly renewed their attacks against democracy after 1945 by placing their pens at the service of that other totalitarian system, that of Stalin. What purpose, then, had their experience served? Even a rat trapped in a labyrinth learns faster than this. And while British, along with Swedish, intellectuals were the only ones in Europe to be spared either Fascist or communist persecution, what is one to think of H. G. Wells and George Bernard Shaw, who made themselves the

---

*Heidegger's futility as a thinker is even more obvious in texts in which his Nazi ontology is not a basic theme. Thus, in *The Origin of the Work of Art,* the banality of which I pointed out years ago in *Pourquoi les philosophes?* (Chap. 5), he accumulates clichés of a devastating boredom about one of Van Gogh's canvases, showing himself incapable even of consulting one or two books about this painting of the master; he manages to misunderstand the subject matter of the work, committing a gross error that demolishes his presumptuous interpretation. On this subject, see Meyer Schapiro, "The Still Life as a Personal Object: A Note on Heidegger and Van Gogh," in *The Reach of Mind: Essays in Memory of Kurt Goldstein* (New York: Springer Publishing Company, 1968).

†Walter Laqueur, *Weimar: A Cultural History, 1918–1933* (New York: Putnam, 1974).

apologists of Mussolini in the 1920s and Stalin in the 1930s? A fine eclecticism in willful blindness!

Indeed, the superiority the intellectual enjoys over the rest of the *homo sapiens* species is due not only to the lazy neglect he displays toward the information available to him, but also to his deliberate readiness to abolish data when they contradict the thesis he wants to put across. This willfulness in falsehood has often produced its baleful effects with respect to questions far more important than Martin Heidegger's Nazi past and the puerile dissimulations that philosophers have resorted to on this subject. Thus, it is generally believed, left-wing intellectuals in the West knew next to nothing of the real nature of the Soviet regime until very late in this century, having first of all been filled with a generous and legitimate confidence in the qualities of the new regime before being deceived by Stalinist censorship and propaganda.

This explanation, however, is false. This is an inversion in the order of events—as Christian Jelen has shown in *L'Aveuglement*—a historical work based on hitherto unpublished documents.* The truth, which Christian Jelen accurately reestablished in the specific case of French socialists, is that *the falsehood was born in the West*. The deception as to the real nature of the Leninist dictatorship was a deliberate operation due to the initiative of French socialists before the crucial split between socialists and communists at the December 1920 Congress of Tours, at a time when the young Bolshevik state lacked a full-fledged service of external propaganda, and when no communist party yet existed in the West to falsify the facts. The deception was invented by those who were deceived, not by the deceivers.

At the outset the truth was known. From 1917 on, the French Left knew and understood in a complete, precise manner the antidemocratic, dictatorial, police-state, and, according to all canonic standards, antisocialist character of the Bolshevik regime. The October coup d'état, which overthrew the Kerensky government, had not yet been baptized a "revolution." Due cognizance was taken of the subsequent elections (in January 1918) to the Constituent Assembly, in which 75 percent of the seats were won by political groups or parties hostile to the Bolsheviks. Using the same logic, the French socialists stigmatized Lenin's second putsch—the forceful dissolution of the Constituent Assembly, whose major "crime" was to include only a minority Bolshevik group—something which revealed that communism did not reflect the general

*"The Blindness," previously cited (Paris: Flammarion, 1984).

will of the Russian people. From October 1917 to January 1918 the correspondent in Russia of the newspaper *L'Humanité,* which was then a purely socialist daily, dispatched a whole series of articles describing what was going on. The products of very competent and honest journalistic coverage, they combined objectivity in reporting concrete events with perspicacity in political analysis.

Even more significantly, from November 1917 until March 1918 the Ligue des Droits de l'Homme (Human Rights League) staged hearings with many qualified French or Russian eyewitnesses, most of whom were socialists or close to the socialists. The commission that heard their accounts comprised some of the greatest French names in literature, science, philosophy, history, economics, sociology, and politics: Anatole France, Paul Langevin, Charles Gide (the economist, uncle of André Gide, the writer), Victor Basch, Celestin Bouglé, Charles Seignobos, Alphonse Aulard, Albert Thomas, Marius Moutet, Marcel Cachin, and Séverine, a former associate of the socialist Jules Vallès. All of them, it should be noted, were intellectuals. Some figured later in the Gotha almanac of the French Communist Party. I was able to read the integral stenographic record of these hearings thanks to Christian Jelen, who was able to obtain a copy preserved in a private library; for the archives of the Ligue des Droits de l'Homme had been destroyed years before in a fire. When I read the record of those hearings, it was as though a veil had been torn from the face of recent history; for what they revealed was that as early as 1918 the highest political and intellectual leaders of socialism already *knew* absolutely all they needed to know about Soviet despotism, since the system in its virtual entirety had been established during the first year of its existence.

What, then, happened in 1918 and 1919? The French socialists began by rejecting the truth. In January 1918 an initially minority but virulent faction of the SFIO (Section Française de l'Internationale Ouvrière— French Section of the Workers' International, as the French socialist party was called right up until 1971) revolted against the—all too accurate!—articles by *L'Humanité*'s correspondent in Russia and persuaded the newspaper's editors not to publish his dispatches. The French Left thus brilliantly inaugurated a tradition of censorship, which has not ceased to flourish right up to the present, varying the doses within the limits of credibility, first on behalf of the USSR, then of Red China, Cuba, Vietnam, Cambodia, Angola, Guinea, Nicaragua, and many self-styled "socialist" Third World countries. One year later, the atrocities the Human Rights League had revealed began to be the object of a cynical compression under the steamroller of historical rewriting, with

unpleasant facts being ground into dust or justified by wily interpretations. The two leading historians of the French Revolution, Alphonse
Aulard and above all Albert Mathiez, absolved Lenin's Bolsheviks for
their mass executions, employing the same arguments they had used to
excuse, even to exalt, the French Terror of 1793–94. Mythical or real,
the "encirclement" of Soviet Russia by foreign foes legitimized proscriptions against internal enemies—which is to say, everyone except the
Bolsheviks. Responsibility for the crimes of communism was blamed on
its adversaries, if possible on real ones but when necessary on imaginary
foes. The first in a long, chronic, and above all persistent series of
economic failures was explained as due to "exceptional circumstances,"
to the "legacy" of the tsarist past, the "blockade" of the capitalist
powers—when in fact President Woodrow Wilson, for the United
States, and Prime Minister Lloyd George, for Great Britain, had made
or were about to make declarations of sympathy and to offer economic
aid to the new regime. And so, without help from outside, the lie
machine began operating on its own.

Intellectuals do not behave differently from the majority of human
beings in their dealings with ideas. Like most of us, they regard ideas
as instruments to be placed in the service not of truth or of a wise
decision, but of a conception of the world that they defend and a cause
they serve, no matter how suicidal it might be. The only exceptions to
this rule are certain well-determined sectors of intellectual activity, in
which scientific constraints eliminate or forcibly reduce the role of
subjectivity, even though scientists too are quick to free themselves of
these constraints once they move away from their constricting sector.
In domains in which a concern for the truth and an impartial receptivity
accorded to all sorts of information depend on sincerity alone, I would
say that the proportion of human beings who, in passing judgment, are
primarily interested in the information available is no greater among
intellectuals than among nonintellectuals—to the extent that a precise
dividing line can be drawn between these two categories. For this reason
the eternally rehashed issue of intellectuals and their role seems to me
to be a bogus problem.

The only real problem is that of our culture—that is, of a culture that
is unable to manage itself in accordance with the criteria it has itself
formulated as conditions for its success. Intellectuals, admittedly, incarnate this contradiction in a more flagrant fashion, simply because they
handle a more abundant conceptual matter; but in reality they do no
more than push normal human behavior to extremes of paroxysm. What
is certain, in any case, is that, contrary to all their aspirations and

pretensions, they do not serve very effectively as guides. While many intellectuals distinguish themselves through the courage and lucidity of their publicly stated attitudes, they do not have a monopoly on such virtues—far from it—and more often than not they have indicated the wrong, rather than the correct, path to be followed by their contemporaries. Ideology naturally creates more havoc among intellectuals than among nonintellectuals; it enriches and encrusts itself through an expenditure of energy which renders it resistant to refutations of reality or contradictory arguments. For this reason, far from correcting the defects of our civilization, intellectuals accentuate them. Far from being the doctors of our ills, they are more like the symptoms. What is wrong and sickly in intellectuals reveals what is wrong and sickly in our civilization as a whole, since they magnify its characteristics.

This they do first of all by rejecting facts contrary to their prejudices. If the World Health Organization publishes a report establishing that schizophrenia manifests itself in identical ways in all forms of society, that it is thus probably an organic malady and not one due to society, immediately the psychiatrists of "antipsychiatry" raise a hullabaloo because this report destroys their own explanation of schizophrenia as caused by the contradictions of capitalism.* They are simply not interested in knowing what is true or false in this matter. This is, admittedly, a widespread attitude, but the hatred of knowledge is particularly astounding in persons whose professional task is to think. Sometimes they admit this hatred with a certain artlessness, but only after the event, when their avowal can no longer modify their acts or rectify the past.

Thus, in *Sens et Non-Sens,* the French philosopher Maurice Merleau-Ponty could after the war describe the prewar state of mind of his friends and the acceptance by some of them of the Munich accords of September 1938 as having been an "occasion to test German goodwill [sic]. This was because we were not guided by facts. We had secretly decided to ignore violence and unhappiness as elements of history, because we were living in a country that was too happy and too weak to envisage them. *To beware of facts had even become a duty for us.*" (Italics mine.) These intellectuals had in fact systematized a passivity which was the same as that of the overwhelming mass of the French people, who welcomed the Munich accords with a blind, enthusiastic feeling of relief. If intellectuals have a greater responsibility than others for the failure of culture—which is to say, for the refusal to use the information at their disposal for analysis and decision making—it is nonetheless true that this failure

*For details on this polemical controversy, see *Le Monde,* September 2, 1986.

was possible in the final analysis because of the passivity of other human beings, whose fear of facing facts led to a desire to be fooled. But the least that can be said is that the intellectuals in general did not do much to undeceive them. Furthermore, Merleau-Ponty's belated realization of his prewar blindness in no way helped after the war to open his eyes, whether in the field of politics or of philosophy. People simply fail to recognize the same pattern of behavior when it is repeated in a different context. When one is similarly mistaken, but with respect to realities different from those of yesterday, one fondly imagines that one has corrected one's mistake.

The same persistent error, whose content but not contextural form constantly changes, is called a fashion. Now, how can intellectuals serve as guides for society when their docility toward the whims of fashion on average exceeds that of other members of society? One is, indeed, struck by the conformism of intellectuals, the frequent lack of originality in the appreciations they display as a social group, and the collective witlessness with which they have rushed headlong to embrace the latest philosophical fads, particularly since World War II—for this failing shows no signs of abating with the passage of time. Contrary to what might be expected of them, they rarely have a personal viewpoint on doctrines that happen to be fashionable. Their capacity for exercising their critical faculties on dominant currents of thought is often very limited indeed. To be sure, not every dominant current is a fashion. The only currents of thought that deserve this appelation are those that appear without justification and which disappear just as irrationally. Roland Barthes' *Le Système de la mode,* an attempt to explain the phenomenon of *haute couture* with the aid of linguistics, was itself a product of fashion.* Being the object of an unmotivated adherence, if not of a snobbish desire to belong to an elite group, a fashion sinks like a stone when the irrational love it once inspired is withdrawn. It is then amusing to see its former lackeys turn savagely against it, multiplying their invectives and attacks and mercilessly grinding underfoot the weaknesses and mystifications they were blissfully unaware of when the beast was full of brawn and muscle. Retrospective lucidity and retroactive courage are one of the forms of useless knowledge, as we have seen in the case of Merleau-Ponty. They serve no purpose if they do not go all the way back to the original sources of the error, but merely consist

*Roland Barthes, *Le Système de la mode* (Paris: Éditions du Seuil, 1967).

of attacking certain ephemeral and episodic actors without analyzing the genesis and the laws governing the evolution of the fashion.

The scientist and the ignoramus do not differ in the least when, thanks to fashion, they commune in a similar exaltation, one in which, as Gustave Le Bon said, "the suffrage of forty academicians is no better than that of forty water carriers."* In Le Bon's notion of a crowd there is no scorn for the people. A human group transforms itself into a crowd when it suddenly responds to a suggestion rather than to reasoning, to an image rather than to an idea, to an affirmation rather than to proof, to the repetition of a phrase rather than to arguments, to prestige rather than to competence. A belief spreads through a crowd not by persuasion but by contagion. The mission of intellectuals should, in theory, be to slow down such irrational mechanisms, but in practice they accelerate them.

How is an intellectual fashion born, how does it reign, how does it vanish? And why?

The question is one of determining, for example, why the same persons who formerly acclaimed Mao Tse-tung or Teilhard de Chardin one day suddenly perceive that their idol sounds hollow, even though this was something that had ceaselessly been pointed out to them. If the criticism suddenly strikes home, it is not merely because it is sound—that is never enough—it is because the hour of downfall has finally struck for this particular craze. The dénouement is as enigmatic as the ascension and the triumph, because every bit as irrational.

Nothing, indeed, is explained if one speaks scornfully of "fashion," for the phenomenon of fashion should itself be explained. An intellectual fashion is a phenomenon whereby a theory, a cluster of enunciations, which often are no more than a set of words, takes possession of a significant number of minds by means other than those of logical demonstration. This fact is paradoxical only when a theory is involved, and a theory furthermore with a scientific ambition. For in everything that is of the domain of taste rather than of knowledge, fashion is the natural order of things. The puzzle begins when something that depends on the criteria of knowledge manages to impose itself without submitting to these same criteria. Not to be rationally verifiable or refutable is perfectly normal for a hat or a dance, but much less so for a psychoanalytical, economic, or biological theory. But it is precisely when such a theory succeeds "outside of the criteria," and when the mere suggestion

*Gustave Le Bon, *La Psychologie des foules* (Paris: 1895).

that it should be subjected to standards of verification becomes a sacrilege, that we find ourselves in the presence of a fashion.

An intellectual fashion cannot be launched haphazardly. Even stubborn repetition, supported by every imaginable kind of publicity, is not enough. It is essential that the theory, its content, and above all its manner of presentation reply to given needs. Dr. Lacan's success offers an exemplary case history of the conditions that must be filled. A psychoanalyst, Lacan refused the technical criteria of the cure, so forthrightly indeed that he was excluded from the International Association of Psychoanalysis. He replaced the real difficulties of scientific research by artificial difficulties, revealed in an obscure, precious, pedantic style, which gave his readers and his listeners the illusion of having to make an effort to understand him, along with the satisfaction of feeling that they had been initiated into a particularly arduous thought process.

These two conditions—real facility and apparent difficulty—provide the recipe which permits a vast clientele to experience a joyous sense of initiation and the privilege of feeing that one belongs to a select minority. This is even the indispensable condition for any intellectual fashion. It can be baptized "mass elitism." To which can be added another ingredient: the resort to a supporting discipline. Dr. Lacan took some time to find it. In a chapter of his *Introduction à la sémiologie,* Georges Mounin undertook a linguistic study of the successive terminological waves that washed over Lacan's style.* The logicomathematical wave was thus followed by the "dialectical" when Hegelianism was in vogue; then came the phenomenological and Heideggerian; and then, around 1960, there emerged structuralism and linguistics.

Naturally, no attempt was made in the Lacan circle to tackle linguistics seriously. Mounin even deplores the fact that "partly because of Lacan, the École Normale, the first place where a linguistic *aggiornamento* of high quality should have appeared, lost ten or fifteen years which it will be hard to retrieve." Lacan did no more than play with linguistics, laying down the principle that "the subconscious is a form of language" or, even better, that "it is structured like a language"— which from the Freudian point of view is utter nonsense. Not wishing to dwell on this confusion, which I have dealt with several times in the past,† I shall simply limit myself to pointing out that those who were

---

*Georges Mounin, *Introduction à la sémiologie* (Paris: Éditions de Minuit, 1970).

†*Pourquoi les philosophes?* 1975, Chap. 6, and the preface to the 1971 Livre de Poche edition, the "Pluriel" collection, pp. 36 ff.

380 The Flight from Truth

responsible for this confusion were following one of the dominant penchants of the period. This penchant consisted of reducing all problems to one of "speech" or "discourse." There was no such thing as medicine, only medical "discourse," no such thing as politics, only political "discourse." Rewriting psychoanalysis or Marxism in the terminology of the discipline that seemed to many people to be the most modern and advanced—structural linguistics (but any other would have served the purpose just as well)—such was the fourth condition of success, that of Roland Barthes and of Michel Foucault. To which must be added a fifth condition, by no means the least significant: the need to come up with a doctrine that seems to provide a global explanation of the human condition, which is to say, a philosophical system. Factual facility, apparent difficulty, an initiatory vocabulary, mass elitism, a supporting discipline, and explanatory globalism—such are the minimal distinguishing traits of a flourishing intellectual fashion. In addition, it acquires an exceptional force of penetration if it is defended and promoted by a "guru" who can be idolized.

Why, then, does an intellectual fashion die? Not because it is refuted, but simply because other doctrines and other currents using another vocabulary succeed in fulfilling the same functions and satisfying the same needs as the old fashion, which then develops wrinkles overnight. Those who now fill the position previously occupied by Lacan are there before our eyes, their names are on everybody's lips, their magic transforms a host of subjects that no one thinks should be submitted to the control of competence, for in any case their incompetence, if proven, would not diminish their audience in the least. And readers who think themselves delivered of the outworn fashion do not realize that what they are acclaiming at this very moment is simply a new incarnation of the illusion that had ceased to please.

Finally, a third characteristic of intellectuals shows that there too, they accentuate rather than correct human error. This is their strange predilection for totalitarian systems. A brief glance over the past three centuries teaches us that only a minority of intellectuals have opted for liberal society. The majority of them preferred to choose projects for training the individual, for producing the "new man." For this majority, culture constitutes a means of domination, reform, propaganda, government—everything except a means of knowledge. Although less often quoted than the chapter on men of letters in *L'Ancien Régime et la Révolution*, Alexis de Tocqueville's chapter on economists (in the same work) is perhaps even more eye-opening.* He lays bare the psychological motives behind the strange pretensions of theorists who would rebuild man and society from scratch. "According to the economists," he writes, "it behooves the state not just to command the nation, but to mold it after a certain fashion; it is up to it to form the minds of citizens according to a certain model which it proposes to itself in advance; its duty is to fill them with certain ideas and to provide their hearts with certain sentiments it deems to be necessary." This is why "not only do they have a hatred of certain privileges; diversity itself is odious to them; they adored equality to the point of servitude."

Since the eighteenth century very few intellectuals have been truly in favor of liberty. Most have fought above all to impose on society their own doctrine of "liberty," if need be by force. Benjamin Constant made fun of the Abbé de Mably, of whom he wrote: "No sooner did he perceive among any given people some vexatious measure than he fancied he had made a discovery and proposed it as a model [for others]; he detested individual freedom as one detests a personal foe."† Is it not disconcerting and a cause for concern that one of the *bêtes noires* of intellectuals over the past three centuries has been what they pejoratively term "individualism"? Save for a handful among them, they too, like the Abbé de Mably and Jean-Jacques Rousseau, regard individual freedom as a personal enemy. Yet should it not be the very opposite?‡ Does not culture afford each and every one of us the means for attaining personal autonomy of judgment and moral choice? Should not the thinker be the one who precedes us and opens the road to the conquest of autonomy? Why, instead of teaching us how to become free, does he turn against us and subject us to a system of his own conception?

The answer, simple enough, is inherent in the question. What most intellectuals up until now have called the triumph of culture is the faculty of imposing their conceptions on all other human beings, not of freeing them intellectually by making available to them the means of thinking for themselves in an original way. If most of the intellectuals living in liberal societies hate those same societies, it is because they prevent them from completely appropriating the intellectual management of others.

*Tocqueville, Book III, Ch. 3: "How the French Wished for Reforms Before Wishing to Have Freedoms."

†Benjamin Constant, *De la liberté des Anciens comparée à celle des Modernes* (Paris: 1819).

‡The devastating history of this fanatical struggle on the part of intellectuals against human freedom has been told by Alain Laurent in two fundamental works: *De l'individualisme* (Paris: Presses Universitaires de France, 1985) and *L'Individu et ses ennemis* (Paris: Pluriel-Hachette, 1987).

Exchanging freedom of expression for the power of oppressing is not always displeasing to intellectuals. Many of them adore regimes or parties that suppress or trim their freedom, offering in return a prodigal wealth of flatteries, honors, and financial rewards. These regimes risk no rebuff when they say in effect, to quote Robert de Jouvenel: "We refuse to recognize your rights. On the other hand, we willingly recognize rights you do not have."*

The Polish socialist Jan Waclav Makhaiski clearly discerned in intellectuals this appetite for domination and monopoly when, around 1900, he developed his theory of the "socialism of the intellectuals," which provoked an uproar at the time. According to Makhaiski, "socialism is a social regime based on the exploitation of the workers by professional intellectuals," and, as his editor, Alexandre Skirda, summed it up with great clarity, "Marx, the founder of scientific socialism, is the prophet of the new, dominant, capable, competent class, which will eliminate the plutocrats, those archaic elements."† One is reminded of the program, which was applied in Italy from 1945 to 1980, of Antonio Gramsci, whom naïve "bourgeois" thinkers took to be a liberal "Eurocommunist"—a misconception that was the height of fantasy, since Gramsci in fact was the most inflexibly Leninist theorist of the total conquest of intellectual power. This *idée fixe* resurfaces periodically, on the Right as on the Left, throughout the entire history of the intelligentsia. In the preface to a new edition of his book *Les Indes rouges,* Bernard-Henri Lévy provides an illuminating testimony: "And, if one wants a more personal and precise anecdote, I still remember those winter mornings when with a brief and deliberately enigmatic telephone call Louis Althusser would summon me to the rue d'Ulm, where, with the air of a conspirator preparing a great philosophical evening far from indiscreet eyes and ears, he would immediately drag me into the school's inner courtyard, where we would stay for a long time, strolling around the " 'Bassin des Ernest,' I listening to him and he, with frowning forehead and his hands in the pockets of his dressing gown and, darting piercing glances intended to make me grasp what was merely half spoken, explaining the place he was reserving for me in his strategy of conquest, of subversion . . . of intellectual power in France!"‡

*Robert de Jouvenel, *La République des camarades* (Paris: Bernard Grasset, 1914).

†Makhaiski's texts, translated with an excellent introduction by Alexandre Skirda, were published by Éditions du Seuil in 1979 under the title *Le Socialisme des intellectuels.*

‡Bernard-Henri Lévy, *Les Indes rouges* (Paris: Grasset and Livre de Poche). The École Normale Supérieure is located not far from the Panthéon, on the rue d'Ulm—which is how

In a book of reminiscences, *Les Royaumes déchirés,* the formerly exiled Spanish novelist Juan Goytisolo describes a most revealing episode concerning the *libido dominandi* that is characteristic of so many intellectuals: "I recall that Arrabal, who had been ferociously insulted by Benigno and by my Party friends, had had one of his plays transmitted to Sartre by [Maurice] Nadeau. The play was due to appear in his review with an introduction written by the philosopher. The news irritated me profoundly, as though an intruder had invaded my territory and his talent might overshadow mine; the comments I added about it likewise scandalized my friends. Heeding their advice, I went very democratically to call on Simone de Beauvoir in order to block the 'offense.' Arrabal, I told her, was an idealist, a reactionary, and he was not solidly committed to our Struggle; many persons would not understand why Sartre was encouraging him, and in any case promoting him would be harmful to the anti-Franco cause. As a result of this intervention Sartre decided not to write his prologue. My friends and I savored our petty victory. As I have sought to explain in *Pièces d'Identité* ["Identity Cards"], such ideological and cultural policing corresponded perfectly to the particular code of the tribe."*

When will intellectuals rid themselves of the perverse illusion that it is their mission to rule the world rather than to enlighten it, to "build" and thus to destroy man rather than to instruct him?

On March 16–17, 1988, a dramatic session of collective exorcism of this kind took place in Rome, where former communist and socialist intellectuals haled the ghost of Palmiro Togliatti before their tribunal, finding him guilty of murder by complicity because of his role in Moscow during the Great Terror of 1937 and the Stalinization of Italian intellectual life, which he imposed on his country after the collapse of Fascism in 1945. Without any qualms and I would even say by lending him a helping hand, Togliatti had let Stalin carry out the shooting of hundreds of anti-Fascist Italians who had taken refuge in the USSR. After the war, furthermore, he had cleverly come to terms with the intellectual world of Italy by proposing a kind of cultural "Gramscian" pact. This pact functioned more or less to everyone's satisfaction for thirty years.

it is often referred to by Parisians. The "Ernest," in ENS slang, are the goldfish to be found in the central basin of the court of honor.

*I have drawn this quotation from the French edition of Goytisolo's memoirs, published by Fayard in 1988. The original Spanish version was published in Barcelona in 1986 by Seix Barral under the title *Lo Reino de Taifa,* available in English as *Realms of Strife: Memoirs, 1957–1982* (Berkeley, CA: North Point Press, 1990).

On the condition that they remain within the zone of attraction of the Italian Communist Party and also of that of Pietro Nenni's Socialist Party, which was then allied with the ICP, intellectuals, writers, and artists were able for three decades to enjoy considerable power, protection, and material security. They were also able to enjoy a considerable, though relative, freedom, since Togliatti was shrewd enough not to muzzle them *à la* Zhdanov and to let them retain their usual preferences, favorite books, and traditions. It is true nonetheless that the functional consequence of this pact was the oppression of Italian culture by an omnipresent ideological bureaucracy. Togliatti's posthumous inculpation at the above-mentioned session, though fascinating from a historical point of view and an important turning point, must nevertheless be added to the catalog of retrospective fits of remorse which suddenly arise at a particular moment when they can no longer alter reality in any way. It was the cultural failure of communism and not the self-criticism of the intellectuals that was the determining cause. To make a great to-do over the evacuation of a shipwrecked vessel requires no particular heroism, even though in this case it gave rise to penetrating analyses and most interesting reminiscences. But the vital question is to know whether or not criticism of the past is likely to prevent a repetition of the same mistakes, made under other forms in the future.

Close observers of contemporary Italy blame the bankruptcy of the "Togliatti pact"—that is, the failure of the cultural conquest of social power within the framework of institutional Marxism—for the fatal orientation of many intellectuals, who from 1968 on turned to terrorism. Even though the ideological and practical failure of the Italian Communist Party may indeed have served as a circumstantial and secondary cause for this philosophical justification of automatic weapons, the primary cause, in my opinion, remains the fundamental hatred for civilizations based on freedom. If not, why, in a politicocultural context and with a historical background that has nothing to do with Italy, should we have witnessed the holding of a symposium devoted to the theme of "Talking Terrorism," which was held on February 4–6, 1988, at Stanford University's prestigious School of Education. The list of invited speakers had been drawn up in such a way as to guarantee that the conference would end up exalting international terrorism and reviving the standard old thesis that it is the democracies that are intrinsically terroristic.

One of the most intriguing manias exhibited by intellectuals consists of projecting onto liberal societies the very defects they refuse to discern in totalitarian societies. We have seen how this mechanism for inverting roles functions in American intellectuals. In Europe one of the thinkers in whom this trait was most surprisingly apparent was Michel Foucault, for Foucault, unlike Sartre and so many others, was never a communist, nor a sympathizer, nor even a Marxist. In his work the "progressive" bias intervenes when he interprets open societies through his theory of confinement, particularly developed in *Surveiller et punir* ("To Supervise and Punish").* Here Foucault described liberal societies as being founded on the principle of generalized confinement: the child at school, the soldier in the barracks, the real or presumed delinquent in prison, the madman or pseudomadman in a psychiatric hospital. When he crammed so many diverse forms of confinement into the same basket in order to accuse democratic societies of totalitarian tendencies—at a moment when they were offering an unprecedented degree of freedom and of liberalization in all of the above-mentioned sectors—one can't help thinking that Foucault in reality was describing another society, a society that fascinated him but which he did not name: communist society. In what other society, indeed, at the time he was elaborating his theory, did confinement reign in such a universal and sovereign fashion? The confinement of the child at school, as everywhere else; of the soldier in his barracks, even more so than anywhere else, with the longest period of compulsory military service on the planet; of the madman, and above all of the phoney "madman," in psychiatric hospitals used for political repression; the confinement not only of common-law criminals in prison, but of many innocent souls in concentration and hard-labor camps; confinement of the population as a whole, thanks to restrictions on free movement, on domestic travel without an internal passport, and on the free choice of one's place of residence; and finally, confinement of the entire population of the country within the frontiers of the USSR by the prohibition imposed on its citizens, who were not allowed to leave the country even for a brief trip abroad, unless they could obtain— always as a special favor, not as a right—an (exceedingly rare) exit visa.

One of the essential components of the totalitarian system, as opposed to liberal civilization, is the vocation to which it lays claim: dominating the world, regenerating it, imposing the type of society it incarnates and which it considers superior to all others. Hence the reigning ideology and the central place it occupies in all those systems and consequently grants to docile intellectuals, who are charged with "supervising" the orthodoxy of society. Totalitarianism alone grants intellectuals this kind of monopoly. In a liberal civilization each intellectual is simply an

*Michel Foucault, *Surveiller et punir* (Paris: Gallimard, 1975).

individual who addresses himself to other individuals, who are free to listen to him or to ignore him, to approve or disapprove him. Each day the work of persuading the public must be started all over again. How wearying, how anguish-inducing! Who among us has not dreamed of exchanging this precariousness for the comfort of a Lysenko or a Heidegger, of receiving the support of the state apparatus in neutralizing all of his contradictors?

We may, according to our temperament and makeup, be either amused or saddened to find Diderot and d'Alembert, editors of the eighteenth-century *Encyclopédie* (theoretically the matrix of so many modern freedoms), intervening with Malesherbes, the magistrate to whom Louis XV had entrusted the administration of printed matter, and asking him to censor and seize the pamphlets of authors who criticized the *Encyclopédie*. In his *Mémoires* the Abbé Morellet, whom d'Alembert had asked to intervene with the magistrate on his behalf, quotes the letter of reply Malesherbes sent him, asking him to transmit it to d'Alembert: "If Monsieur d'Alembert, or any other, can prove that it is against the interest of law and order to allow such critiques to subsist as those by which the *Encyclopédie* has been mistreated in the latest brochures, if any author finds that it be unjust to tolerate such periodical pamphlets, and if he claim that the magistrate himself should judge of the fairness of such literary criticisms before allowing them to appear, in a word, if there is any other part of my administration which is found to be reprehensible, those who complain thereof need but speak out their reasons to the public. I bid them not to name me, for such is not the usage in France; but they can designate me as clearly as they wish, and I promise them every permission thereto. I hope at least that, having exposed myself to their declarations and being unable to impede them, I shall no longer hear of particular complaints, of which I must admit I have had enough."

Malesherbes, in other words, was reminding the Encyclopedists that they should reply to the arguments of their adversaries with other arguments, instead of demanding that the secular branch of the law reduce them to silence. But, Morellet goes on, "when I explained to my friend d'Alembert Monsieur de Malesherbes's principles, I could not prevail upon him to listen to reason; the philosopher raged and cursed, according to his evil habit." For, as d'Alembert went on to claim, resorting to the admirable sophistry that men of letters and philosophers have used down the ages, in the *Encyclopédie* he and his friends "did not transgress the reasonable bounds of philosophical discussion," whereas the accusations of their adversaries were odious personal attacks "which should be prohibited by a government which was the friend of truth and which wished to favor the progress of knowledge." Malesherbes, as is well known, had been openly protecting the Encyclopedists and sparing them trouble with the royal censorship. But this was not enough—in their opinion he should also have had their contradictors placed behind the bars! It was doubtless due to his felonious pluralism and to his pernicious respect for all opinions that in 1794 the disciples of the Encyclopedists, who were then in power, demonstrated their gratitude by having Malesherbes guillotined.

Let me make one thing clear. As far as my personal and relatively unimportant sympathies are concerned, I feel myself to be the distant spiritual descendant of the Encyclopedists, and not of their adversaries. But the point I wish to make is this. As long as intellectuals find it normal to regard "the struggle for the freedom of the mind" and "human rights" as granting them latitude to make abstract pleas on behalf of liberty while refusing the same rights to their contradictors, and as long as they claim to be upholding the truth while in fact cultivating falsehood, the failure of culture and its powerlessness to exert any positive influence on history in the moral sphere will continue on into the future to the greater detriment of mankind.

Still, I venture to hope that we have finally reached the end of an era during which so many intellectuals strove above all to place mankind under their ideological domination, and that we are entering a new epoch in which they will at last settle down to their true vocation, which is to place knowledge at the service of human beings—and not simply in the scientific and technical domains. This transition from the old era, when sterilization of knowledge was regarded as the norm, to a new age is not simply one possible choice among others: it is a necessity. Our civilization is condemned to abide by its underlying principles, or else it will regress toward a primitive stage where there will no longer be a contradiction between knowledge and behavior, knowledge in the meantime having disappeared.

Index

Ochetto, Achille, 123
Ockrent, Christine, 289–90
Ollman, Bertell, 323
Olympia (Manet), 366–67
Omnipotent Government, The (von
  Mises), 149
Oni (Toranska), 42*n*, 359
opinion:
  arbitrary vs. reasoned, 9, 10
  information vs., 231–34, 236–44, 251,
    263, 266–67, 274, 280, 284, 289
  knowledge vs., 7, 9
Order of Saint François de Sales, 178
Organization of African Unity (OAU),
  95, 109, 111*n*
*Origines de la France contemporaine,
  Les* (Taine), 215–16
Origin of the Work of Art, The
  (Heidegger), 372*n*
Ortega, Daniel, 267
Ortega y Gasset, José, 310, 329
Orwell, George, 28
Other Path, The (de Soto), 144–45
Ottone, Piero, 124
Out of Step (Hook), 335, 339

pacifism, 188, 190, 196, 326–27
Painting of Modern Life, The (Clark),
  365–66
País, El, 123, 240–41, 261, 282
Pajetta, Giancarlo, 217, 228
Palme, Olof, 90
Pancino, Gianfranco, 343, 344
Panorama, 253
Papandreou, Andreas, 67, 90, 140
Para Bellum (Zinoviev), 292–93
Pareto, Vilfredo, 168
Parsons, Talcott, 166
Pascal, Blaise, 170, 181–82
Pasqua, Charles, 83, 281, 338
Pasqualini, Jean, 333
Passelecq, Olivier, 62*n*
Pasteur, Louis, 306*n*
Pasteur Institute, 294, 355
Patriot, 293–94
Paulin, Thierry, 281
Pauvert, Jean-Jacques, 58
Pavel, Thomas, 365
Paz, Octavio, 144, 329, 332
pedagogic usurpation, 346
Perestroika (Gorbachev), 156, 163
perestroika, xx, xxiii–xxiv, 68, 248
Perón, Juan, 130

Pershing II missiles, 198, 228
Peru, 142–50
  bank nationalization in, 142–44, 149
  censorship in, 25
  informal commerce of, 144–47, 148
  Shining Path movement in, 167
Pestalozzi, Johann, 302*n*
Petiot, Dr., 281
Petit Parisien, Le, 45
Peyrefitte, Alain, 50
Pham Van Dong, 245
Pham Xuan An, 245
Physicians for Social Responsibility,
  193, 199
Pic, Roger, 120
Pilhes, René-Victor, 311
Piltdown Man, xv
Pinochet, Augusto, 57, 100, 120, 131,
  133, 137, 141–42, 227
Pipes, Richard, xxxv
Pivot, Bernard, 333
Plato, 7, 9, 10, 13, 116
pluralism, journalistic, 236–37, 243, 251
Point, Le, 76*n*, 79, 132*n*
Pokrovsky, Valentin, 295
Polac, Michel, 264–66
Poland, 67, 125, 291, 359–60, 362
Policy Review, 323
political parties, ideological shifts
  within, 123–24
  see also specific political parties
politics, terminology used in, 89–92
Pollack, Robert E., xiv
Pol Pot, 40, 219
Pompidou, Georges, 47, 78, 306*n*
Ponomarev, Boris, 197
Pontalis, J.-B., 339*n*
Pontiki, 140
Popper, Karl, 6
Popular Movement for the Liberation
  of Angola (MPLA), 125, 126, 246
Population Bomb, The (Ehrlich), 197,
  364
Porot, Antoine, 279*n*
Portugal:
  Angolan independence and, 125, 126
  political system in, 177, 285
Possessed, The (Dostoevsky), 167
Pourquoi les philosophes? (Revel), 369,
  372*n*, 379*n*
Pravda, 63*n*, 186, 294
PRI (Revolutionary Institutional
  Party), 143